BUSINESS CHALLENGES IN THE 21st CENTURY

Preparing for the Future

BUSINESS CHALLENGES IN THE 21st CENTURY

Preparing for the Future

Edited by

PREM KUMAR
Director
Sri Aurobindo College of Commerce,
Ludhiana

and

PARVINDER ARORA
Faculty, Institute of Management Technology,
Ghaziabad, U.P.

DEEP & DEEP PUBLICATIONS PVT. LTD.
F-159, Rajouri Garden, New Delhi-110027

BUSINESS CHALLENGES IN THE 21ST CENTURY
PREPARING FOR THE FUTURE

ISBN 978-81-8450-022-6

Typeset by S.S. COMPOSERS,
3190, Mohindra Park, Shakur Basti, Delhi-110034.

Printed in India at NEW ELEGANT PRINTERS,
A-49/1, Maya Puri, Phase-I, New Delhi-110064.

Published by DEEP & DEEP PUBLICATIONS PVT. LTD.
F-159, Rajouri Garden, New Delhi-110027.
Phones: 25435369, 25440916
E-mail: ddpbooks@yahoo.co.in • deep98@del3.vsnl.net.in
Showroom:
2/13, Ansari Road, Daryaganj, New Delhi-110002 • Telefax: 23245122

Contents

Preface

This book is the result of deliberations which took place during National Seminar on *Indian Business: Preparing for the Future* held on March 13-14, 2004 at University School of Management, Punjabi University, Guru Kashi Campus, Talwandi Sabo. The aim of the seminar was to generate ideas aligning management initiatives with the changing demands on the business sector. The Indian business is undergoing massive restructuring in the wake of economic liberalisation, growing regional economic integration and compliance with WTO provisions. The Seminar was an attempt to provide a platform for interaction and knowledge-sharing amongst the experts from academia and the industry on the opportunities and challenges of doing business in the changing environment. The papers which were presented and deliberated upon covered the themes, viz. the changing business environment and its implications for Indian business, emerging opportunities in the manufacturing and service sector, preparing for changing customer expectations and markets, adapting to the new financial order, markets and instruments, managing people and processes for performance excellence, entrepreneurial and leadership challenges in the 21st Century, etc. The book contains the selected papers which were deliberated upon.

We are thankful to Punjabi University authorities for allowing and facilitating the conduct of the seminar. Thanks are also due to all the contributors who contributed the papers and who attended the proceedings of the seminar. We also propose a special word of thanks for all the sponsors of the seminar. Not to forget M/s Deep & Deep Publications Pvt. Ltd., New Delhi for agreeing to publish the collection of papers in the form of a book.

PREM KUMAR
PARVINDER ARORA

List of Contributors

Amandeep Singh, Lecturer, University School of Management, PUGKC, Talwandi Sabo.

Amit Sikka, Department of Business Management, PAU, Ludhiana.

Ashim Raj Singla, Institute of Management Technology, Ghaziabad.

Ashwani Bhalla, Sr. Lecturer in Commerce, SCD Government College, Ludhiana.

Babita Kumar, Associate Professor, Department of Business Management, PAU, Ludhiana.

Balram Dogra, Director, Apeejay Institute of Management, Jalandhar.

Balwinder Singh, Reader, Department of Commerce and Business Management, Guru Nanak Dev University, Amritsar.

Bharatbhushan Singla, Lecturer, Punjabi University, Patiala.

Bikram Singh Virk, Lecturer in Commerce, NJSA Government College, Kapurthala (Punjab).

D.P. Goyal, Institute of Management Technology.

D.P. Warne, Head, Industry-Institute-Partnership Deptt., MIMIT, Malout.

Devinderpal Singh, Lecturer, Punjabi University Regional Centre for IT and Management, Mohali.

Dyal Bhatnagar, Lecturer, University School of Management, Punjabi University, Guru Kashi Campus, Talwandi Sabo.

G.S. Batra, Reader, Punjab School of Management Studies, Punjabi University, Patiala.

Gagandeep Banga, Associate Professor, Department of Business Management, PAU, Ludhiana.

Gianetan Sekhon, Lecturer, Punjabi University, Guru Kashi Campus,Talwandi Sabo.

Harbilas, Lecturer in Commerce, SCD Government College, Ludhiana.

Kesar Singh Bhangoo, Reader in Economics, Punjabi University Regional Centre, Bathinda (Pb.).

M.A. Sahaf, Senior Reader, Department of Management Studies, University of Kashmir, Srinagar, Kashmir.

Manjit Singh, Faculty, Punjabi University, Patiala.

Manveen Saini, Ph.D. Student, Department of Business Management, PAU, Ludhiana.

Mohit Gupta, Assistant Professor of Business Management with the Department of Business Management, Punjab Agricultural University, Ludhiana.

Mushtaq A. Bhat, Senior Lecturer, Department of Commerce, University of Kashmir, Srinagar.

Navdeep Aggarwal, Assistant Professor of Business Management with the Department of Business Management, Punjab Agricultural University, Ludhiana.

P.P. Singh, Asst. Professor, Punjab College of Technical Education, Baddowal, Ferozepur Road, Ludhiana.

Pankaj Madan, Lecturer, Faculty of Management Studies, Gurukul Kangri University, Haridwar (UA).

Parveen Gill, Reader, Punjab School of Management Studies, Punjabi University, Patiala.

Parvinder Arora, Faculty, Institute of Management Technology, Ghaziabad, U.P.

Pawan Kumar Taneja, Asst. Professor, Punjab College of Technical Education, Baddowal, Ferozepur Road, Ludhiana.

Pooja Malhotra, Research Fellow, Department of Commerce and Business Management, Guru Nanak Dev University, Amritsar.

Pratibha Goyal, Assistant Professor of Business Management in Punjab Agricultural University, Ludhiana.

Prem Kumar, Director, Sri Aurobindo College of Commerce, Ludhiana

Purva Kansal, Lecturer, University Business School, Panjab University, Chandigarh.

Pushpinder Gill, Reader, PSMS, Punjabi University, Patiala.

R.K. Mahajan, Professor of Economics, Punjabi University Regional Centre, Bathinda.

R.S. Dhaliwal, Lecturer, University School of Management, Punjabi University, Guru Kashi Campus, Talwandi Sabo.

Rajesh Verma, Lecturer, Apeejay Institute of Management, Jalandhar.

Rajinder Kaur, Lecturer at MIMIT, Malout.

Rajinder Kaur, Reader, Department of Commerce, Punjabi University, Patiala.

Rajiv Arora, Joint DGFT, O/O DGFT, Presently on Training at IIPA.

Rajwinder Singh, Lecturer at MIMIT, Malout.

Riyaz Rainaye, Senior Lecturer in the Department of Commerce, University of Kashmir.

S.K. Singla, Professor of Business Management and Head of Department of Business Management, Punjab Agricultural University, Ludhiana.

Sandeep Kapur, Associate Professor, Department of Business Management, PAU, Ludhiana.

Sarupinder Singh, Lecturer, PSMS, Punjabi University, Patiala.

Selvaarani Shanker, Associate Professor, Department of Business Management, College of Commerce and Business Management, Osmania University, Hyderabad, Andhra Pradesh.

Shailender Saini, Lecturer, Deptt. of Commerce, Punjabi University, Patiala.

CHAPTER

1

Indian Business

Preparing for the Future

PREM KUMAR AND DYAL BHATNAGAR

The world we work in is developing at an exponential rate—a rate that shows no sign of abating. It is only natural that we have a curiosity about how business, work place, institutions and management practices will change in these changing times (Subir Chowdhury, 2000).

The last two decades have seen radical changes in business and economic conditions. And while for the first forty years after independence India fell behind the western world and her neighbours, since liberalization began we have begun to show our paces.

The corporate story since liberalization took root is well known. During the last decade there has been a significant reorganization and shakeout. Those companies that were well managed and were able to respond to the new competitive environment have shaped up well and have emerged stronger. The weaker companies, which depended on licenses and protection, got left behind and in many cases just went under. Fortunately, this shakeout took place when the economy was growing strongly, unlike Europe, where there were large lay-offs when the economy was stagnant.

COMPETING IN THE INFORMATION AGE

Business organizations are in the midst of a revolutionary transformation. With the industrial age paving the way for information age, the critical success factors are shifting in favour of soft skills. The information age competition requires new capabilities for competitive success. Today, the ability of a company to mobilize and exploit its intangible assets has become far more decisive than investing in and managing physical assts. According to Kaplan and Norton (1996), intangible assets enable a business organisation to mange customer relationships, introduce innovative products, mobilize competencies and deploy information technology and systems for sustained success.

NEW OPERATING ENVIRONMENT

The changing operating environment is characterized by integration of business processes enabling innovation, speed and efficiency. The modern organisation is in-fact a network of customers and suppliers.

The modern organisation works in a borderless world and competes against the best companies across the globe. While the companies serve customers world-wide they must develop marketing programmes with sensitivity to local needs and preferences.

The product life cycles are continuously shrinking requiring companies to master rapid technological innovations devising radical new products and services, managing efficient supply chain networks.

The new age companies compete more on the strength of their people—the intellectual elite. The knowledge workers are the backbone of an organisation. Therefore, investing in, managing and using the knowledge of every employee s the most important task in the organisation.

Managerial Challenges in Future

As we enter the new millennium we are on the threshold of a new 'Global Age'. Under the impact of globalization our economy is being integrated with the global economy. It is, therefore, not possible for any company to live in isolation in a business world, which is becoming increasingly integrated. According to Neelamegham (2000), in this new global economy the businesses of the developing nations like India will face a number of challenges.

Technology-related challenges

The world economy of the future will be shaped greatly by technological developments. The rapid technological advances in transport and communication and the emergence of several key industries—microelectronics, biotechnology, telecommunications, robotics and computers would continue to play a major role in integrating the world economy. For example, advances in microelectronics have already accelerated worldwide communication providing the foundation for the emerging global society.

A large part of the Indian manufacturing sector is characterized by old, outdated technologies. Significant investments will be required for technology up-gradation in sectors like textiles, engineering, chemicals, consumer goods, food processing, etc. Similarly, issues of technology absorption, training and development, new management structures and systems in new technology environment will assume increasing importance.

Demographic shift

Another major force that is going to make the world different from that of today is trends in population growth. The population of the world, which is currently 5.8 billion, will reach 8 billion by the year 2020. But almost 95% of the increase in population will take place in developing countries like India and China. Thus, there will be overpopulated developing world and under populated developed world causing demographic imbalances between richer and poorer countries. Also the developed world will have more aged people.

The demographic trends would spawn new opportunities in serving older population in developed countries, out-sourced services, medical tourism, travel and entertainment for the affluent of the developed world. There would also be significant opportunities in value—for money, functional products and cost-effective services in the emerging economies.

When these changes occur especially at a time when sweeping technological changes take place, they are likely to pose several new challenges to the businesses of developing countries. Physical resources may become short in supply and the developing countries may be unable to cope with the new problems related to the environmental degradation.

Change in the role of government

The globalization of financial systems and services has brought in its wake several new challenges to the nation-state. The borderless world implies that government has less control over its currency and fiscal policies compared to what they had in yesteryears. In future government may become smaller leaving many of the business functions to corporate sector. Restructuring disinvestments and privatization of public enterprises are gaining greater importance. In the context of India the government will have a major role to play to design policies and programs necessary to take care of those who may be adversely affected because of deregulation and change over the market economy.

Future of global trading environment

New vision emerged with the establishment of World Trade Organization, to bring together trading partners and achieve a multilateral economic framework covering many areas of common concern to the world economy. At the same time the emergence of powerful trade blocks in the international economy, almost a simultaneous development, creates apprehension about the new forms of protectionism. Further, while the pressure is put on the developing countries for more liberalization and opening up of their economies it is feared that developed countries might use trade as a weapon by their insistence on social clause including labour and environment standards.

While the individual enterprise would get more freedom to operate in the commercial space, the governance issues in terms of compliances, fair practices and social responsibility would assume added importance.

Environmental issues

There is no doubt that with the growth in population and depletion of natural resources there would be growing emphasis on the environmental issues and challenges in the coming decade. While it is true that adoption of environmentally friendly technologies and production processes will in the long-run provide opportunities to improve their sales to environmentally conscious consumers, firms in developing countries are going to face several issues and challenges as they have to incur heavy costs at least in the short-run which might affect their competitiveness.

Emerging Scenario of Governance and Leadership

With the increasing liberalization and globalization of economies, there is a world-wide recognition of higher freedom and role for corporations and mangers, on the one hand, and consequently the need for better governance and effective leadership styles, on the other. Kurup and Pankajam (2000) have outlined seven leadership styles, which according to them, can be suitable for the 21st century leaders. These styles are briefly described below:

1. Visionary leader

A visionary leader means someone who has the capacity to identify the change in products and markets that the business should adopt if it were to out perform its competitors. To develop into a visionary leader a person should read widely, enhance lateral thinking and attend lectures or seminars in his areas of work.

2. Influential leader

Such leaders will be generally those who can push or pull others towards there goals. To become more influential, the leaders have to develop change agent capacities and act in the consultancy role.

3. Facilitative leader

To be a facilitator one should have a level of self-adjustment above average. For this purpose one has to develop his counseling skills through active listening, providing feedback, offering support and encouragement for resolving conflicts.

4. Crisis leader

The successful change leader in a crisis is likely to be relatively independent-minded, self-sufficient and a resilient manager who has a high level of power of thinking and whose leadership and influence style includes a high level of personal power. For this purpose the leader has to be decisive, able to provide feedback, forceful, proactive and assertive.

5. Developmental-Participative leader

In this style the manager will usually be seeking to encourage staff to set their own goals, identify solution tom problems and constantly seek to develop themselves by using learning opportunities. This style is likely to be successful where staff is motivated by the opportunities for self-development.

6. Flexible leader

A leader who can exhibit a flexible response to change will be more successful than someone who can offer only one style of leadership. For this purpose the leader has to empathize with a wide range of staff to understand how the staff feels about particular potential or actual changes.

7. Change Influence Partner

In this case the manager has not only to be fully aware of the strategies but has to be perceived by the colleagues as being able to contribute to the achievement of the strategy. For this purpose one has to improve his understanding of and skills in other management disciplines and change the expectations of others about his contribution.

The corporate governance has succeeded in attracting a good deal of public interest because of its apparent importance for the economic health of corporations and society in general. Corporate Governance has been defined by OECD as "The system by which business corporations are directed and controlled. The corporate governance structure specifies the distribution of rights and responsibilities among different participants in the corporation, such as, the board, managers, and shareholders spells out the rules and procedures for making decisions on corporate affairs. By doing this, it also provides the structure through which the company objectives are set and the means of attaining those objectives and monitoring performance." (OECD April 1999)

The Business Roundtable (May 2000), supports the following guiding principles:

1. The paramount duty of the board of directors of a public corporation is to select a chief executive officer and to observe the CEO and other senior management in the competent and ethical operation of the corporation on a day-to-day basis.
2. It is the responsibility of management to operate the corporation in an effective and ethical manner in order to produce value for stockholders.
3. It is the responsibility of managers to produce financial statements that fairly present the financial condition and results of operations of the company and to make the timely disclosures to the investors.
4. It is the responsibility of the board and its audit committee to engage an independent accounting firm to audit the financial statements prepared by management.
5. It is the responsibility of the independent accounting firm to ensure that it is in fact independent, is without conflicts of interest, employs highly competent staff and carries out its work in accordance with Generally Accepted Accounting Standards.
6. The corporation has a responsibility to deal, with its employees in a fair and equitable manner.

The corporate governance in the 21st century emphasizes the role of shareholders and financial institutions. Shareholders should be involved in all major decisions and financial institutions should appoint functional experts to represent them on the boards of companies in which they have substantial holdings. The importance of corporate governance will be a function of the constituents involved in developing a uniform code. This could be the market, institutions or the government.

MARKET CHALLENGES IN THE NEW AGE

Consumers are evolving, getting richer, more educated and more aware of their rights. Technology is moving so fast that the shelf life of every innovation is dropping exponentially. The media is becoming truly omni-present and providing knowledge and new aspirations to the masses. Liberalization has resulted in an explosion of choices for the consumer.

So how will Markets grow in this new world? First, by accepting that each brand is not merely competing in its category. Rather a shampoo is competing with a mobile phone call to the US or with a meal out in the evening. In this context, businesses must bring to the consumers a continuous flow of new ideas and offerings. To do this they need to be able to sense and predict trends in consumers' lives, economics technology, etc.

To bring up new ideas and to become more innovative the companies must follow these three simple rules advocated by Banga (2003). Firstly, every marketing manager must live the lives of their consumers. Understanding customer is not the prerogative of marketers—each function can contribute to a deeper understanding of the consumer needs and then fulfiling their aspirations. Secondly, there must be a deep conviction that technology is the key to developing new benefits and in making them affordable. This requires an upfront investment in the right scientific talent and infrastructure. Thirdly, companies must build a culture for outstanding execution. Every idea is copied very fast—also the follower has the advantage of learning from the leader. The leader must thus move fast but also very sure-footedly.

Trends to Watch in HR's Future

In the so-called 'better HR decade' with a focus on

improved delivery, HR must function as a technology enabler, leadership developer, knowledge manager and trainer. William Schiemann, Chair and CEO, Metrus Group identified three specific problems in HR area:

1. Focus

There is a lack of clear boundaries. Few organizations want to take the time to think strategically.

2. Balance

Organizations are trying to cater to the demands of multiple stakeholders.

3. Ownership thinking

Organizations are trying to figure out how to bring people into work every day with an ownership mentality.

For managing human resources more effectively and efficiently the future HR managers should take the following points into consideration.

Building leaders

'Make or buy talent'. Either way, you must invest in leader development. While technology is important to HR's future, it cannot replace good leadership.

Managing a changing workforce

It is expected to see more contingent worker in the future, as well as multiple ways to manage them. In addition, we will have to continue addressing the "Remote control mentality" of younger workers, who have options and will move if they are unhappy. The workforce will be more multicultural and in case of India, younger.

Keeping communication open and ongoing

As HR takes on more varied and strategic role, HR professional need to stay close to employees, despite the time and effort this requires.

Focusing on future success strategies and skill acquisition

HR center of power today drives from its ability to

develop relationships and act as strategic partner. For HR to continue to evolve, it must emphasize getting the fundamental rights, developing technologies that can share and manage information, and fostering a business environment of focus rather than control.

OVERVIEW OF INDIAN FINANCIAL SYSTEM

The financial system consists of specialized and non-specialized financial institutions, of organized and unorganized financial markets, of financial instruments and services, which facilitate transfer of funds. Procedures and practices adopted in the markets, and financial interrelationships are also parts of this system.

Financial liberalization is a phenomenon that is almost all pervasive in the world today. While liberalization has led to substantial benefits in terms of increased transparency it has ushered in opportunities of corporate mis-governance. This implies that the mechanism by which legal institutions ensure that suppliers of funds receive the return on investment is not sufficient or appropriate. Recent trends through the 1990s in India and abroad reveal how corporate governance has not been effective permitting unscrupulous and opportunistic individuals to manipulate the market in their favour. The process of financial market regulation ensures that important guidelines are issued regarding how primary dealers (brokers) should operate with regards to mode of operation, conduct, litigation, amount of business to be handled, management of risk, internal control, etc. The security scams and financial scandals involved the manipulation of huge amounts of money.

While the business organisations have increased access to global and domestic funds, the diligence of usage and cross-organisation transfer of funds is the important issues. Added to it is the concern for protecting the interest of small investor.

Future of India's Debt Market

The subject has gained importance over the years, and in particular, more recently after the Monetary and Credit

Policy of April 1997. Some of the reforms in the sector by RBI and Govt. of India have been highlighted here, which can have a probable effect on the debt market—

1. Second, non-banking financial companies are now required to maintain a higher level of liquid assets in the form of government securities and government-guaranteed bonds. This will increase the demand for government paper in the market.
2. Standard practices have to be evolved by the market with regard to the manner of quotes, the conclusion of deals, manner of pricing and accounting standards. In the context of moving towards a liberalized and market-oriented environment in the financial sector, it would be desirable if such standard practices were evolved and accepted in a common forum of a self-regulatory body.
3. Finally, the time has come to accord priority for establishing electronic links between the Deposit Accounts Department and Public Accounts Department/Public Debt Office of the RBI for achieving synchronization of funds and securities transfers.

Recent developments in Indian stock market: The other key area for corporate growth has been the reform of our stock markets. Competition from the National Stock Exchange forced the Bombay Stock Exchange to modernize. A nationwide electronic trading system is in place, shares are transferred electronically in a de-mat form, making issues of bad delivery no longer relevant. SEBI, which has formally established in April 1988, pushed modernization of the stock exchanges. But more importantly, it brought in a modern regulatory regime for Indian companies. For too long, public companies had been treated like the private property of the controlling shareholders. New SEBI norms of disclosure helped bring about greater transparency and accountability. And the corporate sector has learnt quickly how markets reward good corporate governance. And how unforgiving markets can be for failure of governance. The markets have ensured that the promoters with the largest stakes either benefit or hurt the most. While SEBI may not be as sophisticated and well organized as the SEC of USA, and while it may have made several mistakes along the way, it is credible regulatory agency equipped to oversee public companies. Seen against the background, the Indian corporate sector is now placed no differently from the corporate sector in the US or in the major European countries.

The past two years have seen more changes like abolition of *badla* system and the introduction of futures and options trading—putting in place separate markets for cash and forward segments. Indians are now allowed to invest in a limited way abroad in debt and equity. The most substantial change in the past few years, However, has been the ever-increasing responsiveness of the corporates to the markets through greater disclosures and improving corporate governance and the recognition of capital market performance as the benchmark of their success.

Kampani (2003) looks into as what does the future hold for Indian capital markets? We are increasingly being buffeted by far-reaching changes in technology, greater competition, changes in regulations, increasing volatility and greater demands of all participants in the market.

Global platforms for investment will be available for Indian investors in the future with full convertibility of the rupee. Greater integration of the equity and debt markets along with a wide variety of sophisticated financial instruments—equity, debt, commodity and forex—will increase the choice available to investors. Sophisticated hedge mechanisms and synthetic products will be available through the derivatives market. The key to success for investors will be portfolio management and risk management tools, increasing the role of professional financial planners. These changes will also require greater vigilance and responsibility on the part of regulators.

Mutual funds now constitute just about 10 percents of the size of bank deposits. With the increasing complexity of the market, investors will increasingly turn to professionals for managing their money.

With the advancement of technology, Straight-through-processing (STP) will considerably reduce risk through seamless integration of the exchange, banking and custody services.

But the basic rules of investing and psychological aspect of investing will never change—the cycle of fear, greed and hope will continue to lead investors into the capital markets.

Emerging Scenario of Insurance

Resulting from the opening up of insurance sector, policy-holders/investors will find a wide range of products for exercising choice, an obvious consequence of competition. Insurance currently is not considered so important due to lack of awareness, low income and illiteracy.

Market behaviour will undergo change, which will manifest in different market results; freedom to fix prices, the evolution of alternative sales method, stiffer competition from new players will put pressure on premium rates. Insurers will see real opportunity for sales in semi-urban and rural areas and will design suitable products for these markets.

Economic reforms initiated in 1991, swept across the economy. These had impact on the insurance industry also. The Malhotra Committee went into details. It recommended, inter-alia, to open insurance sector to private players.

MANUFACTURING AND SERVICE EXCELLENCE

The Indian Manufacturing sector is a story of lost opportunities, unimaginative government policies and lack of visionary entrepreneurial leadership. The virtual stagnation of jobs in the Indian manufacturing sector during the second half of the 1990s and the massive dip in the graph of manufacturing investments is a small reflection of the stunted sector. These trends were solid enough for industry experts to write-off the future of India's manufacturing. Services is the way ahead, was the unanimous opinion.

Manufacturing has provided enormous gains to the India's neighbouring country China. The secondary sector accounts for as much as 45% of the GDP in China as against

25% in India. While this development process has, by no means, exhausted itself, it has tended to show signs of slowdown principally because the developed world has realized that it can ill-afford to lose jobs on a massive scale both in the large-scale capital intensive manufacturing as well as in the SME sectors. This has given birth to New Global Manufacturing Order where international companies, including Indian multinationals have now come up with a process where they can retain control on markets and other critical drivers of success by developing manufacturing and distribution hubs at cost effective locations. By doing so the developed west seeks to address the critical areas where they have lost out on competitiveness and yet finally retain control on markets and R & D. There is good opportunity for competitive Indian companies to excel in the global market.

However, to make this happen, there has to be an effort for infrastructural development and regulatory structure reforms. Fortunately, in the SEZ policy package of the country, which was announced with much fanfare in the year 2000, we have conductive framework to address both these forces.

Paradoxically, the current setting is highly appropriate principally because it lends balance to the asymmetric perspective that has sought to project that the future of India lies in the service sector and more appropriately in the tertiary sector. In any case, it pays well to remember that tertiary sector is, by and large, a derivative of the growth in both primary and secondary sectors.

The future of service sector is blooming up and chances of India becoming a services hub are very high because of the abundant outsourcing opportunities available in the country. As on 31st March, 2003, the sector employed 171,000 professional. It has $1 billion invested in it. And it generated revenues of $2.3 billion in 2002-03. The sector promises the growth rate of 55 to 60% per annum. Table 1 shows the market potential for various services lines.

Table 2 shows the country-wise weaknesses and strengths in the BPO sector.

The ensuing section discusses as to how India fares on some of thee important parameters for BPO.

TABLE 1

Market Potential for Various Service Lines

Service Line	*Market Potential ($ billion)*
Human resource	3.5-4.0
Customer relationship	7.0
Payment services	3.0-3.5
Content development and others (Like animation)	2.5-3.0
Administration	1.5
Banking, Financial services and Insurance	3.5-4.5
Health care	1.5-2.0

Source: Business World Report.

TABLE 2

The World of BPO

Country	*USP*	*Limitation*
Philippines	Understands the US market; low attrition	More expensive than India; Small talent pool
Canada, Ireland, Australia	Understand the US; High-end skills	High costs
South Africa	Time zone similar to Europe; 25% cost saving; good for niche work	Skill shortage
China	Low costs	No English capability as yet
Russia, Ukraine	Technology skills	Poor infrastructure; Corruption; Language
Czech Republic, Hungary	European language skills	Small talent pool; High costs
Mexico	30% cheaper than the US; Spanish skills	Good only for low end jobs

Source: Business World Report.

Workforce

India produces 2.1 billion graduates, 0.3 million post-graduates and 0.9 million engineers every year. Specifically, the Indian Institute of Management produces 2000 MBAs every year, trained in the American case study format and a good understanding of American business practices.

In the IT sector, India leads the world in the number of companies certified at level 5 of SEI's Capability Maturity model. India has 50 companies at that level compared with just 2 in China and 1 in Canada.

Infrastructure

India operates one of the largest telecom networks in Asia with over 1,000,000 km of optic fiber cables. The power situation has also improved, with 100% power back up in the software technology parks.

Business climate

The Indian government emphasizes in the Cancun Round of WTO negotiations on the cross border delivery of services and the international movement of people to deliver services indicates the realization of the importance of the service industry.

Experience

Technology is the backbone of BPO and India's expertise in IT will definitely help. While domain expertise is key to success in BPO, technology expertise is also required and here Indian companies have a head start.

IT Industry and its Future

Coming to our own country, the Indian IT industry was $16.5 billion in 2002-03. It constitutes 3.2 per cent of the Indian GDP (gross domestic product). While the size is attractive, it is significantly short of our potential. Software services exports have been one of the biggest success stories of independent India. Software exports have grown at a compounded annual growth rate of over 40 per cent in the last five years to $9.9 billion in 2002-03. This has brought in precious foreign currency and developed the local economies of the places where IT companies are situated.

Often, when one speaks about Indian IT, the discussion tends to begin and end with software and services exports. The latent potential of the hardware sector appears to be completely ignored. Yet it is an area of enormous contribution potential. To see what a robust hardware industry can do to a country, just look at Singapore and Malaysia. The truth is that 47 per cent of Singapore's GDP and 65 per cent of Malaysia's GDP come from IT/electronic exports.

The Government of India has recognized the software industry as a high priority industry and has initiated various actions for its growth. Although the software industry has been registering an annual growth of fifty to sixty percent since 1993-94, the increase in value terms has been enormous. Majority of the Internet startups on the west coast of US are Indian. The Indian software companies are gearing up to grab opportunities available in areas like utilities, health care, retail, transportation; new services such as BPO, R & D services, internet-related services, mobile enablement and security and business continuity services.

TRENDS IN FAMILY BUSINESS

According to Pervin (1999), The past fifteen years has witnessed a substantial growth in interest in the family business—among family business members and the rest of the world. No longer are family businesses the butt of jokes or the career of last resort. Indeed, these survey results confirm that both the business family member and the professional who interacts with the family business is becoming more sophisticated in their dealings with each other, the partnership, the family and the business, especially in preventive measures in both the technical and behavioural arenas. Business families now report the changes observed in them and the impact of these changes on future:

1. Accidental partnerships are becoming more complex. Due to this family participation in the firm and number of inactive shareholders will continue to grow and create more partners who have not chosen to be together. This will require different styles of cooperation, communication, organization and governance to ensure a peer relationship and an appropriate level of participation in key decisions.

2. Shared leadership is becoming a reality. So, business families will continue to have an interest in unique and innovative leadership structures. Shared family leadership and teams will become a clear choice—not only for executive leadership but also for family and shareholder leadership.
3. Managing family relationships is becoming critical to business success. Therefore, business families will continue to value and express a strong appreciation for dignified family interaction, listening and communication. The family meeting process and family councils will become critically important to ongoing success. This is due to an expanding need for collaboration and managing positive relationships in the accidental partnership, family and business.
4. Planning for continuity is replacing succession planning. And thus, business families will take a multi-disciplinary approach to continuity planning because succession planning seems to hinge on a single event and is not the whole transition story. Family members have begun to clearly recognize that continuity is about changing relationships, roles, culture, direction, information sharing and entire governance systems and structures. To be effective, continuity planning must address and balance personal, family, business and ownership needs simultaneously within the human and corporate arenas.
5. More professional business practices are becoming the standard. Which leads to a strong preference to balance family and ownership needs within a more professional business environment. More family owners and managers are opting for a different style of organization that incorporates business and strategic plans, governance systems and strategic management methods. They are setting up multiple structures to separate family, estate, business and shareholder decisions, allowing both active and inactive shareholders to

take more responsibility for the present and future performance of the business and the family's wealth.

6. Women are increasingly taking consequential leadership roles. More women are being offered and are pursuing the opportunity to lead or play a consequential role in the business and/or in other areas of the family's wealth. Although gender differences still exist, women armed with education and corporate experience are challenging the historical traditions and are successfully taking on leadership roles in the firm as owners, on the foundation, on the board and/or in the family.
7. Distinct decision-making and accountability are gaining in popularity. As the number of shareholders increases and more business families choose to embrace a participative leadership style, we will see improved accountability, role clarity, sharing of information and more sophisticated governance methods and structures. This will result in more advisory boards, owners' forums and family councils as well as the systems and policies to support them.
8. The business family is becoming more focused on preventing rather than avoiding problems. Families are fighting the instinct to sweep sensitive issues aside. They are becoming more open, focused and interested in corrective action as they deal with issues in a fair, caring, aware and dignified manner. As the next generation takes over, families will begin to manage their relationships and attempt to improve their current family, business and partnership interaction with killed professional help, rather than leaving it to chance. It seems that they are not interested in a long process, but in a solutions-based therapeutic business process.
9. Family business information is becoming comprehensive and more readily available.

Therefore, business family population will continue to seek comprehensive information on family firms that validate and help find solutions to their unique situations. Business families will begin to strongly influence the universities, associations, other learning centers and publishers to produce well developed books, courses and tools to support their ongoing evolution from founder to 10th generation and beyond.

10. Services to the family business client will continue to celebrate their existence. As a result, professional service delivery to the family firm will continue to be more defined and sophisticated as respect for the family enterprise and its ownership relationship increases. As families get clearer when asking for assistance, professional advisors who only purport to be family business consultants will be ill-equipped to provide service. The business family will, therefore, seek those with a documented history of success thereby improving the service and its execution.

CONCLUSIONS

Can you imagine what the future will be like? Life will pop out of the pages of sci-fi. There will be little difference between you and your computer. Health, business, information, travel, in short, your whole life will change.

A decade from now, almost all offices could become paperless organizations. And governments, too, will be following the same route. Electronic corporations will come into being and regulation around the world will have to be completely revamped to deal with such companies. Electronic corporations will also do away with the need to hire humans to staff their offices.

In such a Hi-tech business environment the organization will have to far more competitive than they are now. The issue of competitiveness has been the subject of much economic debate for over a decade now. One can look at competitiveness at various levels—at the individual corporate firms' level, at the industry level and at the national level. Of course, these three are not isolated. The competitiveness environment in which its industry and the national economy operate would determine a large part of an individual firm's competitiveness. On the other hand, the competitiveness of an industry or a nation would be partly explained by the initiatives and innovations of individual firms.

In practical terms, one can also look at the competitiveness of industries from two angles—export competitiveness and import competitiveness. The former relates to a scenario where the domestic manufacturer is competing with global manufacturers for gaining an increasing share of the foreign market. And the latter relates to a scenario where the domestic manufacturer is competing against the importer to fight the import penetration of domestic markets. Thus, export competitiveness is an aggressor's concept and import competitiveness is a defender's concept. While it's worthwhile to distinguish between the two for the sake of analysis, one must remember that attack is the best way of defense. Aiming for export competitiveness is many times the best way to ensure that one retains import competitiveness too.

The next quantum leap is to move onto a regime where there will be fewer regulations and fewer controls. If imports and exports are to be truly free, then they must be rid of licenses. Export promotion must be simple and non-discretionary. And there are ways and means by which such incentives can be introduced.

Further, Special Economic Zones (SEZs) require focus. Still there is not a single SEZ taking off. What one requires for an SEZ is a different kind of constitutional and legal system. Secondly, there is no effort to explore new markets. One of the primary responsibilities of government is to find new market for products.

The challenge is, therefore, how to create an efficient economy which will liberate not only business and industry from rules and regulations that stifle economic growth but at the same time would also strengthen the hands of the government to discharge its social obligations more effectively and efficiently.

References

Athreya, Mrityunjay, "Transforming Corporate Governance", *Paradigm,* Vol. 1, No. 2, January 1998, pp. 10-13.

Bhattacharyya, Dipak Kumar, "Managing Supply Chain Through BPO &HRO" *Productivity,* Vol. 42, No. 4, January-March, 2002. pp. 546-549.

Chowdhury, Subir, "Management 21C", Prentice Hall, London, 2000.

Drucker, Peter, F, "Managing the next society", St. Martin's Press, New York, 2002.

Kurup, B, Shantha; Pankajam, A, "Developing leaders for the 21st century", *Vision,* Special issue—2000, pp. 57-68.

Murthy, Phaneesh; Paul, Jessie, "How India Can be a Service Hub", *The Economic Times,* January 9, 2004.

Neelamegham, S, "Managerial Challenges in the New Millennium", *Journal of Mangement Research* Vol 1. No.1, September-December 2000, pp. 12-17.

Perspective Column, *Business India,* April 14-27, 2003, pp. 44, 76, 86, 96, 140, 150, 154, 162, 222, 226, 232, 238.

Pervin, R., Aron, "Trends in Family Business", June 1999. www.pervinfamilybusiness.com/survey_sum.pdf

Report, "Insurance: emerging scenario", *Contemporary Banking and Finance,* Vol. 1, No. 6, December 2000, pp. 1-5.

Report: "Trends to watch in HR Future", *HR Focus,* December 2002, pp. 7-10

Robert, S., Kaplan; David, P., Norton, "Balance Scorecard", Harward Business Press, 1996.

Sidhu, Hina, " Trade Liberalization and Indian IT Industry" *Productivity* Vol. 43, No. 1, April-June, 2002, pp. 149-155.

Singh, Shelley, "The BPO Status Report", *Business World,* August 2003, pp. 28-35.

Singh, Shelley, "The Next Thirty Years" *Business World,* 3 June, 2002, pp. 27-37.

CHAPTER

2

Women Executives in Changing Times

A Study with Reference to Women Working in Private Sector Banks and Insurance Companies

PARVINDER ARORA AND ASHWANI BHALLA

Though the role of women is changing in every society and India is no exception. However, it has to be seen that how has been this transition phase. This paper is an attempt to highlight what problems women face when they go out for the job, because still it is believed that India is a male dominated country where men and women have traditionally defined roles. The paper focuses on finding out what difficulties women face when they enter into the corporate world, and whether these are the same problems as faced by the men. Moreover, the paper also attempts to see what kind of behaviour or attitude the male colleagues have towards the working women. Are they treated at par with the male colleagues? Another interesting aspect of this would be to study if working women are satisfied with their jobs they are doing and what are their expectations.

INTRODUCTION

Gone are the days when women were confined to the four walls of the house. The stages of development through which our country is going can be seen in every field. In last few decades the role of women has changed to a greater extent. The past century has seen a striking development in the participation rate of women in all sectors whether it is related to business or doing jobs. They have not only begun to play a major role in the workforce, but they have also challenged the persistent barriers in order to enter the traditionally male professions. However, this path has been full of hurdles. Originally the participation of women in field of business and services was very rare. Sex role stereotyping was an evident cause for this phenomenon, where man predominantly carried the role of the bread winner and was perceived as being dominating, aggressive, competitive and assertive. In contrast, women were perceived as being the ultimate child bearer, the dependent housewife with little skills and knowledge and too emotional and passive to handle the stresses associated with professional workforce. But today the scene has changed; today more and more women are taking part in the developmental function. Today nobody can deny the fact that role of women in development of economy is increasing. In each and every field we see women standing head to head with men and contributing sometimes even more than what men do.

In recent times, there has been a lot of debate on the role of women managers in Indian organizations. Traditionally Indian women have been excellent managers as they have managed the institution called home very effectively (Parkash Kewalramani). However, women in India have struggled to establish an identity and create a life space in social as well as work organizations. Though, educational institutions are training women to enter into new professions and to move away from traditional expected roles and low paid jobs (Kalpana). However, the question is whether women make better managers for 21st century. Whatever the difference of detail, managing involves getting things done, making things happen, within a certain period of time and a budgeted cost. Seldom is it possible without working through people (S. Ramachander). The changing nature of work and the workplace due to the effects of technology and social and political changes have been much commented upon. Very soon, the nine to five employer and fixed office space might become anachronisms world over (S. Ramachander). In this changing scenario the question gains a great deal of importance. Let us first try to analyze what are the problems which a working woman faces when she leaves home to go out and work.

There are regional differences in male attitudes towards women colleagues. In north India, men display a lot of aggressive behaviour. They don't say things directly; but the manner and tones makes it quite aggressive. And there, men are not very comfortable with women managers. However, in the southern India, men tend to have more respect for women. Direct fallout of this is that North Indian women tend to be more assertive and sometimes even aggressive, in order to cope (Rasheeda Bhagat). The gender related problem is not specific to Indian society. A Chinese study revealed that in china a woman manager has to do 125% to get 90% appreciation (Rasheeda Bhagat). Management studies on the gender initiatives taken by corporate world shows that companies have followed three approaches. There are some companies that like their women employees to be part pf 'boys', adopt masculine styles of functioning, play golf, takes on tough assignments in factories or overseas and be assertive leaders just like the men. Other companies recognize that women employees do the same but they have different needs which are required to be addressed and accommodated at the workplace (Preeti Mehra). However, all the three approaches have their limitations. That being part of the boy's golf game or making use of flexi hours or even being praised for bringing in the 'feminine' approach to running an organization do not change the essential gender inequity inherent in the system. That would require a larger social change perspective (Preeti Mehra). People in society including employers, have prejudices in their minds both in favour and against women. There are many organizations looking for women on the assumption that women would suit certain vocations better; and there are some employers who don't prefer women for certain jobs thinking that they can't handle them (V. Balaram). Anybody who has worked in an office will be familiar with these notions, a couple positive and rest negative. Women managers are bad; tiresome, sensitive, soft, frustrated, insecure, tough, understanding, and difficult to work with. It immediately becomes a gender issue, as if belonging to a particular gender predisposes on to behaving in a certain way as a manager (Sravanti Challapalli). Another perhaps the biggest challenge faced by women managers today is managing their dual roles of "organizational employees" and "housewives", i.e. working for the organizations as well as their homes (Parkash Kewalramani). The breaking up of joint family system into emerging pattern of nuclear family without the supporting family structure has created the problem of balancing work and family life. The pressures to which women are subjected to at the work place and in the family contrast, and problems encountered after marriages with their spouses and their roles as parents go on increasing (Kalpana).

For the majority of women today parenthood in combined with full time paid work. Although having multiple roles has been found to be beneficial to overall well being for both men and women, multiple roles can also lead to role conflict and negative psychological outcomes. These negative outcomes may be a result of time-based conflict. Working women can be expected to experience higher levels of work family conflict then non-working women. Factors associated with managerial careers, including long hours and psychologically demanding work, have been demonstrated to correlate with work, family conflict. Moreover, job involvement, defined as the extent to which a person identifies with their job and the degree of influence the job has on self-image and self-concept has also been found to have a positive relationship with work family conflict (Apperson and Moore).

Consistently, the managers had not thought about how being women affected their work. For most being a manager does not conflict with their ideas of being an ideal woman. On the contrary, some stated it actually facilitated their goals of being ideal women, because success was a symbol of independence, and the result of one's diligence and intelligence, considered indispensable element of being an ideal women (wang Yi). Many women managers suffer from the fear of success phenomenon and this often results in the woman taking a step backward in her career aspirations, often to modify her husbands and maintain domestic harmony (Rasheeda Bhagat).

Women at the top are still rare. Globally, they comprise only 10% of senior managers in fortune 500 companies, less than 4% are in the uppermost ranks of CEO, president, executive vice-president and COO and less than 3% of them are top corporate earners (Preeti Mehra). In India too, it is no different may be worse. Women in corporate India are aware of the constraints they work under and obviously try to make the best of the bargain. They typically bear a disproportionate amount of responsibility for home and family and thus have more demands on their time outside the office and when they do reach the managerial level, they bring with them both silver lining and dark clouds. Women always being under family pressure, having to take a break due to marriage; deliveries, etc. and hence from the company's point of view are unable to live up to their responsibilities (Preeti Mehra).

The differences one observes between men and women in behaviors and abilities are related more to nurture than nature. What influences women as a group is the societal expectation of what a woman should do and her own psychological consciousness for her being a woman. Many women managers tend to follow their husbands to their new places of work, even if it means sacrificing their career; and this happens even to IIM graduates and the chartered accountants. Women say they do this because they care for their husbands. Obviously, societies conditioning comes into play here (V. Balaram).

SOCIAL AND CULTURAL FORCES

One of the major hurdles in the progress of women is society and culture that prevails in every country. This can be understood better taking example from some Chinese studies.

In order to understand how being women affects their leadership experience, we need to first get a sense of being an urban woman in contemporary Mainland China. There are 3 major social forces that significantly shape this woman's gender identity. The first force is China's longest feudalism history and its legacy on today's society. The feudalistic tradition regards women as inferior to men in all respects. They were considered psychologically weak and intellectually undeveloped. With its deep roots in the culture, this belief is still held by many Chinese men and women. The second is the socialist movement, since the foundation of socialist China in 1949. In this movement, women's equal rights have been stipulated in the constitution. The final major social force shaping Chinese women's gender identity is the economic reform that China is undergoing now (Wand Yi).

The sensitivity of women and their perception of the society, their dilemmas when they are confronted with ideas and expectations of the traditional society and the demands of conforming to a contemporary perceptive code of conduct. It highlights values, attitudes and belief of women in formal work organizations and primary family system (Kalpana).

Do women manage differently in that they can be more humans or understanding? As a matter of fact, good managers both men and women, manage a situation according to the demands of the situation. So they play a role of a friendly persuasive leader when that is required or the role of an assertive leader if that is called for. The fact is that societal expectations and situations often decide what role a woman will play in a certain society. For example see the Iranian society where today one finds a number of women in business. They wear the "Chador", yet they are confident of what they are doing; they are well informed and they take good business decisions. This situation has come about because Iran lost several of its young male population during the prolonged war in Iraq. The Iranian women came to fill the voids left by their men in business and society. So it was a reversal of societal roles in Iran. Even in India the role expected of a man as the bread winner and a woman as the homemaker would be redefined in the years to come; and more opportunities will open up for the women at the workplace. The sheer pressure of ability will paid more and more women into management (V. Balaram).

CHANGING SCENARIO

"A coin has two sides" if we see at its one side we can't see the other, this is true with the women working in the organization. It is true that women face many problems working with the male colleagues but there are some good qualities and positive attitude which can only be seen in a woman. Women establish their own business outside of the traditional corporate because they "want to create their own way to balance what they think is important, their families and work, "says Linda Tarr-Whalen, president and executive director of the center for policy Alternatives in Washington, D.C. "They are not going to try to change the rules, but rather write their own rules so that work doesn't have to be on one side and family on another. They want to live by the rules what women think make sense." The insights that follow are from women whose spirit and creativity has brought great successes to their careers (Ellie Wymard).

"Failures are important because you learn from them", says Clare L. Rothman, president of California Forum. "There's more exhilarating–no money, no power—than knowing deep in your heart you are making the best difference you could possibly make. Once you start taking risks around your values, you get so much psychic energy because you believe in your life. Women need to believe that they have right to live a life that in most inspiring to them, which is a life befitting their values. Until women take risk, they are not going to have the lives that they deserve and that they need, and that we need them to have."

Whatever be the fall of liberalization, one thing is certain—it has opened up immense opportunities. There is a market for everything you can dream of, and the new middle class with buying power is almost adventurous in its task. No one has time. We all need someone who can do it for us. So anything that spells convenience and quality sells! Retailing is a big business and has spawned a host of supplier chains. Women are excelling in the small business sector as they convert their time and talents to green backs!

A woman led office is always a better and brighter place for everybody to work in and there you are bound to find flowers, plants and socially relevant posters. Women managers are more accessible and use a human, participatory approach with their colleagues. But there is a flip side to it—there is often a complaint that woman bosses are aggressive and dominating and push for a job to be completed more than normal. However, Ranjana Kumari, who has specialized in women studies, attempts to explain why this happen. She feels that when women reach the top and it is the anxiety to prove them that gets translated into certain actions. Often women managers tend to subsume their female identity to be a part of the top management. Sue Evans, Principal consultant, A.T. Kearney, has another explanation that involves perspective. She feels it could often be due to double standards. "What's assertive in men is viewed as aggressive in women, and it's mostly who make this complaint", she says and then adds, "But I do believe often women have to overplay their assertiveness in order to be heard. Women have soften voices and have to muscle into get heard at meetings." One of the strongest skills she has found in women managers is their ability at multi-tasking. Women are used to performing different roles and struggling with different tasks at the same time, in the Kitchen, at home also at work. Ritu Nanda CEO at Escolife and Ritu Nanda Insurance Services Pvt. Ltd. (RNIS) is a veteran starting ventures at Escorts. She is categorical in her view that indeed women managers bring with them a different style and different skills. She says, "of course women managers do things differently from men managers because research has shown that women have 40% more nerve connector than man (Preeti Mehra).

Radha Shelat, Technical Director, Veritos Software India, says that initially she had her reservations about not being able to go out often with he make colleagues, but things have changed now and she is a part of the group which goes out for walks, a game or two of tennis or a meal (Sudha Menon). Today in India, many companies bend backward and retain more women and bring them to top levels, Hindustan Levers (HLL) is one of them. There are two reasons for this, The first one being that many products of the HLL are for women and they are HLL's main customers, secondly women form 50% of population and if the company doesn't employ them in an equal proportion, it feels that it cannot be adequately sensitive to the needs of the society (V. Balaram)

Bridget Macaskill says, "Don't get so focused on the obstacles relating to your gender that you are distracted from your ability to get job done, because inevitably you jeopardize yourself. Find ways to cross the obstacles, rather thinking "here's a whole bunch of men who are trying to stop me.

Aditi Malik, Regional Business Manager (India and Middle East), M Phasis, however, differs", I think talented men and women get equal opportunities and if enough women are not seen at the top, I think it is because they are not willing to pay the huge price that is demanded from their personal lives. While men are conditioned to give up a lot of things for their careers, women are not, she says (Sudha Menon).

Though the role of women is changing in every society and India is no exception. However, it has to be seen that how has been this transition phase. This paper is an attempt to highlight what problems women face when they go out for the job, because still it is believed that India is a male dominated country where men and women have traditionally defined roles. The paper focuses on finding out what difficulties women face when they enter into the corporate world, and whether these are the same problems as faced by the men. Moreover, the paper also attempts to see what kind of behaviour or attitude the male colleagues have towards the working women. Are they treated at par with the male colleagues? Another interesting aspect of this would be to study if working women are satisfied with their jobs they are doing and what are their expectations.

For the purpose of the study a very simple research methodology was followed. The paper is based on primary data which has been collected by resorting to questionnaire method of data collection. A pre tested questionnaire was administered to the subjects of the study. Different questionnaires were used for married women and unmarried women. The questionnaire consisted of twenty odd questions which included both open ended and close ended questions.

The size of the sample for the purpose was 100. Hundred women working in the private banks and insurance companies were selected as the respondents. It was not possible to locate the working women in the corporate world so emphasis was put on the service sector. Further amongst the service sector, only private sector banks and private sector insurance companies were selected for the simple reasons that after the opening up of the economy these are two industries which have done the recruitment very heavily in the recent past. The different banks such as ABNAMRO, Standard Chartered, Citibank, Lord Krishna, ICICI Bank, Bank of Punjab, HDFC Bank and Insurance companies like ICICI, HDFC standard life insurance, were identified as all of them have offices in Chandigarh. Chandigarh was chosen for the purpose as most of the banks/companies have their offices there. From each of these banks/companies at least 4 women employees were selected as the respondents on convenience basis.

ANALYSIS AND INTERPRETATION

The research project was undertaken to study the problems which are faced by the Indian working women. As we all know that India is a developing country but still the behaviour adopted towards the women is not acceptable. The mentality of the people living in society is still the same as it was centuries ago that women should not be allowed to go out and work and must follow their husband. In this study an attempt has been made to understand that what level of work family pressure is faced by the working women, how their family members reacts to woman's decision to go out and work. Work-family pressure is the major problem which is faced by the working women. They have to face the work pressure both at the work place and at home. To understand the experience of these women, therefore, one simply needs to extrapolate findings. The experience of Indian working women, their aspirations, difficulties, achievements, satisfaction and cultural identity are largely understudied and this study is just an attempt to explore some of these facts. Joint families are being converted into nuclear family and if in such a nuclear family both husband and wife are working then there can be many good reasons for conflict between them. Moreover, mentality of society plays an important role in success or failure of the people living in it. The people living in our society give more preference to the gender (male). Male domination exists in our society to a great extent and it is also one of the barriers for the woman which restricts them to take any new step. In order to enquire about the general perception that "man is a bread winner and woman is a house keeper", this study has been undertaken. The whole study was focused to determine what place the women occupies today in the society, how she is looked upon by the people living in the society.

For the purpose of the study primary data was collected through a structured questionnaire. Two detailed questionnaire were prepared for this purpose one for the married and other for the unmarried women to collect. The questions focused on their views, attitude towards them of the society, their family, problems they face at home and at workplace, etc. The data thus collected was tabulated and percentage method was used for analysis. No statistical tool other than percentages have been used because the data was so revealing that further analysis would not have made any difference to the inferences.

Today we know that world has become a global village due to which the companies have no national boundaries. In our country too we can see large number of foreign companies operating and this has provided an opportunity to everybody including women to participate and play an important role.

Q I. Since how long are you in job?

	Respondents	*%age*
(a) Less than 1 year	46	46
(b) 1-5 years	46	46

(c) 5-10 years	8	8
(d) 10 or more	-	-
	100	100

As seen traditionally India is a male dominated country where men are supposed to perform the role of bread winner and women would take care of family. However, this viewpoint has been changing for quite sometime and now women realizing their potential and seems to have started working. Out of the total respondents who were subjected to this study majority of the respondents (92%) were working for less than 5 years and only 8% of the total respondents were in job for more than 5 years and surprisingly no respondent was in job for more than 10 years. The reasons behind this may be many; first the selected respondents were from private banks and insurance companies. This phenomenon of private banks and insurance companies is new in India. Secondly, these organizations give chance to young bloods and offer them better opportunity to be a part of their system.

There may be many reasons or factors for which an individual joins a job. The motivating factor could be anything.

Q 2. What made you to go for a job?

	Respondents	*%age*
(a) Self-satisfaction	46	46
(b) Recognition	40	40
(c) Family Compulsion	2	2
(d) Financial Consideration	10	10
(e) Anything else	2	4
	100	100

In order to enquire about the factors responsible for pushing Indian women toward job, when respondents were asked they were put to specific queries. The data reveals that self satisfaction and recognition are the two major factors motivating the Indian women.

As the data reveals that majority of women (45%) joined the job for their self satisfaction and around 40% of women to get recognition in the society in which they live. It may be the desire to prove that they are not less than men. Money is perceived to be the central point which motivates women to go out and work. However, Indian women seem to have different idea. Money is the motivating factor only for 11% whereas more than 85% go out for job because of either self satisfaction or recognition.

Today working women face work-family pressure. Work-family pressure means the burden of work at the work place and at home. Early in the morning they have to cook food for the family members and do a lot more work and then they go out for the job at their workplace so it is a little bit difficult for them.

Q 3. What level of work family pressure do you experience?

	Respondents	*% age*
(a) Very low	42	42
(b) Low	8	8
(c) Moderate	42	42
(d) High	4	4
(e) Very high	4	4
	100	100

There is a general perception that working women face a lot of work- family pressure. When during the study it was tried to find out if this perception is valid or not, surprisingly majority of working women (84%) said they face low and very low level of work-family pressure and out of the total respondents only 8% face high and very high level of work-family pressure. More than 50% of the working women face low or very low level of pressure. The result of the study proves this general perception wrong to a great extent.

When women go out for work sometime they might be asked to work for late hours and it is an important factor that could raise conflict in the family. First in Indian culture women are not allowed to work because it is a kind of mentality which has been developed for many years and secondly working for the late hours at work place adds to their problems.

Q 4. To what extent late hours at work place affects your family life and leads to domestic problems?

	Respondents	%age
(a) To great extent	6	6
(b) To some extent	60	60
(c) Can't Answer.	8	8
(d) To negligible extent	22	22
(e) Not at all	2	4
	100	100

Peculiar to our society is that women should be confined to the four walls of the house and should not go out and work. Because there are many reasons for this, one strong reason is that women have to take care of the family members and have to do all the work at home, so an attempt was made to find out whether for women working during late hours at work places leads to domestic problem. More than half (60%) of the respondents said that it leads to domestic problems but to some extent, and 6% of them said that working late hours at workplace leads to domestic problem to a great extent. 8% of the respondents could not answer the question, 22% said to negligible extent and 4% said there are no domestic problems even if they work late hours. This reveals that working women if work for late hours at work place they do face some domestic problems due to it.

Joint families are converting into nuclear families and if both husband and wife are working in a family then there might be good reasons for clashes between them. Each one of them will be afraid to take upon the family responsibilities. So some of the respondents included in the study were married and to know what kind of problems or tensions are faced by them when both of them are working the question was first put to them about their husband.

Q 5. What is your husband?

(a)	Govt. Employee	
(b)	Private Employee	02
(c)	Businessman	02
(d)	Professional	02

The question about their husband was put to working women which were only three in number. However, as these married women were three in number so no significant results can be drawn.

Working women are generally faced with two type of workload one is work at workplace and second is work at the home. Even if they are properly managing their work then also it is not sure that their job is secure. In order to find out how much their job is secured from the point of view of their family they were put to following queries.

Q 5a. If he is in job and is transferred, will you go along with him and leave our job?

(a)	Most Likely	02
(b)	Likely	00
(c)	Never Thought	02
(d)	Can't Answer	02

However, the result got from the married working women were not surprising because as we all know that India is a male dominated society and woman has to do what their husband tells them to do. Today also they are dependent upon their husband. The response got from married women reveals that even they are working but they have to follow their husband. When they were asked about their viewpoint on the question one respondent said that she would most likely move along with her husband and one respondent said that she has never thought about this and one of them said she can't answer. But significant results can't be drawn from this as the number of married working women were very less, but however, if we take into consideration these responses we can easily make out what reality is.

As we all know that society and culture to which a person belongs play a major role in shaping his/her thought process. A person can't do anything which is not acceptable to society and in case if he/she does so, the problem arises.

Q. 6. If you are transferred will your husband seek transfer and move along?

(a)	Most likely	00
(b)	Likely	00
(c)	Never thought	04
(d)	Can't Answer	02

In our society a person have the attitude that a man is supreme and whatever he does is right even if it is actually wrong, and it is accepted by the majority. But in the case of women it is completely different. Now working women sometimes have to take decisions that are very critical and these decisions are taken within the boundaries of the society and culture in which they live. In order to know how much married working women are affected by these critical decisions they were put to the queries and response were not the shocking one. However, significant results can't be drawn, but if we look at these responses one can make out that how much secure is the job of married working women.

India is a developing country and it is moving through the different stages of development and this kind of development can also the seen in the nuclear families where both husband and wife are working and understand each others needs, responsibilities and problems. Where both husband and wife are working in the family, they help each other in their work. In order to explore this fact, married working women were asked about their experience and how helpful their husbands are and to what extent they are performing their duties at home other than at the work place.

Q 7. Is your husband a good help in household chores?

(a)	To great extent	00
(b)	To some	04

(c) Can't Answer 00
(d) To Negligible 02
(e) Not at all 00

It is true that women have to take care of the family but in many families where the women are working there is a very good understanding between the husband and wife and each one performs his/her responsibilities and take care of their respective partner. As we all know that a working woman have to face work-family pressure, but it can be reduced if husband understands the problem and provides a helping hand to their wives. However, it was found during the study that husbands help their wives in house work to some extent as 2 of the respondents were of this view point and 1 respondent said that her husband help her to a negligible extent. It shows that where both husband and wife are working each one take care of other.

Everyone has ego problem and nobody wants that his/her ego should be harmed. Men are more egoistic and if somebody hurts their ego they take it as their insult. The next question which was put to the married working women was put as a supposition to know how their husband reacts to their success or earning more.

Q 8. Assume you are earning more than your husband; will it lead to any conflict?

(a) Always 00
(b) Quite Sometimes 04
(c) Can't answer 02
(d) Seldom 00
(e) Never 02

The responses got from the respondents were not significant to draw any conclusion as out of 3 respondents 1 was of this viewpoint that it creates problems, whereas one said she can't answer and one of them said it will never had any conflict. The response given by the respondents takes in view the nature of their partner if the partner understands one then there is no problem on other hand if he is egoistic then conflict is obvious.

One of the problems which are faced by the working women at the workplace is the behaviour of their male colleagues towards them. The good behaviour of the male counterparts at the workplace lowers the work pressure.

Q 9. What kind of behaviour more colleagues have toward female counterparts?

	Respondents	*%age*
(a) Aggressive	12	12
(b) Assertive	26	26
(c) Never noticed	38	38
(d) Any other	18	18
(e) Can't Answer	6	6
	100	100

In order to enquire about the behaviour of their male colleagues, the working women were put to the queries. The behaviour of the male colleagues working at the work place can make the working environment for a woman good or worse. Out of the total respondents 12% of them said that the behaviour of their male colleagues toward them is aggressive, 26% said that the behaviour is assertive and 38% said that they never noticed the behaviour because they don't care about the behaviour of their male collogues and take interest in their work, 18% said that they are not able to find out because sometime the behaviour is aggressive and sometime it is assertive and 6% could not answer the question. So it reveals that majority of working women (38%) do not care about the behaviour of their male colleagues because they care about their work. It is also revealed that behaviour to somewhat is assertive because the male colleagues have accepted the women as the part of their system and system can only run without proper co-ordination and a feeling of equality.

When women are at the managerial post and they have to give orders and have to get the work done from the male subordinates it is difficult for both the manager and the subordinates. From the view point of the male subordinate, they feel ashamed when they are criticized by the female boss and from the viewpoint of the female managers it is hard to criticize the male subordinates.

Q 10. Do you think women managers face problems in criticizing their male subordinates? If yes, to what extent?

	Respondents	%age
(a) To great extent	4	4
(b) To some extent	30	30
(c) Can't Answer	18	18
(d) To negligible	18	18
(e) Not at all	30	30
	100	100

It is a general perception that working women face problem in criticizing their male subordinates. In order to find it, they were put to following queries. Majority of respondents (more than 50%) said that they really face problem in criticizing their male subordinates, but the work has to be done. So it reveals that if the male subordinates working under them do not work properly then they get aggressive and do not hesitate to criticize them.

If the manager who has to get the work done is a man then there is no problem for him he can get the work done very easily because it is in a man nature, but when it comes to women they faces complaints because as they adopt aggressive behaviour the male subordinates feels that it is a shame for them. In order to enquire if it is true, the respondents were put to the following queries.

Q 11. There are often complaints by male subordinates that women managers are more aggressive and dominating. Do you agree? If yes, to what extent?

	Respondents	%age
(a) To great extent	6	6
(b) To some extent	44	44
(c) Can't answer	18	18
(d) To negligible extent	12	12

(e) Can't Answer	20	20
	100	100

It was revealed that majority of women (62%) were of the view point that they have to adopt aggressive behaviour for getting the thing done. If they do not act in this manner then their male subordinates don't take their orders seriously and this could affect the overall performance. Therefore, the analysis reveals that if you are not demanding you can't get the work done and if you are demanding you have to face the problems. Moreover, male subordinates do not like to be criticized by a female because of ego problem.

The phenomenon that women are entering into the corporate sector is new in India. In order to enquire about the problem they face in entering into the corporate sector the question was put to them.

Q 12. Do you agree with the fact that the women in Indian corporate sector face the kind of hurdles that men don't especially during initial phase?

	Respondents	*%age*
(a) Always	14	14
(b) Quite sometimes	42	42
(c) Can't answer	16	16
(d) Seldom	20	20
(e) Never	8	8
	100	100

It is a general perception that women face more problems and hurdles at the initial stage of entering into the corporate sector, from the responses it was clear that majority (76%) of women were of the viewpoint that the problem they face is more than that faced by the men. The reason behind this may be the male domination in the corporate sector or due to the mentality of the people that women are not able to face the problem of corporate sector and can only do the house work. Therefore, it reveals that women face a lot of problem at their initial stages.

In very few organizations it has been seen that women reach at the top position. And if they reach there, they have to face criticism and problems and even sometimes their success becomes personal thing for their male colleagues.

Q. 13 Do you think your male colleagues take your success and reaching senior position as a personal thing?

	Respondents	*%age*
(a) Always	4	4
(b) Quite sometimes	34	34
(c) Can't answer	20	20
(d) Seldom	6	6
(e) Never	36	36
	100	100

However, in order to enquire this when the working women were asked about this, majority of them (44%) said that it is true that their male colleagues take their success and reaching top as a personnel thing but this type of mentality does not exist in women. The reason for this may be the society and culture in India where it is peculiar that women should be confined to the four walls of the house and should not go out and work. Most of the respondents were of the viewpoint that reaching at the top or getting promotion hurts a man's ego and they take it as a personal thing.

Indian culture is a male dominated culture where man is given the highest position both in family and at the workplace. So it is very difficult for a woman to prove herself by doing her job. Even if she does her work properly than also she gets less than what she expects.

Q 14. Do you agree with the fact that in male dominated culture women has to do more to get less?

	Respondents	*%age*
(a) Always	16	16
(b) Quite sometimes	38	38
(c) Can't answer	4	4

(d) Seldom	16	16
(e) Never	52	8
	100	100

In order to find if the notion is valid, the queries were put to the respondents. Majority (54%) of the women were of the viewpoint that they have to do more to get little appreciation because of male domination and did not agree with this view point. It reveals that women have to struggle and have to do more to get less. It is not easy for a woman to survive in the corporate world, she has to work hard and has to devote her whole time in her work, and she has to sacrifice a lot in order to get a little appreciation.

Now the picture is changing as more and more women are entering in the corporate world. So the traditional thinking that role of a woman of a housewife and man as a bread winner should be redefined.

Q 15. Don't you think that role expected of a man as bread winner and women as home maker should be redefined?

	Respondents	*%age*
(a) Immediate need	22	22
(b) Its already changed	62	62
(c) No need	12	12
(d) Can't answer	4	4
	100	100

When the working women were asked about this question, majority (62%) of them said that it has already changed as more and more women are entering in the corporate world it is a true example of this and about 22% said that there is an immediate need for the change. Now the traditional thinking that man is a bread winner no longer exists because women also go out and work. They play an equal role in running the family and earning the livelihood.

Working women have to face two types of work load that is called work family pressure. The workload that they face at the workplace can affect their family life because when they go home they don't leave the workload at the doorsteps.

Q 16. How often do you complain about work overload?

	Respondents	%age
(a) Always	2	2
(b) Quite sometimes	56	56
(c) Can't answer	2	2
(d) Seldom	20	20
(e) Never	20	20
	100	100

Workload is a major problem faced today by all because there is competition in every field. For working women also it is a problem because they have to take care of the family also. However, in order to know whether they complain about work overload, majority of working women (54%) said that they often complain about work overload because this workload affects their family life and only 20% said that they never complain about work overload. So it reveals that work overload is a problem and majority of women complain about it.

The factors could be many that motivate women to compete with his male counterparts. In order to enquire what motivates them more they were put to following queries.

Q 17. What motivates you to compete with your male counterparts?

	Respondents	%age
(a) Self-satisfaction	40	40
(b) Recognition	36	36
(c) Financial consideration	10	10
(d) Independent life	34	34
(e) Anything else	4	4
	NA	NA

However, the result obtained revealed that about 80% of the working women are motivated by the factors that are self satisfaction, recognition and independent life. So for most of the women it is not the money which motivates them it is the self-respect which motivates them because they want to prove that they are equal to men. These motivating factors play an important role to boost their morale and compete with their male counterparts.

In India there are many problems or hurdles due to which women are not seen at the top. But for the purpose of the study it was asked from the respondents and they gave different reasons for this problem.

Q 18. Why is more women not seen at the top? (tick whichever you fell is the reason)

	Respondents	*%age*
(a) Family problem	38	38
(b) Society and culture	30	30
(c) Male domination	24	24
(d) More is expected	12	12
(e) Anything else	6	6
	NA	NA

The phenomenon that Indian women started taking part in the corporate sector started few years ago and there are many reasons that women are not seen at the top. When asked from the women majority of them (34%) said due to family problem women are not able to devote much of the time to their work, 27% said it is the attitude of the people living in the society which restricts them to be at the top, 21% said India is a male dominating society and it is one of the reason that more women are not seen at the top, 11% said more is expected from women and 6% said there are many other reasons.

Q 19. If given an option to change, what kind of job will you prefer to take up?

The answer to this question was a mixed one some said they will took up a teacher job, some said a job with more respect, some said a job with more income, etc. so as this question was on open ended question the responses were different.

Q 20. Do you think your job has fulfiled your purpose of joining the job?

It was also an open ended question and responses were different some of them gave the answers in yes/no and some have written few lines. But most of the respondents were satisfied with there job and want to continue it as it has fulfiled their purpose of joining the job?

CONCLUSION

The progress that women have made in the traditionally male dominated Indian culture has been outstanding. However, the survey has revealed that there is still a long way to go before true gender equity exists. Women have failed to progress through the ranks at an equal pace to men and represents a very low proportion of expatriates being sent to global assignment remuneration and workload is also found to be significant area where gender-based differences exists. Discrimination and sea role stereotyping is one possible explanation underlying these inequities. The study conducted by me suggested that now the days were gone when women were only used to take care of kids now time has changed, women are going out to work, this all is possible because proper education is today provided to them and people have realized that girl are equal to boys. Working women face to some extent work/family pressure but they have learned how to manage this problem. The study also reveals that their family also supports them and married women are helped by their husband this all is possible due to proper understanding between the two. From the last 2-3 decades role of women in the service sector has increased this all is possible because of coming up of the private companies. Equal chance is given to them. What needed to be done is that there should be increased awareness of economic implications of women in service sector. The existing barriers should be removed so that woman should take part in the growth of the country. The problems which are faced by a woman at the initials stages of her career are somewhat different from that faced by a man and when women work more is expected from them.

Society also plays a role in participation of women in any field, Indian society where people feel that man can only go out and work and this mentality should also be changed but the respondents of the study revealed that to great extent this mentality has changed and now the people are also helping them. Majority of women I met for the research purpose are satisfied with their jobs because their male counterparts have a right kind of behaviour toward them. but still there is need that something should be done to increase the women role in service sector.

References

Balaraman, V. "Nature versus Nurture", www.successfulmanagers.com, pp. 18-21

Bhagat, Rasheeda. "Facing The Creditability Hurdle", www. successfulmanagers.com, pp. 26-29.

Bhagat, Rasheeda. "Sorry . . . I'm a woman manager", www. successfulmanagers.com, pp. 1-4.

Borozan, Djula. *et al.* "The meaning of differences: working of Croatian Women", www.sbaer.uca.edu/reasearch/2003.

Challapalli, Sravanthi. "There's still room at the top", www.successfulmanagers.com, pp. 22-25.

Creevey Lucy E. *et al.* (1997) "Reports on the impacts of grassroots management training in India", www.worldbank.org, pp. 1-7.

Crotty, Jill Nicholson and Meier, Kenneth J. (2002) "Benevolent Dictator or Queen of Hearts: Women Managers at the top of the organization", Paper presented at Annual meeting of the Midwest political science association.

Culpan, Oya and Wright, Gillian H. (2002) "Women abroad: getting the best results from women managers", *The International Journal of Human Resource Management.*

Davis, Susan. "Make a Difference", President and Founder of Capital Missions Company.

Dunlop, John E and Velkoff, Victoria A.. (1999), "Women and Economy in India", Women of the World, pp. 1-7.

Glover, Jere W. (1998), "Women in Business", U.S. Small Business Administration, Washington, D.C., pp. 1-17.

Hills, Katharine. "Woman Managers' Workplace Relationships: Reflections of Cultural Perception of Gender", www.le.ac.uk, CLMS Working Paper No. 26.

Kalpana, "Women in corporate world in India—Balancing Work and family life" www.successfulmanagers.com, pp. 33-46.

Kewalramane, Prakash, "Role of Indian women managers in today's society", www.successfulmanagers.com

Kim, Soom Nam (April 2001), "Racialized Gendering of the Accountancy Profession: Towards an understanding of Chinese women experiences in accountancy in New Zealand", www. jouranalaccountancy.com

LoRe, Linda, "Act and Concentrate", President and CEO of Giorgio, Beverly Hills.

Marshall, Judi (1994), "Women managers moving in: exploring issues of career", Key note paper presented to third National Women in Leadership Conference, pp. 1-9.

Mehra, Preeti. "Women Managers: To the top and beyond", www. successfulmanagers.com, pp. 5-10.

Menon, Sudha. "Making Choices", www.successfulmanagers.com, pp. 15-17.

Neill, Catheriene, *et al.* (1996), "Women Enterprise Management Training Outreach Program—India", Final Revaluation Report of WEMTOP Pilot Project, pp. 1-6.

Ramachander, S., "They may call difference", www.successfulmanagers.com pp. 30-32.

Ramilo, Chat Garcia, *et al.* (2003), "Using ICT to advance women's empowerment and gender equality in Asia Pacific Region", Statement of the Asia Pacific Gender forum for WSIS Adopted on 12th January 2003, pp. 1-4.

Ramkumar, R., "Where Woman Excel", www.successfulmanagers.com, pp. 11-14.

Rothman, Clare L., "Be a Sponge and turst your intuition."

Schapiro, Mary, "Surround yourself with smart people", National Association of Securities Dealers Regulation."

Macaskill, Bridget. "Forget the Gender issue", President and CEO of Oppenheimer Funds, Inc.

Apperson, Megan, *et al.* (July 2002), "Women Managers and the Experience of Work—Family Conflict", *American Journal of Undergraduate Research*", pp. 9-14.

Vugt, Olivia van, "Gender Inequity in the Accounting Profession", www.worldbank.org, pp. 1-23.

Wang Yi, M.A., "Gendered Leadership Experience of Chinese Women Managers", Ontario Institute of Studies on Education University of Toronto.

Wymard, Elle, "Women and Business: Negotiating the Culture".

CHAPTER

3

Future Challenges to Managing People for Competitive Advantage

RIYAZ RAINAYE

Globalisation implies that all business has to face stiff competitive environment, the key to win lies in the sublimest development of human resources. The business organizations will have to continuously strive to give new thrust and direction to equip their employees to meet emerging challenges. In this paper, some of the challenge that HRD professionals are likely to face, have been discussed. These challenges are: Team building; Intellectual capital; Learning organizations; Performance appraisal; Pay for team performance; Changing environment; Technological development; Business strategy; and, Fun environment.

INTRODUCTION

The world is becoming for more competitive and volatile than ever before, causing organizations to gain competitive advantage, whenever and wherever possible, in todays globalize environment. Organisational survival and success will depend on how they respond to these challenges. Management thinkers are convinced that HRD will play a more distinct and important role, in the decades ahead, in gaining the competitive advantage. One simply can't disagree.

In the past HRD focused on class room training and education of individual employees, and now it focuses on work place learning and enhancement of performance. This in turn was leading to knowledge creation at the macro-organisational level and contribution towards sustainable competitive advantage in the global marketplace.

Plott (1995) advised HRD professionals to recognize and act according to four basic factors in the changing scenario: Firstly, organizations have changed their systems and processes, HRD professionals have to consider themselves as architects of that change; Secondly, HRD professionals' primary aim should not be training individuals but creating shared learning through operating at organisational level; Thirdly, they must encourage them according to change in perspective; and Fourthly, they must initiate and encourage line managers and other key organisational players also thinking in terms of emerging new perspectives. Tichy (1995) advocated for development of three aspects: Firstly, leaders of companies shall have to go beyond their particular national boundaries and cultures, and work in a multi-national and multi-cultural frame.

Secondly, they shall have to accept a global industrial culture sure to be born out of global business. They shall have to transmit this change down throughout the whole establishment. Thirdly, organisational forms shall have to be metamorphosed from national to multi-national kind. In doing so, distribution of tasks, defining of roles, authority relationships, and centres of power shall have to be identified and defined afresh, and appropriate drastic steps shall have to be taken towards new global accomplishments. All recruiting, selecting, developing, rotating and managing shall have to be done on similar lines.

Human resource development issues represent opportunity for performance improvement and a chance to gain competitive advantage. Reading between the lines they also represent challenges to be faced. The organizations are required to develop new capabilities and competencies to face these challenges. Some of the challenges that HRD professionals are faced with are:

- Team building
- Intellectual capital
- Learning organisations
- Performance appraisal
- Pay for team performance
- Changing environment
- Technological development
- Business strategy
- Fun environment

Team Building

Team building encompasses self-managed teams on factory floor, senior-management teams and quality circles. Team work, says Purcell (1996) is the fulcrum of most of the organizations. It is the considered opinion of various luminaries in the field that team work improves decision-making, reduces response time, provides social cohesion, improves employee satisfaction, enhances organisational culture, builds up commitment and sincerity, extols the identity of the firm, and is the great way of doing things. The 21st century will have the concept of team work more and more materializing out. Every organization will be considered as a company of work teams rather than individuals.

Intellectual Capital

HRD envisages that no firm possibly in future can survive without its intellectual capital The intellectual capital, including distinct individual skills and expertise evolved by a firms workers is sometimes called 'Knowledge Theory of the Firm'. That theory visualizes that knowledge is the key to value addition as well as strategic advance (Grant, 1997). Tom Peters put forth the simple concept of Knowledge Management Structure (KMS) wherein he advised the companies to do away with bureaucracy in order to generate knowledge, cultivate skills, and enhance the power in the workplace. Companies in order to survive and progress in the 21st century shall have to advance both in implicit and explicit knowledge. This intellectual capital should not simply be a sum up of inherited past knowledge but must include also the intellectual gains made in the living present and to be passed down to the running company.

Learning Organisations

Trainers in a company have to be learners themselves. This concept materialized in a UK government Green Paper titled the "Learning Age." Herein a number of organizations well established over centuries though, were called learning organizations. Trainer himself being a learner now, HRD terminology changed such as from "Training and Development" to "Learning and Development Services" (Walton, 1999). For a company to transform itself into a learning organization, it is important to put the following the following critical success factors in place—a clear mission statement, long-term approach, a comprehensive business plan, result orientation, right organisational structure, team work, individual drive, customer focus and focus beyond survival.

Performance Appraisal

A distinction of the 21st century may be the performance of an executive being assessed not just by supervisor but by multi rater 360-degree feedback. Self-estimation and estimation by others is often different and the differences are certainly educating; estimation by, say, one boss can never be as valuable. Self-estimation or estimation by a boss is quite often deceptive; whereas that by superiors, subordinates, peers, even outside customers is often informative, educative and indeed precious. It has revolutionized performance management for better. No surprise then that AT&T, Bank of America, Exxon, GE, etc. have been depending on 360-degree feedback for a long time now (Peters, 2001). Multi rater 360 degree feedback shall be more and more used in the 21 century.

Pay for Team Performance

Teamwork and cooperation degenerate unless there is a group-based component in compensation system. Many organizations are often for team work but reward only the individuals and individual outputs (Maury, 2001). That was why quality gurus disqualified this method arguing that it kills much of management time and resources and leaves almost all dissatisfied. They add that 21st century is not going to accept this mode of payment. They uphold that the doctrine of pay for performance calls not only for traditional productivity but also for improvement in customer satisfaction, employee satisfaction, cycle time, and the ability in demonstration of skills (Luthans and Stajkovic, 1999).

Changing Environment

In business world change is endemic. Global managers are becoming pro-active for future requirements, probably, now they are more aware of what lies ahead. Flexibility, that is to say, being adaptive to rapid changes has replaced stability. HRD professionals being the architects of change, have to learn to change faster and be comfortable with it. They have to deal with questions like:

- How do we honour the past and adapt to the future?
- How do we change for every one to change?
- How do we change and learn more rapidly?
- How do we unlearn what we have learned?

(Ulrich, 1998)

Technological Development

New technologies have changed life of the organizations and individuals. Technology has made our world so small that it is being termed as global village. Ideas and massive amounts of information are in a constant movement through fax, e-mail, and other electronic devices. The challenge before managers is to make use of what technology offers. Not all technologies add value. So in coming years managers will need to figure out how to make technology a viable and productive part of the work setting

(Ulrich, 1998). It has accentuated the need to upgrade the employees' skills and competencies. All these changes are already producing a profound impact on how organizations work, how will they restructure themselves, what services they can provide, and, which among the employees they will retain, re skill, or retrench (Shah, 2004)

Business Strategy

Indications are that 21st century may have to adopt Brown and Eisenhardt's Competing on the Edge Model. Both these management thinkers in their *Competing on the Edge* suggest that all companies in the new century will have to go by new ways of thinking, after accepting the hard truth that todays core competencies may be of little value in tomorrow's markets. They also believe that strategic advantage in 2000s will be only temporary. Strategy not being a single approach, but a complex of loosely knit semi-coherent moves in a strategic direction, re invention of business will be name of the game

Naturally then, all enterprises will have to organize and operate differently. The organisational design very likely to be virtual and of network form, sharing authority and resources, among people and among frequently cooperating divisions will begin to replace traditional hierarchial structures. 21st century thus will have to see some new things advancing up—such as, recombinant work teams, co destiny (of the several firms), net woks and webs, virtual offices, portabilities, contingent (disposable) workers, temporary staffers, corporate dowinsizing and so on. This style of thinking meets initiatives needed for the 21st century.

Fun Environment

Organizations, in order to win competitive battles in the 21st century, shall have to create and sustain fun environment. That fun should emerge from mutual respect, fairness, creativity and cordiality. The environment within a company should be all enjoyable, so much so that no replacement costs have to be incurred, nor also that experience based knowledge and customer relations are lost. The spiritual relations long developed among managers, employees and customer base must always be nourished environmentally.

CONCLUSION

Gaining competitive advantage is a must in the 21st century, otherwise, not only profitability, even the survival of the organizations may be threatened. Learning and technology are not enough, the new links between knowledge and learning and performance need to be established. In that great challenge HRD professionals have to play a great role. This will constitute a new shift for HRD function in general and for HRD professionals in particular—a shift that is necessary to prevent from becoming redundant in the changing business environment and making it accountable and proactive.

References

Grant, R.M. (1997), "Strategy at the Leading Edge—the Knowledge Based View of the Firm: Implications for Management Practice", *Long Range Planning*, Vol. 30(3), June.

Luthans, F. and Stajkovi, A.D. (1999) "Reinforce for Performance: The Need to Go Beyond Pay or Even Rewards", *Academy of Management Executive*, Vol. 13(2).

Maury, A. Peiprl (2001), "Getting 360 Feedback Right", *Harvard Business Review*.

Peters Carvey (2001), "Designing a 360 Feedback System to Improve Employee Performance", *HR Focus*.

Plott, Curtis (1998), Introductory Address to Conference of ASTD, Dallas.

Purcell, J. (1996), "People Management Implications of Learner Ways of Working", Quoted in John Walton, *Strategic Human Resource Development*, Prentice Hall.

Shah Parvez A. (2004), "Emerging Issues in Human Resource Development" in Mohi-ud-Din Sangmi and Nazir A Nazir (ed.) 'Emerging Issues of Business', New Century Publications, Delhi

Tichy Nnoel, quoted in Michael, V.P. (1995), Human Resource Management and Human Relations, Himalaya Publishing House.

Ulrich, Dave (1998), "The Future Calls for Change", *Workforce*.

Ulrich, Dave (1998), "A New Mandate for Human Resources", *Harvard Business Review*, Vol. 76.

Walton, John (1999), "Strategic Human Resource Development", Prentice Hall.

CHAPTER

4

Changing Business Scenario and Human Resources

A Case for Acceleration of Burnout amongst Workforce

R.S. DHALIWAL

CHANGING BUSINESS SCENARIO

Just in recent past decades business concerns gave more importance to advance technology for higher productivity surpassing the needs and mental state of its work force. Because of increased competition number of organizations has focused on cost cutting strategies. This created a negative impact on the work force, working conditions and environment. On the other side, organizations the world over have increasingly become aware of the importance of human resources and their optimum utility. This awareness as a sub system is a critical dimension in the organizational effectiveness. The real life experiences substantiate the assumption that no matter how sophisticated and modern the business activities may become, it will be extremely difficult to sustain its growth and effectiveness unless the human resources complementary to its operation. This realization has propelled human resource management as a major field of study in the recent past years this renewed interest has further facilitated the development newer approaches in maintenance and managing human resource. An understanding of work, work environment and human behaviour on experiential and empirical evidences pointed out that the human system is not static. It is being continuously influenced by the ever-changing sub systems in the environment, human resource management could thus be viewed as a dynamic process, which needs to be kept, aligned with the changing realities in the environment.

In the name of globalization privatization liberalization number of work environmental dimensions have been changed. It is quite stressful for an employee to perform the respective job effectively and efficiently in changed working environment. Under high work pressure, hectic schedules, targets to achieve that never seem to end on time, un-cooperative colleagues, impatient bosses, incompetent subordinates and a host of other irritating factors may all have a cumulative effect in making the lives today's job performer quiet complex and miserable. A major change in dynamics of economic growth has made work place a more and more demanding both economically and psychologically. Because of pressure from powerful MNCs and in the name of economic reforms, governments have reduced job security of employees that protected them and their social security by amending prevailing laws. Recommendation of second labour commission is being perceived very serious threat to job security, more freedom is being provided to employer in selection, wage fixation and to show the exit. As a result, instead of providing a foundation for long-term growth to their work force, industrial organizations are cashing in their human resources for short-term stock performances. Because of this enormous and constant pressure these organizations' first priority is to generate cash flow, instead of creating excellent work force or building a stronger community. After the occurrence of the New Economic Reforms employees' job security is under severe threat human resource at of remain in service. After the occurrence of new economy it has emerged that work force must be treated associates, teamwork environment is emerging issue. In this era of global economy, capital now moves around the globe in search of profits more rapidly then ever before. There is no room for labour unions, every individual is considered as a unique, trying to develop his or her full potential as an individual human being, mainly through consumption. Unions imply the loss of the individuality. (Michael D. Yates, 2001) All this, in a way has made the work place more cold and hostile where work has become an obligation rather than resources of growth. Instead of business organizations as existing to extend the capacity of people to earn a living and make significant accomplishments, people working in the business and industrial organizations are sacrificing their aspirations for good of the business concerns. The value of what determines the quality of life is not those of cohesive work groups attempting to provide excellent working conditions or culture.

Thus dynamics of work environment of these factors in performance and productivity of employees is enormously complex, the understanding of contribution of some human factors is an essential part of what we work with in terms of human environment as it is not only the things we work with. It is contended here that burnout is one such psychological factor that tend to have direct effect on performance and output. In order to effectively and efficiently completing the tasks and giving fillip to overall productivity, competitive pressures and new technologies brought about new crises and challenges in the recent context. New stressors acted as catalysts to incapacitate the human work force. Usually researchers have been focusing on factors like psychosocial stressors (Corson, 1971), role ambiguity (Van Sell, *et al.*, 1968), role conflicts (Hall, 1972), anxiety and depression at work place (Caplan and Jones, 1975), under load and overload in working life (Frankenhaeuser and Gardell, 1976), stress-performance (Andrson, 1976), locus of control (Rotter, 1982), personality (Pervin, 1980), interpersonal behaviours (Sundstrom, 1977), etc.

After the initiation of economic reforms, in the name of globalization and liberalization work environment is totally changed. In this changed scenario of work place or work climate these factors do not seem to pave a way for understanding and handling of the said crises. It seems as mismatch between job and the person is increasing. Indicators of this phenomena are obvious, i.e. work overload which means one has to do too much in too little time with too few resources. Lake of control at work place, difficult to update information level at all the times, feeling of inadequate rewards and lake of adequate and meaningful relationship with superiors and co-workers are very problematic. It is a matter not of stretching to meet new challenges but of going far beyond human limits. Majority of work force at work places report that they don't only get recognition rather they are devalued too. They are just as busy as the people they manage. Their working activities and duties are so complex due to interlocking of business in family and family in business. What is proving most devastating is the loss of internal reward that comes when a person takes pride in doing something of importance and value to others and doing that job well. Lack of fairness in the workplace is another serious mismatch problem between people and job. Mutual respect among people who work together is at the heart of any sense of community. Ironically, we find that this is lost today. All this gives rise to a value conflict. Many times jobs can lead people to do things that are unethical and clash with their personal values. People do their best when they believe in what they are doing and when they can maintain their pride, integrity and self-respect. The problematic relationship between individual and situation results in erosion of values, dignity, and spirit and will (Maslach and Leiter, 1997). A large number of researchers have been trying to account for the effects of the adverse reactions to such situations in term of job stress. They viewed job stress as dysfunctional for the organizations and its members which establishes categorical negative relationship between job stress and performance (Buck, 1972). When faced with noxious work environments individuals are more likely to spend sizeable chunk of their time and energy in coping with job stresses. In many instances it may even lead to many undesirable activities in job setting, such as politicking, goofing-off, loafing and sabotaging. (Stears, 1981, Jamal; 1985). For long, this unidimensional model of stress have been serving the purpose but increased complexity of work place situation requires the analysis of individual's stress experience to be done in terms of some multidimensional concept. Burnout is one such construct that conceptualizes individual stress experience embedded in a context of complex social relationship and it involves the personal conceptions of both self and others (Maslach, 1998).

In recent past research shows that burnout is largely a product of the organizational context, even if it is expressed on an individual level (Maslach and Leiter, 1997). Despite the fact that practitioners had identified burnout as an important social problem in the working behaviour, it was long time before it became a focus of systematic study by researchers in the organizational set-ups (Maslach and Schaufeli, 1993). A large number of disruptive changes occurring in working environment in Indian industrial set-ups, because of global competition ringing a bell that its workforce especially managerial and supervisory staff is largely at the risk of burnout.

Herbert Frendenberger in 1974 has been defined the term burnout as to fail, wear out or become exhausted by making excessive demands on energy, strength or resources and recognized as a major occupational hazard among variety of professional groups. Again Frendenberger and Richelson (1980) explained burnout as a state of human resource, fatigue, depression and frustration brought about by devotion to cause, way of life or relationship that failed to produce expected rewards and ultimately led to lessened job involvement as well as lowered job accomplishments. Paine (1982) defines burnout stress syndrome as a consequence of high levels of job stress, personal frustration and inadequate coping skills having major personal, organizational and social costs. Other definitions include a state resulting from repeated work experience in which individuals expect few rewards and considerable punishment in their job and little control of reinforcement (Meier, 1983). Maslach and Jackson (1986) conceived burnout as tri-dimensional syndrome characterized by emotional exhaustion, depersonalization and reduced personnel accomplishment.

Emotional exhaustion characterized by lack of energy refers to feelings of being emotionally overextended and depleted of one's emotional resources.

Depersonalization refers to negative, callous or excessively detached response to others.

Reduced personal accomplishments characterized by tendency to evaluate increased productivity come at the cost of staff members' greater effort.

For long research has been focusing on occupational stress and its negative effect on productivity and performance (Schuler, 1980). But occupational stress being a global and unidimensional construct has not been able to make the situation clear. Hence an individual multiple reactions to different aspects of stress experience in terms of personal, interpersonal and social domains call for a new look into stress experience and stress reactions of managers in various organizations. With regard to specific impact of diverse dimension of the stress experience of managers, executives, supervisor and other employees in organizational set-ups, the present investigation is an attempt tend to look into organizational performance in relation to human factor, i.e. 'burnout'.

In the name of the globalization and due to pressures from MNCs' old style protectionist policies are no more, there to ensure an optimum level of control or take care of work force. Reduced job security and competitive pressures put the work force to abandon traditional ways and adopt the highly productive and efficient focused and cost effective ways where ends are to justify everything and the outcome regarding ends is evaluated in terms of increased productivity and performance

RESPONSIBLE FACTORS FOR BURNOUT

In the past years researchers have made efforts for identifying some predisposing condition of burnout. Some researchers tend to attribute to an individuals inner weakness, flaws in his character or behaviour (Maslach and Leiter, 1997) as the main cause of his burnout. This perspective holds the position that the solution to this problem lies in modification of the person (Maslach and Leiter, 1997). However, the focus of researchers has now shifted on to the situations in which people find themselves, implying that burnout is not a problem of the people themselves but of social environments in which they work (Maslach and Leiter, 1997) as a result, the focus of researchers has shifted to the identification of 'bad' situation rather than 'bad' individuals (Maslach and leiter, 1997).

Over the past few years, have revealed some significant indicators about sources of burnout including personality correlates as well as work related factors. In addition to certain demographic factors, there has been wide consensus among researchers about the six mismatch condition between the job and the person, proposed by Maslach *et al.*, 2001 to have the potential to cause burnout. These condition are: work overload, lack of control, insufficient reward, breakdown of community, absence of fairness and conflicting value at work place. The six mismatch areas attracted the attention of scholars and management thinkers.

(a) Work Overload

In today's work world, workload of individuals is more intense, demands more time and is mush more complex than ever before (Maslach and Leiter, 1997). Moreover, after economic reforms have taken place, in the present world of work, in view of the race of excellence, super success and higher and higher levels of productivity organization thrust man their work force with more and more stress on high quality work, thus pushing and straining there capacity. Excessive workload, beyond the capacity of the individual, has a negative influence on energy, efficiency and productivity levels, which may lead to breakdown. The relationship between work overload and stress and coronary heart disease has been well documented and established (French and Caplan, 1970) Role overload as a type of conflict contributes to increased stress and burnout because of its impact on coping (Cherniss, 1980). Work overload leaves the individual exhausted-emotionally, creatively as well as physically. High degree of work overload with few structured time outs to is escape from role demands has been identified and established as an important factor leading to emotional exhaustion and re burnout (Cherniss, 1980). It is the time, there is no time limit for employees of corporate sector up to late night.

(b) Lack of Control

Lack of control at work place is the second most significant negative condition embedded in the work environment identified by Maslach and Leiter (1997) to have the potential to lead to burnout. Central to being a successful professional as well as in the experience of job satisfaction is the freedom to priorities and make decisions and also autonomy in selecting the relevant approaches to do one's work. However, organizational policies that reduce or undermine an individual's autonomy and curtail his decisions making prevent him from successfully handling work related problems leading to time wastage and dissatisfaction. According to Pines *et al.* (1981) lack of control or autonomy in ones job may contribute to burnout, whereas, increasing participations in the decision-making process enhances the control employees have over there work environment and this may be effective in reducing job-related strain (Jackson, 1983). According to Daniel and Rogers (1981) feeling powerless in ones work setting may contribute to burnout.

Empirical evidence shows that jobs high on demand what low in decisions latitude are source of stress (Smith, Kaminstein and Makadok, 1950). Participation in decision-making has been found to significantly contribute to depersonalization, but not to the other two components of burnout (Schwab, Jackson and Schuler, 1986). Lindsborg's (1988) found among health care workers, that job decision latitude contributed to all there components of burnout. Jackson, Schwab and Schuler (1986) found autonomy in terms of job content to be related to personal accomplishments.

(c) Reward Structure

It is general feeling of work force, working in business and industrial organizations that the respective employer exploits their talent for personal gain not for the welfare of employees. Related to the topic of control and autonomy is the issue of how feedback about performance is communicated to the employees and how their efforts are rewarded. Employees today are expected to give more in terms of time, efforts, skills and flexibility, whereas they receive less in terms of career opportunities, lifetime employment, and job security (Maslach *et al.*, 2001). Reward and punishment structures may have an impact on personal accomplishment and depersonalization components of burnout Schwab *et al.* (1986). When employees do not get information and feedback on how well they are doing and what others think of their work, it may constitute a source of stress, which contributes to burnout. The organization's capacity and effort to reward and appreciate its employees in meaningful ways rarely matches the time, effort and energy being put into their work by most employees. According to Maslach and Leiter (1997), even greater contributor to the experience of burnout is the loss of intrinsic reward of doing enjoyable work and building expertise. This combined loss of extrinsic as well as intrinsic rewards diminishes the potential for the work to be engaging thus paving the way for burnout. Lack of steady financial growth exacerbates the impact of excessive workload making individuals over worked, under satisfied and demotivated to give their best. High turnover ratio among work force is a clear indicator of dissatisfaction.

(d) Personal Relationships at Work

In this area situation is further aggravated by the lack of adequate and meaningful personal relationships at work place. Researchers have emphasized upon the significance of good relationship between the members of a work group as a main factor in individual and organizational health. Lack of trust of people one works with has been positively related to high role ambiguity and it has also been found to lead to inadequate communications between people and to psychological strain in the form of low Job satisfaction and to feelings of job-related threat to one's well being (French and Caplan, 1970). Prevalence of job insecurity and excessive focus on short-term profit undermines the impotence of personal relationship and consideration of others. This atmosphere of distrust and self-centeredness not only fragments of community in an organization but also effect negatively team work which is central too much of organizational activity Maslach and Leiter (1997). Greater conflict, ruthless competition, less mutual support and respect and a growing sense of isolation not only provides conditions for the growing loss of community and degradation of the essential primary values but also paves the way for the feelings of depersonalization amongst professionals.

(e) Absence of Fairness

Work places marked with excessive conflict, and cut-throat competition are likely to lead to the perception of absence of fairness amongst employees, which has been recognized as a potential cause of burnout by researchers (Maslach and Leiter, 1997). Fairness communicates respect and confirms people's self-worth. Work places marked or perceived as fair by employees help them maintain their engagement with work whereas conflict and lack of fairness contributors directly to disinterest in work and ultimately becomes a cause of burnout. Conflict, Distrust and disbelief at work place hinder efficiency and productivity, erodes the value system and promotes stress, strain and burnout. Unfairness can occur when workload and pay is distributed unfairly, when cheating occurs or when performance appraisals, evaluation criteria for financial and non-financial incentives and promotions are handled inappropriately. Perceived inequity has been found to be strong predictor of burnout in several cross-sectional studies among employees. Inequity was found to affect the central component of burnout, i.e. emotional exhaustion in a curvilinear manner. The results revealed that feeling more deprived and feeling more advantaged resulted in higher future emotional exhaustion levels. While no indication was found for a longitudinal relation between inequity and depersonalization, personal accomplishment was found to influence equity.

(f) Value Conflict

A large number of people are shifting their traditional professions for survival. Small-scale industries are having very serious threat from MNCs and are not able to compete with them. Another condition emerges, which can be a potential cause for burnout, is, when the requirements of the job do not match people's personal principles (Maslach and Leiter, 1997). In such situations, people might feel constrained by the job, as they are required to do things that are unethical and not in accord with their own values.

So this is the era of transformation, in each of the six areas if the nature of the job is not in harmony with the nature of the people, the result is increased exhaustion, cynicism and inefficacy of burnout (Maslach, 1998). On the other hand, when a better fit exists in the six areas, then engagement with work is the likely outcome. Engagement has been defined in terms of the same three dimensions as burnout, but the positive end of these dimensions rather than the negative. Thus, engagement consists of a state of high energy, strong involvement, and the sense of efficacy (Maslach, 1998; Maslach *et al.*, 2001).

Six Areas of Job-person Fit (Maslach, 1998)

Six Mismatch Areas

Workload	Control	Reward	Community	Fairness	Values

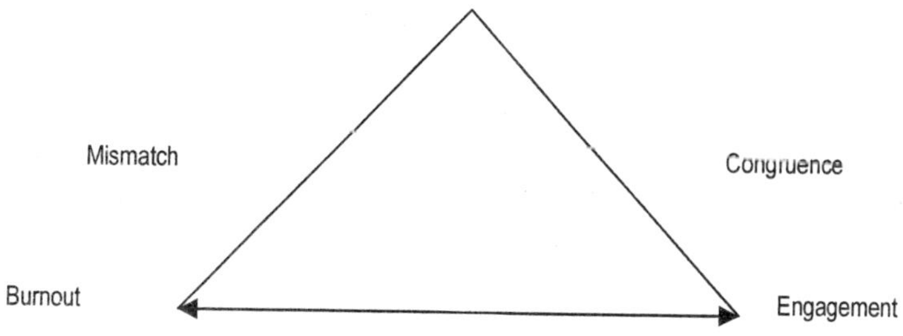

Mismatch

Congruence

Burnout

Engagement

So at the end of discussion we have the opinion that people are the important resources of any organization, these are the humans who can build progressive and growth oriented organizations competent effective and motivated people can make things happen and make enable an organization to achieve its goals. It is hard to find relief at work and jobs are becoming increasingly complex. Increase in non standard jobs mean much less likely to provide pensions, health care and health insurance, job security, and much more likely to pay low wages. It is very much a need of the hour that burnout be analyzed. However, the productivity and performance of an individual is analyzed as a function of burnout.

References

Andrson, C.R. (1976). Coping behaviours as intervening mechanism in the inverted-U stress-performance relationship, *Journal of Applied Psychology*, 61, 30-34.

Breaugh, J.A. (1980). A comparative investigation of three measures of role ambiguity. *Journal of Applied Psychology*, 65, 584-89.

Buck, V. (1972). *Working under pressure*, London, Staples, administrators, engineers and scientists. Unpublished Ph.D. thesis. Ann Arbor: University of Michigan.

Caplan, R.D. and Jones, K.W. (1975). Effects of workload, role ambiguity, and Type A personality on anxiety, depression and heart rate, *Journal of Applied Psychology*, 60, 713-19.

Caplan, R.D., Cobb, S. French, J.R.P., Jr., Harrison, R.V. and Pinneau, S.R. Jr. (1975). Relationship of cessation of smoking with job stress, personality and social support. *Journal of Applied Psychology*, 60, 211-19.

Corson, S.A. (1971). *The lack of feed-back in today's societies a psycho-social stressor*. In L. Levi (ed.) *Society, stress and disease*. London: Oxford University Press, Vol. 1.

Fankenhaeuser, M. and Gardell, B. (1976). Under load and over load in working life: Outline of a multi-disciplinary approach, *Journal of Human Stress*, 2, 35-46.

Freudenberger, H.J. (1974). Staff burnout, *Journal of Social Issues*, 30, 159-64.

Jamal Muhammad, (1985). Relationship of job stress to job performance: A study of managers and blue collar workers, *Human Relations*, 38, No. 5.

Maslach, C. and Jackson, S. (1986), *Maslach burnout investory manual*, Palo Alto: Consulting Psychologist Press.

Maslach, C. and Leiter, M.P. (1997). *The truth about burnout: How organizations cause personal stress and what to do about it*. San Francisco: Jossey-Bass Publishers.

Maslach, C. (1998). *A multidimensional theory of burnout*. In C.L. Cooper (ed.) *Theories of Organizational Stress* (pp. 68-85), New York: Oxford University Press, Inc.

Maslach, C. Schaufeli, W.B. (1993). *Historical and conceptual development of burnout*. In W.B. Schaufeli, C. Maslach and T. Marek (eds.), *Professional burnout: Recent development in theory of research*, London: Taylor and Francis.

Meier, S.T. (1983). *Toward a theory of burnout, Human Relations*, 36, 10, 899-910.

Michael D. Yates (2001). The New Economy and the Labour Movement, *Monthly Review*, Vol. 52.

Paine, W.S. (1982). *Job stress and burnout research, theory and intervention perspectives*, Newbury Park, CA: Sage Publications.

Pervin, L.A., (1989). *Personality theory and research*, John Wiley and Sons.

Rotter, J.B. (1982). *The development and application of social learning theory.* New York: Praeger

Sales, S.M. (1969). Organizational roles as a risk factor in coronary heart disease. *Administrative Science Quarterly*, 14, 325-36.

Schuler, R.S. (1980). Definition and conceptualization of stress in organizations, *Behaviour and Human Performance*, 25, 184-215.

Stears, R.M. (1981). *Introduction to organizational behaviour*, Santa Monica, California: Goodyear Publishing Co.

Sundstorm, E. (1977). *Interpersonal behaviour and the physical environment.* In L. Wrightsman (ed.) *Social Psychology*. Monterey, Calif: Brooks/Cole.

Van Sell, M., Brief, A.P. and Schuler, R.S. (1979). *Role conflict and role ambiguity: Integration of the literature and directions for research,* Working paper, University of Low.

CHAPTER

5

Jobs Satisfaction Level of Bank Employees under Different Situations of Respondent Characteristics and Job Factors

Preparing for the Future

SELVAARANI SHANKER

Job satisfaction refers to a person's feeling of satisfaction on the job, which acts as a motivation to work. It is not self-satisfaction, happiness or self-contentment but satisfaction on the job. The term relates to the total relationship between an individual and the employer for which he is paid. Job saisfaction is an integral component of the organizational climate and an important element in management-employee relationship. In simple words, it is an individual's emotional reaction to the job itself. Job satisfaction is very difficult to define because it is an intangible, unseen, unobserved variable and a complex assemblage of cognition (beliefs or knowledge) and emotion (sentiments or evaluations) and such behavioural tendencies. Job satisfaction may be viewed as the pleasurable emotional state resulting from the perception of one's job fulfiling or allowing the fulfilment of one's important job values, provided these values are compatible with one's needs (Edwin A. Locke). It may be the persistent feeling towards discriminable aspects of a job situation. Job satisfaction may be global or specific. Sometimes it is referred to as an overall feeling of satisfaction, i.e. satisfaction with the situation as a whole. At other times it refers to a person's feelings toward specific dimensions of work environment. A contented and motivated worker is certainly an asset to any organization, and job satisfaction is perhaps essential to the continued high productivity of the employee in his/her field of work.. The present study attempts to locate the influence of some important personal and social characteristics and job factors on the level of satisfaction among the Bank employees.

INTRODUCTION

Job satisfaction plays an important role for an employee in terms of health and well being (Kornhauser, 1965; Khaleque,1981) and for an organization in terms of its productivity, efficiency, employee relations, absenteeism and turnover (Vroom, 1964; Locke, 1976; Khaleque, 1984). Banking job as a whole plays an important role in the economy of any country. It is a service-oriented organization. The quality of banking services to its customers and comminity greatly depends upon the total efforts of the employees. Job satisfaction of bank employees results from the specific likings and dislikings experienced in their jobs. The efficient manpower can best be utilised if they are satisfied with their jobs (McClell, 1961). So, the ways through which authority treats their employees and filfil their needs and expections have a profound impact on the attitudes of the employees towards their jobs which in turn have an effect on the ability to accomplish their work.

Objectives of the Study

The objectives of the study are:

- To predict the level of job satisfaction among the

employees under different situations of (a) Respondent Characteristics, and (b) Job Factors.

- To identify the extent of job satisfaction in the organization as it influences managerial performance both qualitatively and quantitatively.
- To analyse and discuss job security, scope for promotion, etc., for employees in the organization.
- To examine salary and material benefits to its employees

Review of Literature

Different studies have come out with different results on the relationship of respondent characteristics such as age, education, experience with job satifaction. Ageneral consensus among the research was that the relationship between age and job satisfaction was determined by job situations. Similarly, the majority of the studies have reported reverse relationship between educational level and job satisfaction. Again, most of the studies have reported positive relationship between the number of years put in service, the level of an so on. A number of studies regarding the relationship of selected job factors (such as achievement, opportunity for advancement, security, behaviour of the immediate officer, administrative set-up and policies of the organization, salary) with job satisfaction have been conducted. On the whole, the job factors were found to have a positive correlation with the level of job satisfaction. Men work to satisfy their needs and extent of their need satisfaction and dissatisfaction is reflected in their behaviour on the job. Job satisfaction has adjustment value and it has been found that a large part of vacational maladjustment and industrial unrest are secondary to, but a reflection of emotional maladjustment (Kates). Since the modern man spends a major portion of his waking life on his job, it is important, "to know the nature and gratification and deprivation in job performance itself" (Katz). In a developing country like ours where capital and technological resources are scarce and human resource is the only asset, job performance is of prime importance. "Job satifaction", as suggested by Ghiselli Brown, "has many different points of reference, and few workers indeed are satisfied with all aspects of their job." Job satifaction is derived from and is caused by many factors. On reiew of literature, the author found that the results of job satisfaction studies conducted both in India and abroad are far from being unequivocal. Quite a large number of investigators (Hoppock, Inlow Ganguli, Pestonjee, Sinha and Agarwala), have emphasize the role of personality factorsin job satifaction. Studies have also found different results with regard to the relationship of age with job satifaction. Hoppock *et al.*, Super, Morse, Ganguli and Sinha and Sharma have found age to be related to job satisfaction. But the results of the study by Kornhauser and Sharp, Sinha, and Vasudeva and Rajbir indicate no such relationship. Length of service has also been found to be an influencing factor (Hull and Kolstad). Ganguli found the newly joined or people with long service to be more satisfied. Hullin and Smith and Prasad found a positive relationship between length of service and job satisfaction. Similarly, number of dependents also plays a key factor in job satisfaction as reported by Morse, but Sinha and Sinha and Sharma found it in an insignificant factor in job satifaction.Working conditions have been found by Evans and Laseau, Herzberg *et al.*, Siegal and Gosh and Shukla to be an important factor in job satisfaction.

THEORETICAL BASIS OF THE STUDY

Job satifaction has been conceptualized primarily within the psychological frames of reference—the sum total of the feelings one has about the various aspects of one's job. It was viewed as the function of interaction between the job environment and the worker's personality. The need and motivation theories of satisfaction formulated by Maslow and Herzberg *et al.* provided the basis of selection of job factors (Motivator and Hygiene factors) for the study.

RESEARCH METHODLOGY

Methodologically, the case study was adopted to assess the Bank Employees. This method involves a deeper investigation of few banks. To substantiate the intensive study, necessary primary data were collected, by way of questionnaires, oral interviews, enquries and discussions with the persons concerned. The respondents belonged to the executive category of the organization. They were as a target group for the study since executive are part of the management and also the success of an organization largely depends on them. The questionnaires were prepared on a five point scale. The data was collected through random sampling technique The sample size is 250 employees. Job satisfaction can be measured in two ways. One by investigating the specific factors in the job and the resulting attitude. The other, which is much more comprehensive, includes the overall factors that contribute to satisfaction in life. Job satisfaction, is a generalised attitude resulting from many specific attitudes in three areas: specific job factors, individual adjustment and group relationship. The executive or the leader should try to control those factors which produce satisfaction and dissatisfaction, exhibits various qualities like motivation, communication and so on, to make an employee feel happy with his job and stay on in the job to contribute to the organisation's success. A satisfied employee participates in the work whole heartedly and it is the function of the executive to motivate the subordinates and provide the necessary job environment to satisfy the subordinates

FINDINGS AND DISCUSSIONS

Two separate approaches for studying worker's job satisfaction have been followed. In the 'respondent charateristics' approach an overall assessment of the worker's perception of their jobs in totality has been studied, and in the job factor's appoach the worker's satisfaction from various aspects of job such as pay, job security, working conditions, welfare facilities, company policies, supervisory and interpersonal relations, etc. have been studied.

Worker's Satisfaction from Various Aspects of the Job

The responses of the sample employees with regard to their satisfaction from various aspects of job has been shown in Table 1. As regards job satisfagtion from various aspects of job, it is found that majority of the workers were moderately satisfied with salsry, working conditions, job interest and interpersonal relations with colleagues. Employees were found to be highly satisfied with job security. Relatively a higher proportion of the employees expressed dissatisfaction with welfare facilities, supervisory behaviour, policies and promotion opportunities.

TABLE I

Aspects of Job and the Worker's Level of Job Satisfaction

Sl. No.	*Aspects of job*	*Level of satisfaction (%)*		
		High	*Medium*	*Low*
1.	Wages	20.0	52.0	28.0
2.	Job Security	39.0	37.0	24.0
3.	Working conditions	28.0	48.0	24.0
4.	Welfare facilties	22.0	32.0	46.0
5.	Job interest	22.0	42.0	36.0
6.	Supervisory behaviour	28.0	34.0	38.0
7.	Relations with co-workers	34.0	38.0	28.0
8.	Promotion opportunitities	22.0	36.0	42.0
9.	Personal policies of company	24.0	32.0	44.0

Job satisfaction is also viewed in relation to various personal factors such as age, marital status, eduacation, work experience and income, etc. Salaries has turned out to be a significant factor in job satisfaction. There is sufficient evidence that the employees with higher salaries are more satisfied with their jobs as compared to their counter-parts with lower salaries.

Overall Job Satisfaction

Having analysed employee's orientation to various aspects of the job, an attempt is made here to present the picture of overall job satisfaction of the employees. For this purpose the scores of the employees on all aspects of the job discussed above are pooled together to compute the overall index of job satifaction of workers. The index so formulated is described in Table 2. When overall job satisfaction is analysed in totality, it is found that the highest propotion of the workers (42%) were moderately satisfied, while 36% of the employees were found to be at low level satisfaction and only 22% were highly satisfied.

TABLE 2

Index of the Degree of Job Satisfaction

Scores	*Degree of satisfaction*	*No. of workers*	*Percentage*
45-60	High	22	22.0
29-44	Medium	42	42.0
12-28	Low	36	36.0
	Total	100	100.0

It is found that employees of lower age group expressed lesser job satisfaction as compared to the employees of of higher age groups. It is felt that as the person would grow older, he would have greater satisfaction from his work, particularly because of adjustment experience of work. For relationship between length of service and degree of job satisfaction, it is found that the relationship seems to be somewhat complex, but the general impression is that young employees with comparatively less experience, who are at the beginning of their career and filled with high hopes of earning and better career are dissatisfied with their jobs to some extent when they come face to face with real working conditions. As the worker advances in age and experience, dissatisfaction increases due to successive completion and non-progressive career. But the workers who are apporaching towards the end of their career and who take the work as a matter of routine are satified with their jobs due to adjustment with work and settled aspirations.

Level of skill and education seem to bear some kind of relationship with the degree of job satisfaction. Highly qualified employees have strong attachment to their jobs because such jobs generally carry prestige and high remuneration and, therefore, show higher job satisfaction than those with lowly qualified employees. Education generates greater expectancy and aspiration with the conditions of work but the propects of an average worker in India are ill-suited to fulfil them and lead the employees to dissatisfaction.

As to the relatiopnship of personal factors with job satisfaction, marital status is not a significant factor similar to the study by Guha (1965). Number of dependants is also an insignificant factor in job satisfaction as different dependent groups did not make a significant difference as shown by Sinha and Sinha and Sharma (1962). Insignificant difference may be due to the lack of aspiration for high standard of living among bank employees. There is, However, some relationship between job satisfaction and age because job satisfaction scores are significantly high in twenties as compared to forties and fifties. Similarly, job is related with the length of service. Job satisfaction is relatively high at the start, drops during tenth to fifteenth year, and then rises again though this rise is not significant. Smilar results were also obtained by Hull and Kolstad but differ from that of Vasudeva and Rajbir who found an inverse relationship between the two. Thus, this research does not support the contention of Ghosh and Shukla that job satisfaction is more a function of job condition than personal factors.

The findings of the present investigation will demonstrate that the findings are not in complete agreement or disagreement with the earlier studies. However, we may say, in a nutshell, that job satisfaction is more a matter of pay, personality, and personal factors such as age and length of service than of the job conditions. The adverse impact of the employee's job satisfaction on their work is undeniable. The employee dissatisfied with his job is often rigid inflexible, unrealistic in his choice of goals, generally unhappy and dissatisfied. The management must be vigilant about the motivational requirements of these workers, for the effective utilisation of human resources. It should adopt more progressive and challenging opportunities to evolve a proper information system, give the employees fair treatment, make them feel important so that they develop a sense of loyalty.

References

Balaji, C., "Organizational Commitment of Job Satisfaction which explains Intent of Quite Better," *Indian Journal of Industrial Relations,* Vol. 24.

Basu, C.K. "Incentives and Job Satisfaction", *Indian Journal of Industrial Relations,* 1, 3, 289-305.

Blum, M.L., *Industrial Psychology and its Social Foundations,* New York.

Brayfield, A.H. and Rothe, H.F., "An Index of Job Satisfaction", *Journal of Applied Psychology,* 35, 5, 307-11.

Hoppock, R., Job Satisfaction, Harper and Brothers, New York.

Ganguli, H.C., "A Study of some Variables affecting attitudes of Industrial Workers, *Indian Journal of Psychology,* Vol. 30, 45-60.

Ghiselli, E.E. and Brown, C. W., Personnel and Industrial Psychology, New York, McGraw-Hill.

Guha, T.N., Personality Factors and Job Satisfaction among Shoe Factory Workers", *Indian Psychological Review,* 1, 59-64.

Locke, E.A., "The Nature and Cause of Job Satisfaction", M.D. Dunnette (Ed.): *Handbook of Industrial and Organiztional Psychology.*

Kates, S.L., "*Rorschach Responses Related to Vocational Interests and Job Satisfaction,* Psychological Monograph, 64, No. 3.

Kornhauser, A.W. and Sharp, A.A., "Employee Attitudes: Suggestions from a Study in a Factory", *The Personnel Journal,* 393-404.

Sinha, D., "Job Satisfaction in Office and Manual Workers", *Indian Journal of Social Works",* 19, 39-46.

Srivastava, A.K. and Srivastava, Vineta, "Job Satisfaction—Myth and Reality, *Indian Journal of Labour Economics,* Vol. XXVI (1-2), 71-85.

CHAPTER

6

Entrepreneurial and Leadership Challenges in 21st Century

ASHWANI BHALLA AND HARBILAS

With the end of millennium upon us, many writers have put time and ink into considerations of how things will be different in the 21st Century. What type of challenges the entrepreneurs and business leaders for achieving sustainable growth for their business and venture will face? Looking into the future to know, how things will be different, is not an easy task. It is the art of thinking the unthinkable. It needs open and creative mind, and analytical capabilities to envisage different and sometimes, counterintuitive combinations of actors, factors and trends. In this connection a historian notes: "it is desirable, possible and even within certain limits necessary to forecast our future." However, the process of forecasting must be based necessarily on knowledge of the past. If we compare the scenarios of last three centuries then it can be said, "The 19th century was about economic freedom." The 20th Century was about political freedom. This century will be about people deciding for themselves what's moral and what's not. In this changed scenario entrepreneur and business leaders has to gear up their mind to prepare such type of strategies, which suits to people expectations as well. 21st century leaders will need greater awareness of diverse factors and new set of competencies—characteristics that lead to success on the job—to help them make relevant, correct and timely decisions in the leadership of change and leadership of people. Before we discuss the various challenges for the entrepreneur and business leaders in the 21st century, it will be desirable, if we first discuss the scenario of 21st century.

21ST CENTURY—A CHANGED SCENARIO

Besides changes in all the sectors of human life 21st century is witnessing following major changes from the business and economics point of view:

1. The technological structure of today's society has been in a phase of profound transformation.
2. Importance of material resources is reduced in favour of immaterial ones—such as information, and service.
3. Creative capacity has replaced passive learning.
4. Knowledge-based industry is becoming predominant.
5. Development is changing tracks.
6. Structural change of economic development also causes changes to the composition of productive factors.
7. Increase in the contribution of capital and knowledge that incorporates new technological and scientific discoveries.
8. This century will be considered as the cycle of electronic technologies, computers, new materials, and biotechnologies.
9. Faster formation of business networks.
10. Connectivity is becoming essence of every field.
11. The future will be global, hyper competitive, technologically intensive, and rapidly changing.
12. Multinational companies will continue their assault on the Indian developer market.

13. Downsizing policies of the firms through mergers, acquisitions and other restructuring exercises will put the future of existing employment factors at stake.

CHALLENGES FOR THE ENTREPRENEURS AND BUSINESS LEADERS

Keeping in view the above scenario, we perceive the following challenges for the Indian entrepreneurs and business leaders—

1. Redefining the Futuristic Vision

In the changed scenario, business leaders have to draw up their futuristic vision by way of redefining their corporate purpose and mission and resetting their attainable objectives. The older concept of maximizing profit has to be shifted to maximizing market share. To achieve this objective all the policies of the organization has to be re-oriented keeping in view the customer as a central point. In the new order, the customer is all. Satisfying the requirements of the customer, doing it better, quicker and more effectively is the route to survival. Many bureaucratic procedures that existed to enhance regulation and stability also, it turns out, diminish responsiveness across the customer boundary. This shift of objectives and mission may invite stiff criticism from the various stakeholders of business. A rationale has to be developed by the business leaders and the emerging entrepreneurs to manage the stakeholders to accept this shift. A slogan has to be given to the stakeholders that only *"Mool-Mantra"* of survival is the customerisation of business policies.

2. International Competitiveness

With more globalization and removal of local, national and transnational trade-barriers there will be large flow of technologically advanced and quality products at cheaper prices every corner of the earth. At such juncture entrepreneurs and business leaders has to find out the avenues where they have the competitive edge over the other.

3. Threat to the Older Management Styles

In the 21st century a total shift is seen in older management styles. The former approaches to organizing and getting work done has become obsolete. Hierarchies are changing into networks, bosses to coaches, and jobs into ever changing bundles of shifting task assignments. It is a challenge for the business leaders to create highly participative environments in which people at all levels take, and feel, personal responsibility for collective output and in which they are emotionally invested.

4. Management of Information

Highly advanced information technology has flooded the mind of human being and its organizations with data, which is changing every minute. According to one estimate, information supply available to us doubles every 5 years. A small lapse may cost heavily to the organizations. This may need highly conceivable mind to timely interpret the data and transform it into the relevant information. Information management has to be given a prime place in the organizational hierarchy. Towards the end of 20th century information management was considered as secondary aspect. But now business leaders will have to remain updated every minute so that quickly and timely decisions can be taken to combat the threat of large and ever flowing wind of change. Truly successful managers and business leaders of the 21st century will be determined: (a) Not by what they know but by how fast they can learn. (b) Not by how they can access information, but by how they can access most relevant information. It must be borne in mind that 21st century is the age of Connectivity. Though connectivity increases value and innovative capacity but connectivity also increases vulnerability. Virus can cost billions and threaten critical infrastructures. This creates challenges for developing global business models, protecting privacy while bringing the benefits of IT to every sector of business.

5. Challenges of Core Competence

21st century business leaders will need greater awareness of diverse factors and new set-up competencies-characteristics that lead to success on the job—to help them make relevant, correct and timely decisions in the leadership of change and leadership of people. Entrepreneurs and business leaders has to develop core competence to solve their business problems. A tentative list of 21st century core competencies includes:

(a) Tactical, technical and technological (Information/ Computer) Proficiency
(b) Cognitive skills and abilities, such as numerical comprehension, oral communication and problem solving.
(c) Interpersonal skills and abilities, such as skill in human relations and teamwork ability.
(d) Personal characteristics, such as decisiveness and tenacity.

After core-competencies, the business leaders should focus on differentiating competencies that will distinguish between superior and satisfactory leadership in the 21st century. In the new environment strategic focus and vision, coupled with practical sense of when to be flexible and adaptable, will be the most critical for survival. An ability to manage multiple points of view simultaneously will differentiate the best managers. Gone are the days of top-down, hard-nosed direction. Demonstrating flexibility and empathy, while remaining true to the core bivalves of the organization and finding ways to circumvent unpredictable impediments, will be the characteristics of tomorrow's leaders.

6. Market Forces

Business in the 21st century will be more market driven and it will put strong pressure on the business leaders to introduce change in the organizations at a macro-economic level. Here the market forces can be viewed as the cumulative effects of the behaviour and wants of those in the market either demanding or supplying a good or service. These forces include increasing globalization as well as the creation of increasingly massive multinational organizations through mergers and takeovers. Economies of scale, capacity to offer products or services in a variety of countries and cultures, reduction of cost of reaching different geographically dispersed markets will be some of the issues which can pose challenge to entrepreneurs and business leaders in the new environment. However,, the market forces to increase size and go global do not necessarily lead to organizational survival. Of the 100 largest United States companies at the beginning of the 20th century, only 16 are identifiable today.

7. People Issues

With the advent of 21st century people issues are increasingly establishing themselves at center stage. Every year more and more people will be self-employed, temporary or part-time. Expectations of the staff are different today. In the coming years a total change in employer-employee relationship will be witnessed. With their increased complexity and globalization, organizations are demanding skills and abilities from their leaders that are only beginning to be understood, never mind mastered. One of the most important of these will be the ability to balance employee needs (globally) and customer wants (globally and locally)—a balance that will become harder to strike and to strike profitably and efficiently, in the coming years.

Diversity will become a strategic differentiator and merely a desired demographic profile. The managers of tomorrow are growing up in a world where diversity is a productive, exciting and enjoyable reality. As the work force continues to grow more diverse, those able to accept individual differences in the workplace and to look at them as a source of creative energy and productivity will have to access to a larger and more talented work force.

In a quickly changing world, talented human capital will be a prime ingredient of business success. Business leaders will have to accommodate the shift of power from owners and senior management to knowledge workers. Organizations will invest increasing percentages of their revenues in attracting, developing and retaining competent professionals, and this arena will grow to be perhaps the most significant competitive battleground.

In the end we sum up our submission with remarks that entpreneurs and business leaders must keep the following observations in mind while devising their business policies:

1. If innovations and entrepreneurship profoundly shaped the 20th Century, they will define the 21st.
2. Knowledge development and technology commercialization are the new drivers of economic growth.
3. Creating new innovations and harnessing their power will directly impact on prosperity and global influence.
4. Leadership with more competitive technology-based enterprises will be those whose policies promote innovation, promote entrepreneurship and make sustained investment in scientific research and talent.
5. While government have an important role to play in setting the proper business climate to promote innovation and entrepreneurship, private sector leadership is critical to solving the toughest challenges raised by technology convergence

References

Mehlman, Bruce P. (2003), Technology Administration, 21st Century Policy Challenges for American innovation leadership. www.technology.gov.

Emilio Gerelli (2000), Thinking about the future: Economic Aspects. JEL Classification: 20.

Krantz James (1998), Anxiety and the New order, Medison CT: International Universities Press.

Preffer J. (1995), Producing sustainable competitive advantage through effective management of people, The Academy of Management Executive, IX(1), 55-72.

Kenneth H. Pritchard, Lieutenant Colonel, US Army Reserve—Competency Based Leadership for the 21st century. www.cgsc.army.mil.

James H. Johnson, William Rend Kenon (2000), Five Leadership challenges of the 21st century. www.abvision.org/

Mark David Nevins and Stephen A. Stumpf (2000), 21st century leadership: Redefining management education. www.rollins.edu.

CHAPTER

7

Marketing Issues and Challenges in Indian Markets

An Action Agenda for Marketers

M.A. SAHAF

During the past few years marketing in India has witnessed dramatic changes because of new policies of liberalization, privatization, and globalization. In fact, firms in Indian markets have experienced a total overhaul of their philosophies, strategies and frameworks of business in general and of marketing in particular where the tempo and magnitude of change are more significant. Consequently, the marketers need to unlearn major marketing practices of the past and relearn the new strategies and approaches to marketing that would be functional in the changing marketing scenario. Such an approach alone can enable the marketers to translate an environmental change into a strategic operation. To make this happen marketers would face a number of difficulties without having some action agenda capable of providing them a clear path to meet the challenges of the changing environment of marketing in India. It is in this context that the present paper makes a modest attempt to discuss the major challenges of future marketing in India and provide the marketers measures for a creative response.

INTRODUCTION

New policies of liberalization, privatization, and globalization have completely changed the game of business in India. On the one hand such reforms and policies have opened new vistas for the growth and prosperity of firms in India and on the other hand the changing scenario has posed a number of serious challenges to Indian firms. Such challenges have rendered obsolete many of the currently available marketing practices that have driven the business in India for decades and, therefore, require immediate attention of marketers. However, in the turbulent, competitive and frequently hostile Indian market, the success of a firm's business would depend on the ability of its management to anticipate and translate these changes into strategic operations with an objective to capitalize on changes at their appropriate time (Sahaf, 2000). To attain such an objective, a marketer must obtain reliable information about forces shaping the future, finding an appropriate framework to evaluate the effects of those forces, and determine appropriate courses of action. It is in this context that the present paper attempts to discuss present and future challenges in the marketing environment, highlight the implications of these changes for marketing management, and offer suggestions for a creative response.

OBJECTIVES

To define and describe the future of marketing in India and provide a framework for such marketing, the present paper attempts to attain the following objectives:

- To identify the present and future challenges faced by Indian companies;
- To determine the action steps to address each challenge; and
- To assess the priorities for the immediate future.

KEY CHALLENGES AND ACTION AGENDA

Before stressing the critical need to develop effective ways in which to cope with the change in Indian business environment, it would be interesting to summarize some major challenges that influence the success of firms in present competitive and dynamic Indian markets. An examination of existing marketing environment reveals some major challenges as shown in Figure 1.

FIGURE I

Key Challenges and Action Steps

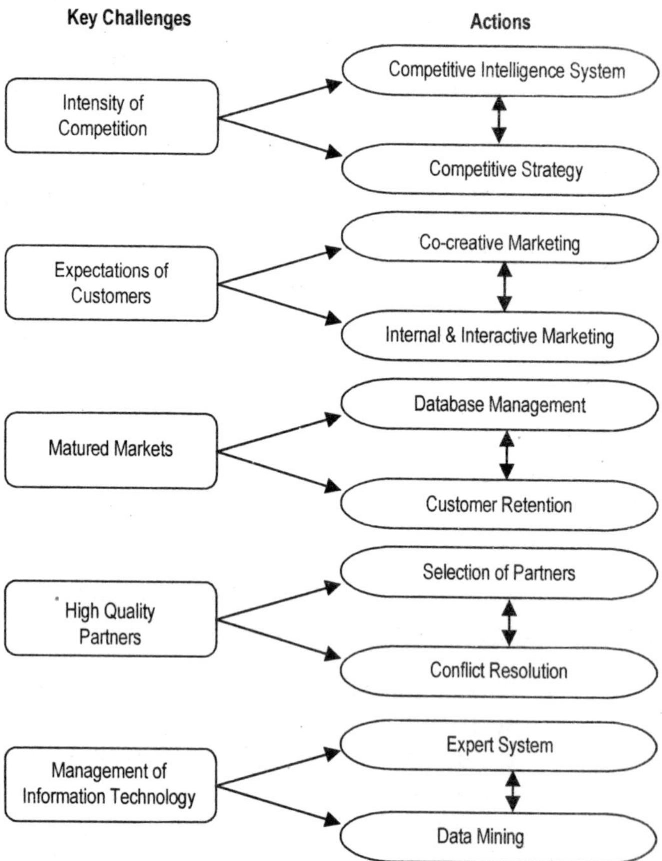

Key Challenge #1

Intensity of Competition

With the presence of multinational companies like Coca-Cola, Pepsi-Cola, Kellogg Cereals, Pizza Hut, Kentucky, Fried Chiken, Morgan Stanley, Peugeot, Colgate, Cadburys, Nestle, Procter and Gamble and General Electric which have entered or reentered the Indian market after liberalization in India in the early 1990, not only has competition increased but consumers' expectations of marketers have multiplied. The increasingly competitive global business environment now means there are few of the protected market circumstances within which an Indian company may operate. In fact, Indian markets have been a source of attraction for multinational companies from all over the world for the last few years because of its population explosion. Thus, with the entrance of the global players in India, not only has competition increased as a result of which domestic companies are finding business operation increasingly difficult, but revenue and profits have also begun to fall and consequently many organizations went out of business. To meet the new challenges, Indian firms need to find new, holistic, and creative ways of sustenance in a highly competitive environment.

Action Steps

Establishment of Competitive Intelligence System

To face the challenges of a highly competitive and increasingly complex competitive environment and to take advantages of emerging opportunities, Indian firms need to possess unprecedented capabilities in understanding and responding to the competition. In fact, a firm's success largely depends on its ability to quickly identify threats and opportunities, respond rapidly to changes in competitors' strategies, and improve the overall effectiveness of the planning process. For this purpose they have to develop detailed information about competitors' characteristics, activities, costs, and strategies. A thorough understanding of the competitive environment enables a marketer not only to identify but also to act on opportunities. However, to achieve this objective the information collected is not only to be collated but also the relevance and significance of its each piece needs to be interpreted and analysed. At the same time, firms have to recognize the fact that every competitor has virtually the same access to every information because of advanced technology. Therefore, the marketer's success depends on his ability to make information work for him—*the conversion of the information into actionable intelligence.* In fact, to reap the rewards of information about the competitive secrets, marketers must know how to use the information which in turn depends on Competitive Intelligence—*an analytical process that acquires, gathers, transmits, evaluates, and analyses raw data about known and potential competitors and makes it available as strategic and tactical knowledge for a marketer to become more efficient and effective competitor* (Sahaf, 2002a). Unfortunately, the majority of Indian marketers have often undermined the strategic importance of competitive intelligence as they interchangeably use the term of intelligence for information. In fact, intelligence is the careful analysis of information that brings critical insight to marketing decision-making by uncovering new patterns or emerging trends. Although competitive information serves as an intellectual asset for a marketer yet he cannot enjoy its healthy returns unless it is converted into intelligence. Competitive intelligence allows marketers to predict changes in business relationships, identify marketplace opportunities, guard against threats, forecast a competitor's strategy, discover new or potential competitors, learn from the success or failures of others, learn about new technologies that can affect the firm, and learn about how government regulations are impacting the competition (McDaniel and Gates,1999). All this has made competitive intelligence an indispensable weapon for marketers in a competitive market. Therefore, every Indian firm must establish a sound and effective CI system capable of providing necessary help to internal decision-makers. Monthly CI reports and newsletter and regular CI meetings should supplement such a system. In fact, CI system must be integrated into firm's strategic planning for better results.

To ensure strategic use of competitive intelligence, firms need to use CI diagnostic—*a device which helps firms to improve their competitive intelligence by identifying their CI needs and comparing the same with their existing CI capabilities*. Such a diagnostic not only helps a firm to identify gaps and problems in its existing system of competitive intelligence but also to establish priorities and options for action (Hall, 2001). The CI diagnostic process comprises of three steps viz.

- Assessment;
- Comparison; and
- Recommendations and Report.

However, before CI process is incorporated in an organization, it needs not only to create CI culture within the organization in which every member should believe, in the sharing of information but an organization has also to impart the necessary training to its employees to enable them to use CI process efficiently and effectively.

Formulation and Execution of Competitive Strategy

Indian marketers can't achieve success in the present competitive business unless they hold some sort of competitive differential advantage over their rivals. In recent years, much attention has been devoted by the marketers to maintain distinctive competence—*a strength that is unique and that makes the organization superior to its competition in the eyes of consumers*. Therefore, distinctive competencies can be exploited in gaining a competitive advantage. Of course, the distinctive competencies must be able to provide incremental value to the market offering when compared to other offerings to the customers. The marketers have been using different sources of competencies at different times. For example, *loyal customers, better product, efficient distribution, research and development, better customer service, low cost*, etc. However, in the past few years Indian marketers have realized the importance of strong relationships with customers and have been using them for this purpose. It is expected that the developments in information and communication technology would definitely bring considerable improvement in such relations. Therefore, Indian marketers must use customer information collected with the help of information technology as basis for a competitive advantage.

Most of the experts on the marketing are of the opinion that in a knowledge-based competition of the future, marketers can use superior knowledge as weapon to sustain competitiveness (Quinn, 1992). With the emphasis on knowledge as competitive weapon, it is essential to make organizational learning a pivot around which a firm's programme for organizational change should revolve. Organizational learning is the combination of discovering new things and acting in new ways that allows an organization to adopt to changes and thereby sustain competitiveness (Miller and Dess, 1996). Therefore, the success of a marketer in a highly dynamic and competitive market shall depends on his ability to learn faster than his competitors. The major challenge before marketers is to find appropriate ways that would help organizations to sustain competitiveness. For this purpose, they can exploit a wide range of sources—*history and experience, customer analysis, experimentation, consultants, management institutions, and benchmarking the best practices of other firms*—to discover what works. However, marketers, in order to make learning possible have to create the combination of culture and climate (Slater and Narver, 1995).

Key Challenge #2

Growing Expectations of Customers

Today's customers in India have become more sophisticated and demanding than ever before. Since a rational customer always evaluates the value of a firm's market offering by comparing his perception of performance with his expectations, therefore, every firm needs to possess complete knowledge and understanding of customer expectations—*customers' beliefs about the performance of a firm's market offering which are used to judge its worth*—if it intends to give value to its customers for their investment. A number of factors have been found to influence customers' expectations, ranging from their personal needs, through the alternative offerings considered, to the specific promises made by a firm with a purpose to win the customers in the first place. Further such expectations are also sensitive to word-of-mouth and customers' past experiences. Consequently, customer expectations keep on changing. This dynamic nature of customer expectations brings to light the important fact that a customer may be satisfied with a particular level of performance from a firm's market offering at a particular time but dissatisfied from the same level of performance another time. On this analogy it is expected that in a highly competitive Indian market customer expectations tend to be very high. In fact, as customers' expectations change, usually becoming more demanding in the benefits they expect from a given product or service, so organizations need continuously to upgrade their offerings to retain position (Hooley *et al.*, 1998). Therefore, an Indian marketer has not only to study customer expectations but has also to link such expectations with his overall strategy in order to ensure superior value for customers' investment. Thus, management of the customer expectations would be a significant factor in the success of any business and would call for a reply from a marketer to the following questions:

- What are the different expectations that a customer holds about a firm's market offering?
- How are such expectations formed?
- How can such expectations be changed?
- What does a firm needs to do if it desires to meet or exceed such expectations?
- What other recourse exists if those expectations aren't met?

Action Steps

Co-creative Marketing

The significance of relationship marketing has tremendously increased among the global marketers in the last part of the 1990's as they realized the importance of customer retention. At the same time the application of relationship marketing has brought a drastic change in the outlook of the global marketers like American Express and British Airways as they began to look upon relationship-based exchanges not only essential for customers but also for their suppliers and distributors. Although it is hard to predict with certainty the future of relationship marketing yet it will be highly influenced by future digitizable technology—*'a blend of digital communications technologies and digital computer technology'*. Such a technology would not only enable the marketers to make relationships with customers more collaborative but also customize all elements of their market offerings to the level of individual customer (Sahaf, 2002b). The collaborative exchange along with the customization of all elements of a market offering would lead to the *'era of co-creative marketing'*—an era that is characterized by such a strong and extensive social and economic ties between a marketer and a customer where a firm's marketing mix is formulated by active participation of both of them (Sheth *et al.*, 2000).

The era of co-creative marketing would not only take marketers back to the micro marketing (i.e., one-to-one interaction) that they thought they had lost because of the wide gap between the point of production and the point of consumption but also offer more opportunities than ever to relate to customers quickly and efficiently. Such an approach to marketing calls for a collaborative approach. This brings to light the important fact that future marketing—*'co-creative'*—would be purely based on the longer-lasting partnering relationships between marketers and customers where both partners would be genuinely interested and committed to match firm's market offering with customer needs. The major features of Co-creative Marketing are:

- Double-win philosophy
- Adaptive
- Customized
- Mutual trust
- Recognition of customer uniqueness
- Circular communication—listening and learning

The co-creative approach towards marketing involves

the process of determining common goals to ensure both partners work in the same direction and the formulation and implementation of the strategies for attaining these goals. Every effort has to be made to develop and maintain partnering relationships so that both partners—marketer and customer—would contribute their best towards the attainment of the mutual goals. Such an arrangement would on the one hand increase the likelihood of offering superior value to the customers for their investment as a result of co-creation of market offering and on the other hand ensure a stream of repeated purchases from delighted customers—both essential for the growth of a business (Sahaf, 2001a). Co-creative marketing is an effective business strategy capable of getting, growing, and retaining the right customers leading to long-term profitability. However, the development and maintenance of successful partnering-type relationship—*prerequisites for successful co-creation*—between a marketer and a customer are no longer an incidental aspect of marketing. In fact, this demands a serious and continuous attention and effort of both the marketer and customer to create rapport, trust and mutual respect that alone can ensure success of co-creative marketing.

Internal and Interactive Marketing

Given the importance of customer value in a competitive market like Indian, it is essential that the firm market the concept of quality internally to its employees—that has been completely ignored in the past—before an attempt is made externally in this direction. Since every member of an organization has to serve someone within it, therefore, the effectiveness within an organization can be enhanced if everyone in the organization treats the other employees as customers. Such an approach formally known as *'internal marketing'* addresses the needs of internal customers, the employees of the firms, who in turn contribute to the external customers—the end users of a firm's product. In fact, it coordinates internal exchanges between the organization and its employees with an objective to achieve successful external exchanges between the organization and its customers (Piercy, 1992). This philosophy recognizes internal marketing equally important with external marketing in a firm's success as it believes that satisfied employees (or well served internal customers) will lead to satisfied external customers. In fact, any attempt to understand the needs and desires of external customers will be of no use unless it is supplemented by a similar attempt for internal customers. Besides traditional methods of marketing research, employee suggestion schemes form an important part of research on employees.

Many global marketers have realized long back the role of their employees in improving the value of their market offerings and have started to look inward for the same. To meet this challenge the Indian firms need to communicate with and motivate employees to share in the goal of improving external marketing through internal marketing. To prepare employees for this challenge, they need to take necessary measures which include *internal research, internal communication,* and *extensive training.*

To prepare employees to meet the demands of internal marketing, firms should organize extensive training programmes for them in which they should be introduced not only to the concept and significance of internal marketing within the marketing environment but also to the customer based culture of the firm. Upon the completion of any training programme in this direction, every effort is to made by every employee to internalize the skills acquired by him in such a programme by applying them continuously at the job.

To meet the expectations of the value conscious customers, Indian marketers have to pay considerable attention towards interactive marketing that identifies the key success factors—*knowledge, skills* and *attitudes*—of a firm's sales force.

Since the salesperson's knowledge is a key ingredient that inspires the customer's confidence in him and enables him to gain the buyer's trust, satisfy customer needs, and practice adaptive selling, therefore, knowledge is among the key resources held by the sales force of an organization. The extensive knowledge enables a salesperson to respond to the queries of the customers confidentially. Thus, knowledge is power—especially when it is offered as proof and support—

without which a salesperson may find it difficult to make the best use of a sales opportunity. To meet the demands and challenges of the competitive markets, a firm's sales force must have a wide exposure in industry trends and developments; product mix, specifications, configuration, service support, and application; company philosophy, mission, culture, organization, and policies and strategies; competitive environment, and competitor's strengths and weaknesses; consumer behaviour, and consumer decision-making process; selling process and techniques; problem-solving process; information and telecommunication technology; and self-management.

Skills are the key to success for a salesperson in marketing task in general and in relationship marketing in particular. However, to meet the challenges of retention marketing, salespeople have to acquire new skills through learning and experience. A successful salesperson must possess communication skills, listening skills, interpersonal skills and technical skills. To ensure better performance at the job, a salesperson must keep a balance in acquiring and using all essential skills.

A salesperson with sufficient knowledge and relevant selling skills cannot be successful in achieving a firm's goals in a competitive market—*customer loyalty*—unless he possesses the right attitude to use that knowledge and practice those skills. The right attitude can make winner out of a mediocre salesperson or help a salesperson bounce back with enthusiasm and drive after being turned down (Kranz and Kranz, 1980). Generally it has been observed that salespeople lack the right attitude, therefore, marketers need to impart training to their sales force which should be not only be professional-based but attitudinal-based as well.

Key Challenge #3

Matured Markets

Customers in India have not only shrunk but also fragmented. As a consequence, conventional mass markets have started to disappear and it is expected that such markets can no longer exist in the future. This change in the market would force marketers to reconsider how they approach their task. Such critical thinking is already beginning to reshape marketing. In future, marketers would prefer to shift from mass marketing to micromarketing, i.e., one-to-one marketing. However, reaching and mitivating fewer customers on a critical thinking is already beginning to reshape marketing. In future, marketers would prefer to shift from mass marketing to micromarketing, i.e., one-to-one marketing. However, reaching and motivating fewer customers on a person basis is more expensive than reaching a mass-market. Efforts are on to make possible the extensive use of micromarketing on profitable basis. It is believed that marketing on one-to-one basis can become cost-efficient if requisite information about customers is made available at a large scale through a customer database that is capable of providing a marketer with the necessary information on the most suitable issues of customers' needs. Therefore, the use of new technology *vis-à-vis* database will help marketers in making micromarketing a reality. Thus, a marketer can meet the challenges of a matured market with the help of *Narrow Targeting Strategy*, the success of which would be dependent on Customer Retention, and Management of Database.

Action Steps

Customer Retention

Traditionally, marketers have been concentrating on customer acquisition and make little effort to retain the customer. A body of recent research highlights the strategic importance of customer retention. The works of Reichheld and Sasser (1990) and others highlighted that a reduction of five percent in defection rate can boost profits ranging from 25 percent to 85 percent, depending on the industry. Further, it takes five times the energy and budget to get a new customer as it does to keep an existing one. In fact, customer retention helps a firm to increase its profitability on the one hand and on the other hand to develop such relations with customers as are essential to understand their preferences and needs. Further, the retained customers create favourable word-of-mouth, pay less attention to competing brands and advertising, and are less price sensitive. Therefore, the ultimate objective of a firm should be to retain customers rather than simply their acquisition. Therefore, marketers have to change this myopic view of transactional marketing and have to make every effort to ensure customer retention. Making this happen requires not only commitment but also effective and efficient marketing efforts capable of meeting the growing demands of customers.

Usually a customer prefers to stay with a firm that meets his needs better than the competitors. At the same time, marketers prefer to stay in relationships that are satisfying; they meet financial objectives; they evidence co-operation, and they can be projected into the future with confidence (Dawner and Tanner, 1999). The mutual relationship—a prerequisite for customer loyalty—that would bind them together with an objective to meet each other's needs, shall be critical determinant of long-term market opportunities in the future. Therefore, one of the major tasks of a marketer in future would be to maintain strong relations with his customers. However, the maintenance of a long-term relationship of a marketer and a customer is highly influenced by the strategy of superior delivered value.

Database Management

The use of database—the creation of a large computerized file of customers' profiles and purchase patterns—has grown dramatically over past few years as it helps marketers to target their efforts with greater efficiency and effectiveness. The beauty of database is that it allows marketers to track information about customer's purchasing habits, preferences, complements, complaints, future needs and other critical issues that can be very helpful in acknowledging and maintaining loyal customers. In fact, database can make marketing programme more flexible and allow a marketer to tailor the programme to the individual needs of each customers. Such an approach can enable a marketer to focus on issues that are most important to his customers. Many successful organizations have realized the significance of customer profiles' as information and intelligence resource and, therefore, they devote a great deal of efforts to building up such profiles (Sahaf, 2001b). Such an attempt not only helps marketers to predict the probability of targeting new customers with their existing marketing programmes but also existing customers with a new marketing programme.

A marketer needs to be careful in deciding what to include in his database. Usually, a customer database contains individual customers' demographics (age, income, family members, birthdays), psychographics (activities, interests, and opinions), past purchases and other relevant information (Kotler, 1997). A marketer can collect data for this purpose from *on going* business (orders, inquiries, and refusals), *external sources* (rented or purchased lists, joint ventures with other companies, and database compilation services), and *customized sources* (primary marketing research, warranty cards, and satisfaction surveys) (Roa and Steckel, 1998). However, an effective database needs to use *transactional data* —an ongoing record of who is using the marketer's services or buying his products (Solomon and Stuart, 1997). Such a data must depict the details of **RFM**—*recency* (when the last purchase was made), *frequency* (how often the customer buys), and *monetary value* (what the customer's annual expenditure is) (Bickert, 1990). Typically, a marketer needs to collect his own information on customers and then enrich the same by external database.

Key Challenge #4

High Quality Business Partners

The higher consumer expectations along with fiercely competition would leave even the most capable companies unable in terms of expertise and economy to meet the requirements of the market in near future. Therefore, companies need to devise new ways of doing business that would offer superior value to the customers. One such way to deal with this situation is strategic alliance—*an arrangement in which organizations join their resources to form a long-term collaboration that is capable of meeting their common goals such as competitive advantage or customer value creation.* To plan strategic alliance, the organizations have to know their respective core competencies because under such an arrangement each collaborator would contribute what it considers its core competencies. However, the identification of core competencies may be far from straight forward within an organization or between partners (Piercy and Cravens, 1995). The depth of commitment required to make a strategic alliance work makes it crucial to choose partners that will have strategic value to both parties and can contribute to viability of the venture. Thus, the selection of quality partners and formulation of a proper system of conflict resolution, in case any dispute arises between the partners crops up during the collaboration, are the two major issues that need attention of the marketers.

Action Steps

Selection of Partners

To ensure superior delivered value to the customers, marketers need to devise a comprehensive system capable of identifying such quality partners whose abilities best match the marketer's unique needs. In fact, such a system should assess each partner's strategic core competences in order judge their significance in the present and future demands of the customers. Such an analysis would enable a marketer not only to choose the right partners for his business but also personalize business programmes according to partners' skills and capabilities. Such an arrangement enables strategic partners to make best use of their resources and capabilities in enhancing customer value of the market offering. Further, a marketer should seek out partners that hold similar vision, values and principles as those of him.

Conflict Resolution

Conflict is unavoidable, perhaps even essential in a creative partnering environment. The impact of the disagreement between partners can vary from a minor irritant to a major problem that can threaten the working of partnering. Therefore, management of conflict needs a careful attention of marketers. In fact, conflict resolution is at the heart of partnering. A badly managed conflict results in distrust and a well managed one always helps in clear communication and finding a solution that everyone can live with. A marketer should always prefer to use the strategy of collaborating—an approach to conflict resolution characterized by a genuine attempt to find a solution ("the win-win" approach) that satisfies all partners—for resolving any conflict in partnering. Further, every effort should be made to prevent the conflict by ensuring (Sahaf, 2001a):

- Well defined roles and positions of the partners;
- Clearly stated goals and programmes of the partnering;
- Effective communication network between the partners;
- Empowerment of the partners to enact their roles;
- Preparation and execution of programme priorities and schedule for partnering; and
- Free access to any information of the partnering business for every partner.

Key Challenge #5

Growth of Information Technology

Information is the most valuable business resource that adds greatest value to modern marketing. Marketers need information to recognize, identify and use marketing opportunities successfully. In fact, the availability of adequate information about the customers, the competitors, and the environment is regarded as a key factor in market planning. As a consequence marketers have begun to recognize information as an important resource that can be utilized for gaining a strategic advantage over their competitors. However, to make it possible a marketer needs to collect and analyze continuously the requisite information. The availability of the requisite information shall enable a marketer to base his decisions on the market realities than on his personal hunches and intuitions. The growth and advancement of technology has made it possible for the firms to collect data on every aspect of their operations. As a consequence, there has been unbridled growth of databases in recent years that enables marketers to have access to an increasing amount of data. Unfortunately data possess little value for decision-makers unless it is transformed into information. In fact, many firms find themselves data rich and information poor (Hair, *et al.*, 2000). Therefore, a marketer has not only to make adequate arrangements for the collection of data but also for its proper interpretation which in turn depends on a marketer's understanding of the relationships existing between different elements of data. How firms best manage information about the different aspects of their businesses is rapidly becoming one of the main concerns of Indian firms. In fact, to deal with such a situation successfully, a number of firms have been using different technology over the past few years. However, to cope with the data deluge of the 2000s, a firm needs to use an integrated approach of Expert system and Data mining.

Action Steps

Expert System

To make sense of a huge volume of data, researchers suggest the application of expert system—*a computer programme that has the capability to generate inferences or arrive at a solution, an answer, or a decision by searching through a large amount of data.* Such a system interacts with the user by asking questions, explaining why it requires certain information; providing advice, justifying the opinion that it offers and explaining which conclusions it reached on the way as well as how these were arrived at (Beerel, 1987). Despite the capabilities of expert system to provide strategic advantage, marketers generally fail to take its advantage as most of them believe that it fails to provide an acceptable return in advance of the system development. However, as people get more and more exposure of using such systems, there is every possibility that its return will enhance.

The technological developments in expert system over the past few years not only have made it possible for it to analyze and assimilate enormous amounts of information in the twinkling of an eye but also to identify new contributions and methods of induction. The author subscribe the view that expert systems will lead to expert marketing managers, managers who will lead the way to highly individualized marketing programmes. Consequently, in the years to come, more and more marketers would be interested to establish an expert system in their organizations to meet the growing demands of competitive market. However, before introducing such a system, a marketer needs to understand its implications. Such an approach alone can remind him to proceed with caution. The establishment of an expert system calls for a larger investment in human capital in order to make firm's working force knowledgeable, adaptable and skillful—*a prerequisite of an expert system.* Therefore, the decision to embark on such a system largely depends on firm's financial capacity and commitment. Once the expert system has been installed, a marketer must ensure its integration with conventional data processing systems in order to experience its real power. At the same time, a marketer needs to update an expert system to maintain its creditability.

Data Mining

Today data mining is one of the hottest topics in information technology. Data mining which is also popularly known as *'knowledge discovery in databases', 'data archeology', 'data exploration', 'data dredging', 'information harvesting'* and *'knowledge extraction'*, is the process of using software technologies to extract the hidden predictive information from large volumes of data. Thus, it calls for exhaustively exploration and analysis of the data existing in a firm's databases from different perspectives to discover consistent patterns, association, and/or systematic relationships between variables related to customers, products, services, processes and other activities that can lead to new and more profitable business opportunities (Sahaf, 2003). Data mining which highlights buying patterns, reveals customer tenancies, cuts redundant costs, or uncovers unseen profitable relationships and opportunities is primarily used today by the companies with strong consumer focus—retail, banking and financial, communication, and marketing organizations. In fact, successful application of data mining has been observed in the areas of direct marketing, retailing industry, business forecasting, quality control, financial services, banking and telecommunication industry (Han and Kamber, 2001). Data mining can be of great help to marketers not only in understanding the relationship between a firm's market offering, marketing environment and customers but also to determine the impact of such a relationship on a firm's sales and profitability, and customer satisfaction.

PRIORITIES OF ACTION STEPS

The author strongly believes that the action steps recommended in this paper vary in terms of urgency and importance for the marketers who intend to operate in Indian markets in future. Therefore, such action steps need to be prioritized so that highly urgent and highly important ones are addressed first by the marketers followed by the action steps that are less urgent and less important. For this purpose the opinion of 90 marketers selected form five top marketing centers in India were sought to rank the action steps identified above in terms of urgency and importance for their respective organizations. The results of the said survey are reflected in two-dimensional matrix (Figure 2). Each respondent was required to select the top-three most-urgent action steps (that call for an immediate address of the marketer) and top-three most-important action steps (that have maximum impact on their businesses).

The top left hand corner is priority I as it constitutes action steps which were considered by the respondents highly urgent and highly important. The top right quadrant which includes the action steps that are highly urgent but less important in the opinion of respondents and, therefore, should be considered priority II. The bottom left quadrant calls for priority III as it represents the action steps that respondents rated as less urgent but highly important. No action step was recommended by the respondents for the bottom right quadrant (priority IV) which reflects less urgent and less important action steps. Thus, on the basis of priority of action steps, the matrix (Figure 2) can easily be interpreted in the fashion of the letter 'z'.

FIGURE 2

Priority Matrix (in terms of Urgency and Importance) of Action Steps

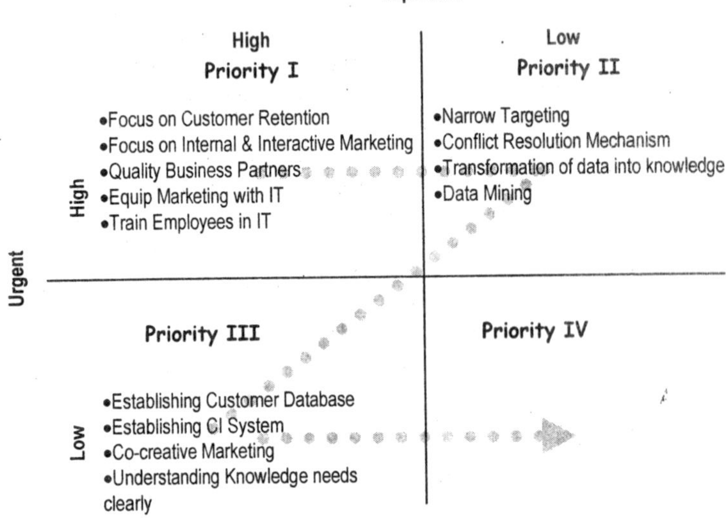

CONCLUSION

The marketing environment in India is constantly changing. These changes can occur any time with any magnitude and would definitely influence the marketing philosophy, principles and practice. At the same time, these changes would open up vast new vistas and opportunities for enterprising marketers. To meet the demands of dynamic and competitive environment, marketers need a framework to address the challenges. The author believes that the framework recommended in this paper will not only help marketers to understand the implications of the environmental changes in India but also identify the necessary measures they need to take to ensure long-term sustainability in a competitive market.

REFERENCES

Beerel, A.C., (1987), *"Expert System—Strategic Implications and Applications"*, Ellis Horwood Limited, England.

Bickert, J., (1990), *"Adventures in Relevance Marketing"*, Briefcase Books, Denver.

Dawner, F.P., Tanner, J.F., (1999), Business Marketing, Irwin McGraw-Hill, Boston.

Hair, J.F. Jr., Bush, R.P., Ortinau D.J., (2000), "Marketing *Research"*, Irwin McGraw-Hill, Boston.

Hall, C. (2001), "The Intelligent Puzzle", *Competitive Intelligence Review*, Vol. 12(4).

Han, J., Kamber, M. (2001), *"Data Mining: Concepts and Techniques"*, Morgan Kaufmann Publishers, San Francisco.

Hooley, G.J., Saunders, J.A. (1998), *"Marketing Strategy and Competitive Positioning"*, London, Prentice-Hall Europe.

Kotler, P. (1997), *"Marketing Management"*, Prentice-Hall, Inc., New Jersey.

Kranz, R.J., Kranz, M.K. (1980), *"Professional Selling: A Practical Approach"*, D. Van Nostrand Company, New York.

McDaniel, C., Gates, R. (1999), *"Contemporary Marketing Research"*, South-Western College Publishing, Cincinnati,

Miller, A., Dess, G.G. (1996). "Strategic *Management"*, McGraw-Hill Companies, Inc., New York.

Piercy, N.F. (1992), *"Market-Led Strategic Change"*, Butterworth-Heinemann, Newton.

Piercy, N.F., Cavens, D.W. (1995), 'The Network Paradigm and the Marketing Organization", *European Journal of Marketing.*

Quinn, J. B. (1992), *"Intelligent Enterprise"*, The Free Press, New York.

Reichheld, F.F., Sasser, W.E. Jr. (1990), "Zero Defection: Quality Comes to Service", *Harvard Business Review*, September-October.

Rao, V.R., Steckel, J.H. (1998), *"Analysis for Strategic Marketing"*, Addison-Wesley, Reading.

Sahaf, M.A., (2000), "Managing the Twenth-First Century: A Guideline to Marketers", *Indore Manager*, Volume IX, No. 1&2, March-May.

Sahaf, M.A. (2001a), "Partnering Relationship Marketing: A Strategic Approach to Success", *NMIMS Management Review*, Vol. XIII, No. 1, January-June.

Sahaf, M.A. (2001b), "Value-Based Micromarketing—A Blend of Narrow Targeting and Information Technology", *The Business Review*, Vol. 7, Nos. 1 and 2, March.

Sahaf, M.A. (2002a), "Competitive Intelligence—An Effective War-Game", *Paradigm*, Volume 2, Issue 2, July-December.

Sahaf, M.A., (2002b), "Co-creative Marketing—An Agenda for the Future", *Business Perspectives*, Volume 4, No. 2, July-December.

Sahaf, M.A. (2003), "Data Mining—A Framework for Marketers in the Age of Information", *The Business Review*, Vol. 9, Nos. 1 and 2, March.

Sheth, J.N., Sisodia, R.S., Sharma, A.. (2000), "The Antecedents and Consequences of Customer-Centric Marketing", *Journal of the Academy of Marketing Science*, 28(1).

Slater, S.F., Narver, J.C. (1995), "Marketing Orientation and the Learning Organization", *Journal of Marketing*, July.

Solomon, M.R., Stuart, E.W. (1997), *"Marketing: Real People, Real Choice"*, Prentice Hall, New Jersey.

CHAPTER

8

Changing Profile of Indian Consumers and Implications for Marketers

Balram Dogra and Rajesh Verma

1.1 INDIAN MARKET: SOME FACTS

177 million households; One thousand million people; Seven hundred and eighty million consumers of cooking oil; Seven hundred and six million consumers of tea; Four hundred and fifty million buyers of casual footwear; Forty million TV owners; Two and a quarter million automobiles owners. This is a market called India.

Income classifications by themselves do not reveal much about the market behaviour and purchasing power, as such. To provide a more realistic picture of the consumption behaviour, the NCAER (National Council of Applied Economic Research) has released a new classification of the market by ownership and propensity to consume various consumer goods[1]—*The Very Rich*: who buy the most expensive consumer products; *The Consuming Classes*: who buy the bulk of all consumer goods marketed in India; *The Climbers*: who

TABLE 1

The Income Classification of Households in India

Household Category	*Annual Income*	*Population Size*	*Share*
Low income	Upto Rs. 22,500	590 million	59%
Lower middle income	22,500 to 45,000	250 million	25%
Middle Income	45,000 to 62,000	100 million	10%
Upper-Middle Income	62,000 to 96,000	40 million	4%
High income	Above Rs. 96,000	20 million	2%

Source: Indian Market Demographic Report, NCAER, 2002.

own some durables; especially, televisions and small home appliances; *The Aspirants*: who possess the most basic durables, such as, transistor radios, bicycles, and aspire for the rest; and *The Destitute*: who are generally not consumers of manufactured goods.

Interestingly, the population of 'Aspirants' and 'Destitutes' is projected to decline in absolute numbers by 2007, based on annual income growth of 7-8%.

TABLE 2

India's Consumer Class

Consumer Group	*Number of Households in Million*			*Growth*
	1995-96	*2001-02*	*2006-07*	*1995-2007*
The Very Rich	1.2	2.0	6.2	416%
The Consuming Class	32.5	54.6	90.9	179%
The Climbers	54.1	71.6	74.1	37%
The Aspirants	44.0	28.1	15.3	-65%
The Destitute	33.0	23.4	12.8	-61%
Total	164.8	180.7	199.2	21%

Source: Indian Market Demographic Report, NCAER, 2002.

The Pricewater-house Coopers (PwC) 2003 report[2] on Global Private Equity says India is the fastest growing market in the world and the 12th biggest, ahead of worthies like Israel and China. In the last five years private equity investments have grown at an astounding CAGR (Compounded Annual Growth Rate) of 82%. Sweden, the next fastest growing private equity market has grown at 57% CAGR.

FIG. I

Top Five Countries on Growth

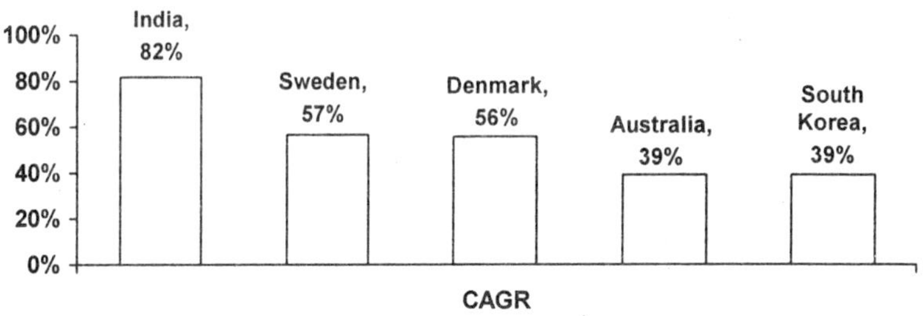

Source: Pricewater-house Coopers Report, 2003.

2. CHANGING PROFILE OF INDIAN CONSUMERS

There is distinct evidence that the Indian consumers, irrespective of socio-economic origin are at various stages of defining their "self." Indian society has changed fundamentally in recent years. Lives no longer follow familiar patterns and that means companies can no longer make broad assumptions about customers' lives, needs and aspirations. So how can one compete in a crowded and shifting marketplace where consumers are increasingly marketing-savvy and marketing spend is ever decreasing? Every day companies are presented with new trends—increasing ethnic diversity, the break-up of the traditional family unit, increasingly ambiguous reactions to the major brands, the growth of online shopping, etc. The list goes on. A driving force behind this changing market is the loss of a single way of living. People no longer have a united set of preferences common to all. Instead, they take on multiple roles and adapt their image to the different situations they face. Some of the significant changes in Indian consumers are:

1. Shifting Choices

The Indian consumer is spending more on apparel, eating out, entertainment, vacations and lifestyle activities.[3] As indicated by *KSA Consumer Outlook 2003,* on an average, spend on personal items, eating out, clothing and vacations has gone up in 2002-03 and per cent spend on regular stuff like grocery has declined to 42% (from 48%).

2. Decreasing Gap between SEC A and SEC B

Between SEC A and B, the gap between spending on Lifestyle-related activities is declining.[4] The *socio-economic classification* (SEC) groups urban Indian households into five segments (SEC A, SEC B, SEC C, SEC D and SEC E households) on the basis of education level and the occupation of the *chief wage earner* (CWE), the person who contributes the most to the house hold expenses.[5] The CWEs of nearly half the SEC A households work in executive position. The other half comprises mainly of industrialists/ businessmen or shop owners. Almost all of them are either graduates or post-graduates. CWEs of SEC B households are primarily employed at clerical or supervisory levels (46%). 29% are shopkeepers while 10% are businessmen. Less than half are graduates or post graduates (45%). 38% are educated till the 10th or 12th grade, while 13% have had some college education. The groups SEC A and SEC B jointly constitute over a quarter of urban Indian population.

The ratio of SEC A to B spending in 2003 in categories of clothing, grocery, movies and theatre has narrowed from 2002. Some select category ratios are—Clothing: 1.25, Eating out: 1.38, Grocery: 1.17, Footwear: 1.37, Savings and Investment: 1.2, Movies and Theatres: 1.19. *(Source: KSA Consumer Outlook, 2003)*

3. Similar Media Influence

Different SEC groups are being exposed to similar media influences owing to rising literacy and increased TV and Cable/Satellite (C & S) penetration. The growth in C & S penetration is more than twice the growth in TV owning homes.[6] Television now reaches 81.6 million Indian homes and reflects a growth of 12% since 1999. Access to C & S homes jumped from 29 million in 1999 to 40 million in 2002; a 31 percent growth rate. C & S subscription has now penetrated 50% of all TV homes. *(Source: National Readership Survey, 2003)*

4. Disposable Incomes

As per annual KSA Indian Retail and Consumer Outlook 2003 there was a rise in discretionary spending across all age groups.[7] Consumer spending in India grew by 12 per cent in 2003, over the previous year and consumer confidence is higher than any other Asia Pacific market. Business World Consumer Satisfaction Survey, 2003 reported that the disposable income of consumer have substantially gone up and consumers were planning to spend 2-3% more on non-grocery items than what they spent last year.[8] Disposable Incomes are up by 10% in Delhi, Hyderabad and Pune; 20% in Ludhiana and Bangalore; and 30% in Mumbai.

5. Rural India on Fast Track

According to the *NCAER Report, 2002*, the lower income group in both rural and urban India is shrinking at the rate of 4.5 per cent.[9] There has been a growth of 14.3 per cent in the Higher Income Group in Rural India and 8.6 per cent growth in the Upper Middle Class Income Group, very close to a 9.9 per cent growth of the same in Urban India.

3. EMERGENCE OF TWENTY-FIRST CENTURY CONSUMERS

"The message of industry was once 'we've made this, so buy it'. Then it was, 'we've made it and it's better, so buy it', then 'we've made it for you, so buy it'. Increasingly it will be 'we've made it with you and personalized it, so buy it." The change in messages is because of rise of 21st century customers. 21st Century customers, because their style of consumption is so distinctive. They have transcended all ages, ethnic groups and even, to some extent, income. Customers are living in economies where their basic needs are quickly and easily satisfied, they are far more concerned with satisfying wants, which now frequently focus on original, innovative and distinctive products and services. As a result they tend to reject mass-produced and mass marketed commodities in favour of products and services that claim to be some way authentic. Independent, individualistic, involved and well informed on consumer matters they are high on aspirations.

Old consumers were beset of scarcities of cash, choice and availability; those confronting the new consumers are shortage of time and attention.

Scarcities of Time

People prefer time and convenience to better bargains and are willing to travel lesser and lesser for standard items in their monthly shopping list. To save on time they are increasingly outsourcing household work as evident by 51 per cent rise in payment to household help.[10] (*Source: Consumer Outlook, 2003*).

Intolerant of delays and frequently cash rich, many consumers are now prepared to pay premium of not being kept waiting.

Scarcities of Attention

Unless consumers are able to understand something quickly and easily it will often be ignored, especially when the personal relevance of the information is unclear. Consumer is today regularly bombarded with advertisements through different medias,[11] as it is evident from the penetration rate of each media shown in the Table 3.

TABLE 3

All India Media Penetration

Media type	*Print*	*Terrestrial TV*	*Cable and Satellite*	*Radio*	*Cinema*	*Internet*
Per cent Penetration	25%	53%	20%	22%	7%	1%

Source: National Readership Survey, 2003.

Partially as result of time scarcity, consumers today have developed greater visual literacy than any generation before and indeed, the perceptual skills are often so advanced that they might spot the strategies behind advertisements, with the result that conventional methods of persuasion often fail to move them.

I. Conventional Consumers *Vs.* 21st Century Consumers

There are three basic forces driving fundamental change in Indian Business: the widening global marketplaces; new technology; and a new species of consumers. Of these three changes, technology provides the tools and expanded markets provide the opportunities but the new consumer will determine the results. Indian consumers are not the same anymore. Table 2 summarizes the key differences between conventional and 21st century consumers.

FIGURE 2

Conventional Consumers *Vs.* 21st Century Consumers

Conventional Consumer		21st Century Consumer
Synchronized		Individual
Time Rich		Time Starved
Authoritarian		Democratic
Seek Convenience		Seek Authenticity
Focused on Basic Needs	⇒	Focus on Discretionary needs
Less Involved		Involved
Conformist		Independent
Less Informed		Well Informed
Liking someone else to organize them		Insisting on organizing their own lives
Avoidance		Experience seeking
Self Denial		Affordable Indulgence
Destiny Driven		Destiny Seeking

The family structure in India has moved from that of a joint family to that of a nuclear family, where family members are highly individualistic, has divergent needs, and have adequate spending power. With both the members of the family often working, there is a constraint on time. This gives rise to a unique need for quality time, which translates into demand for authentic products/services. To ensure authenticity, consumers now involve themselves far more closely with the process of production and/or consumption to ensure that what they buy exactly matches their needs. In this era, it is not just men who make purchase decisions but each family member's choice is taken into account and a collective decision is made. Thus consumer is witnessing a distinct shift from a strict, authoritarian role to a more democratic role. Information is the fuel that drives the new consumers. It has opened up avenues of choice and allows more careful judgments to me made about prospective purchases. Based on this heightened awareness and media exposure consumer now prefers to make their own decisions rather than being told what to buy. By this very nature, it implies an independent approach to consumption and not a conformist approach. Indians have always practiced caution in financial matters and this is reflected in a high personal saving rate. But customers are now saving less and are no longer feeling guilty about occasional indulgence that they previously considered as lavish.

2. A New Consumption Push by 2006-07

Table 4, Shows the income distribution among the Indian households. In this table NCAER has tried to forecast the increase in consumption by the year 2007.

TABLE 4

Income Distribution Among Households in Per cent

	Rural		*Urban*	
	1998-99	*2006-07*	*1998-99*	*2006-07*
High	3	6	13	25
Upper Middle	4	6	12	22
Middle	10	18	23	26
Lower Middle	35	46	34	24
Lower	48	24	19	3

Source: Indian Market Demographic Report, NCAER, 1998.

According to NCAER estimates, in period 1998-99, most of the people were in the lower income group and few in the upper income group.[12] Which indicates that the center of gravity of market consumption was very low. But as the shape of income distribution starts bulging out at the center, the center of gravity of what is consumed should increase. The projected figures suggest that by the year 2007 the center of gravity of what is consumed in case of Urban consumers will be equally distributed among, Lower Middle, Middle, Upper Middle, and High income household; and in case of Rural consumers the bulk purchase will come from Lower middle and Middle income households. This shift in income distribution will be inflection point of consumption that is about to happen.

4. IMPLICATION FOR MARKETERS

It is an accepted fact that today's business has only one boss—The Customer. As India strides into the future with a wave of optimism, one is reminded that the resurgence of the Indian economy has been sustained in the face of the difficult international scenario. Although companies have been shaken, those who have changed along with the needs of the customer have emerged successful.

Product lifecycles shortened; customer behaviour became very fickle and business environment, as a whole turned extremely volatile. Manufacturers can no longer push their products down the supply chain; it is the consumer who pulls the products desired. And the products should be there right where he wants them. Price and quality are no longer sufficient to thrive in this market; speed with which one reaches the market is of paramount importance. To achieve this flexibility, information has to flow freely throughout the Supply chain. The performance of the supply chain needs to be constantly analysed and improved to ensure its survival. A fundamental business shift is taking place in today's business scenario-companies strong focus on products is shifting to an equally strong focus on customers. The entire interaction that a company has with its customers is being scrutinized and dissected with one thought in mind: to win and retain the most loyal and profitable customers. It is thus well established that customer is the one who redefines the business equations.

A lot of little changes are taking place in the market. Each Change when viewed in isolation, could easily be rejected as not being particularly significant. But over a period of time and taken together, they can provide a critical mass of change. It is apparent that the great consumer market has arrived, and is waiting to be served. But the question is: are there enough relevant products and services available to take advantage of this? What are the implications of this rapidly growing dynamic market? A few important trends are discernible.

1. Value Segmentation

As the market matures, and is subjected to multiple changes, segmentation has to go beyond the product-centric paradigm. The question to ask of research is not 'how is the market segmented?', but what is the new way in which to cut it up so that customers can be served better. Segmentation should based on customer needs, preferences, behaviours and economic potential, which provides the basis for resource allocation decisions in marketing, sales and service.

2. Institutional Memory

When the customer interacts with company, everyone in the enterprise must be aware of prior interactions, outstanding issues and pending opportunities. The need of business is custom built databases, which requires constant updating and a dedicated team of people who sift through the data and weed out redundant prospects. This is the area that companies need to invest in.

3. Collaboration

Every purchase consists of three stages: Investigation, acquisition and consumption.[13] Within these three stages there are two key elements—*A Process Dimension* (investigation and acquisition) and an *Outcome Dimension* (consumption). Despite their scarcities of time and attention, consumers are now increasingly introducing a further stage into process dimension by becoming more personally involved in the creation of the product or service they want to purchase.

For marketers, involving consumers provides an opportunity for learning a great deal about their taste and so come up with compelling new value proposition tailored and marketed to groups as small as one.

4. Customer Experience Management

Companies will have to identify the contact points where customers interact with the company. To create a holistic experience, companies need to create a consistent and compelling experience at each of these touch points. Ones companies have mapped all "touch points" between company and their customers they are able to deliver a consistent, high quality experience that provides added value to the customer.

5. Building Organization-wide Commitment

The goal of companies must be to ensure that customer's experience at every level of interface with the company should be satisfying. Every employee in organization must be committed to provide value to customer in his or her own ways.

6. Customer-Centric Revenue Management

The heart of customer orientation is customer centric revenue management, which optimizes profits for each customer relationship based on the price a customer is willing to pay for his or her perceived value. Company will think of profits, which arises because of customer satisfaction.

7. Listen-Understand-Respond

The final ingredient that ties companies to customer in a salutary, lasting relationship is a dialogue where you listen carefully to your customers, understand what they say, and respond by modifying value proposition and brand identity, extending your businesses appropriately to fulfil their desires.

Sustained relations are the result of a continuous communication where one listens carefully to customers, understands what they say and responds to by modifying the value proposition.

8. Use Technology

Rapid changes in technology now allow both collection and processing of data on individual customers. With the help of customer friendly technology companies can now achieve closer and more interactive communication with customer and improve the efficiency and effectiveness of processes that add the value for the customer. As new technologies and channels for communication become established, distance is eliminated or minimized, and information is often available immediately. Today's consumer is a beneficiary of the information explosion. The volume of information available is greater than ever, as is the speed with it is gathered. C mpanies today talk of running on "Internet time", i.e. 24/7/365. Consumers expect these standards to be met in all the transactions. And this expectation should become a benchmark for the companies.

5. CONCLUSION

The emergence of hyper-competition has transferred power to customers. With heightened competition giving them a tremendous sense of freedom and choice, they are becoming more unpredictable in their tastes, preferences and needs. They expect and demand more "value" from companies. In today's competitive world, customers have more information, more choice, more access and, as a result high expectations. The companies that thrive will be the ones that create the most compelling and consistent relationship with their customers. The depth of this relationship will be foundation for ongoing success and sustained competitive advantage despite disruption in market places.

According to a *Meta Group Survey*, 50% of the company's satisfied customer will do business with their competitors.[14] This shows that business today needs to know more and do more than just satisfying there customers. The latest *AC Nielsen Asia-Pacific Consumer Confidence Study* suggests that consumers in the region are so confident about the future of their economies that they are headed for a spending spree.[15] The difference between survival and success of companies will depend on how well they understand consumers' new needs, hopes and aspirations. But feeling the pulse of an Indian consumer will not be an easy task.

NOTES AND REFERENCES

1. India Economic Market Profile, www.aceglobalonline.com/IndiaEconomicProfile.html.
2. Prasad, S., India On Top, Business World, 8 December 2003, p. 10.
3. Singhal, A. and Ghoshal, N., Demystifying The Indian Mass Market, Strategic Marketing, Vol II, Issue V, November-December 2003, p. 11.
4. Singhal, A. and Ghoshal, N., *op. cit.*
5. Inamdar, R., Chandra, M., Targeting New Consumers, www.india-seminar.com/2001/498.
6. Shekhar, R., TV Penetration Growth Flat, Cinema Negative, Radio and Print Positive: NRS 2003, http://www.indiantelevision.com/headlines/y2k3/dec/dec205.htm.
7. Iyengar, J., China, India Confront the Wal-Marts, http://www.atimes.com/atimes/Global_Economy/FA31Dj03.html.
8. Rajshekhar, M., Are Good Times Back? *Business World*, 6 October 2003, p. 63.
9. Sabnavis, M., Getting a Fix on the New Middle-Class Consumer, *Indian Management*, Vol. 41, Issue 7, October, 2002. pp. 52.
10. Jain, S., Changing Profile of the Indian Consumer, *Indian Management*, Vol. 42, Issue 5, May 2003, p. 27.
11. Shekhar, R., *op. cit.*
12. Bijjapurkar, R., The New Improved Indian Consumer, *Business World*, 8 December 2003, p. 32.
13. Lewis, D. and Bridger, D., The Soul of the New Consumer, Nicholas Brealey Publishing, London, 2003, pp. 112-13.
14. Frauenheim, E., Blue Moods in IT shops, http://www.zdnetindia.com/biztech/enterprise/features/stories/79561.html.
15. Datta, K., The New Indian Consumer is on a Spending Spree, http://www. in. rediff. com/money/2004/jan/16guest3.htm.

CHAPTER

9

Changing Role of Women in Purchasing Decisions

A Survey of Patiala and Chandigarh

Parveen Gill, Pushpinder Gill and Bharatbhushan Singla

No study of the Indian consumer is complete if it doesn't look at the Indian family. Unlike in the west, we are a society of consensus seekers. We rely a great deal on our family. Even our purchase decisions are jointly made. Why is this? It could be a hangover from the past when everyone stayed in the large extended families and was used to making decisions through consensus. Or it could be because unlike in the west, we do not have social security to fall back on and family is the only social support system we have.

In the olden days the father was the unquestioned head. Today, there is recognition that even parents don't have all the answers. Kids prefer to go to their peers or seniors for career advice. However, there is greater appreciation of parental advice when it comes to areas like managing interpersonal relationships.

The NUF generation has seen the woman graduate from a housewife to a home manager. The man remains the breadwinner but is more adaptable. Marketers have to target the family as a unit, ironically in an increasingly individualized society. The family as a unit is a complex and ever-evolving institution. This paper is an attempt to analyse the changing role of women in purchase decision-making.

Many people think of marketing as executives taking clients to lunch or playing golf on Friday afternoons. But there is more to marketing than meets the eye. In any type of economy, it is important for companies and non-profit organizations to maintain a visual existence in the public's eye. Marketing is an extremely broad industry with hundreds of departments and areas with each requiring different skills for the overall success of a company. Effective marketing employs a lot of people including promotion analysts, video and commercial writers, directors, designers, art directors, graphic designers, research analysts, survey analysts, marketing specialists and sales positions.

Marketers in India are to face challenging times and situations as Indian consumer has been improving remarkably in terms of socio-economic and cultural dimensions. The beliefs and attitudes of Indian consumers are passing through a *re-socialization* phase. Indian consumer market is a multi-tiered market, with the bicycle and the business class co-existing. It is a market whose potential and desire to consume has perhaps moved ahead of the marketers' mental model of it.

Quantitatively, between 1996-97 and 2000-01, per capita income on an aggregate basis grew by a compounded annual rate of 3.2 per cent. But high-income households grew much faster than by about 20 per cent year after year between 1995-96 and 1998-99 (NCAER, National Council for Applied Economic Research). Falling interest rates, easier consumer credit, increase in variety and quality of products and services at every price point, etc. are also contributing in changing the shape of Indian consumers.

Interestingly, the post-liberalization generation is grown up. There are about 100 million, 17-21 years old in India and six out of 10 households have a liberalization child. This is a generation, which has grown up with no guilt about consumption.

Further, Indian economy is shifting its dependence from agriculture to industry and service sector. Marketers have an eye on rural consumers. "Consumer India will always require strategy complexity far greater than its current market worth, because the number of segments it harbours keeps increasing."[1]

II

The family is the most important consumer-buying organization in society. Family members constitute the most influential primary reference group. One can distinguish between two families in the buyer's life. The *family of orientation* consists of one's parents and siblings. From parents a person acquires an orientation towards religion, politics, and economics and a sense of personal ambition, self-worth, and love? Even if the buyer no longer interacts very much with his or her parents, their influence on the buyer's behaviour can be significant. In countries where parents live with their grown children, their influence can be substantial. A more direct influence on everyday buying behaviour is one's *family of procreation*—namely, one's spouse and children.

Family decisions provide an excellent training ground for thoughtful decision-making. Parents and children can pose the issue, generate a menu of choices and then apply careful research to compare, contrast and ultimately choose one. By sharing the discussion and review, family members increase the likelihood that the group will build consensus around the final decision. A family is considered to be the basic decision-making unit as regards purchases. The decision to purchase a commodity or service is generally combined but every family member is going to influence the decision most. Marketers also acknowledge the fact the consumer behaviour pattern is changing as the influence of the family members among themselves increases

Earlier the family was **'patriarchal'** in which husband/ father plays a dominant role or **'matriarchal'** in which wife/ mother plays a dominant role or a **'equalitarian'** in which both plays combine equal role in family purchasing decisions. In other words, the children could not influence any decision, but contrary to that in the 'nucleus marketing'[2] the man, woman and child plays equal roles for decision-making process. In this concept one can see that no one person can take any decision in this type of democratic family structure. The media choice too gave a high weightage to the family oriented programming, avoiding overtly male or female-targeted slots. Thus, despite the individualism of its members, it chooses buys and uses its products together. The consumption behaviour of each of its constituents—the man/husband/father the woman/wife/mother/equal partner and the son/daughter/child/companion—is being redefined in the context of his/her/relationship with the other members of the family. "The various factors influence the consumer/purchasing behaviour in the family, i.e. parents, child, spouse, sibling. The family communication process has been also changed due to the change in the family structures and patterns. The consumer behaviour and the role perception among the family members is also generally change with the change in the family life cycle at its various stages, i.e. childhood, adolescence, adulthood, late adulthood, etc." (George Moschis, 1985).[3]

Marketers are interested in identifying the changing roles and relative influence of the husband, wife, and children in the purchase of a large variety of products and services. These roles vary widely in different countries and social classes. For the marketer who wants to seize the future, it is paradoxaly, not the individual in India's increasing individualized society who matters but it is the New Urban Family (NUF)—that strictly city bound bundle of wife/mother, husband/father and son/daughter. People, in other words, who are defined less by their individual characteristics than they are by their positions, roles and relationships in the context of their families.

The family structure in India has moved from that of a joint family to that of an NUF, the Nuclear Urban Family (NUF). The NUF family in all probably shall have different buying behaviour. ***The main Characteristics of a NUF family are:*** The members are highly individualistic; the members have divergent tastes; they have adequate spending power; they have unique needs that require unique solutions. Despite the above characteristics, marketers are discovering that it's not just the man, woman or kid but the family that makes the purchase decisions. Herein lies the paradox. Though the family members consume separate products, the choice is taken as one. Also more and more products are being purchased for collective consumption. If a family plans for an evening out, each member's choice is taken into account and a collective decision taken. The family set-up is witnessing a distinct shift from a strict, authoritarian structure to a more democratic set-up.

TABLE I

The Changing Family

	Then	*Now*
Father	Strict, Unemotional, Authoritarian	Caring, Concerned, Sensitive
Mother	Emotional, Caring, Nurturing	Informed, Independent, Enterprising
Children	Self-Indulgent, Irresponsible, Rebellious	Responsible, Disciplined, Career-Minded
Spousal Roles	Strictly, Hierarchical, Rigid	Egalitarian, Flexible
Parental Roles	Controlling, Hierarchical, Distant	Democratic, Companionable, Collegiate

Source: *Business Today*, February 22-March 6, 1999, Vol. 8; No. 4.

In the NUF, the role of each family member has been redefined, as the nature of society has been changes to democratic one from the authoritative/hierarchical setup. The new media/communication plays an important role to influence the decision-making process. Now NUF works/acts as a single unit as a whole. there is a big change in the knowledge, awareness, preferences, conviction and adoption of product/services/ideas for each member of the family. Now the focus is mainly on the understanding to each other as the children are now can be put in the role of companions along with the woman as equal partner for the man in the family. The marketers use children as communication conduit to their parents. It can also be conceived as that the NUF marketing could be the passport to the growth of a marketer in the present environmental setup.

III

The NUF generation has seen the woman graduate from a housewife to a home manager. The man remains the breadwinner but is more adaptable. Marketers have to target the family as a unit, ironically in an increasingly individualized society. The family as a unit is a complex and ever-evolving institution. "The nature of the women decision-maker has been described as more informed decision-maker than men, as men mostly make their buying decisions based on price and availability, and while these play an important role in women's purchasing decisions as well, the need to be informed is just as important. The future of the marketing has been told with the women decision-makers as presently women buy (or influence the purchase of) 80% of today's consumer goods."[4] Women are not only becoming more influential in deciding what car to buy, they are also taking over the traditionally male-dominated responsibility of maintenance and repair, according to the National Institute of Automotive Services Excellence (ASE). The research survey data at AutoNetDirect show that women play a major role in any buying or services issues in the family. Women have influential buying power. **Ford Motor** marketing reports that women influence 80% of all purchases and have 95% veto power regarding automotive purchases. **ASE President, *Ron Weiner*** predicts, "It is inevitable; just as we see more women in the showroom and at the service desk, we will see more women behind the service and parts counter talking to customers, and under the hood diagnosing and repairing automobiles."[5] The challenging careers now not more are gender specific. Over the past three decades (1970-98), while men's median income has barely budged (+0.6% after inflation), women's income has soared a dramatic 63%. "In fact, today, 49% of al professional and managerial level workers are women. Even more interesting to the businesses that sell materials to major companies is the fact that 51% of all purchasing managers and agents are women . . . bringing home on average 68% of household income."[6]

Asian mothers are masters of multitasking, managing to look serene while performing their various roles as wife, mother, career professional and household manager, but these women are simmering within. They maintain a close relationship with their children, while their demotion to others is appreciated. According to researchers, Asian mothers are all too willing to sacrifice their own identity in anticipation of rewards that come in the form of family togetherness, their children's academic and career successes, and their husband's achievements in work. But the women feel that they have little opportunity for their personal fulfilment, and think their accomplishments and their contributions to family and society are unappreciated and not acknowledged enough.

The NUF woman isn't tethered to her mother's territory alone; but also venturing into so-called masculine territory: motoring, banking, and education. The zone of her fulfilment has widens, the NUF Woman is moving closer to the role of decision-maker for the purchase even of the products that are not related to their traditional domain. The older view is represented, for instance, in the depiction of the woman as the arbitrator in the disputes over subjects like the brand of toothpaste—HLL commercial for Pepsodent—or the household cleaner—Reckitt and Colman's commercial for Lizol. For the NUF woman, the husband's approval is not a strong driver any more. The focus is on appreciation and understanding. Realizing how that is being translated into consuming behaviour, Modi-Revlon, for instance, is building its brand through a series of profiles of professionally successful women, who radiate confidence about achievements that have nothing to do with well-cooked meals, well-washed clothes, and well-groomed children. "The mother's role in non-traditional spheres is certainly expanding."[7] Change is stalking as the customer-as-mother too. "Her relationship with the child is changing. It is less of mothering, and more of companionship now. The mother is opening up, becoming indulgent and giving in to her children's demands."[8]

IV

In India only 16 per cent Indian professionals are women. It is believed that 'men still continue to dominate in

India'.[9] In the Indian scenario, a shift from joint family system to nuclear family is necessitated due to migration of people to the cities for employment. A silent revolution is taking place especially in the urban middle class families in the context of greater role of women and their equality with men. Women employment has become a necessity at least for the middle class to maintain the standard of living expected of them. Hence, the role of women in purchasing decisions is also being strengthened. Even non-working woman is aware of the career, and views house-management as career. Gone are the days when she was just minion. She wants to be seen as central of household management. In the new urban family the woman is empowered, possessing a strong voice in the purchase decisions

A survey has been conducting, in the areas of Patiala Municipal Corporation (Punjab) and Chandigarh (U.T.), to record the changing role of women in family purchasing decisions. A random sample of 400 households (each man and woman), that is, 800 respondents in total is selected. Out of the total 200 households from Patiala and 200 households from Chandigarh are taken. The comprehensive study is based on mainly middle class salaried households.

The responses on following statements are recorded on six-point scale:

(1) The purchase decision of the family is a collective decision.
(2) Women do not initiate decisions, but are particular about their responsibility.
(3) Mother and children are able to finance some of their purchase rejected by the father.
(4) The women are ambitious for children and consider her daughter as important as her son.
(5) The increased social interaction of women is determining the purchase decisions.
(6) The women awareness still passes through traditional home environment.

The results depict that majority of the respondents have agreed upon the above statement.

(1) The purchase decision of the family is a collective decision

(% Age)

Group	SA	A	INDIFF	DA	SDA	Total
Patiala Male	39.5	54	3	2.5	1	100
Patiala Female	40	52.5	3.5	3	1	100
All Patiala	**39.75**	**53.25**	**3.25**	**2.75**	**1**	**100**
Chandigarh Male	34	47	.5	7.5	2	100
Chandigarh Female	30	56	10.5	3.5	0	100
All Chandigarh	**32**	**51.5**	**10**	**5.5**	**1**	**100**

Both male and female in both the regions are of almost similar views.

(2) Women do not initiate decisions, but are particular about their responsibility

(% Age)

Group	SA	A	INDIFF	DA	SDA	Total
Patiala Male	20	50	10	18.5	1.5	100
Patiala Female	21.5	45.5	12	18	3	100
All Patiala	**20.75**	**47.75**	**11**	**18.25**	**2.25**	**100**
Chandigarh Male	15	46.5	17	16.5	5	100
Chandigarh Female	14	47	20.5	12	6.5	100
All Chandigarh	**14.5**	**46.75**	**18.75**	**14.25**	**5.75**	**100**

As per the Indian women psyche though they do not initiate the decisions but are fully aware of their responsibilities. Respondents both husbands and wife have favourably responded to the statement. There is no gender bias reflected as such.

As compare to the previous statements, the responses for the third statement are somewhat restricted. May be, the

(3) Mother and children are able to finance some of their purchase rejected by the father

(% Age)

Group	*SA*	*A*	*INDIFF*	*DA*	*SDA*	*Total*
Patiala Male	12	39.5	14	26	8.5	100
Patiala Female	7	45.5	16	26	5.5	100
All Patiala	**9.5**	**42.5**	**15**	**26**	**7**	**100**
Chandigarh Male	7.5	45	16	27.5	4	100
Chandigarh Female	12	47	17.5	22	1.5	100
All Chandigarh	**9.75**	**46**	**16.75**	**24.75**	**2.75**	**100**

professional women can have the freedom to spend independently, but in Indian societies men still dominate in purchase decisions.

(4) The women are ambitious for children and consider her daughter as important as her son

(% Age)

Group	*SA*	*A*	*INDIFF*	*DA*	*SDA*	*Total*
Patiala Male	36	46	10.5	7	0.5	100
Patiala Female	43.5	41.5	10.5	4	0.5	100
All Patiala	**39.75**	**43.75**	**10.5**	**5.5**	**0.5**	**100**
Chandigarh Male	23	45	17	13.5	1.5	100
Chandigarh Female	29	44.5	16	8.5	2	100
All Chandigarh	**26**	**44.75**	**16.5**	**11**	**1.75**	**100**

Certainly, for majority of modern women daughters and sons have same status. Families spend equally on daughter's education as of son. They feel that the daughter should be economically independent. Kids are given due importance in taking purchase decisions, because, they are so well aware of the products that they intervene in any such purchase decision of the family.

(5) The increased social interaction of mother is determining the purchase decisions

(% Age)

Group	*SA*	*A*	*INDIFF*	*DA*	*SDA*	*Total*
Patiala Male	14	58	15.5	11.5	1	100
Patiala Female	10.5	63	12	13	1.5	100
All Patiala	**12.25**	**60.5**	**13.75**	**12.25**	**1.25**	**100**
Chandigarh Male	9.5	60	11	15	4.5	100
Chandigarh Female	19.5	57.5	9	13	1	100
All Chandigarh	**14.5**	**58.75**	**10**	**14**	**2.75**	**100**

Almost 60 per cent respondents agree upon this statement. Being a developing society 'Demonstration Effect' exits in India. Thanks to consumerism, easy availability of credit and glut of products. Indian woman is in a position to purchase the things, her social circle is having.

(6) The women awareness still passes through traditional home environment

(% Age)

Group	*SA*	*A*	*INDIFF*	*DA*	*SDA*	*Total*
Patiala Male	6.5	42	16	30	5.5	100
Patiala Female	8	40	14.5	30.5	7	100
All Patiala	**7.25**	**41**	**15.25**	**30.25**	**6.25**	**100**
Chandigarh Male	6.5	37	22	32.5	2	100
Chandigarh Female	7.5	41.5	21	27.5	2.5	100
All Chandigarh	**7**	**39.25**	**21.5**	**30**	**2.25**	**100**

No doubt, that Indian woman is in transitional phase. Not that simple to detach completely from the old ties, values and traditions. After all, it is a question of changing attitude, psyche. The above results reflect the same.

V

In a Nutshell, in the new family, the women are empowered. Personal gratification, without conflicting with the traditional demands made of her, is moving up the wish-list of women. And the guilt factor involved in self-indulgence dissipates, no longer is the women's consumption executed in secrecy. The women has now a stronger voice in the purchase-decision both of products used by the entire family as well of products used only by specific members of the family. Marketing managers must analyze the household decision process separately for each product category within each target market. Household member participation in the decision process varies by involvement with the specific product, role specialization, personal characteristics, and one's culture and sub-culture. Participation also varies by stage in the decision process. Most decisions are reached by consensus. If not, a variety of conflict resolution strategies may be employed.

Notes and References

1. Dobhal Shailesh (Feb. 22-Mar. 6, 1999), *'NUFgen Marketing'*, *Business Today*, Vol. 8, No. 4, pp. 66-81, http://www.themanagermentor.com
2. *Ibid.*
3. Moschis George, P. (March 1985), *'The Role of the Family Communication in Consumer Socialization of Children and Adolescents'*, *Journal of Consumer Research*, pp. 898-913.
4. *'What Do Women Want?'* (24 July, 2001) *By HitBox.com*, http://www.marketingprofs.com
5. *'Women call the shots on Buying and Maintaining the Family Car!'* AutoNet Direct, http://www.autodirect.com
6. Barletta Martha, (Feb. 2003), *'Build Sales and Boost Share By Tapping into Women's Buying Power'*, *Sales and Marketing Excellence*, www.martha.barletta@trendsight.com
7. *'Asian women simmering within: Study'*, *Inter Press Service* (30 Sept., 1998), http://www.expressindia.com
8. *Ibid.*
9. Riti, M.D. (May 2, 2003), *'Consumer Behaviour: Men still major decision-makers'* http://www.rediff.com.

CHAPTER

10

Managing Customer Expectation in the Next Economy

PAWAN KUMAR TANEJA AND P.P. SINGH

The transition from New Economy to Next Economy has just begun. Are business houses ready to face the challenges of the Next Economy? Rather are businessmen know what are the problems that they are going to face in the Next Economy? Why these problems are coming out? What is the impact of these problems on the Marketing Mix? How to manage these challenges in the Next Economy? In this paper we have tried to come out with answers of all these above questions.

INTRODUCTION

The curve from "Wow!" to "I've got that" to "Isn't here something better?" keeps getting shorter and faster. Nothing works any more? People no longer have the kind of relationship with favourite brands and the companies that provide them that they had 10 years ago or even 5 years ago. One reason is that in the fervour of the New Economy, all kinds of products and services that aren't ready for prime time are rushed to market. The commonly used the rationales are: "Speed to market matters most", and "Get it out today, and fix the bugs tomorrow." As a result, the implied contract between supplier and consumer has been broken. The umbilical cord between brands and people has been cut. Trust has been diminished. The truth is that the New Economy was never the *Ramban* it was supposed to be. It was really just a bridge between two much more significant and substantial eras, the *"Old Economy"* and the *"Next Economy."* The lifespan of both the Old Economy and the Next Economy will be measured in decades; by contrast, the New Economy lasted only months. The past decade we've already passed through one business cycle—the transition from the "Old Economy" to the "New Economy." The New Economy is already shockingly defunct. Long live the Next Economy!

SHIFTS

- The Old Economy was based on products and services; Success was measured by share of market. The focus of the typical enterprise was on scale and efficiency.
- The New Economy was based on information. Success was measured by time to market and site visitation. The focus of the typical enterprise was on evolving technology.
- The Next Economy will be knowledge-based. Success will be measured by profits and share of wallet. And the focus will be on effectiveness in reaching, serving, and retaining customers.

REALITY BITES: CHALLENGES FROM NEW ECONOMY TO NEXT ECONOMY

Changing Houses

Customers no longer seem to respond to brand names the way they once did; they seem shockingly ready to shift their business to rivals from around the corner or around the globe, even to no-name, private-label brands or to upstart firms that may not have existed 5 years ago. It's not imagination—and it's not business alone. In industry after industry, customer loyalty is withering—as are the prospectus for easy, "natural" sales growth. Unable to retain their old customers and grow with them, businesses of every kind are resorting to more and more desperate measures in search of sales increases.

Not One Shop But Shoppers List

Customers short-list-shop banners just as they do brands. As a result, most retailers supply less than half their customers' demand in their category. And this means that they share each customer with at least two other retailers and that the customer views this retail relationship as anything but monogamous. Today, everybody sells everything. It's no wonder that retailer infidelity, once a minor problem, is now the rule rather than the exception. Suddenly the marketing challenge is an entirely new one and a much more difficult one to master.

Internal Mis-marketing

Losing customers is only one part of the vicious "loyalty drain" cycle thy corporation, which loses half its customers every 5 years, also loses half its employees every 4 years and half of its investors every single year. These phenomena are closely interrelated. As customers drift away and business scramble to replace them, it engage in increasingly desperate strategic and tactical ploys—"reinventing" brands and companies, shifting from one target market to another and another, and concoction ill-conceived spin-off products and services that drop almost as quickly as introduce them. In this kind of unstable business climate, it's natural that employees and investors churn their assets, too, in an unending yet ultimately futile search for a safe heaven—a place where they can invest their time, energy, and money for long-term productivity and satisfaction. However, very few businesses today offer such secure long-term prospects. One result is that talented people in today rarely make marketing a lifelong career. They are in a pyramid structure where for every five people, there is one job above. They are often being judged on the basis of sales growth or market share. Their individual goal is to use their stewardships of the brand as a springboard forward in their career. Chaos within marketing infrastructures is there.

Paid, But Impotent

Business not only have jammed more and more ads into the traditional advertising venues—newspapers and magazines, radio and television—but also finding ways to cram ads into spaces that were once ad-free, from grocery shopping carts and school book covers to the lift posts in ski resorts, the urinals in men's rooms and, of course, everybody's Web page. Simultaneously, subtle and not-so-subtle "hidden ads" in the form of product placements have infiltrated movies, TV shows, the print media, theme parks, sports events, concerts—you name it. Even such formerly staid, nonprofit arenas as museums, universities, and public broadcasting are overrun with brand-name promotions (euphemistically called sponsorships, of course). The ads are amusing. But they aren't selling. The problem is that with a very few exceptions, the underlying marketing strategy no longer works. A once-powerful tool has become impotent.

Survival by Sacrifice

Many companies have turned to price promotion as a survival tactic. When used intelligently, price promotions can lure potential customers toward brand, where its innate value can then hook them for life. The problem is that in today's ultra competitive business arena, price promotions are now everywhere, often acting not as a supplement to other marketing strategies but as a substitute for them. Offer products at a reduced price, several messages are sent: our product or services isn't worth paying full price for, when customers pay full price, they're supporting excessive profit margins, all products and services are ultimately the same—the only difference is the price.

Early Death of Life Cycle

"Either sell it or smell it." More and more products are becoming perishable, their value short-lived. As a result, not only are businesspeople forced to run faster and faster to keep up with ever-changing consumer demands; they are also finding that their products are rapidly becoming valueless, putting tremendous downward pressure on prices and profits. One reason is the self-feeding acceleration of technological change. Today, the predictability of decades past is gone. The question facing customers is not whether to buy, but, when to buy. The power belongs to the customers—those fickle, demanding, skeptical, distracted millions who've learned to react according to the split—second attention span of the channel—surfer. If they're bored—even for an instant-your business is history.

Squeezing Coins

New and better products are continually emerging that are cheaper than the goods already in the system. Consumers know this, and they're willing to pay full price for products only for a fleeting moment at the very start of the product cycle. Marketing have educated customers to refuse to pay full price by proliferating outlets where prices are slashed to the bare bones, such as big-box retailers, price clubs, outlet stores, discount catalogues, and Internet auction sites. Profit margins in retailing, distribution, and other marketing-oriented business were never robust, today they are anemic. Businesses have become lean and mean. Yet profits continue to shrivel. Something has to give.

WHY ARE THESE SHAKE-UPS?

Clicking Age The impact of the baby boomers was first felt back in the 1960s, when millions of baby boomers were in their late teens and early twenties. They initiated a value change in society that shocked the system. Fueled by their numbers, they rebelled against mindless acceptance of authority and instilled a concept that the system could be changed if enough people believed in the change. This was a major paradigm shift. The rebellious 1960s, changed all this. If Dad drove a Chevey, son drove anything but a Chevy. The baby-boomer generation took the evolutionary concept of household branding and destroyed in a 10 years period. Long-standing household brands disappeared from shelve.

New ones based on very different values took their place. 1960s "morphed" changed into the "me generation" of 1970s. The "me generation" saw goods and services as an extension and representation of their values structure. In the 1970s, the individualism born in the 1960s, become an economic phenomenon as baby boomers dressed according to their own code, using their fashions and wanting their brands not because they were expensive but because they were different. As the 1970s spilled over into the 1980s, specialty stores proliferated, which drove the need for ever-more, ever-bigger shopping centers. Stores catering to different niches evolved and multiply. In the 1980s, the baby boomers metamorphosed again, entering careers. Many members of this well-educated generation become business professionals, technical experts, or managers. In the 1990s, the baby boomers began to turn 40, and another series of psychological adjustments kicked in.

FIG. I

Consumer Life Cycle

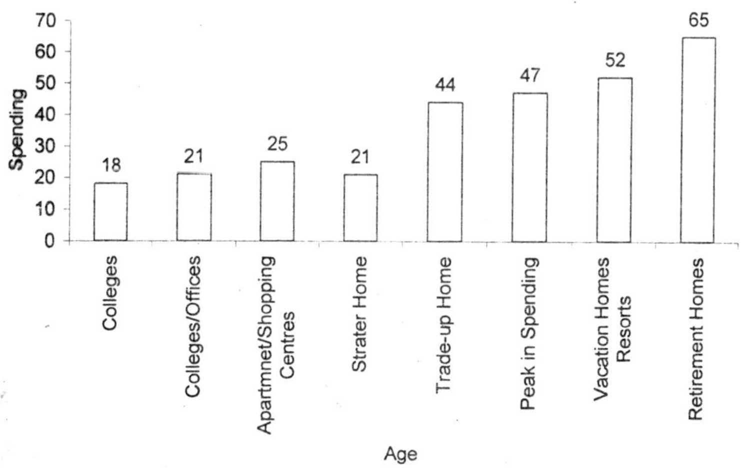

Accelerating Knowledge Today's customers are better educated and understand how to buy better than ever before. Thus they are in a position to demand and wield greater power than previous generations of customers. Traditionally, marketing was defined as managing the flow of goods and services from the supplier to the customer. Today, marketing is a response to the customer. More than ever, business will have to cater to the customer in terms of the physiology of the purchase (i.e., the physical factors of the shopping experience) as well as the psychology of the buying experience. If they don't, customer is gone. And so are businesses.

Ultimate Truth Here's truth most businesses would rather not accept. Most males and females don't really like to shop any longer. As a result, most customers complain about how badly business have mangled their jobs and unnecessarily complicated their lives. They complain about how goods are scattered throughout the mall rather than clustered by category (the way food is clustered in a mall). They complain about the proliferation of look-alike style in every store. They complain about poorly trained and ill-equipped sales staffs.

Traditionally King Present Emperor another reason for this Dyanism is increased competition among sellers. When competition among sellers is intense, what results is a buyers' market. Today's emerging reality is the greatest buyers' market in history. Businesses are terribly over stored.

Technology Excess is Bane The New Economy didn't last long, but its input on consumption and buying behaviour will stand for centuries. The information era made one outstanding change to relationships among merchants, manufacturers, and their customers. It reversed the historical interaction between parties by putting the seller at the back and call of the buyer. The Web changed all this forever.

Report Card of Marketing-Mix

$$\text{Brand Value} = \frac{\text{Product+Place+Promotion}}{\text{Price}}$$

For generations, marketers have been taught the Four P's as the basis of their discipline. Under this doctrine, the definition of brand value grew naturally out of the old definition of marketing. This definition stated that marketing is the management of the flow of goods and services from the manufacturer to the consumer. Under this definition, marketing was focused on two things: what's for sale and how to sell buy. At one time, the Four P's worked reasonably well to define what marketers needed to focus on. This is no longer true.

Product

Copycatting

The Death of the USP is there. Manufacturers used to offer differentiated products, define a unique selling proposition (USP) for the customer base. The focus: What's for sale? The job of the marketer was to say, "Here's what we sell and how it's different." This is not true any more. Reasons may be technology, duplicate, outsourced.

The Temptation of Private Labels

Retail private labeling has been another cause of the death of product. The branded-label companies compounded the problem. They refused to recognize that the private-label brands looked and felt the same as their own products. As a result, they failed to fight back by taking a stand against those who imitated their packaging. When the store brands became common, manufacturers were unable to differentiate their own brands from the store brands.

Place

Death of Distance

Distribution, or "place," meant expertise. Today, keeping up with broadening inventory categories is a challenge. So too are technology changes. Each year new appliances and home electronics products flood the marketplace. If any one needs help today, he will look for it on the Internet—not at the retail level. You'll spend half a day waiting for the tech support department to respond to your question and another half a day figuring out its answer.

Buying Relevancy

Convenience is no longer a differentiating attribute of

place. One can now buy anything anywhere, so place is not going to help in building either brand value or brand equity.

Promotion

Wasted Paid Chaos

Advertising has never been more than a promise. What it has always done is give visible form to the invisible contract that the brand offers its potential customers. The problem is that, as the uniqueness of the offering disappeared, the ability to differentiate one brand from another also disappeared. Since the advertising industry is a well-connected and critical part of the customer relationship, to continue this role, marketers decided that if they had nothing different to say to their customers, they would at least say it differently. Today, advertising is better differentiated than brands. If advertising is a promise, its purpose should be to set an expectation that is deliverable by the brand—to give the consumer contract meaning, to set the criteria for judgment. New Economy was run by 20- and 30-year-old chief executive officers (CEOs) who loved creativity. Finally, creative got through, unscathed by the client Philistines. The result is *"Total Confusion."* No contact was established. In many cases, the advertising conveyed no idea as to what the hell it was selling.

Jumping Jockey Jacks

Instead of coming into the job with the mission of leaving the brand stronger, young marketers come in with the intention of using the brand as a springboard to move up the organization faster than their peers.

Sales Promotion is in the Trap of Law of Diminishing Returns

Sales Promotion does work in the short-term. It artificially inflates the "sugar count." What's worse, it's addictive as "heroin." The Consumer become addicted to discounted prices. It's terribly unhealthy syndrome for all involved. Thus the sales increases produced by promotions are bubble—like both in the speed at which they grow and in their fragility.

Price

Price versus Value

$$\text{Brand Value}=\frac{\text{Equity}}{\text{Price}}=\frac{\text{Place, Product, Promotion}}{\text{Price}}$$

Price is what something costs; value is what it's worth. By focusing on price instead of value, the marketing community failed to build customer loyalty, encouraged short-list alternative-brand shopping, and made substitute shopping a reality.

Perfect Market: But Virtual Think about the shopping to be done, whether it's for laundry detergent, CDs, or prewashed jeans, choose is among from 20 or 30 brands or among 3 or 4? Almost certainly it is the latter. And while this week brand A may have a price advantage, next week it will be brand B, and the week after that brand C. By the end of the year, every major competitor has had its turn—and the market shares are remarkably stable. Because most consumption points are oligopolistic, there are, in practical terms, only two or three price points. All products in a category are promoted at about the same price level (at different times of the year) because nobody can afford to let anyone else get markedly ahead. Since price doesn't really drive branded share, we can see that price—the fought P—has likewise become impotent. Short—term volume increases from temporary reduced prices (TRPs) are offset by competitive TRPs in the next period. Thus, over a full year, price doesn't affect market share-only profitability.

SUGGESTIONS TO MANAGE CUSTOMER EXPECTATION IN THE NEXT ECONOMY

Some of the important strategies which may be implemented to cope up the challenges of Next Economy are discussed as follows:

Upliftment in Definition of Basics from Need to Want

The next economy is all about turning the information into knowledge. Marketers can't just understand what customers are buying; must also understand why they are buying it? And can't use the traditional tool for analyzing customers, i.e. demographics. Demographics is an accounting model, not a marketing model. Instead, another approach is needed, one that more accurately and meaningfully captures how and why customers make the buying decisions they do. Want segmentation has been around since 1960's it is called psychographics. Today the vast majority of people and vast majority of purchases are want-oriented. There are many reasons for this increased influence like credit is available, modern communication technologies, consumption all are aspirational. Thus the old theories about market segmentation by income or geography no longer make much sense. A huge number of people willing to pay premium prices for product they perceived as "real thing." There is no margin in needs. A more profitable option is to segment out your best customers and give them the satisfaction of owing something special. Raise your product or service from fulfiling needs to fulfiling wants. The economics of converting basic services to a stepped up want program are far more attractive because the margins are so much better. There are many want segmentation systems available today, including those from Goldfarb, SRI (VALS), and Thompson Lightstone. It's a way of dividing the market by customer values—what's important to them and their attitudes towards life. These are the critical factors in understanding why people buy. People will pay for why, which satisfies a want. Increasingly the pendulum will swing from global to local marketing priorities.

Rejuvenating Demographics

Finding best customers and focusing business and marketing strategies on serving them will be a prerequisite for success, i.e. "Quintile Marketing." The basic definition of strategy is focus and power. Old quip by legendary retailer John Wanamaker, "I know that half of my advertisement budget is wasted. The only trouble is, I don't know which half." Quintile management is answer. It is simply a segmentation strategy for identifying and focusing on best customers while preventing worst customers from draining away resources. Here's how it works. Start by taking all customers and ranking them in order according to the number of dollars they spend with a particular in course of a year. Depending on the kind of the product or service sold, frequency of purchase may be factor in as well to avoid misranking the person who spends a lot of time, money with particular business without creating a long-term relationship. Once customer data is gathered and ranked customers from those who generate the greatest sales volume down to those who generate the least divide them into five equal groups—quintiles. Each quintile by definition contains an equal number of customers. Q1—contains highest volume customers; through from Q2, Q3, Q4 to Q5—contains customers who buy the least from particular business. They generally break even on sales to Q3 customers and actually loose money when selling to Q4 and Q5 customers (when full market cost is charged). Find this startling? Most business people do.

FIG. 2

Contribution to Profit by Quintile

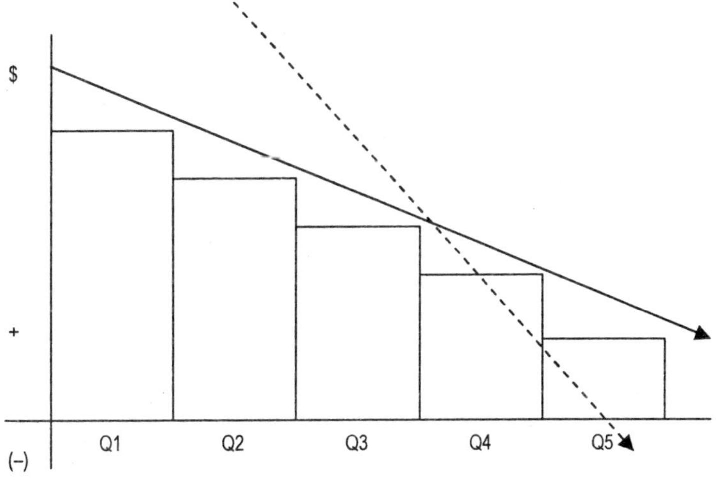

These are wasted expenditures—marketing cost that yield no profit and are a pure loss to business. Quintile marketing doesn't (necessarily) involve increasing marketing budget—it involves redistributing the same money so as to give the "Best Bang for buck." The person who spends every penny of disposable money on his/her car may be a Q1 customer for cars even though his/her income may be relatively low. Demographics can't tell you this—only psychographics and quintile management can. The strategy should be:

- Discourage Q5 customers.
- Ignore Q4 customers.
- Do battle for Q3 customers.
- Wage all-out war to capture and retain Q1 and Q2 customers.

New Ingredients for Marketing-Mix

The marketing equation is :

$$\text{Brand Value} = \frac{\text{Equity}}{\text{Price}}$$

The new equation will be:

$$\text{Brand Value} = \frac{\text{Reengineering, Refocusing, Retrenchment, Relevancy, Rewards, Restructuring}}{\text{Price}}$$

1. Relationship

Marketing must be focused not on individual transactions but on building strong, growing connections between businesses and its best customers. The most meaningful measurement is share of customer spending (SOCS). Whatever is sold—clothing, computers, CDs, food, or financial services—goal should be to become customer's supplier of choice for those products or services. It's a matter of focusing on the target customers rather than on one sale at a time. Two Core Competencies that can be effectively employed in doing this: Service and Experience.

Service

The entire encounter with company and brand. Every customer contact point is a serviceable opportunity—a medium for delighting customer. "Please", "Thank you", "If you want", "If your company plans", "May I call you when they arrive?" should be first phrases of communication with customer. Sales people should function as sales consultants.

Experience

Retailers must relearn the art of delighting the customer by providing a unique, memorable, and enjoyable buying experience.

2. Retrenchment

It involves going to the customers rather than trying to entice him or her to come to business. There are two core competencies that can be used to support a Retrenchment strategy—Technology and Convenience.

Technology

One Retrenchment techniques is to use Technology to bring the store, the brand, or the service in to the customer's home or office.

Convenience

To differentiate brand by offering Convenience. About selling customer in his/her environment rather than coaxing him/her out into business environment.

3. Relevancy

The objective of a relevancy strategy is to tie brand's equity directly to the dominant purchase motivators for the category. It can be done best through Expertise or Merchandising.

Expertise

Means making the company the number one source of ideas and information about the category within which company is competing.

Merchandise

Another way of achieving Relevancy is through a unique mix of Merchandise. By offering products or services that are carefully and intelligently selected to cater specifically to the wants of particular customers, merchandise choices can make company, in effect, the number one procurement manager for its customers—the supplier they trust to make a smart first cut at what they'll be buying.

4. Rewards

Defines strategies built around rewarding consumers for doing business with company. There are, again, two core competencies that a business can employ in carrying out a reward strategy; Stature and Time.

Stature

Certain brands and stores are so respected that simply being a customer of their's carries an intrinsic psychological reward.

Time

The simplest and most obvious form of time strategy is, in fact, saving time for customers. The reason is Time will become a strategic building block in the Next Economy. As for many people it is a scarce resource than money. Time is finite. No one can borrow it or lend it. As a result its value to customers is continually increasing. The Time strategy has many variations:

- Get me in and out quickly.
- Bring the product or service to me.
- Move the store to my block.
- Put it all under one roof.

Similarly, Reengineering, Refocus and Restructuring can be employed

Sponsorship Marketing

In sponsorship marketing, businesses are strategically associating their brand with something important to the customer—an activity, a belief, a cause, a passion. The objective is to link brand to more relevant issues in customers lives in order to increase the involvement level.

Horizontal Marketing

Horizontal marketing will be the big new trend. Here, the idea is to share one Company Q1 and Q2 customers with other companies—companies with whom you have nothing important in common except customers.

Not Master but Jack for all Customers

Co-marketing allows business to focus on its customers by building customized solutions around their needs. Rather than worrying about the people business is having in staff and how businesses are going to keep them busy, business enlist the talents it needs to solve client problems, whether these talents are internal or external. This allows them to keep their cost reasonable, to employ top notch talent for a fraction of a cost, and to present a uniquely customized solution to each client. It's a sure fire recipe for turning customers into best customers.

Intellectual Property/Co-marketing

There is usually one quarterback in a co-marketing deal, and usually this is the company with the initial customer relationship. The quarterback company is the one that figures out what's needed to solve the customers problem and how to do it. The value of these insights is enormous and has to be protected. A lot of work will need to be done over the next several years to develop legal frameworks for the new intellectual capital game. Much old contract law is losing its relevance, and new rules must be established.

People have Read Trust

A concierge is someone who represents the buyer and make sure that his wants are meet in the best possible way. The Next Economy will move millions of customers into more and more relationships like this. This phenomenon is *"Concierge Marketing."* Concierge marketing is the converse of the old ways of buying and selling. The concierge will represent the buyer rather than the seller—a new approach to business. Intermediaries who currently represent sellers as a go—betweens will have to switch sides. If they don't evolve into concierges they'll be ruthlessly eliminated. This includes most retailers.

CONCLUSION

The duration of the Next Economy won't be measured in months, as was true of the New Economy. Therefore, every business should prepare its organization for this transition in to new world. As in New Economy business priorities will shifts to knowledge rather information as in New Economy because coming economy is a knowledge economy. In the Next Economy the success indicator and investment rational of a business will only profit and effectiveness as a well-versed business can only meet social responsibility towards stakeholders. So keys for success in the Next Economy are, customer-centric managerial mindset than web-centric, concentration on marketing function rather than information technology, team-oriented organizational structure and use best combination of debt and equity in its financial structure.

REFERENCES

Alison Stein Wellner (2001), "Beauty in Distress," *American Demographics*, January 2001.

Alonzo Vincent (1998), "What've You Done for us Lately?" *Business Week*, September 14, 1998, pp. 142-48..

Ettenberg, Elliott (2002), *The Next Economy: Will You Know Where Your Customers Are*, Tata McGraw Hills Publishing Company Ltd., New Delhi.

Jonathan Berry (1994), "A Potent New Tool for Selling: Database Marketing," *Business Week*, September 5, 1994, pp. 55-62.

Matthew Schwartz (2001), "The Care and Keeping of Online Customers," *Computer World*, January 2001.

Quelch, J.A. and L.R. Klein (1996), "The Internet and International Marketing," *Sloan Management Review*, 1996, pp. 60-75.

Richard K. Green (1998), "Demographics Don't Support New-Store Boom," *Chain Store Age*, May 1, 1998.

Stanley F. Slater and John C. Narver (1994), "Market Orientation, Customer Value, and Superior Performance," *Business Horizons*, March-April 1994, pp. 22-28.

Stephanie Armour (1998), " Companies Grapple with Gripes Posted on Web," *USA Today*, September 16, 1998, p. 5B.

CHAPTER

11

Changing Dimensions of Marketing in India

An Analysis of Viral Marketing

PUSHPINDER GILL AND SARUPINDER SINGH

Viral marketing describes any strategy that encourages individuals to pass on a marketing message to others, creating the potential for exponential growth in the message's exposure and influence. Like viruses, such strategies take advantage of rapid multiplication to explode the message to thousands, to millions. This Paper is an attempt to explore various dimensions of Viral Marketing.

INTRODUCTION

In 21st century technology brought renaissance in the life style of people. The world was transformed to a Global village. Communication subsided the physical barriers. Unique concepts in technology continued to surface and affect the lives of people in on way or the other.

Internet changed the scenario in ail aspects. Business too galloped in synchronization with technology. In the Internet era, a company's competitiveness seems to depend on its velocity of thought and action. Companies can grow more rapidly than ever before, but so too may they suddenly die from obsolescence Internet shopping or e-commerce commenced and gradually became famous. This incited new concepts in Marketing. Promoters, Advertisers and Marketers commenced to take Internet Marketing seriously and found out new strategies too woo e-customers.

Word of mouth marketing strategy and word of mouse marketing strategy became the new tools for marketing a product. New businesses also want to let the world know their name, but they do not want to be annoying, and thus, they must provide a compelling reason for customers to help spread the word.

On the Internet, word of mouse marketing is called "viral marketing." Viral marketing is any marketing technique that induces Web sites or users to pass on a marketing message to other sites or users, creating a potentially exponential growth in the message's visibility and effect.

WHAT IS A VIRUS?

Virus has a way of living in secrecy until he is so numerous that he wins by sheer weight of numbers. He piggybacks on other hosts and uses their resources to increase his tribe. And in the right environment, he grows exponentially. A virus don't even have to mate—he just replicates, again and again with geometrically increasing power, doubling with each iteration:

Viral Marketing—Definition

What does a virus have to do with marketing?

Viral marketing describes any strategy that encourages individuals to pass on a marketing message to others, creating the potential for exponential growth in the message's exposure and influence. Like viruses, such strategies take advantage of rapid multiplication to explode the message to thousands, to millions.

In simple words, viral marketing means creating messages that contain concepts within them that are absorbed by the people that come into contact with the messages. And making these messages compelling enough so that people pass them on and in this manner the marketing message flows on and on.

Off the Internet, viral marketing has been referred to as:

1. Word-of-mouth,
2. Creating a buzz,
3. Leveraging the media, and
4. Network marketing.

But on the Internet its called "Viral marketing."

A good example of viral marketing is many of the free e-mail services available on the internet. The messages that one sends from these free services invariably contain promotion for the company providing the service.

This form of Internet marketing is extremely effective. If someone utilizes the mail service on average only twice a day, in the period of a year the service is advertised approximately 730 times. Multiply this number by the number of registered users (if the users are approximately 30,000,000, and the service provider has 21,900,000,000 advertisements per year. OK, so those are pretty huge figures that most of us can only dream of achieving, so how does the little guy utilize the viral marketing concept on a budget of say . . . $ 0.

THE CLASSIC HOTMAIL.COM EXAMPLE

The classic example of viral marketing is Hotmail.com, one of the first free Web-based e-mail services. The strategy was simple:

1. Gave away free e-mail addresses and services,
2. Attached a simple tag at the bottom of every free message sent out: "Get your private, free e-mail at http://www.hotmail.com",
3. Then stood back while people e-mailed to their own network of friends and associates,
4. Who saw the message,

5. Signed up for their own free e-mail service, and then
6. Propelled the message still wider to their own ever-increasing circles of friends and associates.

Hotmail's Amazing Growth

- Hotmail grew a subscriber base more rapidly than any company in the history of the world ...faster than any new online, Internet, or print publication ever.
- Hotmail is the largest e-mail provider in the world.
- In its first 1.5 years, Hotmail signed up over 12 million subscribers.
- A traditional print publication would hope to reach a total of 100,000 subscribers within a few years of launch. Hotmail signs up more than 150,000 subscribers every day, seven days a week.
- Every Hotmail subscriber, without exception, has filled out a detailed demographic and psychographic profile including occupation and salary. This is an unprecedented supply of personal information.
- Yet, from company launch to 12 million users, Hotmail spent less than $500K on marketing, advertising and promotion. This compares to over $20 million spent on advertising and brand promotion by Juno, Hotmail's closest competitor with a fraction of the users.
- Hotmail became the largest e-mail provider in several countries, like Sweden and India, where it had done no marketing whatsoever.
- Hotmail is in 220 countries beside the fact that it is only available in one language English.

From the example of Hotmail.com it can be inferred that:

1. Viral marketing is perceived as calorie-free, no

pain—all gain path to customer acquisition.

2. Viral marketing is the wave of online advertising future.
3. Viral marketing is what will get the company all the customers to survive as a business without much cost.

REASONS FOR THE POPULARITY OF VIRAL MARKETING

1. Technology has made world a Global village. The urge to communicate produces millions of Websites and billions of e-mail messages. Internet has made communication faster.
2. A good idea can spread more quickly over the Internet than had ever been possible before in the physical world, where manufacturing and distribution fundamentally limit the rate of product adoption. Especially in the Internet era, a company's competitiveness seems to depend on its velocity of thought and action. Companies can grow more rapidly than ever before.
3. Entire social networks have migrated to the web. A large proportion of everyone's friends and family members are now online or soon will be.
4. Contacting individuals on the web is virtually cost-free or very inexpensive. It is possible for one individual to contact hundreds in one day who can contact hundreds more, etc. Pyramids of network can be built in a day, not years.
5. The network effect plays an important role: as more and more people sign up, they can contact many more people and in this manner the message can propel from tens to hundreds and to thousands and so on.

SIX FUNDAMENTAL ELEMENTS OF A VIRAL MARKETING STRATEGY

A viral marketing strategy comprises of six basic elements :

1. Gives away products or services.
2. Provides for effortless transfer to others.
3. Scales easily from small to very large.
4. Exploits common motivations and behaviors.
5. Utilizes existing communication networks.
6. Takes advantage of others' resources.

1. Gives away valuable products or services

"Free" is the most powerful word in a marketer's vocabulary. Most viral marketing programs give away valuable products or services to attract attention. Free e-mail services, free information, free "cool" buttons, free software programs attract most of the attention. Cheap or inexpensive may generate a wave of interest, but "free" attracts eyeballs. Eyeballs then see other desirable things that the company is selling, and, in this way company earns money. Eyeballs bring valuable e-mail addresses, advertising revenue, and e-commerce sales opportunities. Give away something, sell something.

2. Provides for effortless transfer to others

Viruses only spread when they're easy to transmit. The medium that carries the marketing message must be easy to transfer and replicate: e-mail, website, graphic, software download. Viral marketing works famously on the Internet because instant communication has become so easy and inexpensive. Digital format make copying simple. From a marketing standpoint, one must simplify the marketing message so it can be transmitted easily and without degradation. Short is better. The classic is: "Get your private, free e-mail at http://www.hotmail.com." The message is compelling, compressed, and copied at the bottom of every free e-mail message.

3. Scales easily from small to very large

To spread like wildfire the transmission method must be rapidly scalable from small to very large. The weakness of the Hotmail model is that a free e-mail service requires its own mail servers to transmit the message. If the strategy is wildly successful, mail servers must be added very quickly or the rapid growth will bog down and die. The viral model must have scalability in it.

4. Exploits common motivations and behaviours

Clever viral marketing plans take advantage of common human motivations. Greed drives people. So does the hunger to be popular, loved, and understood. The resulting urge to communicate produces millions of websites and billions of e-mail messages. Design a marketing strategy that builds on common motivations and behaviours for its transmission.

5. Utilizes existing communication networks

Most people are social. Social scientists tell that each person has a network of 8 to 12 people in their close network of friends, family, and associates. A person's broader network may consist of scores, hundreds, or thousands of people, depending upon her position in society. People on the Internet develop networks of relationships, too. They collect e-mail addresses and favourite website URLs. Learn to place the message into existing communications between people.

6. Takes advantage of others' resources

The most creative viral marketing plans use others' resources to get the word out. Affiliate programs, for example, place text or graphic links on others' websites. Authors who give away free articles, seek to position their articles on others' web pages. A news release can be picked up by hundreds of periodicals and form the basis of articles seen by hundreds of thousands of readers. Now someone else's newsprint or web page is relaying someone others marketing message.

TYPES OF VIRAL MARKETING

There are five types of Viral Marketing:

1. Value Viral
2. Guile Viral

3. Vital Viral
4. Spiral Viral
5. Vile Viral

1. Value Viral

What it is: People share quality experiences with others.

How it works: Joe tries product X and finds it to be very good. He then tells Jane to try it.

Product examples: Hotmail, Harry Potter books.

Web site examples: Amazon, Yahoo!

How to "make it viral": The products alone must be good enough to foster user chatter. "Tell a Friend" technologies do not make a product viral; they merely allow users to tell others about good products.

2. Guile Viral

What it is: People try to "sell" to others in exchange for incentives.

How it works: Joe tries to convince Jane to try product X because Joe may receive a reward if Jane tries it.

Product examples: Amway, Tupperware.

Web site examples: Quixtar, MyPoints.

How to "make it viral": Users must feel that the reward is worth it and that the products are good enough to risk the possible displeasure of others. Simply adding a reward when the products are not of sufficient quality might result in user backlash against being "sold."

3. Vital Viral

What it is: People want to share experiences with others, which requires certain products.

How it works: Joe wants to share experience Y with Jane, and Jane needs product X to do so.

Product examples: ICQ, RealPlayer, Macromedia Flash, Adobe Acrobat.

Web site examples: AOL, MSN Messenger.

How to "make it viral": Users must feel that the experience and the product are worth it to make a change for themselves, let alone to convince others to do likewise. Simply creating a user-to-user standard without making it worthwhile and enjoyable might only serve to inhibit adoption.

4. Spiral Viral

What it is: People want to share funny, and/or interesting experiences with others.

How it works: Joe wants to share experience Y with Jane because Joe thinks that Jane will also find it funny, and/ or interesting.

Product examples: numerous jokes, Hampster Dance, Frog Blender

Web site examples: Mahir Cagri's Home Page, JenniCam , Sanatabanta.com

How to "make it viral": Success stories in this category were rarely intended to be "viral," rather, they were intended to be funny, and/or interesting.

5. Vile Viral

What it is: People warn others of negative experiences.

How it works: Joe tries product X and finds it very bad. He then tells Jane to avoid it.

Product examples: Many failed dot-coms, Apple Newton.

Web site examples: Real.com (for the RealJukebox fiasco).

How to "make it viral": Simply create products that are of poor quality, are not designed with the user in mind, or are perceived by the user to be marketed in an underhanded manner.

WHAT MAKES A MARKETING CAMPAIGN VIRAL?

The newest buzzword to hit e-mail marketing these days has to be "viral." Every company wants his marketing slogan to be viral, have a viral aspect, and capitalize on viral marketing.

Viral marketing is not an objective

IT IS AN INTEGRAL PART OF A CAMPAIGN

STRATEGY THAT IS USED TO ACHIEVE OBJECTIVES. If the main objective of an e-mail campaign is branding, in order to achieve greater branding success, the message must be crafted in such a manner that it encourages pass-along.

Producing a message with a quality offer or an incentive for pass-along is what viral marketing is all about.

Its Viral:

1. Offer something worthy of sharing.
2. A valuable discount.
3. Vital information.
4. Offer an incentive for sharing.
5. Additional entries into a sweepstakes or an added discount or premium service and viral marketing happens naturally . . . and often quite successfully.

Its not Viral

Merely *suggesting* e-mail recipients forward your message to others is not viral marketing. Adding a line at the bottom of your e-mail that reads "Feel free to forward this message to a friend" is not viral marketing at its best.

For example:

If there are two e-commerce offers in your mailbox. One e-mail offers a substantial discount on electronics (25 percent), and the other offer is also an electronics offer but offers free shipping on any purchase. Neither offer is terrible nor uncommon. But free shipping is pretty much expected these days and often is not perceived as a great value anymore. Of the two offers, which offer are you more likely to forward to a friend?

OK, would it make a difference in your selection if the free-shipping offer told you to "Feel free to forward this offer to your friends"? Probably not. You would choose the offer you deemed more valuable as the one to pass along to a friend if, in fact, either offer enticed you at all.

The bottom line is that the message must be perceived as having value.

KEY CONSIDERATIONS WHILE PLANNING A VIRAL CAMPAIGN

1. Pick the initial recipients of the message carefully

The whole viral marketing process starts off with the first few message recipients. They have to pass the message on to others who will then pass it on to others, etc.

These viral pioneers must be popular (i.e., have access to large social network), influential (i.e., have persuasive power over others) and representative of your target market. One of the mistakes that firms make in putting together viral campaigns is to choose these individuals out of convenience (e.g. the friends of employees) rather than by any strategic consideration.

2. Pick the message carefully

Design a message that communicates the value proposition clearly and simply. Make it easy for consumers to pass the message on to others. Strive for methods that will ensure consistency of the brand image. If you are going to provide consumers incentives for passing on the message, think about how it will affect the final results. For example, incentives can reduce the credibility of the sender in some cases.

3. Put control mechanisms in place

Think about how you will measure the impact of your viral marketing campaign. One simple way of doing this may be to ask new customers where they heard about the service. The company must constantly monitor how consumers are spreading the message. Many companies have now hired full-time employees who constantly monitor public forums to see what is being said about them.

INSIGHTS ON HOW TO EXECUTE A VIRAL MARKETING CAMPAIGN EFFECTIVELY

1. Make it easy to spread the word

A key element of viral marketing is to make it simple for people to convey the message you want them to send.

One of the most popular methods for accomplishing this is the "E-mail this to a friend" feature. E-mail is the primary method in which viral marketing is spread online, it's ideal to have the brand missionaries send a message that allows their "friends" to interact with the viral content in the e-mail (that is, rich media/HTML e-mail). This allows the new user the benefits of a carefully crafted user experience in their e-mail without having to surf the web.

2. Include links in all outbound communications

The Hotmail example is classic—a pitch for the service every time someone uses Hotmail—but it is not the only way to use e-mail to encourage viral marketing. One of the easiest ways to drive site traffic is to include a pitch as a standard element in all e-mail messages you send. Include a link at the end of all company e-mails to a product special, the newsletter sign up form or another promotion—ready feature.

3. Reward your "marketers"

Providing a payback for referrals to the company can encourage people to spread the word. For example, the company can offer extended weeks or months of a subscription service in exchange for customer referrals. Businesses such as health clubs do this all the time in the offline world by adding extra months of membership to club-goers who send business their way.

4. Think value

Viral marketing works when you provide something that people care about. Let's be honest: Few people are going to forward copies of a company press release or a purely self-serving article. They are likely to forward high-value tips, resources that help them make decisions, very funny content, or information on a free product. When you are designing something that you hope will encourage viral marketing, create it with your customers in mind. Give them a reason to be viral for the company.

5. Track and analyze the results

As with any marketing campaign tracking the results

and optimizing performance over time is absolutely necessary. Thankfully, sophisticated e-mail marketers can track insightful and actionable data that can be used to evaluate performance. Important metrics to analyze are pass-along, click-through, and conversion rates. Marketers should separate the click-through and conversion rates by original customer from referrals and evaluate their respective performances.

6. Continually promote friendly referrals

Marketers who want to have their messages frequently forwarded should place a viral marketing offer in every relevant outgoing e-mail message. Viral marketing makes for a great one-time campaign, but it can also be a very effective tool for continuing to broaden the reach of your marketing messages over time.

HOW VIRAL MARKETING STRATEGY WORKS?

By implementing viral marketing strategies, the company provides an incentive for web site visitors to carry a sales message. This incentive is usually a free "carrier" tool for that marketing message or a means by which it is easier for people to spread the word about the products and services. The idea is not to push the visitors into delivering the sales message to others, but as a side effect of them gaining benefit from a utility or service that the company offer.

VIRAL MARKETING TECHNIQUES THAT A TYPICAL BUSINESS WEBSITE CAN DEPLOY

1. Encourage link to the site Register with search engines, of course, and seek reciprocal links. Here are some approaches designed to set-up an exponential response to your efforts.
2. Write articles and encourage other to post them free as content for their site. If you're an expert in a particular area, write an article about an aspect of it. Then offer it to complementary sites to post

on their site as free content, so long as the article contains links to your site. Your article could go far and wide, especially if it is carried on the wings of e-mail to others who will distribute the same article to their network of contacts

3. Set-up an affiliate program to encourage links to your products. Affiliate programs are a form of network marketing that provides financial incentive for other sites to link to yours. Make sure you pay enough to make this attractive to already-saturated site owners.
4. Send out news releases concerning a free service or product available on your site. The key here is to have a truly newsworthy event, contest, free service, or digital download. If your news release is carried by just 5% of the media you send it to, you could have your URL in front of tens of thousands of readers quite inexpensively.
5. Install a Recommend-It.com referral system. Recommend-It won't save a dismal site, but it will help your visitors promote your site to their network of friends.
6. Encourage people to forward your newsletter to friends. Always encourage readers to forward your e-mail newsletter to their friends. Do this at the end of a newsletter, and you may jog some readers to do it immediately. It's easy.

COMPARING VIRAL MARKETING STRATEGIES TO THE SIX PRINCIPLES

1. Gives away products or services.
2. Provides for effortless transfer to others.
3. Scales easily from small to very large.
4. Exploits common motivations and behaviours.
5. Utilizes existing communication networks.
6. Takes advantage of others' resources.

Example	*1. Free*	*2. Transfer*	*3. Scales*	*4. Motivations*	*5. Network*	*6. Resource*
Amazon.com (http://www.amazon.com). Affiliate program with 300,000 links on member websites.	Yes	Copy HTML code	Requires robust database	Revenue	Affiliates' site visitors and ezines	Affiliate's website and e-mail
Geocities (http://www.geocities.com) allows members to construct free websites who they invite their friends to see. On each visit an interstitial ad Geocities pops up to invite visitor to Geocities.	Yes	Builds website with wizard	Requires larger servers and more disk space	Pride in creativity, family bonds	E-mail personal friends and family	Members' e-mail
eGroups (http://www.egroups.com) allows members to set-up discussion and work groups on line, and then invite their friends to be a part, who can then begin a group of their own. Invitations use eGroups resources.	Yes	Wizard sets-up a group	Requires larger servers	Work productivity, family connectivity	Family, work, and academic associates	
ICQ (http://www.icq.com)	Yes	Easy set-up	Requires larger	Love, keep-in-	Family, work	Invite friends

(Contd.)

Example	*1. Free*	*2. Transfer*	*3. Scales*	*4. Motivations*	*5. Network*	*6. Resource*
instant messaging system allows members to set-up accounts, who then invite friends to sign up for the service themselves.			servers	touch, chat	associates	using own e-mail
Blue Mountain Arts (http://www.bluemountain.com) provides greeting cards which can be e-mailed to friends, who then are invited to send their own; cards. Uses Blue Mountain's mail server to send e-mail	Yes	Easy wizard, wide selection	Requires larger servers	Love, friendship, sympathy, loyalty	Personal friends and family	
The Success Doctor (http://www.successdoctor.com), Michel Fortin, allows any site to use his free articles as content, provided they include links to his site.	Yes	Easy download, requires HTML skills	Easily scalable	Growth, desire for content	Visitors to hosts websites	Uses hosts' websites
GoLinQ.com (http://www.GoLinQ.com), provides free e-commerce services to retailers, distributes through chambers of commerce partners.	Yes	Wizard set-up	Requires larger servers	Desire to serve members	Local business members	Uses Chambers' traditional communication channels

VIRAL MARKETING: PITFALLS AND SOLUTIONS

Viral marketing is a form of *motivated* word of mouth that works offline as well as online. The marketer encourage its customers to do the legwork for the company by motivating them with:

- Really valuable service or content (natural word of mouth).
- Bribery (in the form of contests or kickback schemes).
- The prestige of being associated with your brand
- Entertainment (animations, postcards, etc.).

But viral marketing has some pitfalls. There are four key problems in viral marketing. All four problems are explained below with their respective solutions.

Problem: Diluting your brand by letting others be your mouthpiece.

The problem with viral marketing is that the company has no control over its branding. Nobody knows ahead of time whom an individual is going to contact. As a result, many of the messages may end up with people outside the target audience. Moreover, in some cases, individuals may modify the message or add something to it. This leads to variability in how the company's brand is perceived, something you don't want. The company don't have control over its branding because customers are mouthpiece of the company.

Solution: Create a brand strong enough to endure interpretation, or invent a brandless approach.

(a) If the company has a household name, it probably doesn't matter. The brand identity is firmly established, and probably reinforced by ongoing print, web and TV campaigns. So when anyone say "Go see Coca-Cola's web site," the message doesn't matter because the brand is already there.

(b) If the company is not a household name, there are two options. One can carefully construct the scheme to reinforce the brand, by keeping the message, prize, design, and verbiage concentrated on customers. Instead of asking visitors to pass on the word, have them enter addresses at the site and the company people then contact the list with their own message. But note that the more the marketer tries to control a viral campaign, the smaller that campaign will be.

(c) The second solution: Don't worry about it. Use the virus to pull people to the site in large numbers, whether or not they understand the message. Then use the site to educate, brand and target after the fact.

Problem: Uncharted growth

Viral marketing can lead to unanticipated growth paths. For example, Hotmail is now one of the leading e-mail providers in India. It is not clear if it expected that or even wanted that. However, many individuals started e-mailing friends in India who e-mailed many more. Such growth paths may lead to abrupt changes in strategic direction, which can be problematic. The weakness of the Hotmail model was that a free e-mail service requires its own mail servers to transmit the message. If strategy is wildly successful, mail servers must be added very quickly or the rapid growth will bog down and die.

When the company is dealing with web promotion, the action might involve the respondents hitting your web site, registering, downloading a large file, requesting a freebie, or buying something.

If the promotion is big enough and response strong enough, the site might see a ten- or 100-fold increase in traffic within a day. Is the web server ready? Is the response staff ready? Is the budget ready?

Solution: Keep the spread of the virus properly valued, paced and targeted.

Target, target, target. Again, viral marketing works best as a community-based event. Visitors should be spreading the word to friends that will be interested in the topic, not to everyone in the world.

How can you make sure your visitors properly target their word-of-mouth, when they may not even know what targeting means? The reward should be relevant to your market. The reward shouldn't be so large that it motivates cheating or over-spread. The reward should have your message or brand all over it, so that everybody knows this is about *you*.

Some examples: CNET's concept of giving away content lets users put tech news on their web sites, in exchange for a link to CNET. People who participate in the program will naturally place the stories in front of their visitors who care about industry news. It's automatically targeted by the relevancy of the giveaway.

Problem: Spam Threats

Finally, if done poorly, viral marketing can lead to large-scale spam issues. Consider a company that pays individuals to e-mail their friends to convince them to buy one of its products. In this case, the individual who receives the e-mail had only given the friend permission to send e-mail of a personal nature. The one friend's receiving an unsolicited commercial e-mail can weaken his or her relationship with the person who sent it. This can lead to the recipient of the e-mail dropping a friend and becoming angry with the marketer for sending an unsolicited message. Flames may result, leading to damage to the advertiser's reputation. In some cases, individuals who want to earn more money simply go out and spam people. This can be problematic for your company image.

Solution: Know the rules, and educate minions

1. Remember the basic premise of viral marketing: The company is MOTIVATING the customers by offering something positive. "Motivation" does not mean force, threats, dishonesty or stealth.
2. Remember the basic rule of business: Build a customer base through good service, good

products and trust. Whatever tactics the companies tries, don't violate or breach the trust the customers that the company has already won.

CONCLUSION

Companies planning to implement viral marketing programs must carefully consider these problems and devise plans to overcome them. Certainly, viral marketing must be part of a comprehensive marketing strategy. But relying on viral marketing to do all the marketing grunt-work may be placing too much stock in the latest fad.

CASE STUDY—NAUKRI.COM

Introduction

Up until five years ago, job hunters would wait the whole week for the weekly supplements with various newspapers or sundry employment journals and gazettes to learn about the vacancies and job openings in the industry. Then came the Internet and threatened to push the days of white envelopes to oblivion.

A forerunner in ushering in the change in the way we look at job hunting today is none other than naukri.com which is regarded as one of the more resourceful destinations for job hunters—be it a seasoned professional or a fresher who has just got his/her degree.

The big idea

Sanjeev Bikchandani, an IIM graduate is the founder of naukri.com. Bikchandani came up with the idea of starting an online employment exchange. At that time there was no Internet in India and no online exchange. According to him people used to wait for weekly supplements with various newspaper or journals to learn about the vacancies. This sparked a thought in his mind about creating a centralized database of jobs that working professionals could access. At that time the Internet was non-existent. Once the net made its way to India, naukri.com was launched on April 1, 1997.

Opening doors

The single most important factor that made naukri.com profitable was the founder's tight leash on the purse strings. Started with self-funding in 1997, naukri.com didn't have deep pockets to start with. The investment in the first three years was to the tune of Rs. 25 lakh. The company kept its overheads low, refused to splurge on advertising and promotions and sailed through the dotcom bust with little problem.

In mid-2000, the company approached ICICI, which in turn picked up a stake in the venture, providing it with the capital needed to spread its wings.

From just one office in Delhi in the year 2000, the company then crossed state borders to have 15 offices in 13 cities nationwide. naukri.com now covers Noida, Gurgaon, Mumbai, Pune, Ahmedabad, Baroda, Indore, Chennai, Hyderabad, Bangalore, Cochi, Coimbatore and Kolkata.

Measuring succes

1. naukri.com's database is the largest with more than 50,000 jobs listed on the website, which is, "three times the jobs listed in any other job portals in the country."
2. The site provides its headhunting services to 9,500 different corporates from various sectors such as FMCG, IT/telecom, IT-enabled services, bank/ financial institutions, engineering/automobile sectors and healthcare. naukri.com claims it provides better response than its offline competitors at a-tenth of their total cost.
3. naukri.com gets 90 million page views a month (as of June 2003) serving over 9,500 clients in India and abroad.
4. It gets about 2,500 new CVs posted on the site on a daily basis and an equal number of people who modify or edit their CVs already posted on the site.
5. Global Alexa Rankings (an independent traffic ranking service) has adjudged that naukri.com is India's No. 1 job site on all parameters—page views, reach and traffic.

6. While in the financial year of 2002-03 its revenues stood at Rs. 10 crore, the company hopes to double it to Rs. 20 crore by the end of the current financial year.

Revenue Model

Naukri.com has had a clear revenue model since its inception. While it has a select few services that are free to both job-seekers and job providers, the majority of its services are paid for by recruiters.

The company has three paid services—Job Posting Services, Response Management Software (e-application through which recruiters can manage response collected to advertised vacancies and reduce time spent on handling applications by over 80 per cent), and Resume Database Product or RESDEX through which it grants access to its registered CVs to corporate clients and placement agencies.

The company also offers services such as organising walk-in interviews, resume short-listing, and conducting first-cut interviews for recruiters. Additional services for job-seekers include Resume Development, Resume Splash, Job Alert, etc.

Advertising strategy

The company calls its advertising and promotional strategy based on "word of mouth as well as word of mouse" marketing strategy. The company never had the huge advertising budgets that many other online ventures had. Instead, the company used viral marketing, events, and to some extent press and TV to build its brand.

The company advertised by both ways:

1. Online—Viral marketing
2. Offline—Word of mouth, Press

CONCLUSION

It is observed that naukri.com reached to unbelievable heights and created permanent niche for itself in its respective field in a very short span of time. The company never had the huge advertising budgets that many other online ventures had. Viral marketing was AN INTEGRAL PART OF A CAMPAIGN STRATEGY THAT WAS USED TO ACHIEVE OBJECTIVES. Naukri.com had all the essential elements that an effective viral marketing campaign has—

1. It provided valuable service that was necessary for any seasoned professional or a fresher who has just got his/her degree.
2. It was a unique concept. It attracted people because it was first online job exchange in India.
3. It touched the right chord by targeting the right customer. The next logical step that naukri.com developed was to form a set of loyal clients who used its services on a regular basis.
4. It imparted more services than other sites for example. Unlike some other sites, there were no convoluted registration forms to apply for jobs. Job-seekers used Resume Manager as a convenient centralized space in which they stored their CVs for easy access.
5. The company kept its overheads low, refused to splurge on advertising and promotions. It primarily adopted viral marketing as strategic marketing tool and it paid-off well.

References

www.wilsonweb.com/wmt5/viral-principles-clean.htm
www.clickz.com/mkt/emkt_strat/article.php/817461
www.wilsonweb.com/wmt5/viral-principles-clean.htm
http://www.wilsonweb.com/wmt5/viral-principles-clean.htm
www.clickz.com/mkt/onl_mkt_comm/article/1646534785
www.clickz.com/ad/online_ad/article.php/830021
www.wilsonweb.com/wmt5/viral-principles-clean.htm
www.bloggerheads.com
www.clickz.com/crm/crm_strat/article.php/831941
www.clickz.com/em_mkt/comm/article.php/826091
www.publish.com/
www.iabuk.net/index.php

www.express-marketing.com

www.bloggerheads.com

www.wilson.web.com_www.clickz.com/mkt/onl_mkt_comm/article/164653478_www.clickz.com/mkt/onl_mkt_comm/article.php/821371

Case study—naukri.com—www.agencyfaqs.com/interactive/ht_new_media/the_net_at_work/10.html

www.emediaplan.com/Internet/ViralMarketing.asp

CHAPTER

12

Service Quality Perceptions in Banks

A Comparative Analysis

MUSHTAQ A. BHAT

Delivering higher levels of service quality is the strategy that is increasingly being offered as a key to service provider's efforts to position themselves more effectively in the marketplace. Almost all banks perform same functions. Therefore, customer takes into account the relative efficiency while choosing a particular bank. Moreover, banks carry on business with public money and, therefore, customers expect better services from them. Under such circumstances customer's decision to patronize one and not the other is based on quality service offered to him. He takes into account relative efficiency while choosing a particular service firm. Firms, therefore, prosper or decline, depending upon the quality of service they provide to their customers. As a result of this widespread belief, service organisations have placed service quality at the top of the list of strategic constructs. In view of its strategic importance, an attempt has been made in the present paper to make a comparative study of service quality perceptions in banks with their respective customers so as to know whether the banks are at, above or below the perceptions of their respective customers and to offer suggestions to make the overall banking service more effective and efficient. The results of the study lead us to the conclusion that Indian banks fall much below the expectations of their customers on service quality in comparison to foreign banks, and suggests heavy investment on tangibility and improvement in other dimensions of service quality.

BACKGROUND

Service quality is about meeting customers' needs and requirements, and how well the service level delivered matches customer expectations. Service quality in banking implies consistently anticipating and satisfying the needs and expectations of customer (Howcroft, 1991). Raddon (1987) while emphasizing the importance of service quality in banks reported that 40% of those customers switching financial institutions in the USA did so because of service problems. Improving quality in the eyes of customers pays-off for the companies that provide it. Data from the Profit Impact of Market Strategy (PIMS) research show that a perceived quality advantage leads to higher profits (Buzzell and Gale, 1987). Berry and Parasuraman (1991) also hold the view that high quality service gives credibility to the field sales force and advertising, stimulates favourable word-of-mouth communications, enhances customers' perception of value, and boosts the morale and loyalty of employees and customers alike. Heskett, Sasser, and Hart (1990) observed that across a wide range of businesses, the pattern is the same: the longer a company keeps a customer, the more money it stands to make.

Increased competition, slower growth, and mature markets are also forcing many businesses to review their customer service strategy. Many businesses are channeling more efforts to retain existing customers rather than to acquire new ones. It has been estimated that the cost of acquiring a new customer is about five to eight times more than retaining an existing one. Maximizing customer satisfaction through quality customer service has been described as the 'the ultimate weapon" by Davidow and Uttal (1989) in their book "Total Customer Service." According to them, ". . . in all industries, when competitors are roughly matched, those that stress customer service will win.

In light of above research findings, interest in service quality is, thus, unarguably high, particularly when one thinks about it. Poor quality places a firm at a competitive disadvantage. It customers perceive quality as unsatisfactory; they may be quick to take their business elsewhere. Thus, it is clear that service quality offers a way of achieving success among competing services. Particularly where a number of firms that offer nearly identical services are competing within a small area, such as banks, establishing service quality may be the only way of differentiating oneself. Such differentiation can yield a higher proportion of consumers' choices and, hence, mean the difference between financial success and failure. In a liberalized and competitive environment, therefore, only those banks would be effective in delivering goods which provide excellent service quality. Almost, all banks perform same functions. Therefore, the customer takes into account the relative efficiency while choosing a particular bank. Moreover, banks carry on business with public money and, therefore, customers expect better services from them.

In view of above facts, interest in the measurement of service quality becomes fundamental concern for every successful service organization. Measurement is both the last and the first step in producing superior service quality (Davidow and Uttal, 1989). It has been said that what gets measured, gets done. While the importance of service quality to businesses is unequivocal, its measurement and explication have presented problems to researchers and managers. To a large extent, this is due to three unique characteristics of services, namely, intangibility, heterogeneity, and inseparability. Measuring service quality is quite different from measuring product quality because service is an experience. To date, probably the most significant contribution towards the development of a quantitative yardstick for assessing a firm's service quality is the work conducted by Parasuraman, *et al.* (1985, 1988).

LITERATURE REVIEW

Service Quality Concept and Measurement

Although researchers have studied the concept of service for several decades, there is no consensus about the conceptualization of service quality (Cronin and Taylor, 1992; Rust and Oliver, 1994). Different researchers focused on different aspects of service quality. The most common definition is the traditional notion that views quality as the customer's perception of service excellence. That is to say, quality is defined by the customer's impression of the service provided (Berry, *et al.*, 1988; Parasuraman, *et al.*, 1985). The assumption behind this definition is that customers form the perception of service quality according to the service performance they experience and based on past experiences of service performance. It is, therefore, the customer's perception that categorizes service quality.

There are number of definitions that refer to the importance of the client's/customer's perceptions of quality (Takeuchi and Quelch, 1983) which are consumer's attitudes or judgements resulting from comparisons by consumers of expectations of service with their perceptions of actual service performance (Berry, *et al.*, 1988; Gronroos, 1982; Lewis and Boom, 1983). Berry (1980), along with Booms and Bitner (1981), argue that, due to intangible nature of services, customer use elements associated with the physical environment when evaluating service quality. Managing the evidence and using the environmental psychology are often seen as important marketing tools. Levitt (1981) proposes that customers use appearances to make judgements about realities, and less tangible a product the more powerful is the effect of packaging in judging that product. Hostage (1975) for his part, believes that a service firm's contact personnel comprise the major determinant of service quality, while Lewis and Booms (1983) propose that service quality resides in the ability of the service firm to satisfy its customer needs, i.e. customer satisfaction. The traditional approach for defining service quality emphasizes that service quality perception is a comparison of consumer expectations with actual performance (Gronroos, 1984; Lewis and Booms, 1983; Parasuraman, *et al.*, 1985; Parasuraman, *et al.*, 1990).

Parasuraman, *et al.*, (1985) viewed quality as "the degree and direction of discrepancy between customers' service perception and expectations." According to this approach, services are different from goods because they are intangible, heterogeneous and are simultaneously produced and consumed. Additionally, as the disconfirmation paradigm states, service quality is a comparison between consumers' expectations and their perceptions of the service they actually receive.

The roots of service quality research lie in early conceptual work from Carson and Gilmore (1989), Gronroos (1983), Lehtinan and Lehtinan (1982). The catalyst for much of the programme research work in the management domain of services is the conceptual model of 'SERVQUAL' presented by Parasuraman, *et al.* (1985; 1988). The foundation and focus of their model lay in identifying the key components of service quality, namely customer expectations and perceptions and the service delivery associated with these. The basic premise of the model is that there exists a gap between customer expectations and perceptions and the actual delivery of the service. They established that a mismatch between expectations and perceptions causes dissatisfaction, a 'performance' gap as they call it. As found by other writers, the process of service delivery was considered to be a key feature in the assessment of quality (Cronin and Taylor, 1992; Liljander and Strandrik, 1994). Parasuraman *et al.* (1985) have originally identified ten determinants of service quality generic to the service industry. These determinants were Tangibles, Reliability, Responsiveness, Competence, Courtesy, Credibility, Security, Access, Communication, and Understanding the customer. At a later stage, Parasuraman *et al.*, (1988) developed a twenty-two item instrument, recognized as SERVQUAL, that has become widely used as a generic instrument for measuring service quality. SERVQUAL consists of two sections. A twenty-two item section measuring the service quality expectation within a specific sector and a corresponding twenty-two item section measuring the perception of service quality of a particular company in that sector (Prasuraman *et al.*, 1988, 1991). SERVQUAL scores were defined as the differences between the expected service quality and the perceived one. The innovators Parasuraman,

Zeithaml and Berry have further developed promulgated and promoted SERVQUAL through a series of publications (Parasuraman *et al.*, 1985; 1988; 1990; 1991; 1994; 1997; Zeithaml *et al.*, 1990; 1993; 1996, Berry and Parasuraman, 1997). SERVQUAL examines five dimensions that have been consistently ranked by customers to be most important for service quality, regardless of service industry. These five dimensions of service quality are:

1. *Tangibles*: Physical facilities, equipment, and appearance of personnel.
2. *Reliability*: Ability to perform the promised service dependably and accurately.
3. *Responsiveness*: Willingness to help customers and provide prompt service.
4. *Assurance*: Knowledge and courtesy of employees and their ability to inspire trust and confidence.
5. *Empathy*: Caring, individualized attention the firm provides its customers.

Limitations with SERVQUAL are highlighted by the authors themselves (Parasuraman, *et al.*, 1991) and in other research studies (Babakhus and Boller, 1992; Carman, 1990; Lewis and Mitchell, 1990; Lewis, 1993; and Smith, 1992). They relate to respondent's difficulties with negatively worded statements; using two lists of statements for the same items, the number of dimensions of service being assessed; ease of consumer assessment and timing of measurement—before, during or after a service encounter. While there is a healthy and for most part a productive debate regarding the dimensionality of SERVQUAL across industries, and the precise wording of the SERVQUAL items, researchers generally agree that the scale items are good predictors of overall service quality. (Babakus and Boller, 1992; Bolton and Drew, 1991; Brown and Swartz, 1989; Carman, 1990; Cronon and Taylor, 1992; Parasuraman *et al.*, 1991). The debate underscores the importance of the subject and the significance of the contribution to date. Such interchange will help refine the meaning of service quality.

RESEARCH OBJECTIVES

The study has been conducted with the following precise objectives in view:

1. To make a comparative study of service quality perceptions in banks, under study, with their respective customers and to know whether the banks are at, above or below the perceptions of their respective customers.
2. To suggest, on the basis of study results, ways and means for improving service quality in banks with a view to make overall banking service more effective and efficient.

Research Instrument

The SERVQUAL measuring instrument developed by Parasuraman *et al.* (1988) was adapted and used for the present study. It was pre-tested among a number of customers and all its dimensions were felt important. A number of other industry specific empirical studies have been conducted using SERVQUAL Model which include some mostly cited studies carried out in car retailing (Carman1990), travel and tourism (Fick and Ritchie, 1991), hospitality (Saleh and Ryan 1991), banks (Lewis, 1991; Lassar, *et al.*, 2000; Angur, *et al.*, 1999; Blanchard, *et al.*, 1994), medical services (Brown and Swartz, 1989). SERVQUAL was, therefore, chosen as an ideal instrument for studying service quality in banks.

Sample Profile

The present study has been conducted in some states of Northern India which include J&K State, Punjab, Haryana and Delhi. The study is further limited to five banks in Northern India, namely State Bank of India (SBI) and Punjab National Bank (PNB), in the public sector banks being the largest and oldest banks in India, Jammu and Kashmir Bank (JKB) which is the largest private sector bank in the country and, City Bank (CB) and Standard Chartered Grindlays Bank (SCGB) having the maximum operations in India among the foreign banks. These banks were also purposely selected for the present study keeping in view their role and involvement in shaping the economic destiny and in instrumentalising the process of social and economic transformation in Northern India. Specifically, in terms of advancing credit and deposits, employee strength and branch network, they stand at the top (IBA Bulletin, 2002: 264-99). Further, present study is limited to retail banking only as it constitutes nearly eighty per cent of the total banking business (Srivastava, 1994).

The sample for the study comprises of eight hundred bank customers. This represents 50% bank customers from nationalized banks, 25% from private banks, while as the remaining 25% are from foreign banks. While choosing a bank customer, the method of simple random sampling was followed. All important demographic characteristics like age, level of education, level of income, profession and geographic location of the bank were taken into consideration. All these characteristics have an important bearing upon bank customers' evaluation (regarding expectations and perceptions) of service quality. In the same way three hundred seventy bank officials of the sample organisations, were approached by the scholar to fill up the SERVQUAL instrument with a view to measure the perceptions about service quality they are delivering to their respective customers. This represents 54% bank officials from nationalized banks, 27% from private banks, while as the remaining 19% are from foreign banks. While choosing bank officials, the method of convenience sampling was used. All other important factors about bank officials like age, level of education, scale of pay and location of bank were taken into consideration while approaching the bank official.

Results and Discussion

In line with the objective of the study the main areas of questioning and analysis concerned perceptions of service quality and its dimensions: tangibility, reliability, responsiveness, assurance and empathy. Perceptions were measured on a seven point strongly disagree/strongly agree scale. Mean differences between service quality perceptions of banks and their respective customers' were calculated separately for all the banks followed by a T. Test to determine the level of significant difference. The results obtained from this computation are presented in Tables 1 to 6.

Overall Service Quality

The analysis of Table 1 clearly reveals that there exists wide perceptual difference among Indian banks with their respective customers regarding overall service quality in banks while as the said perceptual difference between foreign banks and their customers is narrow. The high mean difference of JKB (25.36) followed by SBI (20.68) and PNB (18.17) shows that these banks have incorrect assessment about the quality of service they are delivering to their respective customers. A low mean difference of SCGB (1.67) followed by CB (4.91) shows that there is negligible perceptual difference between foreign banks and their respective customers about the quality of service they are delivering to their customers. For a comprehensive analysis regarding service quality in banks, see also Mushtaq, 2003; Gani and Mushtaq, 2003.

DIMENSION-WISE ANALYSIS

Tangibility

The data on Table 1 brings to light high differences in the perceptions of Indian banks with their respective customers on tangibles. The data on tangibility (–1.13 and –0.90) reveals that foreign banks (CB followed by SCGB) are exceeds the perceptions of their customers while as Indian banks with high mean difference, particularly SBI (5.28) followed by JKB (4.25) and PNB (4.16), fall much below the perceptions of their customers on this dimensions. The element-wise analysis of tangibility shows serious shortfall of perceptions among Indian banks on up-to-date equipments and physical facilities available in a bank as perceived by their respective customers.

TABLE I

Comparative Perceptions of Bank Officers and Customers about Tangibility

Sl. No. Elements of Service Quality Dimension (Tangibility)	Group	BANKS																			
		SBI				PNB				JKB				CB				SCGB			
		Mean	STD. Dev.	M.D.	T. Value	Mean	STD. Dev.	M.D.	T. Value	Mean	STD. Dev.	M.D.	T. Value	Mean	STD. Dev.	M.D.	T. Value	Mean	STD. Dev.	M.D.	T. Value
1. Up-to-date equipment	BO	5.63	0.68	1.53***	15.04	5.39	1.01	0.97***	8.38	5.86	1.09	1.10***	7.06	6.24	0.51	-0.28***	-2.66	6.05	0.45	-0.25	-1.23
	BC	4.10	0.89			4.42	0.91			4.76	1.36			6.53	0.50			6.30	1.24		
2. Physical Facilities	BO	5.35	0.97	1.89***	15.42	5.56	0.90	1.57***	12.20	5.86	0.98	1.30***	8.71	6.28	0.53	-0.30***	-2.73	6.05	0.68	-0.22	-0.96
	BC	3.47	1.00			4.00	1.11			4.56	1.33			6.58	0.52			6.27	1.37		
3. Neatness of Employees	BO	6.16	0.63	0.98***	11.48	6.29	0.55	0.85***	9.59	5.87	1.35	0.89***	5.45	6.97	0.19	0.02	0.35	6.53	0.51	-0.13	-1.03
	BC	5.18	0.72			5.44	0.80			4.98	1.32			6.95	0.22			6.65	0.72		
4. Communication material	BO	5.99	0.08	-0.88***	6.72	5.97	0.71	0.77***	7.20	5.71	0.92	0.96***	5.76	6.31	0.54	-0.58***	-7.25	6.45	0.60	-0.30***	2.58
	BC	5.11	1.18			5.20	0.95			4.75	1.55			6.89	0.32			6.75	0.63		
Tangibility (1+2+3+4)	BO	23.13	2.21	5.28***	18.46	23.20	2.14	4.15***	13.17	23.30	2.60	4.25***	9.07	25.79	1.37	-1.14***	-4.75	25.07	1.57	-0.89	-1.44
	BC	17.84	2.37			19.04	2.78			19.05	4.33			26.93	1.06			25.97	3.79		

Reliability

As is evident from the data on Table 2 on reliability dimension, there exists a wide gap in the perceptions of Indian banks and their respective customers. The JKB's high mean difference (5.55) followed by SBI (3.37) and PNB (2.58) shows the level of incorrect assessment about the quality of service they are delivering to their respective customers. Foreign banks are exceeding the perceptions of their customers on this dimension. The element wise analysis of reliability shows that Indian banks fall short of correct assessment on their respective consumer perceptions as far as keeping the promise and being sincere in solving the problems are concerned.

Responsiveness

The data on responsiveness (Table 3) shows that there is marginal perceptual difference in foreign banks with their respective customers. However, among Indian banks, particularly JKB followed by SBI's, the perceptual difference between banks and their respective customers is wide on said dimension. High mean difference of 5.01 and 3.64 of JKB followed by SBI respectively shows that there exists a wide gap in the perceptions of these banks and their respective customers regarding the delivery of quality service. The element-wise analysis shows that Indian banks are falling below the perceptions of their respective customers as far as employees providing prompt services are concerned.

Assurance

The perceptual difference between JKB and its customers on service quality (assurance dimension) is high as is evident from the mean difference (3.9) in Table 4. The respondents of SBI and PNB have also given low rating on assurance dimension to their respective banks compared to the ratings of their respective banks. It is clear that Indian banks fall below the perceptions of their respective customers on said dimension. Contrary to Indian banks, the perceptual difference, on assurance, between foreign banks and their respective customers is relatively low. The data on Table 4 clearly brings to light that SCGB followed by CB are exceeding the perceptions of their customers on

TABLE 2

Comparative Perceptions of Bank Officers and Customers about Reliability

Sl. No. Elements of Service Quality Dimension (Reliability)	Group	BANKS																			
		SBI				PNB				JKB				CB				SCGB			
		Mean	STD. Dev.	M.D.	T. Value	Mean	STD. Dev.	M.D.	T. Value	Mean	STD. Dev.	M.D.	T. Value	Mean	STD. Dev.	M.D.	T. Value	Mean	STD. Dev.	M.D.	T. Value
5. Promise to do some thing by a certain time, doing it.	BO	6.06	0.71	0.46***	3.92	6.19	0.64	0.59***	6.85	6.27	0.63	1.28***	8.51	6.14	0.35	-0.29***	-2.89	6.45	0.60	-0.04	0.40
	BC	5.60	1.05			5.60	0.74			4.98	1.44			6.42	0.50			6.49	0.52		
6. Being sincere in solving the problem	BO	6.32	0.67	0.69***	5.54	6.28	0.65	0.63***	6.28	6.54	0.57	1.45***	8.98	6.97	0.19	0.50***	5.06	6.90	0.30	0.25***	2.66
	BC	5.63	1.15			5.65	0.89			5.09	1.57			6.46	0.52			6.65	0.55		
7. Performing the service right the first time	BO	6.13	0.74	0.58***	4.66	6.16	0.50	0.56***	5.96	6.24	0.85	1.20***	8.06	6.21	0.41	-0.36***	-3.53	6.50	0.60	-0.05	-0.55
	BC	5.55	1.13			5.60	0.87			5.04	1.36			6.57	0.50			6.56	0.54		
8. Providing the service at the promised time	BO	6.02	0.67	0.31***	2.82	6.20	0.62	0.49***	5.40	5.76	1.19	0.79***	4.57	6.03	0.19	-0.09	-1.47	6.23	0.53	-0.21**	-2.14
	BC	5.71	1.00			5.71	0.79			4.97	1.51			6.13	0.34			6.43	0.52		
9. Keeping records correctly	BO	6.85	0.36	0.39***	4.09	6.87	0.34	0.31***	5.13	6.53	0.76	0.81***	4.88	6.97	0.19	-0.02	-0.92	6.78	0.53	-0.21***	-3.66
	BC	6.46	0.92			6.56	0.56			5.72	1.58			6.99	0.10			6.98	0.14		
Reliability (5+6+7+8+9)	BO	31.37	2.16	2.43***	4.88	31.69	1.72	2.57***	7.46	31.34	2.77	5.53***	8.48	32.31	0.76	-0.26	-1.50	32.85	1.90	-0.26	-0.88
	BC	28.94	4.69			29.11	3.23			25.81	6.24			32.57	0.85			33.11	1.48		

TABLE 3

Comparative Perceptions of Bank Officers and Customers about Responsiveness

Sl. No. Elements of Service Quality Dimension (Responsiveness)	Group	BANKS																			
		SBI				PNB				JKB				CB				SCGB			
		Mean	STD. Dev.	M.D.	T. Value	Mean	STD. Dev.	M.D.	T. Value	Mean	STD. Dev.	M.D.	T. Value	Mean	STD. Dev.	M.D.	T. Value	Mean	STD. Dev.	M.D.	T. Value
10. Telling customers exactly when services will be performed	BO	6.11	0.62	0.73	6.53***	6.01	0.52	0.51	5.41***	6.13	0.65	1.15	7.76***	6.21	0.41	-0.13	-1.21	6.40	0.50	-0.06	-0.14
	BC	5.39	1.01			5.50	0.87			4.98	1.41			6.33	0.52			6.46	0.52		
11. Employees providing prompt service to customers	BO	5.86	0.88	1.20	7.72***	5.52	1.08	0.73	4.80***	6.26	0.76	1.52	8.44***	6.21	0.41	0.09	0.71	6.73	0.45	0.21	1.73*
	BC	4.65	1.42			4.79	1.33			4.74	1.72			6.11	0.68			6.52	0.70		
12. Employees who are always willing to help	BO	6.10	0.74	0.92	6.47***	5.89	0.92	0.67	5.14***	6.50	0.56	1.62	9.37***	6.79	0.41	0.46	3.43***	6.63	0.49	0.06	0.60
	BC	5.18	1.32			5.22	1.14			4.87	1.69			6.33	0.69			6.56	0.64		
13. Employees who are never too busy to respond to customers requests	BO	5.31	1.24	0.80	4.70***	5.40	1.11	0.86	5.31***	5.43	1.47	0.78	4.18***	6.28	0.45	0.24	1.59*	6.60	0.50	0.24	1.99**
	BC	4.52	1.43			4.54	1.42			4.65	1.55			6.04	0.75			6.36	0.71		
Responsiveness (10+11+12+13)	BO	23.38	2.66	3.64	7.21***	22.82	2.94	2.77	5.91***	24.31	2.59	5.06	8.41***	25.48	0.94	0.66	1.97**	26.35	1.18	0.45	1.32
	BC	19.73	4.65			20.04	4.22			19.24	5.73			24.81	1.73			25.89	2.03		

TABLE 4

Comparative Perceptions of Bank Officers and Customers about Assurance

Sl. No.	Elements of Service Quality Dimension (Assurance)	Group	BANKS																			
			SBI				PNB				JKB				CB				SCGB			
			Mean	STD. Dev.	M.D.	T. Value	Mean	STD. Dev.	M.D.	T. Value	Mean	STD. Dev.	M.D.	T. Value	Mean	STD. Dev.	M.D.	T. Value	Mean	STD. Dev.	M.D.	T. Value
14.	Employees who are trustworthy	BO	6.04	0.53	0.73	5.89***	6.02	0.58	0.70	6.46***	6.24	0.59	1.17	7.16***	6.24	0.44	0.09	0.79	6.38	0.49	-0.21	-1.90**
		BC	5.31	1.17			5.32	1.01			5.07	1.59			6.15	0.56			6.59	0.63		
15.	Feeling safe in transacting with the Banks	BO	6.88	0.33	0.26	3.70***	6.80	0.42	0.28	0.36***	6.72	0.51	0.63	4.49***	6.97	0.19	-2.02	-0.92	6.88	0.33	-0.09	-2.02**
		BC	6.62	0.66			6.52	0.70			6.09	1.36			6.99	0.10			6.97	0.22		
16.	Employees who are consistently courteous	BO	6.12	0.69	1.09	8.22***	5.93	0.79	0.88	7.15***	6.26	0.56	1.14	7.66***	6.48	0.51	0.70	5.90***	6.63	0.49	0.14	1.37
		BC	5.03	1.22			5.05	1.10			5.12	1.44			5.78	0.58			6.48	0.59		
17.	Employees who have the knowledge to answer the customers questions	BO	6.05	0.63	0.81	6.60***	6.01	1.03	0.81	6.59***	6.34	0.53	1.14	7.86***	6.24	0.44	0.75	4.32***	6.63	0.59	0.54	3.42***
		BC	5.24	1.14			5.20	0.99			5.20	1.40			5.49	0.90			6.09	0.93		
	Assurance (14+15+16+17)	BO	25.09	1.64	2.89	7.58***	24.76	2.20	2.66	7.44***	25.55	1.52	4.08	8.29***	25.93	0.70	1.51	5.43***	26.50	1.37	0.37	1.17
		BC	22.19	3.60			22.09	3.24			21.47	4.82			24.41	1.44			26.12	1.83		

trustworthiness of employees and employees providing prompt services to their customers.

Empathy

The data analysis of Table 5 discloses the fact that Indian banks stand for away from their respective customers regarding delivery of quality services. There exists a wide gap between the perceptions of Indian banks (especially JKB followed by PNB and SBI) and their respective customers as is evident from their high mean differences (7.46, 6.05 and 5.50 respectively). However, it is surprising to note that even CB is falling below the perceptions of their customers (4.09) on this dimension. Its element-wise analysis shows that foreign banks (CB followed by SCGB) are exceeding the perceptions of their customers on banks individualized attention and convenient operating hours.

CONCLUSION AND SUGGESTIONS

To sum-up, the results of the study lead us to the conclusion that Indian banks fall much below the perceptions of their customers on all the dimensions of service quality in comparison to foreign banks. Foreign banks, in particular, are exceeding the perceptions of their customers on tangibility and reliability dimensions of service quality. These banks are not far away from the perceptions of their customers as far as other dimensions of service quality are concerned. In other words foreign banks have correct assessment about the quality of services they are delivering to their customers in comparison to Indian banks. Two major reasons can be identified for such high service quality variation: first, foreign banks operate in selected markets and offer selected services; secondly, foreign banks are backed by state of art banking technology which gives them differential/competitive edge in financial services markets. SBI followed by JKB are much below the perceptions of their customers regarding the delivery of quality services. In particular, JKB falls comparatively much below the perceptions of its customers as far as reliability is concerned. The study leads us to the conclusion that all Indian banks, under study, especially JKB

TABLE 5

Comparative Perceptions of Bank Officers and Customers about Empathy

Sl. No.	Elements of Service Quality Dimension (Empathy)	Group	BANKS																			
			SBI				PNB				JKB				CB				SCGB			
			Mean	STD. Dev.	M.D.	T. Value	Mean	STD. Dev.	M.D.	T. Value	Mean	STD. Dev.	M.D.	T. Value	Mean	STD. Dev.	M.D.	T. Value	Mean	STD. Dev.	M.D.	T. Value
18.	Bank that give individual attention	BO	6.02	0.68	0.74	5.69***	6.06	0.72	0.74	6.34***	6.26	0.64	1.33	7.81***	6.28	0.45	-0.01	0.15	6.58	0.59	0.15	1.31
		BC	5.28	1.19			5.32	1.05			4.92	1.65			6.29	0.56			6.42	0.63		
19.	Convenient operating hours	BO	6.23	0.88	1.38	8.12***	6.11	0.81	1.45	9.48***	6.18	0.89	1.63	9.12***	7.00	0.00	0.12	1.98**	6.70	0.46	-0.14	-1.20
		BC	4.85	1.57			4.66	1.43			4.55	1.67			6.88	0.33			6.84	0.66		
20.	Employees who give personal attention	BO	6.16	0.60	0.99	7.51***	6.02	0.65	0.83	7.16***	6.27	0.65	1.40	8.22***	6.21	0.41	0.15	1.57*	6.65	0.48	0.25	1.96**
		BC	5.17	1.24			5.19	1.07			4.86	1.65			6.06	0.45			6.40	0.73		
21.	Bank which has your best interests at least	BO	6.24	0.67	1.25	9.84***	6.17	0.66	1.28	10.54***	6.40	0.69	1.67	10.27***	7.00	.00	2.36	11.82***	6.78	0.42	1.04	5.70***
		BC	4.99	1.17			4.89	1.13			4.73	1.55			4.64	1.07			5.73	1.13		
22.	Employees who understand specific needs of the customer	BO	5.98	0.68	1.14	8.32***	5.94	0.61	1.19	9.76***	6.22	0.61	1.41	8.95***	6.62	0.49	1.47	-9.64***	6.53	0.51	0.49	3.21***
		BC	4.84	1.28			4.75	1.14			4.81	1.52			5.15	0.77			6.04	0.90		
	Empathy (18+19+20+21+22)	BO	30.63	2.37	5.49	9.59***	30.29	2.25	5.49	10.17***	31.31	2.34	7.43	10.49***	33.10	0.90	4.08	10.92***	33.22	1.73	1.79	3.24***
		BC	25.13	5.47			24.80	5.18			23.87	6.91			29.02	1.94			31.43	3.32		

TABLE 6

Comparative Perceptions of Bank Officers and Customers about Overall Service Quality in Banks

Overall Service Quality	*Group*	*BANKS*																			
		SBI				*PNB*				*JKB*				*CB*				*SCGB*			
		Mean	*STD. Dev.*	*M.D.*	*T. Value*	*Mean*	*STD. Dev.*	*M.D.*	*T. Value*	*Mean*	*STD. Dev.*	*M.D.*	*T. Value*	*Mean*	*STD. Dev.*	*M.D.*	*T. Value*	*Mean*	*STD. Dev.*	*M.D.*	*T. Value*
Overall Service Quality	BO	133.52	8.64	19.65	10.37***	132.78	8.01	17.66	10.43***	135.82	9.23	26.36	10.69***	142.62	2.62	4.85	5.84***	144.00	6.21	1.46	0.85
	CO	113.86	17.72			115.11	16.01			109.45	23.73			137.76	4.23			142.53	10.10		

Note: BO and BC denotes Bank Officials and Bank Customers respectively. *p < 0.01; **p < 0.05; ***p < 0.10.

Bank :	SBI	PNB	JKB	CB	SCGB
Number | BC	200	200	200	100	100
| BO:	100	100	100	30	40
df :	298	298	298	128	138

followed by SBI and PNB do not have correct assessment of the quality of service they are delivering to their respective customers. This observation undoubtedly reveals bleak reality that Indian banks do not meet the expectations of their customers. Foreign banks, including private banks and non-banking institutions, backed by state-of-art banking technology, have spurred the aspirations of customers of other banks. As compared to foreign banks, our banks are trailing far behind in offering/delivering quality service. In delivery of quality service in banks, it is speed, accuracy, promptness, reliability, individualised attention, etc. which matters and which can be achieved through relevant banking technology wherein our banks are lagging behind. This is one of the main contributing factors for high level of customer dissatisfaction particularly in public sector banks where retail banking constitutes nearly eighty percent of the total banking business (Srivastava, 1994).

In the light of above findings it is suggested that banks should continually assess and reassess how customers perceive bank services so as to know whether the bank meets or exceeds or is below the expectations of their customers. Such an appraisal, however, is a tedious task because customer service is complex in nature and dynamic in action. What is good service today may become indifferent service tomorrow and bad service the next day. Frequent customer surveys, therefore, throw light on ratification and refinement, which will go a long way to improve service quality in banks.

Customer service must match with marketing efforts otherwise a customer would remain a dissatisfied soul and all marketing efforts will go down the drain. The process of fulfiling customer needs, therefore, requires tailoring bank services to what customer wants, rather than making them to accept whatever banks can conveniently provide. The needs and expectations of the customer changes from time to time and as such innovating of new services and refinement of existing services is imperative. Today customers are exposed to the standards of international banking and expect same range of service quality from Indian banks. If Indian banks fail to regulate their financial services to that of foreign banks, time is not far away when they will loose substantial market share to foreign banks.

In order to overcome growing consumer dissatisfaction it is suggested that banks should make commitment to service quality and the creation of an appropriate culture. The organizational culture may require change, towards employee orientation to the company, and everyone's orientation to the external customer. This change starts at the top; the customer care process must begin with senior management's commitment to employees and customers, ideally with strong and visible leaders.

Banks must pay attention to potential failure points and service recovery procedures, which become integral to employees training. In other words, it amounts to empowering employees to exercise responsibility, judgement and creativity in responding to customers' problems.

A bank of tomorrow has to forget the branch of all trades. Our public sector banks operate in almost all segments, which increase the workload of front line staff thereby leaving them less time to provide individualized or personalized service. This has become one of the major reasons of growing customer dissatisfaction (Bhattacharya, 1989 and Muniraj, 1994). The research findings of present study corroborate the findings of above-mentioned scholars. In the light of these research findings, it is suggested that banks must create branches dedicated to specific lines of business and specific customers. As the number of players is increasing, clients opt for the best service, setting aside the traditional banker customer relationship that covers every service. In other words, in today's liberalized and competitive environment, customers will look for the best bank in each area of business rather than depending upon any one as a one-stop shop. It is, therefore, necessary that banks should specialize in those customer segments where they are strong, which will go a long way in improving service quality. In the same way banks should create separate branches in each town/ local area to take care of government related financial transactions like salaries to government employees, pension holders, sales tax, excise duties, electricity bills, telephone bills, etc in each state.

Lastly, managing the perceived service quality means

that the firm has to match the expected service and the perceived service to each other so that consumer satisfaction is achieved. In order to keep the gap between the expected service and the perceived service as small as possible it is important that the promises about how the service will perform, given by traditional marketing activities, and communicated by word of mouth, must not be unrealistic when compared to the service the customers eventually will perceive. Hence efforts of the banking think tank should not be only to equationalise the customer expectations with what the banks offer but endeavours have to be put in to ensure that Indian banks provide such a level of quality service which exceeds the perceived expectations of customers and thus creates a 'wow' syndrome among all visiting clientele/ customers.

. References

Angur, M.G., Nataraajan, R. and Jahera Jr, J.S., 1999, "Service Quality in the Banking Industry: An assessment in a developing economy", *International Journal of Bank Marketing,* Vol. 17, No. 3: 116-23.

Babakus, E. and Boller, G.W. (1992), "An Empirical Assessment of the SERVQUAL Scale", *Journal of Business Research,* Vol. 24, May, pp. 253-68.

Berry, L.L., Parasuraman, A. and Zeithaml, V.A. (1988), "The Service Quality Puzzle." Business Horizon, 31(5), 35-43.

Berry, L.L. (1980), "Services Marketing is Different", *Business,* Vol. 30, (May-June), pp. 8-30

Berry, L.L. and Parasuraman, A. (1991), "Marketing Services: Competing Through Quality", Maxwell Macmillan International, New York, pp. 175-203.

Berry, L.L. and Parasuraman, A. (1997), "Listening to the Customer—the Concept of a Service-Quality Information System", Sloan Management Review, Spring: 65-76.

Blanchard, R.F. and Galloway, R.L. (1994), "Quality in Retail Banking", *International Journal of Service Industry Management,* 5: 5-23.

Bolton, R.N. and Drew J.H. (1991), "A Multistage Model of Customer's Assessment of Service Quality and Value", *Journal of Consumer Research,* Vol. 17, No. 4., pp. 375-84.

Booms, B.H. and Bitner, M.J. (1981), "Marketing Strategies and Organisation Structures for Services Firms", in Zeithaml, V.A., Panasuraman, A. and Berry, L.L (1985), "Problems and Strategies in Service Marketing", *Journal of Marketing,* Vol. 49, No. 2, pp. 33-46.

Brown, S.W. and Swartz, T.A. (1989), "A Gap Analysis of Professional Service Quality", *Journal of Marketing*, Vol. 53, April, pp. 92-100.

Buzzell, R. and Gale, B. (1987), The PIMS Principles, Free Press, New York.

Carman, J.M. (1990), "Consumer Perceptions of Service Quality": An Assessment of the SERVQUAL Dimensions", *Journal of Retailing*, Vol. 66, Spring, pp. 33-56.

Carson, D. and Gilmore, A. (1989), "Customer Care: The Neglected Domain", *Irish Marketing Review*, Vol. 4, No. 3, pp. 49-61.

Cronin, J.J. and Taylor, S.A. (1992), "Measuring Service Quality: A Re-examination and Extension", *Journal of Marketing*, Vol. 56, July, pp. 55-68.

Davidow, A., and B. Uttal (1989), "Total Customer Service: The Ultimate Weapon", New York: Harper and Row.

Fick, G.R. and Ritchie, J.R.B. (1991), "Measuring Service Quality in the Travel and Tourism Industry", *Journal of Travel Research*, Vol. 30, No. 3, pp. 2-9.

Gani, A. and Mushtaq, B.A. (2003), "Service Quality in Commercial Banks: A Comparative Study", *Paradigm*, Vol. VII, No. 1, January-June, pp. 24-36.

Gronroos, C. (1982), "Strategic Management and Marketing in the Services Sector" in Parasuraman, A., Zeithaml, V.A and Berry, L.L (1985), "A Conceptual Model of Service Quality and its Implications for Future Research", *Journal of Marketing*, Fall, Vol. 49, pp. 41-50.

Gronroos, C. (1984), "A Service Quality Model and its Marketing Implications", *European Journal of Marketing*, Vol., 18, No. 4, pp. 36-50.

Gronross, C. (1983), "Strategic Management and Marketing in the Service Sector" in Lovelock, C.H. (1996), "Service Marketing", Prentice Hall, New Jersey, p. 85.

Heskett, J., E. Sasser and C. Hart (1990), "Service Breakthrough: Changing the Rules of the Game", New York: Free Press.

Hostage, G.M. (1975), "Quality Control in a Service Business", *Harvard Business Review*, July-August, pp. 98-106.

Howcroft, J.B. (1991), "Customer Satisfaction in Retail Banking", *Service Industry Journal*, January: 11-17.

Journal of the Academy of Marketing Science, Vol. 25 No. 2, pp. 154-61.

Lassar, W.M., Manolis, C. and Winsor, R.D. (2000), "Service Quality Perspectives and Satisfaction in Private Banking", *Journal of Services Marketing*, 14 (2/3): 244-72.

Lehtinen, U. and Lehtinan, J.R. (1982), "Service Quality: A Study of Quality Dimensions", Working Paper, Service Management Institute, Helsinki, Finland.

Levitt, T. (1981), "Marketing Intangible Products and Product Intangibles", *Harvard Business Review*, May-June, pp. 94-102.

Lewis, B. (1991), "Service Quality: An International Comparison of Bank Customers Expectations and Perceptions", *Journal of Marketing Management*, Vol. 7, pp. 47-62.

Lewis, B.R. (1993), "Service Quality Measurement", *Marketing Intelligence and Planning*, Vol. 11, No. 4, pp. 4-12.

Lewis, B.R. and Mitchell, V.W. (1990), "Defining and Measuring the Quality of Customer Service", *Marketing Intelligence and Planning*, Vol. 8, No. 6, pp. 11-18.

Lewis, R.C. and Booms, B.H. (1983), "The Marketing Aspect of Service Quality" in Lewis, B.R. (1981), "Service Quality: An International Comparison of Bank Customers Expectations and Perceptions", *Journal of Marketing Management*, Vol. 7, pp. 47-62.

Linjander, V. and Strandrik, T. (1994), "The Nature of Relationship Quality" in Carson, D. and Gilmore, A. (1996) "Services Marketing, Text and Readings" (Eds.), Mercury Publications Ltd. Dublin, pp. 41-49, 255-277.

Mushtaq, B.A. (2003), "Service Quality in Public Sector Banks: An Empirical Investigation", *Business Review*, Vol. 9, No. 2, pp. 44-52.

Parasuraman, A. (1997), "Reflections on gaining competitive advantage through customer value".

Parasuraman, A., Berry, L. and Zeithaml, V. (1985), "A conceptual model of SQ and its implications for future research," *Journal of Marketing*, Vol. 49, Fall, 41-50.

Parasuraman, A., Berry, L. and Zeithaml, V. (1988), "SERVQUAL: a multi-item scale for measuring consumer perceptions of SQ", *Journal of Retailing*, Vol. 64, Spring, 12-40.

Parasuraman, A., Berry, L. and Zeithaml, V.A. (1990), "Guidelines for Conducting Service Quality Research", *Marketing Research* (December), 34-44.

Parasuraman, A., Berry, L. and Zeithaml, V.A. (1991) "Perceived Service Quality as a Customer-Based Performance Measure: An Empirical Examination of Organizational Barriers Using an Extended Service Quality Model", *Human Resource Management*, Vol. 30, No. 3, pp. 335-64.

Parasuraman, A., Berry, L.L. and Zeithaml, V.A. (1991), "Refinement and Reassessment of the SERVQUAL Scale", *Journal of Retailing*, Vol. 67, Winter, pp. 420-50.

Parasuraman, A., Zeithaml, V.A. and Barry, L.L. (1994), "Reassessment of Expectations as a Comparison Standard in Measuring Service Quality: Implications from Further Research", *Journal of Marketing*, Vol. 58, No. 1. pp. 111-24.

Raddon, G. H. (1987), "Quality Service—A Low Cost Profit Strategy", *Bank Marketing*, Vol. 19, No. 9; 10-12

Rust, R.T. and Oliver, R.L. (1994), "Service quality: Insights and managerial implications from the frontier" in Rust, R.T. and Oliver, R. L. (Eds.), "Service Quality: New Directions in Theory and Practice", Thousand Oaks, CA: Sage Publications.

Rust, R.T. and Oliver, R., (1994) "Service Quality", SEGE Publications: London.

Saleh, F. and Ryan, C. (1991), "Analysing Service Quality in the Hospitality Industry Using the SERVQUAL Model", *Service Industries Journal*, Vol. 11, No. 3, pp. 324-43.

Smith, S. (1987), "How to Quantify Quality", *Management Today*, October, pp. 86-94.

Srivastava, A.K. (1994) "Customer Service in Banks: Need for a Marketing Approach" in Bidhi, C. (1994) "Marketing of Services" (Ed.), Rawat Publications, New Delhi, pp. 25-38.

Takeuchi, H. and Quelch, J.A. (1983), "Quality is more than Making a Good Product", *Harvard Business Review*, July-Aug., pp. 139-45.

Zeithaml, V.A., Berry, L.L. and Parasuraman, A. (1993), "The nature and determinants ofconsumer expectations of service", *Journal of Academy of Marketing Science*, 21, (1): 1-12.

Zeithaml, V.A., Parasuraman, A. and Berry, L.L. (1990), "Delivering Quality Service: Balancing Customer Perceptions and Expectations (New York: Free Press) p. 28.

Zeithaml, V.A., Parasuraman, A. and Berry, L.L. (1996), "The Behavioral Consequences of Service Quality", *Journal of Marketing*, April, 31-46.

Zeithaml, V.A., Parasuraman, A. and Berry, L.L. (1992), "Strategic positioning on the dimensions of service quality", in Swartz, T.A., Bowen, D.E. and Brown, S.W. (Eds), Advances in Services

CHAPTER

13

Conceptual Model of Banking Service Quality

NAVDEEP AGGARWAL, MOHIT GUPTA AND S.K. SINGLA

While extensive research has been carried out in the field of service quality, no work is universally acceptable. Further, all the available approaches to determination of service quality are abstract and subjective in nature; consequently of no practical utility to the managers. Keeping this gap in mind, the authors have attempted to develop a model of banking service quality. Specifically, Dabholkar, Thorpe, and Rentz (1996) multilevel-multidimensional model of service quality which presents service quality as consisting of primary and secondary dimensions has been used as the building block for this model. Secondary dimensions were identified using qualitative research and were condensed into primary dimensions using factor analysis. Authors identified four primary dimensions namely, 'Service time', 'Interaction with bank's staff', 'Ambience and infrastructure', and 'Services and banking channels.' Details of these primary dimensions and their managerial implications have been discussed.

Keywords: Service quality, Banking, Multilevel, Multidimensional.

- A high level of service quality is related to key organisational outcomes viz., market share (Buzzel and Gale, 1987), improved profitability relative to competitors, enhanced customer loyalty (Reicheld and Sasser, Jr., 1990), realization of competitive price premium, and increased probability of purchase (Zeithaml, Berry, and Parasuraman, 1996). These research findings indicate that when an organisation provides quality services to its customers, it ensures its survival with increased profitability.

Therefore, every manager must keep track of quality of service, his/her organisation is providing to the customers. However, the task may not be as simple as it would appear. This is so because service quality has proved to be a difficult concept to understand (Brady and Cronin, Jr., 2001) and the research related to the construct is still considered inconclusive. Problem is compounded when there is no consensus as to the nature or content or the number of dimensions of service quality. Two (e.g., Gronroos, 1984), three (e.g., Rust and Oliver, 1994), five (e.g., Parasuraman, Zeithaml, and Berry, 1985), and even ten (e.g., Parasuraman, Zeithaml, and Berry, 1985) dimensions have been proposed to constitute service quality. But, a conceptualization that reflects the complexity and the nature of the construct has been a major missing link. Moreover, most of the research has focused on the objective of developing a generalized model of service quality—applicable to a variety of services from wide industry spectrum, which unfortunately, has not been a great success till date. Consequently, whatever models had been developed, have proved to be of little value to practicing managers. For example, what constitutes reliability, responsiveness, empathy - the dimensions of service quality as proposed in SERVQUAL (Parasuraman, Zeithaml, and Berry, 1985) or other dimensions are not clear (Brady and Cronin, Jr., 2001). In this research, therefore, we intend to plug this gap by developing a model of service quality applicable specifically to Indian banking sector, which has turned out to be one of the most vibrant sectors in service industry in post-liberalization era of Indian economy.

CONCEPTUAL BACKGROUND

Review of literature suggests that early conceptualizations (e.g., Parasuraman, Zeithaml, and Berry, 1985) were developed on the foundation of the disconfirmation paradigm employed in the physical goods literature. This suggests that service quality results from a comparison of perceived with expected performance. For instance, Gronroos's (1984) Nordic model of service quality puts the perceived service against the expected service. He has identified two dimensions for service quality viz., functional quality and technical quality. Functional quality represents how the service is delivered, that is, it defines customer's perceptions of the interactions that take place during service delivery. Technical quality reflects the outcome of the service act, or what the customer receives in the service encounter.

Similarly, Parasuraman, Zeithaml, and Berry's (1985) SERVQUAL model, popularly known as American Model, views service quality as the gap between the expected level of service and customer perceptions of the level received. Whereas Gronroos (1982) suggests two dimensions, Parasuraman, Zeithaml, and Berry (1988) propose five dimensions, viz., the reliability, responsiveness, assurance, empathy, and tangibility characteristics of the service experience.

While these two themes have dominated the service quality literature, many modified versions of the SERVQUAL model have been proposed either by dropping expectations altogether (e.g., Cronin and Taylor, 1992), adding dimensions to the expectations portion of the model, such as "will" and "should" expectations (Boulding *et al.*, 1993), or employing alternative methodologies (such as conjoint analysis) to assess service quality perceptions (Carman, 2000).

Other researchers who have shown interest in Gronroos's (1984) technical and functional quality dimensions have also come out with alternative conceptualizations. Rust and Oliver (1994) for instance, have offered a three- component model: the service product (that is, technical quality), the service delivery (that is, functional quality), and the service environment.

Another theme relates to the structure of the service quality construct (Dabholkar, Thorpe, and Rentz, 1996). For example, Dabholkar, Thorpe and Rentz (1996) have identified and tested a hierarchical conceptualization of service quality that proposes three levels: (1) customers' overall perception of service quality, (2) primary dimensions, and (3) sub-dimensions. In other words, service quality is viewed as a higher-order factor that is determined by two lower levels of attributes.

The foregone discussion signifies that there is no universally accepted structure/model of service quality. Further, operational points of services marketing are so dynamic that whatever is applicable to retail may not be suitable to banking. This itself talks of the need for a study with respect to a specific industry and to add practical value to theoretical models/research carried out in the realm of services marketing literature.

RESEARCH METHODOLOGY

We adopted Dabholkar, Thorpe, and Rentz's (1996) idea that service quality perceptions are multilevel and multidimensional as such a structure takes a holistic view of the complexity of human perceptions (Carman, 1990). At the same time, it does not prefix the dimensions of service quality as in case of SERVQUAL or other schemes, thus providing for the scope of flexibility. To develop such a model for service quality in banking sector, identification of both primary dimensions and their sub-dimensions was required. Contrary to earlier approaches, we adopted a bottom-up approach in this regard, that is, we first focused on identification of sub-dimensions and then developed the primary dimensions based on them.

IDENTIFICATION OF SUB-DIMENSIONS

While many existing researches are helpful in identifying the primary dimensions of service quality (e.g., Gronroos, 1984; Parasuraman, Zeithaml, and Berry, 1985), little effort has been made to identify the factors that constitute these primary dimensions (Brady and Cronin, Jr., 2000). Therefore, the first activity carried out was to identify them.

A review of marketing literature reveals many examples of qualitative research being applied to clarify the domain of inquiry and to enable the development of precise hypotheses (e.g., Parasuraman, Zeithaml, and Berry, 1985; Bitner, Booms, and Mohr, 1994; Grove and Fisk, 1997; Harris, 1999). We used qualitative research to identify the factors customers consider while evaluating the quality of the services provided by a bank. For this purpose, first of all a thorough review of literature was carried out to discern the various aspects of service quality (e.g., Gronroos, 1982, Parasuraman, Zeithaml, and Berry, 1985; Baker, Grewal, and Parasuraman, 1994; Bitner, Booms, and Mohr, 1994; Brady and Cronin, Jr., 2000). Informal, unstructured interviews were then conducted with five branch managers, five academicians, and 30 bank customers selected at random at banks' premises. Based on the outcome of the interview process, 39 variables, which could have a bearing on banking service quality, were generated. Broadly, these variables focused on interpersonal interaction, service environment, facilities provided by the bank, service outcome, etc.

Using these 39 variables, a formal questionnaire focusing on the customer perceived importance of these variables was developed. Importance of each variable was measured on a nine-point scale, to enable respondents to make better discriminations (see Andrews, 1984) with 'unimportant' and 'important' as the anchors. The developed questionnaire was then pre-tested with 30 bank customers selected at random at banks' premises. This led to modifications in the questionnaire and finally a questionnaire with 29 variables was utilized to collect data.

In the course of interview and pre-testing, many customers and some managers talked about the service charges/price and interest rates charged. However, these were not included in the questionnaire as price/interest charged, which represents the sacrifice made by the customer, is a determinant of value of the service to the customer (Brady and Cronin, Jr., 2000) and should not be included in quality assessment (Dabholkar, Thorpe, and Rentz, 1996).

DATA COLLECTION

The study was limited to the city of Ludhiana, a major commercial center in North India. It was further restricted to the customers of private sector banks only. The rationale for the same can be sought in the fact that the private sector banks have existed in India only for last ten to twelve years. Most of their customers are those who have defected either from public sector banks or other private sector banks. Certainly, these customers are more service quality conscious and can better discriminate between more important and less important aspects of service quality. Therefore, inclusion of these customers in the sample will lead to more reliable and practicable findings. Further, only customers had been included in the sample because it is the customer only who knows the best—what he/she wants and what he/she gets.

Data collection was carried at the Feroze Gandhi Market, the banking hub of Ludhiana city. Data were collected by randomly selecting customers, who came to the bank premises to avail of banking services, by personally administering the questionnaire. A total of 200 customers were included in the sample. These customers are of various types, viz., saving bank account, current account, cash credit accounts, loan account, NRI/foreign currency account, and others. An effort was made to have nearly equal number of customers from each category. In case of current account, cash credit and some loan accounts, it was observed that the account holders themselves did not come to bank, but sent their employees or representatives. In such accounts, due care was taken that only the actual account-holders are contacted for data collection.

DATA ANALYSIS

The objective of the research was to develop a multilevel and multidimensional model of service quality in banking sector, which could be of utility to the practicing managers. As discussed earlier, a total of 29 variables related to banking service were studied. However, many of these variables could be correlated to each other. Also taking all these variables into one model would present, although exhaustive but a cumbersome and voluminous picture of little practical value. A more precise picture with independent variables affecting banking service quality would provide better insights. Therefore, the technique of factor analysis was utilised to reduce the original 29 variables into small number of synthetic variables, called factors (Tull and Hawkins, 1999), which would represent the primary dimensions of banking service quality. The factor loadings were extracted by using the method of principal components and rotated, for better interpretability, using varimax rotation (Singh and Singla, 1998). Finally, only those factors were retained which enjoyed Eigen Value of 1.00 at least. Further, only those variables were considered which had a factor loading of 0.5 minimum (Shenoy and Pant, 1994).

ANALYSIS AND DISCUSSION

The study was carried out with the objective of developing a banking service quality model, which could be of utility to practicing managers. Specifically, Dabholkar, Thorpe, and Rentz (1996) multidimensional-multilevel model of service quality which presents service quality as consisting of primary and secondary dimensions was adopted as a guiding principle for structuring the model under study. Consumer perceptions regarding the importance of 29 variables, which represent 'secondary dimensions' of banking service quality, were studied. The mean and standard deviation of the perceived importance of these variables have been presented in Annexure I.

As it was envisaged that many of these 29 variables could be overlapping, therefore, in order to develop a concise and clearer picture, the same were condensed into primary dimensions of service quality using factor analysis. Only those factors were retained which had Eigen value of 1.00 atleast. In addition only those variables were retained which enjoyed factor loading of 0.5 minimum. The details of the factors arrived at (primary dimensions) have been summarized in Table 1. Further, the factors have been discussed in decreasing order of the variance explained by them.

The factor 'Service time' explains 38.79% of the variance. As depicted, the variables which constitute this factor are 'banking hours', 'time taken in cash transactions', 'time taken in clearance of cheques', and 'timely information about services/changes'. As most of these variables are related to time taken in provision of services, the factor has been named as 'Service time'.

This factor, which accounts for the largest proportion of variance explained, is the most important primary dimension of banking service quality. Therefore, the managers should focus their maximum attention and effort on minimizing the time taken in provision of banking services and also try to offer longer banking hours.

The second most important factor influencing the banking service quality explains 25.02% of total variance. It consists of a number of variables namely, 'availability of staff', 'courteousness of staff', 'availability of branch manager', 'staff's knowledge about banking products/ services', 'grievance handling'. As all of these variables focus on interpersonal interaction of the bank's staff with the customer, the factor has been named as 'Interaction with the bank's staff'. This clearly indicates that customer no longer accepts the apathetic and non-professional attitude of the bank staff, which usually was the practice when number of banks was less and most of them were in the public sector. Therefore, the managers must be clear that the harmonious interpersonal relationships between the customers and the banking staff will play an important role in today's cut throat competition.

Apart from 'Service time' and 'Interaction with the bank's staff', ambience and infrastructural facilities play an important role in perception of service quality as 18.08% of total variance is explained by this factor. This 'Ambience and infrastructure' includes variables as 'spacious and uncluttered layout', 'location of bank', 'parking facility', 'branching network', 'technology used by the bank'. Evidently, the customers are not looking at just the core service but also towards the environment in the bank and the infrastructure.

Moreover, infrastructure has expanded from the concept of 'brick and mortar' to include technological networks, information sharing and modern information technology tools. Further, banks have now become the places to visit not only by the businessmen but almost every individual who does any commercial transaction. Therefore, the location of the bank needs to be convenient, fully visible and supported by adequate parking infrastructure.

The last in the series of factors influencing banking

TABLE I

Summary of Factor Analysis

Variable	*Factor 1*	*Factor 2*	*Factor 3*	*Factor 4*	*Factor Name*
Banking hours	0.824				Service time
Time taken in cash transactions	0.795				
Time taken in clearance of cheques	0.726				
Timely information about services/changes	0.571				
Availability of staff		0.752			Interaction with bank's staff
Courteousness of staff		0.741			
Availability of branch manager		0.685			
Staffs' knowledge about banking products/services		0.621			
Grievance handling		0.615			
Spacious and uncluttered layout			0.662		Ambience and infrastructure
Location of bank			0.613		
Parking facility			0.582		
Branching network			0.571		
Technology used by the bank			0.520		
Network of banking services				0.725	Services and banking channels
Facilities like ATM, lockers, kiosks				0.716	
Phone banking				0.681	
Additional benefits like free credit/ debit card, etc.				0.517	
Eigen Value	7.249	5.110	3.190	2.214	
Variance Explained	38.790	25.025	18.078	11.911	
Cumulative Variance Explained	38.790	63.815	81.893	93.804	

service quality explains 11.91% of total variance and has been named as 'Services and banking channels'. This factor which consists of 'network of banking services', 'facilities like ATM, lockers, kiosks', 'phone banking', 'additional benefits like debit card/credit card'. This shows that the banking in the current business scenario has become the center stage of all the monetary transactions. No longer it caters to the basic depositing and withdrawal of money, it now fulfils other needs like any time banking, investment needs, personal loans and convenience banking like ATM, net and phone banking. In order to attract and retain its customers, therefore, banks will have to provide these benefits to the customers.

CONCLUSIONS AND MANAGERIAL IMPLICATIONS

The last two decades of study, research and much lively debate on conceptual framework of service quality can best be described as divergent and chaotic. At the core of debate are two competing perspectives—Nordic and American schools and their extensions. Both perspectives highlight important aspects of service quality, but neither fully captures the construct. Moreover, all the available approaches are generalist and abstract in nature. As a result, the existing body of limited knowledge does not guide practicing managers to pinpoint the significant service dimensions. With little pieces of study as relevant to India, has led to the call for this research that reconsiders the various dimensions of service quality, as applicable to Indian banking service sector—one of the most vibrant service sectors.

We premise our research on the Dabholkar, Thorpe, and Rentz (1996) multilevel-multidimensional model of service quality which presents service quality as consisting of primary and secondary dimensions. Using qualitative research we identified secondary dimensions, primary dimensions were extracted from the secondary dimensions by applying factor analysis. The results show that banking service quality can best be described through four dimensions namely, 'Service time', 'Interaction with bank's staff', 'Ambience and infrastructure', and 'Services and banking channels.' These dimensions further comprise their sub-dimensions.

This model can greatly assist practicing managers in understanding how their customers assess the quality of service experiences and guide them in their endeavour to enhance customers' service experiences. With this kind of focused information managers not only can diagnose service failures but also can isolate their origins. Using this model, relative performance of organisational units across primary and secondary dimensions can also be tracked. From a competitive point of view the identified dimensions can be utilized to compare the service levels of competitors' offerings.

References

Andrews, F.M. (1984), "Construct Validity and Error Components of Survey Measures: A Structural Modeling Approach," *Public Opinion Quarterly*, 48, 409-42.

Baker, J., D. Grewal, and A. Parasuraman (1994), "The Influence of Service Environment in Quality Inferences and Store Image," *Journal of Academy of Marketing Science*, 22(4), 328-39.

Bitner, M.J., B.H. Booms, and L.A. Mohr (1994), "Critical Service Encounters: The Employee's View," *Journal of Marketing*, 58 (October), 95-106.

Boulding, W., A. Kalra, R. Staelin, and V.A. Zeithaml (1993), "A Dynamic Model of Service Quality: From Expectations to Behavioural Intentions," *Journal of Marketing Research*, 30 (February), 7-27.

Brady, M.K. and J.J. Cronin, Jr. (2001), "Some New Thoughts on Conceptualising Perceived Service Quality: A Hierarchical Approach," *Journal of Marketing*, 65 (July), 34-49.

Buzzel, R.D. and B.T. Gale (1987), *The PIMS Principles*. New York: The Free Press.

Dabholkar, P.C., D.I. Thorpe, and J.O. Rentz (1996), "A Measure of Service Quality for Retail Stores," *Journal of Academy of Marketing Science*, 24 (Winter), 3-16.

Ganesh, J, M.J. Arnold, and K.E. Reynolds (2000), "Understanding the Customer Base of Service Providers: An Examination of the Differences Between Switchers and Stayers," *Journal of Marketing*, 64 (July), 65-87.

Gronroos, C. (1984), "A Service Quality Model and its Marketing Implications," *European Journal of Marketing*, 18(4), 36-44.

Grove, S.J. and R.P. Fisk (1997), "The Impact of Other Customers on Service Experiences: A Critical Incident Examination of 'Getting Along'," *Journal of Retailing*, 73(1), 63-85.

Harris, C.L. (1999), "The Organisational Barriers to Developing Market Orientation," *European Journal of Marketing*, 34 (5-6), 598-624.

Parasuraman, A., V.A. Zeithaml, and L.L. Berry (1985), "A Conceptual Model of Service Quality and its Implications for Future Research," *Journal of Marketing*, 49 (Fall), 41-50.

Reicheld, F.F. (1996), "Learning from Customer Defections," *Harvard Business Review*, 74 (March/April), 56-69.

Reicheld, F.F. and W.E. Sasser, Jr. (1990), "Zero Defections: Quality Comes to Services," *Harvard Business Review*, 68 (September/October), 105-111.

Shenoy, G.V. and M. Pant (1994), *Statistical Methods in Business and Social Sciences*. New Delhi: Macmillan India Ltd.

Singh, P. and S.K. Singla (1998), "Performance of Mutual Funds: A Factor Analysis Approach," *Effective Management*, 8(1), 48-53.

Tull, D.S. and D.I. Hawkins (1999), *Marketing Research: Measurement and Method*, New Delhi: Prentice Hall of India.

ANNEXURE I

Mean and Standard Deviation of Perceived Importance of Variables Influencing Banking Service Quality

Variable	*Mean*	*Standard Deviation*
Banking hours	7.64	2.79
Time taken in cash transactions	7.22	2.77
Time taken in clearance of cheques	7.34	2.46
Time taken in issuance of drafts	6.76	2.81
Quick rectification of mistakes	5.84	3.03
Timely information about services/changes	7.02	2.61
Availability of staff	7.50	1.78
Courteousness of staff	5.70	2.84
Availability of branch manager	7.04	2.32
Staffs' knowledge about banking products/services	4.88	3.09
Grievance handling	7.04	2.16
Pleasant atmosphere in the bank	8.18	2.05
Spacious and uncluttered layout	7.88	2.46
Location of bank	6.44	2.48
Parking facility	6.26	2.34
Branching network	6.52	2.60
Technology used by the bank	7.18	2.33
Accessible and visible display of information	6.20	2.71
Network of banking services	5.90	2.45
Facilities like ATM, lockers, kiosks	7.30	2.58
Phone banking	7.32	1.90
Width of banking services/products	7.64	2.30
Additional benefits like free credit/debit card, etc.	7.02	2.55
Accurate handling of accounts	7.66	2.43
Extra effort by staff to resolve problems	5.76	3.62
Efficient and quick handling of phone calls	6.08	2.96
Electronic fund transfers	6.22	2.74
Provision of annual/quarterly statements	6.28	2.47
Safety of investments	5.22	2.32

CHAPTER

14

Performance of Indian Capital Market and Financial Reporting Tradeoffs

A Case for Corporate Governance

G.S. BATRA

The need for financial reporting arises to comply with the statutory requirements, public opinion and the logic of public accountability. The increasing importance of the corporate sector in the Indian economy has necessitated a complete and analytical disclosure of accounting information to the various interested parties. The capital market, which is one of the very important segments of the Indian financial system, has of late helped in the spectacular performance of its corporate Sector. There has been a vast increase in the number and type of capital issues, capital raised and the market capitalization in the Indian capital market.

The investment in the capital market is being seen as a trade off of so many factors like risk, return, safety, liquidity and marketability. The investment decisions are being guided by the disclosure of information in the prospectus and the financial reporting by the companies. The common investor which represents vast Indian population has become much more mature. It is not only the investor but also the various stakeholders and users of the accounting information like lenders, creditors, suppliers, government, financial analysts, brokers, stock exchanges and trade associations who have become much more interested in the disclosure of information by the corporations.

Keeping in view its GDP growth rate and performance in the stock market, India is being considered as a powerful engine of growth. Nonetheless there are vast market imperfections like lack of adequate regulation of the corporate securities market and its integration with the International capital markets. The availability of the desired financial information through corporate financial reporting is also being considered as a key factor in the efficient allocation of limited resources. Since the Corporate disclosures in India as well as in the number of other emerging economies is being governed by various capital market developments and market imperfections, therefore, an attempt has been made here in this paper to analyze the financial reporting and capital market trade offs.

I. INTRODUTION

The need for financial reporting arises to comply with the statutory requirements, public opinion and the logic of public accountability. The increasing importance of the corporations in the Indian economy has necessitated a complete and analytical disclosure of accounting information to various interest groups. The Public interest in the efficient operation and conduct of corporate enterprises has been increasing and, therefore, it expects that the management as the trustee and custodian of public funds should make adequate corporate disclosures in an appropriate manner to investors, creditors, consumers, government and the public at large so as to fully satisfy them as to the working and performance of the corporations in which they have or they intend to invest money. However, the accountability of the government owned corporations is much more wide because of massive public money invested in these corporations and the poor rate of return on Investment. Therefore, the objectives of financial reporting in these set of corporations is aimed at attaining the following objectives:

(a) to comply with the various statutory requirements,
(b) to make available the interested parties the desired information and details as to the activities and achievements of the corporations for the period under review,
(c) to highlight clearly the policies and programs of the corporations, and
(d) to indicate in absolute terms the efficiency, performance and skill within which the corporations have been working.

There are inter-linkages between the capital market structure and the regulatory framework for governance of the Indian Corporate Sector. The reform process in the capital market started in India since 1991-92 has certainly improved the performance of the Capital Market and strengthened its regulatory framework, which in turn has a bearing on the corporate financial reporting by the corporations in India. The Indian Corporate sector has started realizing the need for adequate corporate disclosures in order to repose the confidence of the stakeholders in the working of their enterprises and performance in the stock market (Sharma and Batra 2000).

The integration of Indian financial markets at the global level also requires convergence to global standards of transparency and financial reporting. Another important issue is that while developed economies have performed well on the whole in the globalized financial structure, the emerging economies faced lot of volatility in the financial markets.

The Asian Crisis of 1997-98 affected all emerging markets open to capital flows (Johnson, Boone, Breach and Friedman 2001). The South East Asian economies faced financial crisis during 1997 period where as India as one of the regulated market performed well and remained largely unaffected by the capital market volatility and the flight of capital. This indicates that in order to truly integrate the

Indian Capital Market with the global financial structure, there is a need for strengthening its accountability regime and ensuring the adequate corporate disclosures by corporate enterprises.

In this paper an attempt has been made to analyze the Performance of the Corporate Securities Market and financial reporting trade-offs. This study is based on the data collected from various Published sources. In the section 2 review of previous research has been made. In section 3 motivations behind carrying out this study have been given. The section 4 deals with a brief overview of the economic potential of India as an emerging market and the performance of corporate securities market. In section 5, an attempt has also been made to study the framework of corporate financial reporting and disclosure practices. In the section 6 summary and conclusions have been given.

2. PREVIOUS RESEARCH

Some studies have already been conducted in India and abroad covering different aspects of Corporate Financial Reporting. A brief overview of these studies has been given here in this section.

An analysis of financial reporting practices prevalent in India was made to examine the various practices adopted in this regard. It was suggested that statements of highlights, summarized balance sheet and profit and loss account, narrative Statements, statistical records, diagrams and charts should be included in annual reports so as to make these reports more informative and to serve the increasing needs of their Users (Gupta, 1977).

The disclosure of financial and non-financial information in the annual reports of 40 public sector enterprises on the basis of index of disclosure consisting of 35 items indicated that there are vast differences in the quality of disclosure made by the sample companies (Singh and Bhargva, 1978).

The disclosure practices of Manufacturing Companies in the Private sector during the period 1965-75 covering a broad range of 50 items for measuring the extent and quality of disclosure in annual reports of selected companies indicated that over a period of ten years, there has been an improvement in the disclosure quality during the period under study (Lal, 1985).

A comparison of financial reporting practices in United Kingdom and India; firstly by examining influences on accounting practices in the two countries and secondly by comparing the actual accounting practices and the level of disclosure of information in financial reports was carried out in this study. The study concluded that since early times most of India was administered directly by United Kingdom, therefore, the accounting and financial reporting practices were largely based on United Kingdom model, although since independence significance differences have arisen. On the basis of his study he concluded that the overall disclosure in the United Kingdom was greater than as compared to India (Marston, 1986).

A study on Industrial giants in India points out that certain items like ratios, budgeting forecast, etc. were not disclosed by majority of Indian Corporation. He gave various suggestions and asserted that if these were implemented, these would go a long way in making disclosure more meaningful for the users of financial statements (Man Mohan, 1986).

A study of 45 Indian Companies to evaluate the relationship of quality of disclosures and various company characteristics concluded that the companies having large shareholding base and the higher rate of return have better quality of disclosure (Saeed, 1990).

A study on the pattern of preparing the annual report by the public limited companies pointed out that the size of annual reports of companies varies from company to company and the arrangement of Statutory material and non-statutory material was in sequence in case of the reports under study (Rathod, 1990)

A corporate analysis of the disclosure practices of the public and private sector giants in India for the period 1980-81 to 1984-85 concluded that the quality of disclosure both item wise and company wise is significantly better in case of public sector as compared to private sector. A large number of items have very low disclosure score in both the public sector and private sector during all the five years under study. However, there has been improvement in the disclosure practices of public and private sector giants in 1984-85 over 1980-81 (Chander, 1992).

In a comparative study of financial reporting in Britain and Australia, various reporting practices and standards were examined. The study concluded that the legislative enactments in both the countries require annual presentation by companies and the copies of annual accounts are required to be filed with the Registrar of companies in Britain and with various State Corporate Commissions in Australia (Standish, 1994).

The disclosure requirements in Germany are stringent for public companies and there is increased uniformity in the preparation of financial statements by companies. The directives of the European Economic Community on corporate financial reporting have been included in the German Publicity laws (Macharzing, 1994).

In a study on corporate published accounting information and investors, a vast gap was found between the information supplied by companies in their annual reports and the investor needs. The study suggested that the managements of the companies should be broad based and must insist on the incorporation of statutory and non-statutory information in the corporate reports (Bhattar, 1994).

The corporate reporting practices of public enterprises of Madhya Pradesh with reference to extent of disclosure, timelines and readability indicates that the disclosure of information in state level public enterprises is very scanty and delayed and even the guidelines of the bureau of public enterprises and state Government were not adhered to. The study itself revealed the gaps in the sphere of extent of reporting, quantum of reporting, various time lags and readability aspects. The study clearly revealed that the management has ignored its social and statutory obligations regarding disclosure requirements (Meena, 1995).

A study made to assess the degree of compliance by the Indian Companies with the disclosures requirements under the existing listing agreements pointed out that most of the Indian Companies do prepare interim reports in time. However, most of them do not release this information for publication within the prescribed time and the SEBI should exercise its powers as a statutory body. There is need of concerted efforts on the part of law enactment and law enforcement agencies and the development of a voluntary disclosure culture to improve the overall investment climate in the country (Vasal, 1997).

In a study on financial reporting practices of local authorities in two different economies—the UK and Malaysia indicated that there is a significant difference in the accounting disclosure practices in the two set of countries. The comparative development of local authority accounting in the two different countries studied is very much influenced by the level of interest expressed by the central/state authorities, professional bodies and user groups (Coombs and Tayib, 1998).

The measures of corporate governance particularly the effectiveness of protection for shareholders explain the extent of exchange rate depreciation and stock market decline better than do standard macroeconomic measures. The countries with weak corporate governance and worse economic prospects result in more expropriation by managers and thus a larger fall in asset prices (Johnson, Boone, Breach and Friedman, 2000).

The investor's requirements in the light of the present reporting practices of companies for the period 1989-96 to 1993-94 pointed out that there exists wide variation in the reporting of statutory and non-statutory items of information. The companies under study disclosed the statutory information like profit and loss account; Balance sheet, Director's report; Auditor's report, etc. and only a very small number of companies disclosed the non-voluntary disclosure. As far as investor's requirements are concerned, he concluded that the annual reports which have been considered most important and significant media of disclosure have been used by very less number of investors while making financial decisions (Ubha, 2001).

A discussion focus on the empirical Voluntary disclosure literature assumes that the same forces that shape firms' governance structures and management incentives endogenously determine firms' disclosure policies. In this study corporate finance theory has been used to expand and provide an alternative analysis of the voluntary disclosure literature (Core, 2001).

There is a need for reduction of information asymmetry in order to build a starting point for a comprehensive theory of disclosure which is basically a vehicle to integrate the efficiency of disclosure choice, the incentives to disclose and the endogeneity of the capital market process as it involves the interrelations among individual and diverse investors (Verrecchia, 2001).

Financial reporting and disclosures are potentially important means for management to communicate firm performance and governance to outside investors. A framework for analyzing managers reporting and disclosure decisions in a capital market setting indicates that the globalization of capital markets has been accompanied by calls for globalization of financial reporting (Healy and Palepu, 2001).

In a study on empirical investigation of the true and fair view, a survey of financial directors, auditors and shareholders of Newzeland listed companies were conducted to know their preferences and perceptions for true and fair view *versus* other standards for financial statements. The results show that a clear majority of all three groups share similar perceptions of the meaning of true and fair view to other items including fairly present in conformity with GAAP, result consistent with previous comparisons of UK and USA investor's opinions. This indicates that the true and fair view remains an important international overall standard for financial reporting quality (Kirk, 2001).

A study relating to financial reporting framework for intangibles in Australia provides that the Australian GAAP leaves corporate managers wide discretion to capitalize intangibles assets irrespective of whether the assets are acquired or generated internally. Evidence to date suggests that Australian equity markets are no less efficient than US markets (Wyatt, 2002).

The above review of studies indicates that some studies

have been made in India with reference to Financial Reporting but none of the works carried out analyzed the Capital market and Financial Reporting trade offs. Hence the proposed study.

3. MOTIVATION

The corporate financial reporting is a system of communication between the management and the user of the financial statements in order to report the performance and activities and to highlight the accountability and credibility of its working. There has been a lot of controversy about the accuracy, authenticity, reliability and transparency of the financial reports of the corporations. The disclosure of financial information benefits various users of the financial statements such as lenders, suppliers, creditors, customers, employees, financial analysts, brokers, underwriters, stock exchange authorities, Government, reporting agencies and trade associations, etc.

The corporations closely link the capital market performance with the extent, quality and timeliness of disclosure. The increasing trend towards liberalization and globalization demands increased financial market integration and the convergence to global accounting standards. Therefore, it is not only important for the corporations to be transparent, accountable and socially responsible but also to ensure adequate returns to the shareholders and satisfy various stakeholders and society at large about their conduct. The growth of corporate sector in India has been accompanied by cases of mismanagement, shareholders dissatisfaction and cases of vanishing companies (Department of Company Affairs, 2000).

Various regulatory bodies of the government like the Department of company Affairs and Securities and Exchange Board of India have adopted certain legislative measures and issued guidelines for governance of the corporations. At the same time it is being felt that in the long-run, the legislative interventions should be minimum leaving adoption of such measures on voluntary basis subject to the demand of market forces and various externalities. Therefore, in this paper an attempt has been made to study the tradeoffs between performance of Indian corporate securities market and financial reporting by corporations. This study is an attempt toward building a case for adequate corporate disclosures by Indian corporations, which in turn has implications for improved performance and efficiency of the Capital market structure.

4. INDIA'S EMERGING MARKET POTENTIAL AND THE PERFORMANCE OF CORPORATE SECURITIES MARKET

The India adopted a policy of self-reliance on the eve of independence, which included protecting the home industry and import substitution. The other important planks of the economic policy at that time were export promotion, promotion of the public Sector and the greater role of the state in the commercial and business ventures. Over a period of five decades of its development, India has emerged as a mature and dynamic business market. It accounts for 2.4% of the world surface area and Supports 16.7% of the world population. The population of India as on March1, 2002 crossed one billion and was enumerated at 1.027 billion (Indian Census, 2001). As a fast developing industrial economy, India has the potential of emerging as a separate trading block in the Asia-Pacific region. Given the availability of vast natural and physical resources, the entrepreneurial instincts of the people and the new economic policy regime, Indian Economy is bound to perform well in the different Sectors. In its bid to open up the country's economy, the Government of India has geared up its Corporate Sector to meet the growing economic challenges, which the economy is likely to face (Batra, G.S., 2001). The other economic policy changes include trade sector reforms, industrial sector reforms and agriculture and the infrastructure sector reforms. India's strong democracy, stable polity, consensus of economic reforms, a good legal System, competitive private sector and the growing skilled manpower makes India an economic opportunity. The average economic growth during the ninth five-year economic plan 1997-2002 was estimated at 5.4%, which is lower than the plan target of 6.5%. This deviation has posed a challenge for ensuring much better growth in the Tenth Five Year Plan. However, the Indian Economy has not been adversely affected much due to external factors such as East-Asian Crisis of 1997, Oil price increase of 2000-01 and the global economic slow down (Economic Survey, 2001-02).

The various macro economic parameters indicate that the overall growth rate of 5.5% is supported by a growth rate of 5.7% in agriculture and allied sectors, 3.3% in industry and 6.5% in services. The wholesale price index was recorded at 4.7% in January 2002. The balance of Payment position remained reasonably stable during 2000-01 and 2001-02. The current account deficit as a% of GDP declined from 1.1% in 1999-2000 to 0.5% in 2000-01 due to better export performance. The exports grew by 19.6% in 2000-01 as compared to 9.5% in the previous year and imports recorded a moderate growth rate of 7% during 2000-01 much lower than the previous year, i.e. 16.5%. The export policy 2002 announced dismantling of the Quantitative restrictions on exports to give a boost to the agricultural and industrial exports' (Export Policy, 2002).

4.1 Performance of Securities Market

The Capital Market Reforms have given a much-needed boost to the financial institutions, capital market and the inflow of funds through the channel of foreign direct and foreign institutional investment. The resource mobilization from the primary market by way of public issue and right issue was Rs. 28.58 billion and Rs. 9.19 billion respectively during 2000-01. The percentage of the funds raised through equity and debt issues were 5% and 95% respectively, which indicate about the growing debt market in India. The turnover in the derivative products in the National Stock Exchange and the Bombay Stock Exchange was Rs. 138.91 billion and Rs. 10.89 billion during April-December, 2001 (Economic Survey, 2001-01 and SEBI Annual Reports).

As per Table 1 of the 93 issues during 1999-2000, 28 were right issues which entered the market for raising Rs. 15.60 billion while during 1998-99, 26 issues out of 58 issues were right issues for Rs. 5.67 billion. Total of 65 public issues entered the market for raising Rs. 62.56 billion during

1999-2000 while during 1998-99, 32 public issues raised Rs. 50.19 billion. In terms of percentage increase, public issues were higher by about 25 per cent, whereas rights issues nearly tripled from Rs. 5.67 billion during 1998-99 to Rs. 15.60 billion, i.e. an increase of 175 per cent during the year under review (SEBI Annual Report, 1999-00). The growth recorded as to the amount raised through rights issues led to an increase in the share of right issues from 10 per cent to 20 per cent reflecting that the issuers are increasingly relying on the existing shareholders to meet requirement of additional capital for growth or diversification of their business activities.

TABLE I

Capital Raised from the Securities Market

(Rs. Billion)

	Number of Issues and Amount						% increase/decrease Type of Issue		
	1997-98		1998-99		1999-2000		1997-98	1998-99	1999-2000
	No.	Rs.	No.	Rs.	No.	Rs.			
Public	62	28.61	32	50.18	65	62.56	-75.2	75.4	24.66
Right	49	17.08	26	5.67	28	15.60	-37.2	-66.8	174.90
Total	111	45.69	58	55.85	93	78.16	-67.9	22.2	39.92

Source: Securities and Exchange Board of India, Annual Reports, 1997-2000.

During 1999-2000, the listed companies mobilized Rs. 50.97 billion through 42 issues as compared to Rs. 51.82 billion mobilized through 40 capital issues during 1998-99 registering a marginal decline of nearly 2 per cent. As per Table 2, however, there was a marked increase in the number of IPOs during 1999-2000 to 51 from 18 IPOs issued during 1998-99. In terms of amount, IPOs mobilized Rs. 27.19 billion during 1999-2000 as compared to an amount of Rs. 4.04 billion during 1998-99 (SEBI Annual Report, 1999-00).

The vast increase in IPOs and their subscription indicates the increase in confidence of investors to invest in new companies in information technology and healthcare sector, which entered the market in a big way. The average size of an issue of IPO was half billion, smaller than the average size of Rs. 1.21 billion for listed companies during 1999-2000 because of a larger number of small size new companies entering the market. In terms of percentage, IPOs accounted for 35 per cent during 1999-2000 as compared to a share of 7 per cent during 1998-99. An increase in the share of IPOs proves that the investment pattern is changing towards new enterprises with latest Information technology (SEBI Annual Report 1999-00). As a result of the above, the entry of new companies with IPOs on a fast pace is expected to provide fresh equity for trading in the secondary market also.

TABLE 2

Listed and IPO Issues

(Rs. Billion)

	No. and Amount						*% Increase/Type of*	
	1999-00	*1998-99*	*1997-98*	*1999-2000*	*1998-99*		*Decrease*	*Issue*
	No.	*Rs.*	*No.*	*Rs.*	*No.*	*Rs.*		
Listed	42	50.97	40	51.82	59	35.22	-1.63	47.12
IPOs	51	27.19	18	4.04	52	10.47	572.68	-61.41
Total	93	78.16	58	55.86	101	45.69		

Source: Securities and Exchange Board of India, Annual Reports, 1997-2000.

The private sector companies mobilized maximum amount of capital during 1999-2000. The total amount of Rs. 76.03 billion through 90 issues was mobilized by the companies in the private sector during 1999-2000 which formed 97 per cent of total capital mobilized as compared to Rs. 54.83 billion mobilized through 55 issues accounting for 98 per cent during 1998-99. The public sector raised Rs. 2.00 billion through 2 issues during 1999-2000 as against 1 issue for Rs. 0.70 billion by the public sector during 1998-99. The resource mobilization was, however, maximum during this period by the private sector (SEBI Annual Report 1999-00).

The amount allotted on the basis of firm allotment was Rs. 2.02 billion during 1999-2000 as compared to Rs. 1.42 billion during the previous year. The total capital raised through firm allotment during 1999-00 indicates that the non resident indians got the highest share of Rs. 0.75 billion followed by promoters with Rs. 0.48 billion, employees with Rs. 0.34 billion and others with Rs. 0.16 billion, Financial Institution with Rs. 0.16 billion and mutual funds with Rs. 0.11 billion. The Foreign Institutional Investors could raise only about Rs. 0.01 billion whereas money market funds could not mobilize any amount from the capital market (SEBI Annual Report, 1999-00).

The various capital Market reforms have been undertaken to promote efficiency, transparency, safety and stability in the capital market. All the above indicators point out that India is one of the vast emerging market capable of raising vast resources from the capital market. Despite its vast economic potential, the efficiency in the real sectors of the Indian Economy have remained poor. The investor's confidence from home and abroad has eroded. The overall performance and the capacity utilization of the industrial sector has not been as projected. There has been lack of transparency and the poor disclosure of information in the corporate sector, which has a strong bearing on the performance of the corporate securities market.

5. CORPORATE FINANCIAL REPORTING AND DISCLOSURES IN INDIA

The objective of corporate financial reporting is to disclose the information about the resources and performance of the enterprise to various stakeholders. In a constant changing environment, it is very difficult to fix the objectives of corporate financial reporting as the objectives are not only limited to measurement of economic and financial performance of the company. The International Accounting Standard Committee has given framework for the Corporate Financial Reporting. According to it, corporate financial reporting includes showing the results of the stewardship of management or the accountability of management for resources entrusted to it (IASC, 1919).

The Corporate Financial Reporting is of great significance in the accomplishment of financial accounting objectives and in contributing to the efficient allocation of resources through sound economic decisions. The financial reporting framework in this study is supposed to be analyzed with reference to corporate sector in India; hence it is of significance to highlight the growth of corporate sector in India.

5.1 Growth of Corporate Sector

A glance at the table 3 indicates about the growth of corporate sector otherwise described/named as Companies in India. The number of working companies as on Feb. 28, 2002 stood at 5,91,036, of which 5,87,557 were companies limited by shares and 2995 companies limited by guarantee. The table indicates that the Private sector accounts for the 90% of the companies incorporated till date.

TABLE 3

Number of Working Companies in India

Category of Companies	*Govt./Non-Govt.*	*Public/Private*	*Number of Companies*
Companies Limited by Shares	Govt.	Public	658
		Private	603
	Non-Govt.	Public	75595
		Private	510701
	Sub-Total		587557
Guarantee Companies	Govt.		5
	Non-Govt.		2995
Unlimited Liability Companies			479
Total			5,91,036

Source: Government of India, Department of Company Affairs, 2002

5.2 Financial Reporting and Disclosure Practices

As Corporations have multiplied in number and size, correspondingly the supply of the capital and the risk taking have also increased manifold. This has created a considerable public interest in business activity among shareholders, lenders, creditors, employees, customers, government authorities and the general public which in turn has caused business enterprises to accept social, economic, financial and legal responsibilities and a growing need for the communication of information to account for results which are of considerable interest to the various stakeholders. The financial reporting is not an end itself but is intended to provide information that is useful in making business and economic decisions.

As the corporate performance is influenced by the micro and macro-aspects of the business environment in the different set of situations, in the same way financial reporting is affected by the economic, technological legal, political, and social environment of corporations in which they have to function.

The primary focus of financial reporting is to disclose the information about earnings and its components. The studies conducted by Allan R. Cerf (1961) and Copeland and Frederick (1968) researched the issues relating to corporate reporting and investments decisions and measuring corporate disclosure respectively.

The accounting policies of companies have a tremendous impact on the resulting financial statements. In some accounting areas, managers are relatively free to choose from among several competing alternatives. In such a case, equity investment decision is seriously affected unless the user knows the accounting policies followed during a period and changes introduced therein. Thus, accounting policy disclosure at the same time help the financial statement reader in interpretation of operational results and financial position. It also reveals the uniqueness of accounting practices followed by the corporations.

A glance at the annual reports of Corporations indicates that the large number of items of information is not presented in the corporate annual reports. Such items are various efficiency and liquidity ratios like current ratio, quick ratio, inventory turnover; dividend ratios such as dividend per share, dividend payout ratio; Profitability ratios such as gross profit to sales, net profit to sales, earning per share and rate of return on investment or return on capital employed; financial statements such as statement of gross profit, net profit, sales, net worth; capital investments such as capital expenditure budgeted for next year; data about performance budgeting, share held by directors, human resources accounting; capital, labour and machine productivity; information on number of employees, sales turnover, production Performance; inflation-adjusted accounts; cash flow statement; statement of sources and application of fund and cash budget forecasts, etc. The information presented under accounting ratios is piecemeal. The accounting ratios are a powerful tool of analysis of financial performance. The investors while making investment decisions attach importance to earning per share, dividend payout ratio, net profit ratio, gross profit ratio and return on investment ratio.

The disclosure practices have improved in government owned corporations in India. The concept of disclosure has grown and expanded considerably in diverse ways in response to the evolution of corporate form of business organization and the statutory requirements of Indian Companies Act 1956 to prevent fraud and manipulation and to protect innocent shareholders and/or would be investors, and also on account of emergence of accounting and auditing as a recognized profession and convergence to global accounting standards.

There are statutory requirements to disclose the information relating to profit or loss and state of financial affairs in profit and loss account and Balance Sheet respectively (Indian Companies Act, 1956).

It is worth noting that inspite of the efforts on the part of corporate management to improve the purposefulness of the annual reports; there are many users of these published corporate annual reports that continue to show their dissatisfaction with the overall quality and quantity of disclosure expressed therein. The presentations of Corporate Financial Reporting have undergone vital changes from time to time. The micro and macro-aspects of environmental forces have shaped new face of corporate financial reporting in terms of issue of accounting standards and strengthening of the corporate governance over the corporations. To make the corporate report more useful to the users, the same should include the inflation Accounting, Human Resource Accounting, Social Accounting, Environmental Accounting, Values Added Accounting and the extent of convergence to Accounting standards.

The financial reporting practices in India are reflected by the Annual Reports prepared by the companies both in the public and private sector. A glance at the Table 4 indicates the type of information disclosed in the annual reports of companies. The statutory requirements of the company Act 1956 are to disclose only the financial information as at the end of a particular period. The profit and Loss Account and Balance Sheet, Auditors Report, Directors Report and Schedules and Notes are prepared and disclosed by the all corporations as per statutory requirements.

TABLE 4

Type of Disclosures made by Corporate Enterprises

1. Profit and Loss Account
2. Balance Sheet
3. Director's reports
4. Auditor's reports
5. Schedules and Notes
6. Statement of sources and applications of funds
7. Cash Flow Statement
8. Statement of Company Highlights
9. Statement of Accounting Policies
10. Accounting Ratios
11. Inflation Accounting
12. Value-Added Statement
13. Social Accounting
14. Human Resource Accounting
15. Environment Accounting
16. Chairman's Speech
17. List of Directors
18. Statement Relating to Subsidiary Companies

A study in this regard indicates that these items are considered less useful by the investors as compared to accounting ratios while taking investment decisions. The cash flow statement and the Statement of Sources and Applications of Funds is disclosed insignificantly by the corporations though these have been made mandatory recently (Ubha, 2001). The disclosure of information as to Human Resource Accounting, Social Accounting and Environment Accounting, Value added Accounting and preparation of various reports highlighting about the company performance is voluntary in nature.

The above items are relevant to the investors and various users of accounting information in making investment decisions. The relevance of information to users' decision-making is being considered as information selection parameter. These items of information are quite helpful in understanding the past and present performance and future plans of the corporations.

5.3. Corporate Securities Market and Financial Reporting Trade-offs

The Securities market in India has a long history. The Bombay stock exchange as one of the oldest and the first stock exchange established in India has its roots in brokers coming together in the 1860's to trade in shares issued by various companies. The informal group of brokers gradually grew into stock exchanges of which Bombay Stock Exchange established in 1875 is one of the oldest Stock Exchange. The raising of capital from the securities market was free from controls until the Second World War when the Defense of India rules were introduced which imposed the severe restrictions on the issue of capital. The controls on capital issues were incorporated in 1947 (Capital Issue Control Act, 1947).

The government at that time followed the policy of giving predominance to public sector, which in fact did not access the securities market significantly. At the same time the Private Enterprises were restricted from investing in response to market forces by a system of industrial licensing. Their access to capital market was restricted through the institution of CCI and their debt requirements were met through loans from nationalized banks and from public sector development banks. The regime of administered interest rate also did not offer many incentives to access the securities markets for debt. As a result of the limits on the role of the private sector and the issue of securities by it, Indian securities market did not develop in consonance with the growth in the rest of country. The trading and settlement infrastructure remained poor and the market intermediaries were largely unregulated. The disclosure requirements were inadequate and of an *adhoc* nature and there was no apex authority for regulation of the securities market.

A peep in to the past would be adequately helpful in understanding the linkages between Corporate Securities market and Financial Reporting. The broad picture of securities market before liberalization (Sharma and Batra, 2000) could be described as under:

(1) Fragmented regulation and multiplicity of administering agencies.
(2) Primary markets not in to the mainstream of financial system.
(3) Poor disclosure in prospectus.
(4) Problems of refund and transfer delays, etc.
(5) Stock exchanges regulated through Securities Contract Regulation Act.
(6) Stock exchanges run as brokers clubs and the management of stock exchange dominated by brokers.
(7) Merchant bankers and other intermediaries unregulated.
(8) No concept of capital adequacy.
(9) Mutual funds virtually unregulated with potential for conflicts of interest in structure.
(10) Poor disclosure by mutual funds, Net Asset Value not published and no valuation norms.
(11) Takeovers regulated only through listing agreement between the stock exchange and the company.
(12) No prohibition of insider trading and fraudulent and unfair trade practices.

Though India has a long history of stock exchanges, the

securities market really emerged from the periphery into the mainstream of the country's financial system only after 1991 when the era of economic reforms started in the country.

In order to have orderly development of securities market, the Government Budget 1987-88 provided for the establishment of a regulatory body of stock exchanges and securities market namely Securities Exchange Board of India. Initially in April 1988 by a notification it was constituted as an interim administrative body to function under the overall administrative control of the Ministry of Finance of the Central Government. It is only in April 1992, it became a statutory body after enactment of Securities Exchange Board of India Act (SEBI Act, 1992). The basic objectives of the SEBI are:

1. to protect the interest of investors in securities market,
2. to promote the development of the securities market,
3. to regulate the securities market, and
4. to provide for the matters connected with or incidental to the aforesaid purposes.

In India SEBI is the primary body responsible for the regulation of the securities market. SEBI derives its powers of registration and enforcement primarily from SEBI Act. (Sharma and Batra, 2000). Earlier there was a regulatory framework for the Securities market provided by Securities Contract Regulation Act, 1956 and now most of the powers and functions under the Security Contract Regulation Act have been delegated to the Securities and Exchange Board of India. The Ministry of Finance controls the SEBI whereas the Department of Company Affairs is controlled by the Ministry of Law, Justice and company affairs of the Government of India.

In addition to registration and regulation of intermediaries, service providers, mutual funds, collective investment schemes, venture capital funds, regulating takeovers, prohibiting insiders' trading and fraudulent practices, SEBI is also empowered to issue directions to any person or persons related to the securities markets or companies in the matter of issue of capital, transfer of securities and disclosures (SEBI Act, 1992).

The Department of company affairs administers the Companies Act, 1956, which is the cornerstone for corporate governance in India (Report on Corporate Excellence through Governance, 2000).

The powers under the Companies Act are to grant incorporation of companies, act against issuers for violations related to issue of capital and also includes regulation of the companies as to corporate governance and inspecting the companies' affairs.

The Bureau of Public Enterprises has issued guidelines from time to time for presentation of accounts by public sector undertakings (Bureau of Public Enterprises, 1990-2000).

The Institute of Chartered Accountant has issued so far only three accounting standards as to corporate disclosure by companies in India (ICAI, 2001). These are as following:

AS 1 Disclosure of Accounting Policies
AS 17 Segment Reporting
AS 25 Interim Financial Reporting

The awareness of and the interest in the investment opportunities in the securities markets and the need for adequate corporate disclosures have grown significantly in recent years. This awareness and interest in it has However, not resulted into a committed, confident and growing pool of investors. Some of the main constraining factors have been the high volatility in the market prices, lack of adequate disclosures, several undesirable practices and the structural inadequacies, which have led to an erosion of investor's confidence. At the same time, this has infact affected the desired growth of the securities market.

Another important development in India has been the mobilization of resources from the capital market by the new economy stock of the information technology sector, which alone accounted for a share of more than 20 per cent in the total funds mobilized. Several factors which includes adequate disclosures by the corporations, regulation of corporate securities market by Securities and Exchange Board of India and the regulation of Companies by Company Law Board and the Accounting Standard Board of the Institute of Chartered Accountants of India have contributed and accelerated the growth and Performance of the corporate sector and the Securities Market in India. The performance of the capital market is being increasingly influenced by the quantum and quality of disclosures by the corporate sector in India.

5.4 Case for Corporate Disclosure

The increased awareness and active interest being taken by the shareholders in the disclosures by the corporations, an increase in the number of corporate failures, pressure on the regulators to provide an environment to protect the interest of shareholders and awareness on the part of corporations to become competitive and global has led to a need for creating a congenial environment by the corporations, regulators, directors and management of Corporations in order to ensure accountability to various stakeholders.

It is not only important for the corporations to be transparent, accountable, socially responsible and ethical but also ensure adequate returns to the shareholders and satisfy the various stakeholders and society at large about their conduct. The growth of corporate sector has been accompanied by cases of mismanagement, shareholders dissatisfaction and cases of vanishing companies. Various regulatory bodies like the Department of company Affairs and Securities and Exchange Board of India have taken the legislative measures and issued guidelines for governance of the corporations. At the same time it is being felt that in the long-run, the legislative interventions should be minimum leaving adoption of such measures on voluntary basis subject to the demand of market forces. The listed companies should publish their annual reports and accounts in a desired format for circulation of these to various stakeholders. The returns with the Registrar of companies and SEBI/Stock exchanges shall be displayed by listed companies and by SEBI and stock exchanges on their respective web sites. The Chief Executive Officer and the Financial Controller of all public listed and unlisted companies should provide a statement in each annual report to shareholders about financial matters that the financial statements have been prepared in accordance with the accepted accounting standards and practices and explaining the reasons as to deviations emerging from set standards and practices at large. The statutory auditors should be required to qualify their audit certification and the audit committees should be free to disclose any concerns affecting the shareholders in their reports to the shareholders (Department of Company Affairs, 2000). All these measures are expected to lead to an increased accountability of the corporations to the stakeholders and various regulatory bodies.

6. SUMMARY AND CONCLUSIONS

The financial reporting practices have improved in corporate enterprises in India. The concept of disclosure has grown and expanded in diverse ways in response to the evolution of corporate form of business organizations and the statutory requirements of Indian Companies Act, 1956, the enactment of securities and exchange Board of India Act, 1992 and also on account of emergence of accountancy and auditing as a distinct profession.

It is worth noting that inspite of the efforts on the part of corporate management to improve the meaningfulness of the annual reports; there are many users of these published corporate annual reports that continue to show their dissatisfaction with the overall quality and quantity of disclosure expressed therein. More specific deficiencies are inadequate disclosure of pertinent data, lack of uniform employment of alternative approximation methods and lack of sufficient voluntary disclosures.

The rapid growth of the business and industry has led to the vast expansion in the supply of capital through capital market. The capital market in turn by providing investment opportunities has helped in directing the flow of funds to those corporations, which can make use of it more effectively. The availability of the desired financial information through corporate financial reporting is being increasingly recognized as a key factor in the efficient allocation of limited resources.

The capital market, which is one of the very important sectors of its financial market, has helped in the spectacular performance of the corporate Sector after start of the liberalization process in the country since 1991-92. There has been vast increase in the number and types of capital issues, capital raised and the equity base in the capital market. The common investor which represents vast Indian population has become much more mature. The investment in the capital market is being seen as a trade off of so many factors like risk, return, safety, liquidity and marketability. The investment decisions are being guided by the disclosure of information in the prospectus and the financial reports of the companies. It is not only the investor but also the various stakeholders and users of the accounting information like lenders, creditors, suppliers, government, financial analysts, brokers, stock exchanges and trade associations who have become more interested in the disclosure of information by corporations.

In the liberalized economic regime, the new perspectives in corporate financial reporting have given a new dimension to the corporate enterprises. The present practice of financial reporting is not complete and perfect in Indian context. The financial statements should not be silent with regard to social, economic and political conditions in which the business is operating. The non-statutory reporting has to play a vital role in the disclosure of accounting as well as non-accounting information in the annual reports.

It is suggested that the guidelines issued by the Accounting Standard Board and the corporations should follow various regulatory bodies. This would lead to full disclosures of information by the corporations, which in turn could be a decisive factor for the investors in decision-making as to the investment in capital market. It is also suggested that all the companies should make available various annual reports and disclose the material information on their website. The disclosure of information and the preparation of annual reports should be timely, transparent, and reliable and ensure transparency so that the various stakeholders and users of such information are able to make use of it.

The presentation of Corporate Financial Reports has undergone vital changes from time to time. The micro and macro-aspects of environmental forces have shaped new face of corporate financial reporting in terms of issue of accounting standards and strengthening the corporate governance over the corporations. The present practices indicate that the corporations disclose only the statutory information pertaining to profit and loss account and Balance Sheet, Director's Report, Auditor Report and Schedules and Notes. It is suggested that in order to make the corporate report more useful to the users, the same should include the inflation Accounting, Human Resource Accounting, Social Accounting, Environmental Accounting, Values Added Accounting and the extent of convergence to Accounting standards.

References

Batra, G.S (2001). Financial Markets and Services, Deep and Deep Publication.

Bhatter, M.M. (1994). Corporate Published Accounting Information and Investors, Books Treasure

Cerf, Alan Robert (1961). Corporate Reporting and Investment Decisions, Berkeley, The University of California Press.

Chander, Subhash. (1992). Corporate Reporting Practices in Public and Private Sector, Deep and Deep Publication.

Coombs, Hugh, M., and Tayib, Mohamad. (1998). Developing a Disclosure Index for Local Authority Published Accounts-A Comparative study of Local Authority Published Financial Reports between the UK and Malaysia, Asia Pacific Inter-disciplinary Research Conference, Osaka.

Copeland, Ronal, M., and Frederick, William, (1968). Extent of Disclosures, *Journal of Accounting Research*, 106-13.

Core, John, E. (2001). A Review of the Empirical Disclosure Literature: Discussion, *Journal of Accounting and Economics*, 31, 441-56.

Government of India (1990-2000). Bureau of Public Enterprises, Various Annual Reports.

Government of India (1947). Capital Issue Control Act.

Government of India (2000). Department of Company Affairs, Report on Corporate Excellence through Governance, 1-75.

Government of India (2001-02). Economic Survey.

Government of India (2002). Export Policy.

Government of India (2001). Indian Census.

Government of India, The Indian Companies Act, 1956.

Government of India (1997-02). Ninth Five-Year Plan.

Gupta, Das. N. (1977). Financial Reporting in India, Sultan Chand and Sons.

Healy, Paul. M and Palepu, Krishna G (2001). Information Asymmetry, Corporate Disclosure and the Capital Markets: A Review of the Empirical Disclosure Literature, *Journal of Accounting and Economics,* 31, 405-40.

Johnson, Simon. Boone, Peter. Breach, Alasdair. and Friedman, Eric. (2000). Corporate Governance in the Asian Financial Crisis, *Journal of Financial Economics*, 58, 141-86.

Kirk, N.E (2001). True and Fair View versus present Fairly in Conformity with Generally Accepted Accounting Principles. A Discussion Paper. Massey University, Newzeland.

Lal, Jawahar (1985). Corporate Annual Reports—Theory and Practice, Sterling.

Machanzina, Klaus (1994). Financial Reporting in West Germany, in Christopher Nobes and Robert Parker (ed.), Comparative International Accounting, Heritage, 97-125.

Marston, Claire (1986). Financial Reporting in India, Billing and Sons Limited, Great Britain.

Meena, D.D. (1995). Corporate Reporting Practices in Public Enterprises, Ess Ess Publications.

Rathod, R.K. (1990). Recent Trends in Financial Reporting by Corporate Sector in India, in M Saeed (ed.), Corporate Financial Reporting, Anmol Publications.

Saeed, M. (1990). Corporate Financial Reporting, Anmol Publications.

Securities and Exchange Board of India Act, 1992.

Securities and Exchange Board of India, (1995-2001). Annual Reports.

Sharma, A.K. and Batra, G.S. (2000). Indian Stock Market-Regulation, Performance and Policy Perspective, Deep and Deep Publication.

Singh, D.R and Bhargava, S.K (1978). Quality of Disclosure in the Public Sector Enterprises, *Indian Journal of Accounting*, 7, 21-37.

Standish, Peter (1994). Financial Reporting in Britain and Australia, in Christopher Nobes and Robert Parker (ed.), *Comparative International Accounting*, Heritage, 44-74.

The Institute of Chartered Accountants of India (2001). *Accounting Standards.*

The International Accounting Standard Committee, 1919.

Ubha, Dharminder Singh (2001). Corporate Disclosure Practices, Deep & Deep Publication.

Vasal, V.K., (1997). Interim Reporting Practices: A Research Study, *The Chartered Accountant*, Vol. 45, 24-36.

Verrecchia, Robert, E., (2001). Essays on Disclosure, *Journal of Accounting and Economics*, 32, 97-180.

Wyatt, Anne (2002). Towards a Financial Reporting Framework for Intangibles: Insights from the Australian Experience, *Journal of Intellectual Capital*, 3, 71-86.

CHAPTER

15

Corporate Governance and Disclosure Practices

Indian Experience

Rajinder Kaur

In the era of Globalisation, major institutional investors move beyond domestic markets in search of attractive investment opportunities to spread geographical risk. With this they want high standard of financial reporting and equally high standards of treatment of shareholders interest. With this, the need for companies to be self regulating in their behaviour has increased. The companies are expected to accountable to all its shareholders, employees, customers, suppliers and society. Companies make themself accountable to world through disclosure made with the help of reports.

The promptness, completeness and correctness with which the companies declare the Annual results and honesty with which the functioning and future outlook is discussed in Annual reports shows the extent to which the companies are responsive to shareholders. Companies provide statutory and non-statutory information through reports. Besides the statutory information, non-statutory information enables company to convince the general public about is honesty, credibility and reliability.

Non-statutory information includes corporate objectives and profile, business policies, statistical presentation social accounting, human resource accounting, statement of value added, national and international development of industry, etc.

Opening up of world economy has highlighted the concept of corporate governance. Corporate governance is as old as corporates themselfs. This concept can be defined as set of systems which ensures that a company is managed in best interest of all stakeholders. It is all about conducting the affairs of a company in a manner so as to ensure fairness to customers, employees, investors, vendors, the government and society at large. It includes the information and disclosure obligations. Ultimately, it is about accountability of board of directors.

The cadbury committee defines corporate governance as the system by which companies are directed and controlled by placing board of directors of the company in the centre of governance system.

According to CII draft, corporate governance deals with laws, procedures, practices and implicit rules that determine the company's ability to take managerial decisions, particularly regarding its shareholders, creditors, the state and employees.

The prominance of the concept began with the cadbury committee report after facing financial crisis due to business failure in U.K. On this issue, a committee on financial aspects of corporate governance under the chairmanship of Adriam Cabdury, was established in May 1991 by the Financial reporting council, the London stock exchange and accounting profession. The major chunk of the report dealt with the aspect of financial transparency and related role of directors and auditors. Transparency is considered as hallmark of corporate governance where no vital information is concealed by the board.

Besides this a number of reports have also been published internationally which include—Report of Greenburg Committee, The Combined Code of London Stock

Exchange, The OECD Code on Corporate Governance, The Blue Ribbon Committee on Corporate Governance, etc.

In India, investors' confidence is low due to the number of financial scams during the lat few years. Now, investors' protection is the basic agenda before SEBI (Regulatory body of securities markets) which can be achieved through corporate governance. Besides this, increase inflow of foreign capital made the concept of corporate governance popular. Separate codes for corporate governance were issued by trade and industry associations in 1997, which included the recommendations for management and supervisory categories of board, consolidation of accounts, limited directorship to increase accountability and efficiency, etc. Taking into consideration, the urgency of corporate governance, SEBI appointed a committee headed by Kumar Mangalam Birla on corporate governance in 1999. Committee has formed the codes of corporate governance and suggested implementation of code through stock exchanges and non-compliance should be resulted to delisting of such companies by stock exchanges. Based on the Report of Kumar Mangalam Birla Report, SEBI has directed all Stock Exchanges to amend listing agreements between them and entities whose securities are listed or have applied for listing with them, so as to implement the prescribed code of corporate governance. This provision has been inserted under clause 49 of the listing agreement.

Accounting has an important place in corporate governance as accounting is the ultimate way through which the performance of a company can be measured. Present paper is an attempt to analyse the reporting practices of various companies with regard to corporate governance. For this purpose, Annual reports of 10 companies for the year 2002-03 have been analysed. Information given under "Report on Corporate Governance" is divided into various broad categories.

PHILOSOPHY ON CORPORATE GOVERNANCE

Corporate governance is about promoting corporate fairness, transparency and accountability. This has been the philosophy of majority of the companies. As 80 percent companies have reported to believe in conducting the business in transparent manner. Same percentage of companies have reported that they work to enhance the value of its shareholders. 10 per cent companies have informed that they have received two awards for corporate governance viz. "Second ICAI National Award for Excellence in Corporate Governance" and "Golden Peacock Award for Excellence in Corporate Governance."

Similarly 10 per cent companies get rated themself to examine whether the company is being run on the Principles of Corporate Governance and whether the practices followed by company lead to value creation for all its shareholders. Companies got the symbols for rating by ICRA are; one is Corporate Governance Rating 2 (CGR2) and other is stake holders value creation and Governance Rating 2 (SVG2). These symbols denote belongingness of these companies to high category for Corporate Governance practices. 10 per cent of companies have emphasised on substance of Corporate Governance over form.

TABLE I

Philosophy of Companies on Corporate Governance

Item	*Percentage of companies*
Enhance the value of shareholders and fulfil the obligations of stakeholders	80
Integrity, accountability, transparency and compliance of law.	80
Award for excellence in corporate governance	10
Rating on good corporate governance	10
Effective management control by board and adequate presentation.	30
Emphasis on substance of corporate governance over form	10

BOARD OF DIRECTORS

Companies have given sufficient space to directors in the Report of Corporate Governance.

TABLE 2

Composition of Board

Item	*Percentage of companies*
Details of directors	100
Number of directorships held	100
Board meetings	100
Board functions and procedure	10
Number of board meetings attended	100
Number of membership of other board committees	100
Appointment or reappointment of directors	10

All companies have given details about their directors, categorizing them as executive and non-executive directors. Companies have also given details about number of directorships held by each director including private, public and foreign companies. Similarly, board meetings held and number of board meetings attended by directors is also disclosed by all companies. Whereas 10 percent companies have disclosed board functions and procedure adopted for performing those functions. 10 per cent companies have given information about directors who have been appointed or reappointed during the year.

COMMITTEES

Companies have constituted various committees consisting board of directors for looking into various matters.

TABLE 3

Committees of Board

Item	*Percentage of companies*
Audit committee	100
Shareholders/investors' grievence committee	100
Remuneration committee	40
Ethics and compliance committee	30
Committee of directors	10
Human resource committee	10

All companies under the study have constituted the shareholders committees to look into redressal of shareholders complaints like transfer of shares, non-receipt of annual reports, non-receipt of declared dividend, etc. Audit committee is also formed by all companies to looking into the matters regarding internal control systems, internal and external auditors, to review quarterly, half yearly and annual results of company before submission of those to board. Remuneration committees have been set-up by 40 per cent companies to determine the companies policies regarding remuneration package of senior management members. While fixing the remuneration committees adopt various remuneration policies. Committees of director have been formed by 10 per cent companies to approved the routine matters of the company. 30 per cent of the companies have also formed the ethics and compliance committee in which companies have adopted specific code of conduct. 10 per cent companies have set-up human resource committee to review human resource policies and practices of the company.

MEANS OF COMMUNICATION

Companies are using various means of communication for disclosing their results. All companies have published their half yearly results in newspapers whereas 10 percent companies have also sent their half yearly results to its shareholders. Besides sending the annual reports to its investors companies have also filed the reports to various

TABLE 4

Means of Communication

Item	*Percentage of companies*
Publication of results in newspapers	100
Filing reports and returns to various statutory bodies	100
Annual reports	100
Half yearly report sent to each shareholder	10
Web-sites	80

statutory bodies. 80 percent companies have displayed their annual results on websites.

GENERAL INFORMATION

A wide variety of information has been found under this head as, as many as 22 items are included by companies for giving general information to shareholders.

TABLE 5

Shareholders' Information

Item	*Percentage of companies*
Date, time and venue of last AGM	100
Date, time and venue of last thee annual general meetings	80
Date of book closure	90
Listing on stock exchanges	100
Listing fee	40
Stock code	80
Share transfer system	90
Registrars and share transfer Agent	80
Number of shares in D-mat form	70
Market price data	100
Dividend payment date	80
Shareholding pattern	80
Nomination facility with regard to shares	20
Financial calender	100
Outstanding GDR/ADR/Warrants	60
Registered office	30
Plant location	80
Address for correspondence	100
Investors service department	10
Public funding in last three years	10
Directors seeking appointment/reappointment	10
Code of corporate Ethics	10

All companies have informed about Date, time and venue of their last Annual General Meeting. Whereas 80 per cent companies have given this information regarding last three annual general meetings. All companies have given details about their listing with various stock exchanges. Whereas only 40 percent companies have talked about listing fee paid by them. 80 percent companies have given their stock codes at stock exchanges. 70 percent companies have informed about their shares in dematerialised form. All companies have given the market price of their securities. 80 percent companies have detailed about shareholding pattern. Similarly, 80 percent companies have included the dividend payment date.

Address for correspondence is given by all companies whereas 80 percent companies have given the addresses of their plant locations also. 10 percent companies have maintained investors service department. Same percentage of companies have made details about public fundings in last three years.

CONCLUSION

It is now becoming a habit among the corporate watchers to think of the governance of a company when something is heard of a company. SEBI has come out with helping hands for stakeholders by including various provisions relating to disclosure and transparency in clause 49 of Listing Agreement. This has helped in establishing the accountability of management to stakeholders in corporate affairs. Now companies are showing a white variety of information under the name "Report on Corporate Governance." These types of information were no where in annual reports of companies in recent past.

REFERENCES

Annual Reports of various Companies.

Awasthi, Arvind Kumar (2001). "Corporate Governance and The Auditor", *The Chartered Accountant*, August.

Garg, Lakshmi Kant (2001). "Corporate Governance—Implications for Accountants," *The Chartered Accountant*, October.

Gopalsamy, N. (1998). Corporate Governance: The New Paradigm, Wheeler Publishing, New Delhi.

http://www.corpgov.net/

Report of Kumarmangalam Birla Committee on Corporate Governance (2000), *Chartered Secretary*, March.

Sharma, Anil (2001). "Disclosure and Transparency: New Dimensions in Corporate Governance," *The Chartered Accountant*, October.

Singh, Devi and Garg Subhash (2001). "Corporate Governance", Excel Books, New Delhi.

Sundaraman (2001). "Accounting Implications of Corporate Governance: The Growing Clout of Accounting Standards", *The Chartered Accountant*, October.

CHAPTER

16

Activity-based Costing
A Conceptual Understanding

PARVINDER ARORA

Activity-Based Costing (ABC) has been one of the most significant innovations in the area of cost/management accounting systems. The concept does not seem to be bereft of the conceptual soundness. However, in order to grasp the idea of Activity-Based Costing, one has to understand first what went wrong with traditional systems. In fact before understanding *How* of ABC, it is necessary to understand *Why* ABC. This paper attempts to throw some light on the problem areas of traditional cost systems which gave rise to the concept of ABC. The paper also aims at understanding the conceptualities of ABC.

Key Words: Activity-Based Costing, Cost Drivers, Traditional Systems.

ACTIVITY-BASED COSTING: AN INSIGHT

The last two decades of the twentieth century have seen the accounting fraternity deliberating on certain latest developments in the area of cost/management accounting systems. Activity-Based Costing (ABC) has been one of the most talked about developments in the said area. In fact, ABC is one of the two or three most important management innovations in the 20th century and arguably the most written and talked about management accounting topic since 1985 (Brown, 2001). The decades of late, eighties and nineties were witness of the most rigorous debate in the area of cost accounting. There had been a sort of consensus that the traditional cost accounting failed to provide the managers with the information they needed to manage their operations in times when they were facing stiff competition and survival was the first thing on their minds.

The story began with the American giants loosing to their global competitors especially the Japanese. The Japanese were on a market-capturing spree in the United States, leaving the Americans wondering what was going wrong with them. Was it the quality of goods or prices or something else where they were not able to compete? The strong Japanese competition of the 1970s and 80s threatened the viability of several major segments of U.S. industry. After losing dominance of the consumer electronics, automobile and semiconductor processing industries, American industry was forced to look for something new to be more competitive. This led to a wide spread sole searching to find out the reasons of this wholesale failure of American companies. The results of this sole searching process led to different suggestions. The strategic process of Japanese companies, Japanese management styles, Japanese cost management, etc. everything was brought to the microscopic scrutiny. This scrutiny resulted in different views coming from different quarters amongst the management experts.

One school of thought emerged with a strong belief that the organizations, which were finding it difficult to compete, were not being supported by the cost information systems of the organizations. If those companies were losing business to the competitors, it was due to the inefficient cost accounting systems the companies were relying upon. There is no denying the fact that an inefficient cost system can play havoc with the business of a particular organization. The scholars who took this belief to its logical conclusion had amongst its front-runners Robert Kaplan, H.T. Johnson, and Robin Cooper among others.

The initiative can be found in Kaplan's study (Kaplan, 1986) focusing on the obsolescence of the cost accounting systems of certain companies, which could not weather the winds of competition. This was followed by the joint effort of Johnson and Kaplan's Relevance Lost (Johnson and Kaplan, 1987) and furthered by Cooper and Kaplan's (1988) and Cooper's (Cooper, 1989) systematic description of how the cost accounting systems then existing can distort the cost information being provided to the decision-makers. All this has led to one factor, i.e. the traditional cost accounting was found faltering in provision of timely, precise and accurate information to the managers thus leading to dysfunctional decisions and consequently leading to failure of such companies. All this criticism was taken to its logical conclusion by Mr. Cooper (Cooper, 1988, 1988a) in the form of introduction of new refined costing system that was named as Activity-Based Costing (ABC). This concept of Activity-Based Costing since its inception has been widely hailed by all and sundry. However, one can wonder how the cost accounting systems which have taken centuries to come to its final shape can be discarded at the spur of the moment by labeling them as obsolete and irrelevant. Were the systems based on certain ill thought foundations or those foundations themselves have crumbled? There may be a section of concerned people for whom this new development was difficult to digest as the only solution for the organizations looking for something new. Nevertheless to present and understand the conceptual foundations of Activity-Based Costing one has to understand first of all the historical description of the cost accounting as such and then the events responsible for turning the traditional costing systems into absolutely obsolete. In the following pages an attempt has been made to present the history of cost accounting in brief and then a critical evaluation of the same in order to understand this newly developed system which is called as Activity-Based Costing and which is the central point of the current study.

TRADITIONAL SYSTEMS: THE OBSOLESCENCE

Johnson and Kaplan argue that virtually all cost/ management accounting practices being practiced in today's world had been developed by 1925 and since then the cost/ management accounting has stood still. (Johnson and Kaplan, 1987, 125). During the period 1925-80s, the corporate world did not witness any significant development in the area of cost/management accounting. The practices emerged till 1920s continued to be the standard practices and continued to be followed by virtually all the organizations hereafter for next 50 years or so. Nevertheless, these practices were developed to cater to the informational and control needs of the managers of increasingly complex and diverse organizations. And these practices did serve the purpose very well during those periods. Afterwards no visible innovative ideas had come up in the area of cost/management accounting, argue Johnson and Kaplan. One reason of this stagnation could be that there was possibly no change in the corporate organizational form. The corporate organizational structures of the likes of Du Pont and General Motors continued to be the model structures and continued to be followed by most of the organizations thereafter for next 50 years or so.

However, this does not mean that the diversity and complexity of the manufacturing (process) was not increasing during the said period of 1925-80s. Even without significant innovations in organizational forms, However, the diversity of products and complexity of manufacturing processes continued to increase in the decades after 1920. Thus, the need for accurate product costs and effective process control should have imposed new demands on organizations' management accounting systems. The matter of the fact is that during this period the corporate world witnessed some sharp and radical changes in the manufacturing environment. But the costing practices could not keep pace with the improvements in the organizations' product and process technologies.

The corporate world witnessed two fundamental changes in the business scenario during the decades of 1960s to 1980s viz. vigorous global competition and technological revolution virtually reshaping the manufacturing environment. Global competition has made the managers' job more difficult by putting an additional demand on them to take quick, accurate and timely decisions. This in turn has increased the information needs of the mangers manifold. In fact this has redefined the informational needs of the managers. Similarly, to manage the products and process in modern technological environment, managers need relevant information in a timely and precise manner and which supports the manufacturing environment.

Unfortunately amidst all these changes one constant factor has been the firm's cost/management accounting system (Kaplan, 1986, 193). Management/cost accounting has been found lagging far behind the improving organization and technology of manufacturing process. This stagnation or what could be called as *'accounting lag'* had turned the systems absolutely obsolete. This really is baffling for the experts. As Kaplan asserts. . . .

> Relative to the real changes occurring in the firms manufacturing operations, it would seem to be simple for accountants to change the way they move the numbers around on their ledgers or in their computers. Transforming numbers should be easier than transforming real objects or motivating, educating, and training real people. Yet, when manufacturing operations change, the last and the most difficult component to change is the accounting system. Ironically if the accounting system is not representative of actual operations, and not useful in understanding and controlling these operations, it has little other justification for existence.
>
> (Kaplan, 1986, 194)

Because of this accounting lag, the cost/management accounting systems produce information that is "*too late, too aggregate, and too distorted to be relevant for managers' decision-making.*" (Johnson and Kaplan, 1987a, 22).

Consequently:

- Management accounting reports are of little help to operating managers attempting to reduce costs and improve productivity.
- Managers spend too much time on understanding and explaining reported variances that have little to do with the economic and technological realities of their operations. Too much focus on inputs like direct labour, which is not a significant factor in today's manufacturing, could be a causal factor for this distortion in product cost.
- Managers' horizons contract to short-term cycle of their monthly profit/loss statement. With too much emphasis on short-term profitability, managers sometime reduce certain discretionary investments that have future bearings but unfortunately are treated as expense in the period these are incurred.

Today's manager needs timely, accurate and precise information to:

- Control costs;
- Measure and improve productivity;
- Support pricing decisions;
- Introduction of new products;
- Abandonment of obsolete products;
- Response to the appearance of rival products; and
- Even to motivate and evaluate the performance of mangers.

No denying fact that an excellent accounting system cannot guarantee success. But an inefficient system can undermine even the best of the efforts. A costing system has always to be based on and is supposed to support the manufacturing environment. If it fails to fulfil even one of the conditions it would tend to produce information which is not relevant and may lead to dysfunctional decisions by the managers.

Unfortunately, the present day costing (of eighties) has been found to be distorting the product costs in a very systematic manner (Cooper and Kaplan, 1988). Not being able to exactly identify the functions to be addressed by a cost system is perhaps one of the major reasons for using such systems. Too much attention paid to inventory valuation for financial reporting and tax purposes remain to be at the top of agenda in minds of cost system designers. Where as the designers must realize that the cost system needs tom address the different functions viz.

- Inventory valuation,
- Operational control, and
- Individual product cost measurement (Kaplan, 1988).

In part, this too much emphasis on inventory valuation can be attributed to the dominance of the external financial accounting statements during the twentieth century. With more widespread public ownership of corporations' securities, and periodic crises in capital markets, the demand for audited financial statements increased. Auditors and regulators, mindful of their responsibility to users of financial statements, preferred conservative accounting practices based on objective, verifiable, and realized financial transactions. When measuring cost of goods sold and valuing inventory, auditors insisted on product costs based on the historical transactions recorded in the firms' ledger accounts. Further, they wanted the financial statements to be integrated. It did not matter for the summary financial statements if the inventory costing procedures distorted or cross-subsidized individual product costs as long as the total value recorded in the inventory accounts was derived from transactions recorded in the ledgers. Thus, simple methods were used to assign direct and period costs to products.

Because of these costing systems, the modern organizations have been found to be distorting the product cost information systematically. The source of this distortion could be:

1. Misunderstanding as to the definition of variable cost fitting to the modern day operations. (Cooper and Kaplan, 1988, 21).
2. Faulty overhead allocation system used in traditional costing systems.

The latter part is the actual bone of contention and the focal point for the present study. Cooper and Kaplan have beautifully exemplified the systematic distortion in reported product cost on the basis of their experience with 20 companies they have picked up for the study. Most of these companies:

1. Were multi-product companies, i.e. producing large number of distinct products in a single facility and subsequently selling these products through diverse marketing channels.
2. The range in demand volume for products within a product line was high.
3. Product cost played an important role in decisions viz. introduction, pricing and discontinuance of products.

The other significant aspect was that high volume products faced direct competition and consequently were subject to frequent price revisions. Whereas no market prices existed for low volume products as they were specially designed products. Significantly, companies tried to obtain larger margins for its low volume products to compensate for the gross underestimates that were perceived to be reported for these products. Those big companies were loosing business in high volume product segment to smaller companies with practically no economic or technological advantage. Surprisingly some of the products, which were considered to be unprofitable by production managers as these were so difficult to produce, were reported as most profitable by the cost systems. As one of the companies reported that *'they often won bids that had been over priced because it did not really want the business, and lost bids it had deliberately overpriced in order to get the business'* (Cooper and Kaplan, 1988, 21).

THE PROBLEM

The problem actually lies with the two-stage overhead allocation mechanism used in traditional cost systems. The context in which the term traditional is used refers to the cost systems with two major characteristics: one, inputs limited to actual historical cost, and the absorption of fixed and joint cost by each product. Traditional systems assume that products consume resources. Hence, justifying the joint and fixed costs to products. Generally this allocation is done through the two-stage allocation mechanism found in most of the organization.

Overhead costs are generally combined into large, frequently plant wide, overhead pools. The costs from overhead pools are then allocated to cost centers using different bases for allocation. For example, building expenses (depreciation, taxes, heat, light, etc.) and housekeeping can be allocated on the basis of floor space, electricity by machine hours, supervision by labour hours, etc. This is called as first stage of overhead allocation.

However, these cost centre costs are then, in second stage of allocation, are allocated to products using direct labour as basis of allocation. Generally predetermined rate is used for applying these overheads to products. This predetermined rate is arrived at by allocating the costs to cost centers and then dividing the costs of cost centers by the direct labour hours to be worked in the respective cost centers in the event of doing the forecasted production in the coming period.

Surprisingly, the labour hours are used by most of the organizations in the second stage allocation even if the production processes are highly automated and this overhead burden rate exceeds 11000% in some cases (Cooper and Kaplan, 1988, 21).

Typically this fully burden cost centre labour rate is at least four times the actual labour rate paid to the workers. In some highly automated cost centers, it is not unusual for the rate to be ten or even 15 and 20 times the hourly labour rate (Johnson and Kaplan, 1987, 184).

Johnson and Kaplan have highlighted this problem by taking a real life example. This really magnifies the problem underlying the whole criticism of overhead allocation. Just imagine the overheads, which represent 60% of the costs attributed to the product, are distributed on the basis of direct labour cost which is smallest (merely 11%) of the three cost categories. This really is baffling as to why companies keep on using such measurements, which go entirely against common sense.

Another problem with this kind of cost systems is that these tend to combine material, labour, and overhead costs at each stage into a single cost that, when transfer to the next stage is identified as the material input cost to that stage. While, in this case the final product cost will remain same, as it obviously must be, all semblance of cost structure will be destroyed. Because material cost at final stage includes labour and overhead costs from all previous stages, it is impossible to make any estimate of direct or prime costs. Companies that wish to understand the value added of their production process, for pricing or productivity analyses, would have to special studies and costing system would be of no use. Anyways we would be sticking to one basic problem that is the overhead allocation mechanism and consequent distortion in the product cost. Cooper (1987, 1990) has further illustrated this distortion in reported product cost information in a systematic manner.

GENESIS OF THE PROBLEM

The genesis of the problem lies in basically:

- Using direct labour as basis for overhead allocation
- Ignoring the product diversity

The problem arises from the use of direct labour as the basis for allocation in the second stage of two-stage allocation mechanism. This practice seems to have its roots in the later part of nineteenth century cost accounting in metal working shops of scientific management era (Kaplan and Atkinson,

1992, 5). Moreover, this practice is not totally bereft of conceptual support. This practice seems to have done well in the times when it was actually invented. This procedure may have been adequate even some decades ago when labour was the principle value adding activity (Cooper and Kaplan, 1988, 22). But, with technology changing, processes being automated, the labour is no more a causal factor for the incurrence of most of the overhead costs. Thus, labour no longer represents a reasonable surrogate for resource demands by the products.

However, some companies have moved to certain other bases for allocation in the second stage of two-stage mechanism, such as material cost (Specifically companies using JIT, etc.) and machine hours. This introduction of new bases to some extent gives some relief from the problem of using unrealistic basis for attaching costs to products. Some companies have even been found to be using all three viz. labour, material, and machine hours simultaneously. This definitely results in a finer attribution of costs to products responsible for the incurrence of these costs. In fact, using these bases simultaneously will definitely help especially in case where labour hours, material costs, and machine hours are not consumed in same proportion by the products. Machine hours as a basis for allocation had, however, been used extensively in nineteenth century in process industry like chemicals, glass and petroleum where labour costs were relatively small and processing time had to be measured in order to control the physical conversion process (Kaplan and Atkinson, 1992, 6) . The problem is in fact two-fold. One, direct labour (or for that matter material cost and machine hours) do no more have the cause and effect relationship with the incurrence of overheads which are to be distributed to the products. As a matter of fact direct labour is no more a causal factor for most of the resources demanded by the products. This in no way is a surrogate of demands put on the resources by different products in the modern day manufacturing facilities. Second, direct labour hours along with the two other measures, viz. machine hours and material cost failed to capture the product diversity/complexity. Reason being all these bases are volume related bases. The use of volume related bases underlies the basic assumption that all the costs, allocated or to be allocated, have the same behaviour, i.e. they increase in direct proportion to the volume of product items manufactured. Surprisingly, the use of labour as a basis of overhead allocation was criticized even at the beginning of 20th century (Church, 1908) but the practice still remains in vogue even after so many decades.

As a consequence of using these allocation bases especially the direct labour hours the cost centre managers are forced solely to focus on direct labour savings in order to reduce the costs. With overhead burden rates of 400-1000 percent, small savings in direct labour time would have large impacts on cost distributions and thus on product cost. Amusingly, little attention is paid to the actual overhead accounts, where costs actually increase rapidly. Let's assume a manager succeeds in reducing the growth in some overhead category, the benefit would be distributed to all the cost centers and products in the factory because of this allocation procedure (Johnson and Kaplan, 1987, 188). In that situation it would be a smarter move on the part of the managers to slightly reduce the direct labour charge since that is the account by which all other costs are attached to their cost centers and products. Consequently, less attention is devoted to escalating overhead costs than to small increments in labour costs.

As Johnson and Kaplan state that managers soon discover that any process that requires relatively large amounts of direct labour seems very expensive. In fact, it usually becomes easier to find a supplier that can produce the labour intense component or subassembly cheaper than the cost center can fabricate it. In such case costs are apparently lowered by sub-contracting and companies would start buying than manufacturing. This happens ignoring the fact that factory overheads are no linger driven by the labour hours and outsourcing saves only relatively small fraction of the component's costs.

Further, the use of direct labour hours leads to cross subsidization amongst different products. Robin Cooper has highlighted this cross subsidization in a very convincing manner (Cooper, 1988). Cooper asserts that in a multi-product, multi-process manufacturing facility where products are volume diverse as well as size diverse, the use of direct labour hours or any other volume related allocation basis would lead to

- Over costing of high volume products and of large size products.
- *Under costing of low volume products and small sized products.*
- These two factors would reinforce each other.

The usage of volume related bases result in high volume, large size products receiving excessively high fraction of support department costs, Therefore, subsidizing small size and low volume products. This cross-subsidization in reported product cost can be lethal if this information is used in decisions like discontinuance of a product. Then in all possibilities a high volume or large size product, because over costed, would be dropped despite actually being a profitable product. Though, by dropping/eliminating that product may not lead to elimination of overheads. Then this overhead cost will have to be shared by the remaining products. This can well be a beginning of putting the products into what could be called as *"product death spiral."*

To sum this up, the distortions or biases in the reported product caused by volume or size diversity are in fact variants of the same underlying phenomenon, which can succinctly be stated as:

> 'when the quantity of volume related input that a product consumes does not vary in direct proportion to the quantity of volume unrelated input consumed, volume based systems will report distorted product costs.' (Cooper, 1988, 54).

This non-proportionality can be due to

- Production volume diversity,
- Size diversity, complexity diversity—complex products may consume more volume related input though not necessarily volume unrelated resources,

- Material diversity—materials that take longer to machine may consume more volume related input relative to volume unrelated resources, and
- Setup diversity—the time required to set-up a machine varies depending upon the product being manufactured, so that the proportion of the volume unrelated to volume related input consumed may vary by product to product. (Cooper, 1988, 54). The types of diversity that lead to distortion in the product cost reported by traditional systems are numerous and common.

THE REMEDY: ACTIVITY-BASED COSTING

To curtail this distortion in product cost information, the blueprint to newly suggested refined systems can be found in Johnson and Kaplan's Relevance Lost.

Transaction Costing is what primarily has been suggested as a remedy to the problem discussed above (Cooper and Kaplan, 1988, 24). The proposed system would use transactions as a basis for overhead allocation instead of the above-discussed volume related bases. Instead of trying to trace the costs to products as is done in traditional systems the costs are assigned to the units that cause the transaction to originate. The costing element would no longer be the product but those elements the transaction effects. Eventually, unit cost of product will be determined by dividing the cost of transactions by number of units in the costing elements. (Cooper and Kaplan, 1988, 25).

The more elaborative and persuasive presentation of transaction costing comes from Cooper's pioneering works introducing the concept of Activity-Based Costing (ABC). If 1880s can be termed as period of Costing Renaissance in English speaking word then 1980s can definitely be earmarked as the period of second costing renaissance. Emergence of ABC has probably been the most talked about development in the area of cost/management accounting. Robin Cooper and Robert Kaplan conceived this idea of ABC that has guaranteed them a permanent place in the history of cost/management accounting.

ACTIVITY-BASED COSTING: THE CONCEPT

The basic distinction between traditional cost accounting and ABC is as follows: Traditional cost-accounting techniques allocate costs to products based on attributes of a single unit. Typical attributes include the number of direct labour hours required to manufacture a unit, purchase cost of merchandise resold, or machine hours. Allocations, therefore, vary directly with the volume of units produced. In contrast, ABC systems focus on activities required to produce each product or provide each service based on each product or service's consumption of the activities.

Using ABC, overhead costs are traced to products and services by identifying the resources, activities, and their costs and quantities to produce output. A unit of output (a driver) is used to calculate the cost of each activity. Cost is traced to the product or service by determining how many units of output each activity consumed during any given period of time.

ABC does not only apply to manufacturing organizations: it is also appropriate for service organizations such as financial institutions (Mobberley, 1993), medical care providers (Lawson, 1994), and government units. In fact, some banking organizations (Mays and Sweeney, 1994) have been applying the concept for years under a different name—unit costing. Unit costing is used to calculate the cost of banking services by determining the cost and consumption of each unit of output of functions required to deliver the service.

As Cooper would say *'ABC represents an evolutionary extension of the two-stage procedure that underlies most modern cost systems'* (Cooper,1988, 45). ABC differs from traditional systems in the following ways:

1. Product is not the costing element as is in the traditional systems. Activities are the focal point in an ABC system. Instead of tracing the costs to products as is done in conventional systems, in ABC systems costs are first traced to activities and then to products from activity pools on the basis of products' demand fro these activities during the production process. This is based on very simple notion, i.e.

the products do not consume resources, as is assumed by the traditional systems; rather products consume activities which in turn consume the resources. Hence, it would be a common sense to trace the flow of costs to activities and from activities to products.

2. Allocation bases used in ABC differ from those used in traditional systems on two accounts:

- Nature of allocation bases to be used, and
- Number of allocation base to be used.

The traditional systems primarily use only three allocation bases, viz. direct labour, material cost and machine hours. By nature all of the above said bases are volume related. The volume related bases are always based on one inherent assumption, i.e. more the volume of products to be produced; more will be the consumption of resources, which may not be true in case of number of overhead items which are volume un-related. Moreover, apart from above said three bases there can be possibly number of transaction/activities that facilitate the production and consume the resources as well. ABC systems take care of that fact by using a large number of cost allocation bases, which include volume-related as well as volume un-related bases. These allocation bases used in ABC systems are termed as cost drivers (Cooper, 1988, 48). A cost driver is an event, associated with an activity that results in consumption of firm's resources (Babad, *et al.*, 1993). Variety of cost drivers can be used in ABC systems to allocate overheads that are not volume related. The examples can be:

- Set-up hours,
- Number of set-ups,
- Material hours,
- Number of times handled,
- Number of items ordered,
- Ordering hours,
- Inspection time,
- Number of inspections, etc.

The cost drivers used in ABC are thus measures of activity performed. Many of activities may not be related to the value of production run. For example doubling the volume of a product does not require the number of set-ups or part orders. A simple volume related allocation base can not capture the complexity of the relationship between volume and a lot or order, rather it measure only attributes of product item viz. the number of labour hours, machine hours, and material rupees consumed. So, to trace costs deriving from activities which are not related to volume requires allocation bases which themselves are independent of volume (Cooper, 1988, 49). The most significant feature of Activity-Based Costing system is it uses multiple cost drivers in order to improve the accuracy of reported product cost. These cost drivers help in capturing the economic non-proportionalities in production. Every cost driver used in ABC requires measuring some unique feature of each product. This perhaps is the major and significant contribution of ABC. Nevertheless, the same characteristic of ABC can be a limiting factor as well.

Every additional cost driver introduced in the system would significantly reduce the distortion in reported product cost thereby providing more accurate information to the managers and thus reducing the chances of making poor decisions, i.e. reducing the cost of errors. However, on the other hand every additional cost driver introduced means putting demands for some additional measurements, hence increasing the cost of measurements. The basic problem hereby is that these two costs are inversely related and there always exist trade-off between the two. So, finding the optimum number of cost drivers can be one major issue.

SUMMARY

The emergence of ABC has been an offshoot of the inability of the traditional systems to come up to the growing information needs of the managers in rapidly changing business scenario all over the globe. ABC focuses on activities required to manufacture the products rather than focusing on the product itself. The most significant feature of Activity-

Based Costing system is it uses multiple cost drivers for allocation of overheads in order to improve the accuracy of reported product cost. These cost drivers help in capturing the economic non-proportionalities in production. Every cost driver used in ABC requires measuring some unique feature of each product. This perhaps is the major and significant contribution of ABC.

References

Babad, Y.M. and B.N. Balachanderan, 1993. Cost Driver Optimization in Activity Based Costing. *The Accounting Review* (July): 563-575.

Brown, A.D., *et al.*, 2001. Organizational Influences, Ownership, and Adoption of Activity Accounting in Australian Firms. *School of Accounting Working Paper 46*. Sydney: University of Technology.

Church, H. 1908. The Proper Distribution of Expense Burden. New York: The Engineering Magazine Co.

Cooper, R. 1988. The Rise of Activity-Based Costing—Part-I: What is an Activity-Based Costing System. *Journal of Cost Management* (summer), 45-54.

Cooper, R. 1988a. The Rise of Activity Based Costing—Part-II: When Do I Need Activity-Based Costing System? *The Journal of Cost Management* (Fall): 41-48.

Cooper, R., 1987. Two Stage Procedure in Cost Accounting: Part-I: *The Journal of Cost Management,* (summer): 43-51.

Cooper, R. and R.S. Kaplan, 1988. How Cost Accounting Distorts Product Costs. *Management Accounting,* (April): pp. 20-27.

Cooper, R., 1990. Implementing Activity-Based Costing System. *The Journal of Cost Management,* (Spring): 33-42.

Johnson, H.T. and R.S. Kaplan. 1987. Relevance Lost—The Rise and Fall of Management Accounting. Boston. Harvard Business School Press.

Kaplan, R.S. 1986. Accounting Lag: The Obsolescence of Cost Accounting System, *California Management Review,* (Winter): 174-99.

Kaplan, R.S. 1988. One Cost System Isn't Enough, *Harvard Business Review,* (Jan.-Feb.): 61-66.

Kaplan, R.S. and A.A Atkinson, 1992. Advanced Management Accounting, N. Delhi: Prentice Hall of India.

Lawson, R.A. 1994. Activity-Based Costing System for Hospital Management. *CMA Magazine.* (June)

Mays, J.W. and R.B. Sweeney. 1994. Activity-Based Costing System in Banking. *CMA Magazine.* (May)

Mobberley, Julie. 1993. Activity-Based Costing in Financial Institutions. Pitman Publishing, London.

CHAPTER

17

Issues in Activity-based Costing

PARVINDER ARORA

The concept of Activity-Based Costing (ABC) does not seem to be bereft of conceptual soundness. However, designing and implementation of ABC can pose some problems. Occurrence of these problems can be attributed to different reasons. The problems can be categorized into two categories one behaviour-related problems and the other technical problems. Understanding of these problems can be of a real help for a person or organization which is going to have an ABC system. In the following discussion some of these issues have been discussed in detail.

PLANNING THE SYSTEM

Before embarking on any project, it is important to know what the project is expected to accomplish. A project to implement ABC is no exception. Without a fairly precise definition of its purpose, the project will result in an ABC system designed to solve the general problems of some hypothetical organization, not the specific problems of a real organization. There are various approaches for designing and implementing an ABC system. For example, Cooper has suggested a structured approach to ABC design and implementation (Cooper, 1990). Burch (1994) has recommended Activity-Based Costing systems life development life cycle. There is no "one approach fits all" solution.

The system-planning phase establishes the broad strategic framework and clear vision of the enterprise and an understanding as to how the Activity-Based Costing system will serve the enterprise. The very first thing would be to decide on the objective of the system. The costing system may be required for product costing, operational control, business reengineering, etc. If the objective of the ABC system is simply to provide improved information for evaluating pricing opportunities, a different solution would be required than if one of the objectives was to devise and track new methods of performance measurement on a day-to-day basis. Similarly, if the objective is to develop the system in stages or through a pilot project rather than on an organization-wide basis, a different approach might be in order. However, we will be focusing only on product costing as an objective of the Activity-Based Costing systems. One must be cautious, however, with any approach that addresses only a sub-set of its activities. Such an approach contains the danger of over looking activities or costs from areas in the organization not being studied.

After the decision as to the objective(s) of the Activity-Based Costing system has been taken before moving to next phase we must find the answers to certain queries, which form a crucial part of planning the system. There are certain examples:

Who will own the new ABC system?

Ownership of the new system should be consistent with its primary objective.

How complex and detailed should the system be?

To be effective, the ABC system must make the appropriate trade-offs between accuracy, flexibility and cost (Cooper, 1989).

What degree of accuracy is required and what precision level will it produces?

Again, the system's objectives are key to making the precision *versus* accuracy determination. If the new system is to be used to support strategic decisions, a lower level of precision can be acceptable than if the system is to be used to support tactical and other day-to-day decisions.

Will the system be integrated into the day-to-day financial accounting system, or will it be a stand-alone system maintained off-line?

An ABC system can be viewed in two different ways. There is the cost assignment view and the process view. The cost assignment view provides information about resources, activities and cost objects. The process view provides operational (often non-financial) information about activities.

What approach to the cost assignment view should be taken?

The approaches to the cost assignment view fall into two general categories: a two-stage approach and a multiple-stage approach.

Once these questions are answered, planning for the ABC project can move forward. Like any major organization-wide systems project, a formal project management structure and project plan is necessary for an effective implementation. The structure includes a steering committee (Cooper, 1990).

ANALYZE AND IDENTIFY ACTIVITIES

Theoretically, even a small organization can identify an almost limitless number of activities. The identification process should, however, be guided by materiality and the objectives of the ABC system. For example, if the objective is strategic (e.g., product line profitability, pricing policies), the primary need is to accurately assign costs to cost objects. In such cases, activities can be broadly defined. If, on the other hand, the intent is to improve operations (e.g. eliminate non-value-added processes), the need is for information about activities as well as cost objects. In these cases, activities must be defined more narrowly. However, materiality will also impact activity definitions. For example, an organization with only two individuals in the purchasing function will not gain as much by dividing the function into twenty separate activities, as will an organization with fifty individuals. Decomposing functional areas into their constituent activities can identify activities.

SELECTION OF COST DRIVERS

Cost drivers are the variables that can be used to explain the behaviour of activity costs. They reflect the consumption of costs by activities and the consumption of activities by other activities, products, or services. The most significant feature of Activity-Based Costing system is it uses multiple cost drivers in order to improve the accuracy of reported product cost. These cost drivers help in capturing the economic non-proportionalities in production. Every cost driver used in ABC requires measuring some unique feature of each product. This perhaps is the major and significant contribution of ABC. Nevertheless, the same characteristic of ABC can be a limiting factor as well. Activities being the focus of Activity-Based Costing systems, the costs are first traced to activities on the basis of the demands these activities put on the resources of the organization. Then cost of activities is assigned to the products on the basis of magnitude of activities consumed by the products respectively. The cost drivers corresponding to each activity represent magnitude of activities consumed. Theoretically speaking a separate cost driver should be used for each activity which performed and which consume resources in a production facility. But activities performed in typical facility are so great that using a separate cost driver for each activity will not be economically feasible. On the other hand not using a separate cost driver means compromising with the accuracy in reported product cost.

Every additional cost driver introduced in the system would significantly reduce the distortion in reported product cost thereby providing more accurate information to the managers and thus reducing the chances of making poor decisions, i.e. reducing the cost of errors. However, on the other hand every additional cost driver introduced means putting demands for some additional measurements, hence increasing the cost of measurements. The basic problem hereby is that these two costs are inversely related and there always exist trade-off between the two. So, finding the optimum number of cost drivers can be one major issue. Cost of errors may come in different ways;

- Making poor product-related decisions.
- Making poor product-design decisions.
- Making poor capital investment decisions.
- Making inaccurate budgeting decisions about the level of operating expenses required.

Similarly the cost of measurement may consist of—

- The cost of routing the information to cost system.
- The cost of undertaking the calculations required computing product cost.

Decision as to what number of cost drivers to be used would entirely depend upon (1) what is the desired level of accuracy in reported product cost, and (2) affordability of the firm as regard to cost of generating the information. Basically here we are talking about the trade-off between cost of errors and cost of measurement. An optimal cost system is a system whereby marginal cost of improvement in reported product cost just equals the marginal benefits from any such improvement. But remember an optimal cost system would not be the most accurate system but an efficient system. An efficient system is that which is economical to maintain and which does not introduce excessive distortions. As discussed earlier minimum number of cost drivers required would depend upon the desired level of accuracy in reported product cost. The greater the required accuracy the greater will be the number of cost drivers. The complexity of the product mix being produced does also play a significant role. The problem is not that simple it's a two-fold problem. If, as we find it, it is not economically feasible to use a different cost driver for the activities being performed then we will have to aggregate the two or more activity pools and use a single cost driver to trace the costs of the aggregate pools by eliminating one or more cost drivers. The second related problem would be then which cost driver to be eliminated. In fact while designing an Activity-Based Costing system one has to take two different but related decisions as how many cost drivers to be used and which cost drivers to be used. Here are certain suggestions as regard to the above said decisions;

The cost of two or more activities can be aggregated and single cost driver can be used subject the fulfilment of certain conditions. Provided there is positive correlation between the activities and frequency of cost drivers for the said activities is almost same. However, the complexity of the product mix plays a more subtle and complex role in determining if the costs of two (or more) activities can be aggregated and traced using a single cost driver without introducing unacceptable levels of distortion (Cooper, 1989, 35).

Three factors viz., (i) product diversity, (ii) relative cost of activities aggregated, and (iii) volume diversity, are responsible for a decision as to accepting or not accepting a single cost driver for two (or more) activities. (Cooper, 1989, 35).

Product Diversity

Two products will be called as diverse if these consume activities in different proportions and the degree of diversity between the two products is measured by the ratio of activities consumed by each product. The greater the degree of diversity stronger will be the recommendation of not clubbing it together. If the degree is less aggregate it.

Relative Cost of Aggregated Activities

The relative cost of various activities is a measure of how much each activity costs as a percentage of the total cost of the production process. If the relative costs of activities represent significant proportions of total cost then do not aggregate it. If otherwise those can be aggregated. Because higher the higher the relative cost the larger will be the distortion that will be introduced be inaccurately tracing it to the products.

Volume Diversity

This occurs products are manufactured in batches of different sizes. If products are high volume diverse use different cost drivers and no aggregation of activities should be done.

These are certain broad guidelines to take two different but related decisions as to how many and what cost drivers to be used. However, this decisions to this effect calls for a mixture of judgment and analysis (Cooper, 1989, 43).

Babad, *et al.* (1993) have made an attempt to optimize the number of cost drivers. Their model states that perfectly correlated cost drivers can be combined, i.e. can be represented by one of the correlated cost drivers, after dropping the other correlated cost drivers without losing any level of accuracy in product cost.

A multiple combination of cost drivers can be replaced by a set of pair wise combinations of cost drivers. But if the cost drivers are not perfectly correlated then there is bound to be a loss of accuracy and that can be measured as:

$$U_i - U_i^{km} = D_k * (V_{ik} - V_{im})$$

where:

U_i = Total cost of product i.

U_{ikm} = Cost of product i, after taking into account the contribution of all the cost drivers and merging cost drivers k and m into cost driver m.

D_k = Total dollar expense of activities associated with cost driver k

V_{ik} = Volume of the actual absolute frequency of use of cost driver k by product i.

V_{im} = Volume of the actual relative frequency of use of cost driver m by product i.

On the other hand there will occur some savings (C_k) in the form of lesser cost of measurement, if we drop one cost driver (suppose k). So, the optimum number of cost drivers will be reached where we maximize the total weighted savings minus weighted distance costs.

$$\text{Max. } \sum_{\substack{\text{All Pairs}\\(k,m)}} X_{km} \left(C_k - \text{SQRT}\left[\sum_{\substack{\text{All Pairs}\\(k,m)}} \sum_i W_i (U_i - U_{ik.m})^2\right]\right)$$

The second major issue while selecting the cost drivers relates to the nature of cost drivers to be. While selecting cost drivers, one has to be aware of the fact that there is sometimes interdependence among different activities. As firms frequently choose the amounts to expend in various activities simultaneously rather than sequentially, the interdependence among activities must be estimated simultaneously (Datar *et al*, 1993).

Moreover product and process design also influence the consumption of overheads. The problem is two fold. One, there is simultaneity among activities (which are endogenous variables, e.g. supervision, tool maintenance, quality control, scrap, etc.) resulting into simultaneity among overhead costs. The other is that product and process features affect these overhead costs (exogenous variables like shape, size, etc.)

Thus, while selecting cost drivers, simultaneity and influence of product design must be taken into consideration. Datar teal recommends use of econometric methodology to determine the interaction between endogenous variables. In such a case resources consumed within the plant can be estimated as system of simultaneous equation.

Till now the entire discussion has been evolving around minimizing two errors, viz. specification errors and aggregation errors. Specification errors arise when methods used to trace costs to products do not reflect the demand placed on the resources by individual products. However, aggregation errors occur when costs and units of a resource are aggregated over heterogeneous activities to derive a single cost allocation rate. Aggregation errors could also be viewed as a special case of specification errors.

The need for refined systems, e.g. Activity-Based Costing systems arises from the desire to reduce the above said errors. However, this endeavours to reduce these two errors by changing (and increasing the number of) the cost drivers and disaggregating of cost pools may result in increasing the measurement errors. That is, improved specification of cause and effect relations and less aggregation could increase the problems of identifying costs with a particular cost pool and measuring the specific units of resources consumed by individual products (Datar and Gupta, 1994, 569). Thus, the benefit of reduction in aggregation errors and specification errors may be offset by the increase in the measurement errors. Hence there might not always be visible improvements in product cost information (Datar and Gupta, 1994 and Foster and Gupta, 1990).

SOURCES OF ABC SYSTEM

There are three primary sources for the information needed to develop an ABC system: people, the general ledger, and the organization's computer system. The people who do the work are a major source of information. They can provide information about the organization's activities, the resources consumed, and the performance measures used. The general ledger provides information about the organization's elements of cost and the outputs produced. The organization's system should contain information about some of the cost objects and cost drivers. For example, the number of invoices paid (a potential cost driver) should be available through the accounts payable system.

A review of organization charts, facility floor plans, marketing materials, and detailed financial information can also give some clues as to the organization's major activities and costs. They are helpful in getting the information-gathering process started and also provide the basis for selecting strategic cost drivers around which the subsequent interview process can be designed. Including representatives from Management Information Systems (MIS) on the cross-functional ABC project team will also help to determine whether the required information is already available in the system and will facilitate the capturing and processing of information. The majority of the information to be used in developing the system, however, should come from interviews and questionnaires directed to the organization's personnel because they are the best source to ensure that all the bases are covered. If there are hundreds of individuals to interview, questionnaires may be the only feasible alternative. Such questionnaires must be carefully designed if they are to be effective. They must be complete and they must ask the right questions in an appropriate manner. For example, if a question relates to cost drivers without first defining cost drivers, an incorrect answer may result. However, the main drawback to questionnaires is that they do not provide for dialogue that may lead to important insights.

References

Babad, Y.M. and B.N. Balachandaran. 1993. Cost Driver Optimization in Activity Based Costing. *The Accounting Review* (July): 563-75.

Burch, J.G., 1994. Cost and Management Accounting: A Modern Approach. St. Paul: West Publishing.

Cooper, R., 1989. The Rise of Activity-Based Costing—Part Three: How Many Cost Driver Do You Need, and How You Select Them? *The Journal of Cost Management,* (Winter): 34-46.

Cooper, R., 1990. Implementing Activity-Based Costing System. *The Journal of Cost Management,* (Spring): 33-42.

Datar, S. and M. Gupta, 1994. Aggregation, Specification and Measurement Errors in Product Costing, *The Accounting Review,* (Oct.): 567-91.

Datar, S.M. *et al.,* 1993. Simultaneous Estimation of Cost Drivers. *The Accounting Review* (July): 602-14.

Foster and M. Gupta. 1990.

CHAPTER

18

Emerging Trends in the NPA Management in the Indian Banking Industry

MANJIT SINGH AND AMANDEEP SINGH

INTRODUCTION

As the thrust of the second phase of reform is on improvement in the organizational efficiency of banks, the most critical area in the improvement of profitability of the banks is the reduction of Non-Performing Assets (NPA). This issue is intimately connected with the overall stability of the financial system. Poor recoveries are going to block huge funds in non-performing assets and it compelled bankers to consider recovery as a key performance area. Accordingly, this aspect drew the serious attention of bankers and academicians. Because balance sheet is to reflect the banks actual financial health, a proper system for recognitions of income, classification of assets and provisioning for bad debts on a prudential basis is imperative. (RBI 2001)

Reserve Bank of India has released 'Report on Trends and Progress in Banking 2002-03' makes clear that privatization is no guarantee of banking health. Consider the new private sector banks, set-up with much fanfare in the mid-90s. In their haste to grow they have over-reached themselves. The result is that while their balance sheets have grown at a much faster pace for the industry as a whole, so have their bad debts. The new private sector banks have been unduly aggressive in their pursuit of new avenues of business. For instance their lending to capital market, generally regarded as more risky than other sectors.

OBJECTIVES

The principle objectives of the study are:

1. To examine the trends of non-performing assets in Indian Banking Industry
2. To make a comparative analysis of non-performing assets in private and public sector banks.
3. Suggest a model for proper management of NPA's in the banks.

SCOPE AND METHODOLOGY

Data Base

Both primary data and secondary data has been used for the purpose of the study. Primary data has been collected from the employees of private and public banks. Unstructured interview method has been used for obtaining the opinions of bank employees. Secondary data has been obtained from various reports including RBI Manuals and Circulars, Various Journals and Newspapers, etc.

Trends in NPA's in Indian Banking Industry

The health of the financial sector is a matter of great concern, especially in developing countries where failure in financial intermediation can disrupt the development process. Indian financial system has undergone significant changes during last few years. These changes were necessitated due to inefficiencies cropped up in public sector banks. The inefficiencies had decreased productiveness of banks assets and problem of over dues had assumed alarming proportions. As a result of that Reserve bank of India advised the banks to concentrate on performance of their assets and to bring down the percentage of Non-performing Assets

The trends in NPAs of commercial banks on the basis of data available over a period of five years ending from 1999 to 2003 have been examined in this part of the paper. The exercise is confined to 27 government owned banks and 31 private sector banks.

TABLE I

Gross NPA of Commercial Banks in Indian Banking Industry

(in crores)

	1999	*2000*	*2001*	*2002*	*2003*
Gross Advances	399436	475113	558766	680958	778043
Non-Performing assets	58722	60408	63883	70861	68714
% Gross to Advance	14.7	12.7	11.4	10.4	8.8
% Gross to Assets	6.2	5.5	4.9	4.6	4.4

Source: Compiled from Report, *Trend and Progress of Banking in India, RBI 2002-03.*

As is evident from the Table 1, the NPAs in the scheduled commercial banks are declining in absolute terms and as % of gross advances and assets. The decline is more visible in 2003 when NPAs declined from Rs. 70861 crores to 68714 crores and NPAs as percentage of advances declined from 10.4% to 8.8%.

Group-wise NPA trends explain that gross NPAs decreased in Public sector banks where as in the Private Sector Banks, an increasing trend is visible, as at end March 2003. The percentage of gross NPAs of public sector banks have reduced from 15.9% to 9.4% while in private sector banks, percentage has increased from 6.2% to 7.6% and the increase is more prominent in new private sector banks than old private sector banks. Because as the time is passing more NPAs of new private sector banks are coming.

TABLE 2

Gross NPAs of SCB—Bank Group-wise

(in crores)

Bank Group/Year	*Gross Advances*	*Gross NPA*	*% to Advances*	*% to total Assets*
Public Sector Banks				
1999	325328	51710	15.9	6.7
2000	379461	53033	14	6
2001	442134	54773	12.4	5.3
2002	509368	56473	11.1	4.9
2003	577813	54086	9.4	4.2
Old Pvt. Sector Banks				
1999	28979	3784	13.1	5.8
2000	35404	3815	10.8	5.2
2001	39738	4420	10.9	5.2
2002	44057	4851	11	5.2
2003	51329	4568	8.9	4.3
New Pvt. Sector Banks				
1999	14070	871	6.2	2.3
2000	22816	946	4.1	1.6
2001	31499	1619	5.1	2.1
2002	76901	6811	8.9	3.9
2003	94718	7232	7.6	3.8

Source: Compiled from Report, *Trend and Progress of Banking in India, RBI 2002-03.*

So comparing the trends of private and public sector banks, private sector banks NPAs are showing much volatility than decreasing trend of NPAs in public sector banks.

It is clear from Table 3 that public sector banks have improved in net NPAs, as there is a declining trend as from 8.1% in 1999 to 4.57% in 2003. On the other hand, the NPA's in private sector banks have increased substantially. The comparative performance amongst private sector banks, i.e. between old private sector banks and new private sector banks reveals that the percentage increase in NPAs new private sector banks has more NPAs as compared to old

TABLE 3

Group-wise Net NPAs of SCB

Bank groups/year	*Net NPA as percentage of Advances*	*Net NPA as percentage to Total Assets*
Public Sector Banks		
1999	8.1	3.1
2000	7.4	2.9
2001	6.7	2.7
2002	5.8	2.4
2003	4.5	1.9
Old Pvt. Sector Banks		
1999	6.5	2.9
2000	7.1	3.3
2001	7.3	3.3
2002	7.1	3.2
2003	5.5	2.6
New Pvt. Sector Banks		
1999	2.6	1.6
2000	2.9	1.1
2001	3.1	1.2
2002	4.9	2.1
2003	4.6	2.2

Source: Compiled from Report, *Trend and Progress of Banking in India, RBI 2002-2003.*

private sector banks (i.e. 2.6% to 4.6% in case of New Pvt. sector banks from 1999 to 2003 and old Pvt. sector banks have shown a marginal decline in the year 2003 despite the fact that NPAs are still alarmingly high). As a percentage of NPAs to total assets also, NPAs in public sector banks have declined from 3.1% in 1999 to 1.9% in 2003. On the other hand, new private banks percentage increased from 1.6% to 2.2% during the same period, which is a pointer that private sector banks are in a grip of NPA menace and it is the high time to come up with strategy to overcome the problem of increasing NPAs.

Table 4 highlights sector wise NPAs of public and private sector banks. Public sector banks NPAs are dominated by priority sector lending while private sector banks are not that much involved in priority sector lending and the proportion of NPAs in non-priority sector are dominating in the private sector banks.

TABLE 4

Sector-wise NPAs of Public and Private Sector Banks

	Agriculture sector	*Small scale Industry*	*Others*
Public Sector Banks	14.6	19.24	13.39
Old Private Sector Banks	6.47	18.27	13.27
New Private Sector Banks	3.28	5.74	0.44

Source: Compiled from Report, *Trend and Progress of Banking in India, RBI 2002-03.*

The reason for more percentage of NPAs in public sector banks is due to government interference. Government launches various schemes timely for providing loans to various sectors and probability of default in priority sector is move as compared to non-priority sector Therefore, Public sector banks have move NPAs in priority sectors as compared to private sector banks. It can be concluded from the trend analysis of NPAs of public sector banks and private sector banks that public sector banks are showing declining trend of NPAs while there is much volatility in private sector banks NPAs and among private sector banks. Though the percentage of NPAs is declining in public sector banks but on the basis of primary survey (i.e., with interviews of bank employees) it has came to existence that public sector banks have more NPAs increase than decreasing trend. The fact has came to existence that on average Public Sector Banks are concealing about 40% of NPAs. Moreover public sector banks are going for more compromising policies, restructuring of accounts, etc. which results in decrease in NPAs and put bad effect on profitability of banks. This type of practice is followed because public bankers don't want to damage the image of the banks. On the other hand, in private sector banks also NPAs are increasing this is due to fact that as the time is passing more advances are becoming NPAs. Because these banks have established in mid-90s. Since the introduction of economic liberalisation and financial sector reforms, banks are undergoing pressure to bring down their NPAs so as to improve their performance and validity. The asset quality and recovery mechanism of the commercial banks have a crucial bearing on the viability of overall credit system.

SUMMARY OF FINDINGS

Apart from internal factors such as weak credit appraisal, non-compliance and wilful default, there are several external factors such as preponderance of certain traditional industries in the credit portfolio of certain banks, majority of which are suffering from serious inherent operational problems, and other such factors, which are not within the control of banks. While banks cannot be blamed for advances becoming non-performing due to external factors, there is an urgent need that the banks address the problems arising out of banks. A clear thrust on improving the skills of officials for proper assessment of credit proposal should be given.

Though there are problems in effecting recoveries and write offs and in compromise settlement. It is of utmost importance that necessary changes are brought about in the related legislations for making recovery process more smooth and less time consuming. Many steps have already been taken to tighten the noose of defaulters but still a lot needs to be done. With respect to objectives of study, i.e. to study trends of NPAs bank wise and sector wise and to review management of NPAs following findings came out.

- Large amount of funds are blocked in NPA accounts.
- NPAs in public sector banks are showing declining trend.
- Private sector banks are showing increasing trend in NPAs.

- As comparison to private banks public sector banks give more percentage of advances to priority sector and agriculture sector.
- For removing NPAs from balance sheet public sector banks are going for more compromising and restructuring policies as compared to private sector banks.
- Compared to public sector banks private sector banks have inefficient staff for assessing credit proposal.
- On average public sector banks are not disclosing NPAs about 40%. Thus, balance sheet does not disclose proper transparency.

RECOMMENDATIONS

Containing NPAs has been in focus ever in focus ever since the banking sector reforms were initiated in 1992 and RBI issued guidelines on income recognition, asset classification and provisioning norms. All banks have been making efforts to contain the NPA level and reduce the drag on their profitability. Now they are fully vigilant about the quality of their loan assets. Though it is always wise to follow-up of advances to avoid NPAs but risks attached to lending cannot be completely eliminated. Aiming for a zero-level of NPAs in the banks would be un-realistic and would be like looking for an ideal situation. So, if certain advances are converted into NPAs, it is necessary to efficiently manage them and appropriate and timely corrective steps must be taken. Reduction in NPAs is necessary to improve profitability of the banks. By the adoption of these measures banks can reduce their NPAs.

- Persuasion is one of the best method of recovery so, regular following up with borrower through correspondence and personal visit to borrower.
- Educating loanee about genuine loan requirement
- All loans should be fully secured by primary as well as collateral securities.

- Government should pass laws to give powers to bank officers for recovery of banks dues in case of wilful defaulters.
- Names of defaulters should be shown in newspapers and in websites.
- Political interference should be checked and all the risk of sponsored cases should be born by Government.
- The legal action should be taken against willful defaulter immediately.
- Proper monitoring should be during the loan period.
- Full transparency should be in disclosing NPAs so that need can be felt out for reducing NPAs.
- In line with annual business targets, budgets for reduction in NPA should be fixed. The branch-wise target may be given on the basis of an action plan that can be prepared by the branches.
- Staff accountability should be fixed for becoming bad loans and specific guidelines.

CONCLUSION

The study stresses on the emerging trends in NPAs in banking industry in India and in the new scenario the private sector banks are experiencing a dangerous trend in increasing NPA. However, the percentages of NPAs in Private sector banks are still below the international norm of NPA, i.e. 5% but it is the high time for the banks to take lessons from the public sector banks and be cautious in their lending policies.

REFERENCES

Circular of RBI No. GMO/REC/GEN/3, dated May 19, 2001.

Circular of RBI No. GMO/REC/GEN/30, dated Feb. 2, 2002.

Op. cit. Ref. No. 2.

Circular of RBI C&I/17, dated July 3, 1996.

Circular of RBI No. GMO/REC/GEN/30, dated Feb. 2, 2002.

Circular of RBI No. GMO/REC/GEN/21, dated Oct. 11, 2001.

FM May Set ARC *'The Economic Times'*, March 3, 2002.

Report, Trend and Progress of Banking in India, RBI 2002-03.

CHAPTER

19

New Revolution in the Indian Banking Industry

Internet Banking

BALWINDER SINGH AND POOJA MALHOTRA

The revolutionary developments in information and communications technology have had and will continue to have a profound impact on the banking and the financial services industry. The competitive pressures and the evolving requirements of consumers have required the banks to develop new technologies and tools. Internet banking will be an important part of these developments. It has turned out to be the nucleus issue of various studies all over the world. The present study has provided a picture of the concept of Internet banking and the scope of services offered along with the key risks associated with the adoption of this technology. The paper also describes the current state of Internet banking in India. Such a picture can provide an initial step for the likely future impact of Internet banking on the banking industry.

INTRODUCTION

With the rapid improvements in electronic technology and availability of higher computer power and faster communication technology we have more sophisticated society than in the older days. We have a better educated, better informed and better organized customer who want to be more financially sophisticated, that is, more aware of the value of funds, time and convenience. What does it require?—An efficient banking system that can provide an efficient payment system with lesser time and cost. It has resulted in more competition among the banks and also stimulated more technological developments. Internet banking that has revolutionized the banking industry world-wide is the product of this innovation. Internet banking involves consumers using the Internet to access their bank and account, to undertake banking transactions. The banks are using the electronic technology to meet the ever-increasing competition in banking which has converted the traditional brick and mortar banking into Electronic Banking (E-Banking).

We can define the electronic banking as, "delivery of bank's services to a customer at his office or home by using electronic technology."

The following developments in the Indian banking system have made it possible to use Electronic Technology to each banking transaction like cash receipts, cash payments, transfer of funds, payment of utility bills and payment of dividends and interests, etc.:

1. Automated Teller Machines (ATM)
2. Electronic Funds Transfer (EFT)
3. Electronic Data Interchange (EDI)
4. Electronic Clearing System (ECS)
5. Shared Payment Network System (SPNS)
6. Debit Cards/Credit Cards
7. Telephone Banking
8. PC Banking
9. Internet Banking
10. Mobile Banking

Internet banking is the latest and the cheapest technology introduced in the banking industry. It is acknowledged that the Internet has already had a profound effect on delivery of financial services and is likely to bring more radical changes. At the basic level, Internet banking can mean the setting up of a Web page by a bank to give information about its product and services. At an advance level, it involves provision of facilities such as accessing accounts, funds transfer, and buying financial products or services online. This is called "transactional" online banking (Sathye, 1999).

In general, Internet banking refers to the use of Internet as a delivery channel for the banking services, including traditional services, such as opening an account or transferring funds among different accounts, as well as new banking services, such as electronic bill presentment and payment, which allow the customers to pay and receive the bills on a bank's web site.

There are two ways to offer Internet banking. First, an existing bank with physical offices can establish a web site and offer Internet banking in addition to its traditional delivery channels. Second, a bank may be established as a "branchless," "Internet only," or "virtual" bank. Further Internet banking sites offer financial services products to customers in three basic formats:

Informational only

Presents online information about the different bank services and products to the customer as well as the general public and may include unsecured e-mail contact, with no customer identification or verification required.

Information exchange

Customer information such as name, address and account information may be collected or displayed, with possible secure e-mail and/or data transfer, with verification of customer identification (authentication) required. No financial transactions are to be made.

Transactional

Customer account information enquiry, financial transactions such as transfer of funds, payment of bills, application for loans and a variety of other financial transactions, with strong customer authentication required.

When first introduced, Internet banking was used mainly as an information presentation medium in which banks marketed their products and services on their Web sites. With the development of asynchronous technologies and secured electronic transaction technologies, however, more banks have come forward to use Internet banking both as a transactional as well as an informational medium. As a result, registered Internet banking users can now perform common banking transactions such as writing checks, paying bills, transferring funds, printing statements, and inquiring about account balances.

CURRENT INTERNET BANKING PRODUCTS

In general, Internet banking products are offered in a two-tiered structure. A basic tier of Internet banking products includes customer account inquiry, funds transfer and electronic bill payment. A second or premium tier includes basic services plus one or more additional services.

Basic

(1) Account inquiry.
(2) Funds transfer.
(3) Electronic bill presentment and payment.

Premium

(1) Brokerage.
(2) Cash management.
(3) Credit applications.
(4) Credit and debit cards.
(5) Customer correspondence.
(6) Demat holdings.
(7) Financial advice.

(8) Foreign exchange trading.
(9) Insurance.
(10) Online trading.
(11) Opening accounts.
(12) Requests and intimations.
(13) Tax services.
(14) E-shopping.
(15) Standing instructions.
(16) Investments.
(17) Asset management services.

PROS AND CONS

Internet banking model offers advantages for both banks and customers. The Internet provides the banks with the ability to deliver products and services to customers at a cost that is lower than any existing mode of delivery. A survey conducted in U.S. shows that of all the modes of transactions, Internet banking is the cheapest for the banks, as depicted below:

Type of Delivery Mode	*Avg. Cost*
Normal Branch Transaction	$ 1.07
Telephone Banking	$ 0.54
ATM	$ 0.27
PC Banking	$ 0.02
Internet	$ 0.01

Source: Booz Allen and Hamilton, *Banking Survey*, July, 1996 as quoted in Palsokar (2000).

Customers benefit not only from the increased convenience but also from higher interest rates resulting from cost savings by the banks. The ability to pay higher interest rate with a much wider potential of customers, allows these banks to grow faster than traditional banks.

While we feel that Online Banking is an excellent idea there are still pros and cons to banking by computer that need to be addressed.

Pros

- Consumers can use their computers and a telephone modem to dial in from home or any site where they access to a computer.
- The services are available seven days a week, 24 hours a day.
- Transactions are executed and confirmed quickly, although not instantaneously. Processing time is comparable to that of an ATM transaction.
- The range of transactions available is fairly broad. Customers can do everything from simply checking on an account balance to applying a mortgage.
- Financial planning capability. Online Banking can give fingertip access to all areas of personal money management, such as budgeting and forecasting.
- Low cost. Coastal Union will offer free software and charge minimal amounts for services.

Cons

- One must be comfortable using a computer.
- Investment of time upfront can be formidable. After several hours of peering into a computer terminal at work, the last thing you may want to do is go home and pay bills by PC.
- Switching software or banks can mean re-entry of data.
- Growing Pains. Some online banking services are coming to market before they're ready.
- One can't get cash from a PC.

The Pros are something we won't have to worry about as much as the cons. We will have to research to try and make some of the cons work for us. The primary goal of online banking is to apply convenience to the customers.

KEY INTERNET BANKING RISKS

A major driving force behind the success of I-banking all over the world is its acceptance as an extremely cost effective delivery channel of banking services as compared to other existing channels. However, Internet is not a pure blessing to the banking sector. Along with reduction in cost of transactions, it has also brought about a new orientation to risks and even new forms of risks to which banks conducting I-banking expose themselves. Regulators and supervisors all over the world are concerned that while banks should remain efficient and cost effective, they must be aware of different types of risks this form of banking entails and have systems in place to manage the same.

1. Operational Risk

Operational risk, also referred to, as transactional risk is the most common form of risk associated with I-banking. It takes the form of inaccurate processing of transactions, non-enforceability of contracts, compromises in data integrity, data privacy and confidentiality, unauthorized access/intrusion to bank's systems and transactions, etc. Such risks can arise out of weaknesses in design, implementation and monitoring of banks' information system. Besides inadequacies in technology, human factors like negligence by customers and employees, fraudulent activity of employees and crackers/ hackers, etc. can become potential source of operational risk.

2. Security Risk

Security is the biggest concern with both current and potential users of online banking services. Security risk arises on account of illegal access to a bank's critical information stores like accounting system, risk management system, portfolio management system, etc. A breach of security could result in direct financial loss to the bank. For example, hackers operating via the Internet could access, retrieve and use confidential customer information and also can embed virus. This may result in loss of data, theft of or tampering with customer information, disabling of a significant portion of bank's internal computer system thus denying service, cost of repairing these, etc. Other related risks are loss of reputation, infringing customers' privacy and its legal implications, etc. It is, therefore, necessary that banks critically assess all interrelated systems and have access control measures in place in each of them.

Though secure electronic transaction (SET) and other encryption schemes have made the actual transaction instructions relatively secure and while there haven't been reports of any of the Indian banks being hacked into, one question still nags users: nothing on the Internet is 100 percent secure and customers fear that their money is vulnerable to attack

Another path breaking technology, which could provide enhanced security to e-banking operations, is Biometrics, the science of verifying an individual's identity by means of personal characteristics, such as voice, retina, face or fingerprint. It advances the security paradigm by empowering banks to verify the actual identity of a person, and not a password or PIN code.

LBV, or Layered Biometric Verification, is one such technology, which is based not just on a single biometric verification, but also on several layered verification technologies (voice, face and fingerprint).

3. Privacy

Consumers are concerned about privacy and expect to see a privacy statement on a web site. Has a privacy policy and statement been developed for the online banking site? Can the consumer opt-in or opt-out? Are appropriate controls in place to ensure privacy and confidentiality? Does the site inform the customer of the controls in place? Are consumers informed of their rights and any limits on liability?

4. Reputational Risk

Reputational risk is the risk of getting considerable negative public opinion, which may result in a critical loss of funding or customers. Such risks arise from actions that cause major loss of the public confidence in the banks' ability to perform critical functions or impair bank-customer relationship. The main reasons for this risk may be system or product not working to the expectations of the customers, significant system deficiencies, significant security, breach (both due to internal and external attack) inadequate information to customers about product use and problem resolution procedures, significant problems with communication networks that impair customers' access to their funds or account information especially if there are no alternative means of account access. Such situation may cause customer-discontinuing use of product or the service.

Possible measures to avoid this risk are to test the system before implementation, backup facilities, contingency plans including plans to address customer problems during system disruptions, deploying virus checking, deployment of ethical hackers for plugging the loopholes and other security measures.

5. Legal Risk

Legal risk arises from violation of, or non-conformance with laws, rules, regulations, or prescribed practices, or when the legal rights and obligations of parties to a transaction are not well established. In some cases, rights and obligations are uncertain and applicability of laws and rules is uncertain or ambiguous, due to the relatively new nature of Internet banking, thus causing legal risk.

Other reasons for legal risks are uncertainty about the validity of some agreements formed via electronic media and law regarding customer disclosures and privacy protection. A customer inadequately informed about his rights and obligations, may not take proper precautions in using Internet banking products or services, leading to disputed transactions, unwanted suits against the bank or other regulatory sanctions. In the enthusiasm of enhancing customer service, bank may link their Internet site to other sites also. This may cause legal risk. Further, a hacker may use the linked site to defraud a bank customer.

6. Money Laundering Risk

As Internet banking transactions are conducted remotely banks may find it difficult to apply traditional method for detecting and preventing undesirable criminal activities. Application of money laundering rules may also be inappropriate for some forms of electronic payments. Thus banks expose themselves to the money laundering risk. This may result in legal sanctions for non-compliance with "know your customer" laws.

To avoid this, banks need to design proper customer identification and screening techniques, develop audit trails, conduct periodic compliance reviews, frame policies and procedures to spot and report suspicious activities in Internet transactions.

7. Cross Border Risks

Internet banking is based on technology that is designed to extend the geographic reach of banks and customers. Such market expansion can extend beyond national borders. This causes various risks. It includes legal and regulatory risks, as there may be uncertainty about legal requirements in some countries and jurisdiction ambiguities with respect to the responsibilities of different national authorities. Such considerations may expose banks to legal risks associated with non-compliance of different national laws and regulations, including consumer protection laws, record-keeping and reporting requirements, privacy rules and money laundering laws.

8. Strategic Risk

This risk is associated with the introduction of a new product or service. Internet banking can be seen both as a discreet business and as one of several delivery channels. Has the bank developed a realistic Internet banking business strategy that is consistent with the bank's overall strategy and aligned with the bank's other lines of business? Degree of this risk depends upon how well the institution has addressed the various issues related to development of a business plan, availability of sufficient resources to support this plan, credibility of the vendor (if outsourced) and level of the technology used in comparison to the available technology, etc.

For reducing such risk, banks need to conduct proper survey, consult experts from various fields, establish achievable goals and monitor performance. Also they need to analyze the availability and cost of additional resources, provision of adequate supporting staff, proper training of staff and adequate insurance coverage.

9. Other Risks

Traditional banking risks such as credit risk, liquidity risk, interest rate risk and market risk are also present in Internet banking. These risks get intensified due to the very nature of Internet banking on account of use of electronic channels as well as absence of geographical limits. However, their practical consequences may be of a different magnitude for banks and supervisors than operational, reputational and legal risks.

9.1 Credit Risk

It is the risk that a counter party will not settle an obligation for full value, either when due or at any time thereafter. Banks may not be able to properly evaluate the credit worthiness of the customer while extending credit through remote banking procedures, which could enhance the credit risk. Presently, banks generally deal with more familiar customer base. Facility of electronic bill payment in Internet banking may cause credit risk if a third party intermediary fails to carry out its obligations with respect to payment. Proper evaluation of the creditworthiness of a customer and audit of lending process are a must to avoid such risk.

9.2 Liquidity Risk

It arises out of a bank's inability to meet its obligations when they become due without incurring unacceptable losses, even though the bank may ultimately be able to meet its obligations. It is important for a bank engaged in electronic money transfer activities that it ensures that funds are adequate to cover redemption and settlement demands at any particular time. Failure to do so, besides exposing the bank to liquidity risk, may even give rise to legal action and reputational risk.

ANALYSIS OF INTERNET BANKING IN INDIA

In India, slowly but steadily, the Indian customer is moving towards Internet banking. While the world has seen corporate banking as the first choice for Net bankers, India seems to be reversing the trend and most initial developments seem to be in the retail banking area.

A number of banks have either adopted Internet Banking or are on the threshold of adopting it. The banks started Internet banking initially with simple functions such as getting information about interest rates, checking account balances and computing loan eligibility. Then the services were extended to online bill payment, transfer of funds between accounts and cash management services for corporate. Recently, banks have started to facilitate payment for e-commerce transactions by directly debiting bank accounts or through credit cards. It will add to the revenues of the banks.

Profile of Banks

Presently there are 30 private sector banks (21 old and 9 new), 27 public sector banks and 36 foreign banks operating in India. The paper studies the current state of Internet banking services offered by private and foreign banks operating in India. Almost all the banks are having websites; however, only 47 banks are providing transactional banking services in one form or the other which represents nearly 51 percent of total Indian commercial banks (excluding regional rural banks operating in India). Table 1 shows the adoption rates of the Internet banks.

TABLE I

Adoption Rates of Internet Banks (As on December end 2003)

	Number of Banks	*Number of Banks with Websites*	*Number of Banks with Transactional Sites*
Private Sector Banks	30	28	14 (46.7)
New	9	9	9 (100)
Old	21	19	5 (23.8)
Public Sector Banks	27	27	13(48.1)
Foreign Banks	36	35	20(55.6)
All Banks	93	90	47 (50.5)

Note: Figures in bracket denote percentage.

Source: Websites of the individual banks available at www.banknetindia.com/banklinks.htm (accessed during December, 2003).

As evidenced from Table 1, number of banks that offer Internet banking services in one form or the other, are 47 representing nearly 51 percent of the banks. Foreign banks offering Internet banking services represent 55.6 percent and banks in private sector comprise 46.7 percent. However, the true position of foreign banks offering Internet banking services in different countries is different as shown in Table 2.

TABLE 2

Position of Foreign Banks providing Internet Banking in India

No. of Banks	*Banks with Websites*	*Banks providing Internet Banking in India*	*Banks providing Internet banking*	*Accessible Websites*
36	35	25	20	16

Currently, Internet banking in India is in the form of 'online versions' of traditional banks. ICICI and HDFC for example, are working at migrating their existing customer base online. There are also 'Standalone' Internet banks such as Egg from Prudential UK, Wingspanbank, and First-e, which are predominant worldwide.

ICICI was the first bank to initiate the Internet banking revolution in India as early as 1997 under the brand name 'Infinity'. This was soon followed by HDFC, IndusInd Bank, Global Trust Bank, Federal Bank. Large public sector banks like SBI and UTI, initially slow to adopt online banking, have jumped into the fray with Bank of Baroda too planning to invest around Rs. 250 crore for its online banking operations.

Surprisingly, Indian private sector banks have outnumbered foreign banks like Standard Chartered Grindlays in the Internet banking arena with Citibank, the only foreign bank offering retail Net banking. Deutsche Bank has launched db-direct Internet, a browser-based electronic banking system for a range of corporate banking products, in place of its earlier PC-based system, where customers had to dial up to access their network. HSBC and Centurion Bank are also all set to kick off Net banking but only for employees.

Worldwide, Internet banking has witnessed a healthy growth from 2.5 million users less than four years ago, to seven million users. In India, given the low PC penetration in the country, HDFC bank alone claims to have more than 140,000 customers since they launched 'Net Banking' in September 1999.

Internet banking services offered by Indian banks range from basic 'entry level' services like accessing and tracking transactions on various accounts you have with the bank like savings accounts, fixed deposit accounts and demat accounts, to advanced services like online fund transfer transactions to facilitate bill payment. Customers can also securely move money to and from different accounts anywhere within India. However, this is restricted to self and third party accounts within the bank only.

Some of the forerunners in the Net banking arena, such as HDFC, ICICI and Citibank, are beginning to offer integrated financial services like applying for loans or paying your credit card bills online. Currently, all banks offer Internet banking services at no extra charge.

SUMMARY AND CONCLUSIONS

Information technology allows the banking industry to establish a direct link to customers. Bank customers can bank online, including viewing their account banlances, and transaction histories, paying bills, transferring funds between accounts, requesting credit card advances and ordering checks.

The banking industry also recognizes that the internet must be secure to achieve a high level of confidence with both customers and businesses. Internet banking creates new challenges for banks which must be addressed to before the adoption of this new technology. The regulator would also be concerned with whether the nature of products and services offered are within the regulatory framework and whether the transactions do not camouflage money-laundering operations. In such a scenario, the thrust of regulatory thinking has been to ensure that while the banks remain efficient and cost effective, they must be aware of the risks involved and have proper built-in safeguards, machinery and systems to manage the emerging risks. It is not enough for banks to have systems in place, but the systems must be constantly upgraded to changing and well-tested technologies, which is a much bigger challenge.

The present study has also provided a picture of the current market for Internet banking and the scope of services offered in India. Presently, most of the banks use the internet as a presentation media of various banking products and services as well as of bank information. However, complete internet banking services are provided by only a few banks. Only 47 banks provide internet banking services in one form or the other which represents only 50 percent of the total banks operating in India. Among these banks the share of new private sector banks is higher.

The market of internet banking in India is still untapped. There is a lot of scope for the Indian banks to expand their internet banking services to have a more sophisticated customer. However, the banks will have to remove the hindrances of security, reluctance to change, lack of awareness among the customers. The banks will have to provide better products and services and at lowest cost which the traditional banks can't provide.

References

All banking sites available in India at http://www.eastindiavyapaar.com/trade/bank/bank_links_websites.htm and, www.banknetindia.com/banklinks.htm accessed during December, 2003

Banknet India (2002), "Internet Banking." available at www.banknetindia.com, December.

Chou, C.D. and Chou, Y.A. (2000), "A Guide to the Internet Revolution in Banking," Information Systems Management Spring, pp. 51-57.

Corrocher, N. (2002), "Does Internet banking substitute traditional banking? Empirical evidence from Italy," Working Paper, CESPRI, No. 134, November.

Dasgupta, P. (2002), "Future of E-banking in India," available at www.projectshub.com December, accessed as on August 16, 2003.

Diniz, E. (1998). "Web Banking In USA," *Journal of Internet Banking and Commerce*, Vol. 3, No. 2, June.

Furst, K., Lang, W., William and Nolle, E., Daniel (2000), "Who Offers Internet Banking?" Office of the Comptroller of the Currency, *Quarterly Journal*, Vol. 19, No. 2, June.

Furst, K., Lang, W., William and Nolle, E. Daniel (2002), "Internet Banking: Developments and Prospects," Center for Information Policy Research, April.

Gupta, D. (1999), "Internet Banking: Where does India Stand?", *Journal of Contemporary Management*, Volume 2, No. 1, December.

Rao, G. R. and Prathima, K. (2003), "Internet Banking in India," *Mondaq Business Briefing*, April 11.

Reserve Bank of India (2001), "Report on Internet Banking" available at www.rbi.org.in, June 22.

Sathye, M. (1997), "Internet Banking In Australia," *Journal of Internet Banking and Commerce*, Vol. 2, No. 4, September.

Saxena, A. (2003) "Risks in Internet Banking," *IBA Bulletin*, September, pp. 24-30.

Seitz, J. and Stickel, E. (1998), "Internet Banking—An Overview," *Journal of Internet Banking and Commerce*, Vol. 3, No. 1, January.

Suganthi, Balachander and Balachandran (2001), "Internet Banking Patronage: An Empirical Investigation of Malaysia," *Journal of Internet Banking and Commerce*, Vol. 6, No. 1, May.

Sullivan, R.J. (2000), "How has the Adoption of Internet Banking Affected Performance and Risk at Banks? A Look at Internet Banking in the Tenth Federal Reserve District," Financial Industry Perspectives, Federal Reserve Bank of Kansas City, December.

Unnithan, C.R. and Swatman, P. (2001), "Ebanking Adaptation and Dot.Com Viability—A Comparison of Australian and Indian Experiences in the Banking Sector," Working Paper, School of Management Information Systems, Deakin University, No. 14.

Wenninger J. (2000), "The Emerging Role of Banks in E-Commerce," *Current Issues in Economics and Finance*, Volume 6, No. 3, March.

CHAPTER

20

Using Internet as a Research Tool

A Study of Consumption Patterns of the Global Online Communities

DEVINDERPAL SINGH

The globalization and proliferation of new technologies has resulted in the emergence of global communities on the World Wide Web. In these communities the members across the political borders coalesce around common interests, needs, and experiences. An attempt is here made to provide insight into consumption patterns of these online communities. This paper provides information about various methods for conducting research on these online communities, as it becomes imperative to understand this ubiquitous contemporary global social order, to understand the contemporary consumption patterns of consumers.

INTRODUCTION

Globalization of economies is transforming India and world, and especially the business world. Indian business organizations are facing intense competition from marketing savvy and high–quality foreign producers. Old marketing strategies no longer come as aid to the products and the companies in this new marketing arena. The old style marketing messages convince fewer consumers as the information explosion along with the Internet revolution has made consumers "better informed, sceptical and resistant to manipulation" (Gupta and Rajshekhar 2002). To maintain long-term profitability and market share, marketers have continuously devised strategies to build brand loyalty. In the quest for customer retention the marketers ventured into places where they could find loyal customers. This has led us to customer relationship marketing, a panacea which aimed at building brand loyalty through maintaining relationships with the customers. But this approach of building one to one relationship with customers has failed to take off because it focussed on the customer–company relationship, a view which stressed on being closest to known customers, without sharing any emotion with them. It failed to appreciate the other facets of relationship like customer-customers relationship, which emerged as a central point in this vortex of relationships. This phenomenon of relationships, which fosters a sense of belonging and 'community' has been observed as a major reason behind the success of a number of brands (Muniz and O'Guinn, 2001). The Linux users group represents a community of consumers who are champions of free software .Similarly the return of software professionals who lost their jobs as a result of global slowdown and were shown pink slips resulted in the emergence of Pink Clubs in Banglore and Hyderabad in which the members discussed their problems and found a solace in their 'community'. The consumers today have more power than before (Schiffman and Kanuk, 2004) and he is more informed, connected and active. The technologies of today have made it possible for the consumer to socialize across the world and it has resulted in the emergence of global communities or "virtual communities" on the world wide web, in which consumers coalesce around common interests, needs, and experiences, without regard for geographic or social barriers.

COMMUNITY

The term 'community' a core concept in sociology refers to a group of people, who share social interaction and some common ties between themselves and the other members of the group and who share an area for at least some of the time. Traditional communities have been based mainly on geography which included the town or village, the workplace or the café.

The concept of community was mainly confined to social thought and was rarely mentioned in the consumer behaviour, until the advent of Post Modern period—a period marked by "the sign system, hyperreality, particularism, fragmentation and the symbolic nature of consumption" (Venkatesh, 1999).

Postmodernism witnessed the beginning of end of individualism and the emergence of communities or "tribes" in the consumer culture (Cova, 1996).

Communities are identified on the basis of commonality or identification among their members, which could be "a neighbourhood, an occupation, a leisure pursuit, or devotion to a brand." People in these communities share essential resources that could be "cognitive, emotional or material in nature" (McAlexander Schouten and Koeing, 2002). McAlexander *et al.* (2002) find that market place communities were first described by Boorstin (1974) which he mentions as consumption communities. Community members in these communities may place special emphasis on some type of consumption, which could be food, drink, gifts, celebration or ritual (Muniz and O'Guinn, 2001). Consumers in these communities may coalesce around a tradition (Belk and Costa, 1998), social identity (Steven Kates, 2002), value system (Thompson and Troester 2002), entertainment (Kozinets 1997, 2002), body modification (Foster and Hammel, 2000), product (Cova and Cova, 2001) or a brand (Schouten and McAlexander, 1995; Muniz and O'Guinn, 2001).

Friends, family and community represent crucial anchors for consumers. At a time when the pace of life is accelerating for many, the sense of "belonging" becomes increasingly important. The deconstruction of old communities through the breakdown of families, greater employment mobility, decline of traditional religion and other reasons remove this anchor. New communities provide new anchors. For some, football may be seen as the new religion. It has places of worship, ritual chants, icons and sacred clothing. Like the old religion, a lack of acceptance of others' beliefs can sometimes cause friction. "Tribes" exist in both real and virtual worlds. Other anchors may be provided through communities such as support groups for single people, for sufferers of certain illnesses, enjoyment of specific leisure pursuits, etc.

Muniz and O'Guinn (2001) reveal that there are at least three core components of a community. The first is "the conscious of a kind or a way of thinking about things that is more than shared attitudes or perceived similarity." The second feature of community is the presence of shared rituals and traditions and the third is a sense of moral responsibility towards the community and it's members. In contrast, to the traditional communities, these communities are no longer restricted by geography as modern marketing, consumer culture and mass media have catalyzed the omnipresent global communities.

These communities bring to fore the importance of inter-customer relationships, which are prominently responsible for brand loyalty (Muniz and O'Guinn, 2001). This social integration results in more loyalty (Oliver, 1999). The customer advocacy (Kozinets, 2002) and sociality (Holt, 2002) influence brand equity for one brand over another. The consumers experience a sense of utopia in these aggregates (Kozinets, 2001) and construct themselves as sovereign consumers (Thompson and Haytko, 1997).

ONLINE COMMUNITIES

The communities on Internet have been variously termed as "online," "virtual," or "computer-mediated" communities (Kozinets, 1999). Kozinets finds work of Rheingold, (1993) a good starting point for any investigation of online communities. Rheingold was probably the first to write of the existence of online communities, saying that

"Virtual communities are cultural aggregations that emerge when enough people bump into each other often enough in cyberspace." These virtual communities are based around online third places such as chat rooms and conferencing systems. Rheingold goes on to say that members of virtual communities join together online to do everything that others do in the physical world. The obvious difference is that members of online communities interact, many times exclusively, via text on computer screens. This means a change in the nature of a community even if many of the traits displayed are similar. New communities are not so much linked by location but more by common interests.

Many of the new communities arise through the ability of new communications media to reach people with similar interests around the globe. The media channels bring together people with the same interests and geography is no longer a limiting factor. As before, the community members share a common territory although this territory is no longer based on location. This allows members to belong to many communities based on work or leisure interests or beliefs. Consumption knowledge is learned along with the knowledge of the online group's cultural norms, specialized jargon and language, concepts, and the identities of other group members. What had started as a search for information transforms into a source of community (Kozinets, 1999). As such, the new communities have the potential to be more fluid than old communities as members opt in and out as they wish. Flexibility is important, not just for the community but also for the members.

New communities are frequently based on the Web or via e-mail discussion lists. Moonfruit.com, for example, invites you to "share your passion" and build your own Web site within the Moonfruit community. Similarly major search engines like MSN search encourage people to form own groups.

SIGNIFICANCE TO MARKETING

These Internet communities "signal a power shift from manufacturers to customers: the communities are information gathering and information-disseminating conduits"

(Venkatraman and Henderson 1998). Marketers have recognized the importance of these online communities as they provide a platform for the advocacy of the brands and provide a source to the market researchers to study the tastes, desires, and other needs of consumers who interact in online communities (Kozinets, 2002). Yahoo's acquisition of e-Groups in July 2000 is a clear indication of the interest that marketers are taking in the development of new communities. e-Groups uses e-mail to target consumers, using permission marketing, or opt-in-e-mail, that is constructed around different interest groups or communities. By 2000, e-Groups had 600,000 groups in 22 countries and 14 languages. e-Groups and the rise of other companies that enable consumers to construct on-line communities such as Geo-Cities (also owned by Yahoo!), Tripod, Moonfruit and Sony's Friend Factory are indicative of some of the new types of community that are evolving and that are proving to be increasingly attractive to marketers.

The Swedish site Dobedo has been extensively advertised to encourage new members and hence advertisers. It even enables advertisers to attach real brands to virtual messages. Brands are often used by consumers as totemistic symbols to say something about who they are and what values they have. This applies in new communities as much if not more than before.

However, the new communities are not just places for consumers to meet. There are clear businesses to business opportunities too. Communities are evolving for different reasons. They may connect small business owners, teleworkers, working women or other interest groups. Communities such as First Tuesday, for example, have represented the venture capital industry, a worldwide initiative made up of virtual and real-world meetings.

First Tuesday is an example of a community that has developed further into a company. It may help to promote investment in Internet start-ups but it is the regular meetings in 100 cities around the world that form the backbone of its success. Similarly, FitnessJumpsite.com has evolved from e-mail communication and Internet discussion groups to a wider community based around quality fitness, health and nutrition-related education around the world.

Many marketers are starting to view the new communities as ways in which they can reach like-minded people. Unilever, Johnson and Johnson and Tesco are all involved in the Web-based women's community i-Village. Recently Tesco and i-Village announced a joint venture to develop a UK version of the community that has been running in the USA since 1995. This is i-Village's first initiative outside the UK and represents a means for Tesco, the world's largest on-line grocer to reach one of its key target markets. Women are rapidly growing as a proportion of the on-line market and are estimated to account for 60% by 2005. Unilever sees its involvement in i-Village and the teenage portal wowgo.com as an important way to reach its target audience.

Word of mouth is arguably the most effective form of marketing communications and hence numerous companies have recently investigated viral marketing to help promote their brands. Community involvement is one way to further encourage this. Just as the adoption of products and brands by "leaders" of old communities can help spread consumption through the community members, the new communities also have opinion leaders. The targeting of marketing communications through relevant communities can help a product or brand gain acceptance and even prestige. The mere presence of a brand within a specific community can provide a positive association if it is correctly managed and accepted by the community.

Some of the larger communities represent huge potential markets. The US portal gay.com claimed some 8 million visitors during December 1999. Moreover, they tend to have incomes well over the national average! iVillage membership reached over 5 million in the second quarter of 2000 with year-on-year revenue growth over 200%. As such, they represent major marketing opportunities.

METHODS FOR STUDY

Marketing researchers employ different methods to understand the consumer behaviour. Qualitative methods are useful to reveal the underlying "needs, desires, meanings and choice" (Kozinets, 2002). Focus groups, personal interviews and ethnography are the widely used methods for understanding consumer behaviour. Focus groups and personal interviews even though less time consuming and simple are more obtrusive and artificial. The respondents tend to give cognitive answers to emotional issues. The main problem is that consumers often buy emotionally and justify rationally. The focus group discussion and interviews tend to trigger rational thoughts because in such a formal setting, people do not like to concede that they are influenced in a irrational manner. Moreover, a respondent may not recall certain issues arising during shopping or product use.

Ethnography is a marketing research methodology that emulates an anthropological method of study in which naturalistic observation and semi-structured interviewing are combined to see how consumers behave in their natural setting. It is an open-ended technique based on participation and observation in a natural setting. This method, even though less obtrusive than focus groups and personal interviews but it is time consuming and involves more research resources and skill (Kozinets, 2002).

"Netnography" or ethnography on the Internet is a new qualitative research method that extends ethnographic research techniques to study online communities. It utilizes the information that is available on Internet and understands the various aspects of relevant on online consumer groups. It is less time consuming, less costly, naturalistic and unobtrusive but it has a narrow focus on online communities.

ETHNOGRAPHY ON NET

The researcher having specific question of interest to him must gain information about the forums, groups and other participants relevant to his area of interest. A forum is any discussion group accessible through a dial-in bulletin board service, a mailing list, or a news group. The various types of groups on Internet are usually free websites that are created and managed by a group manager group may have features like message boards, chat rooms and photo albums. The boards are also known as Usenet groups or newsgroups or discussion forums.

Usenet is, in many ways, like a worldwide bulletin board where people around the globe read and post messages. While the exact figures are unknown, millions of people participate in this discussion on a daily basis. Millions of messages are posted to this global message board every day. These messages are then automatically sorted into thousands of different categories. Each category is known as a newsgroup. At current count, there are approximately 20,000 different newsgroups with subjects ranging from the serious to the trivial to the offensive.

The naming and organization of newsgroups follows a somewhat hierarchical structure. Each newsgroup has a name consisting of multiple parts separated by periods or dots. The first part is an identifier indicating the broadest topic category. The second part narrows the topic, and so on. One example is rec.food.recipes. The first part, *rec,* is at the top of the naming hierarchy. It indicates that the topic of this group is recreational. The second part, *food,* narrows the subject specifically while the third, *recipes,* indicates that this is not a general discussion of food, but that it deals with recipes (unlike <rec.food.cooking>, <rec.food.chocolate>, or <rec.food.restaurants>).

Most newsgroups are oriented towards discussion. This makes Usenet an ideal source of material for critiquing and analyzing not only argument, but also language. Someone would start a topic with a posting on a bulletin board. Someone else would reply. This initial post and response now constituted a "thread" on the topic. The thread might grow to include dozens or even hundreds of individuals responding to the first post or any that came after it. They might start threads of their own as offshoots of the original discussion. For example, discussion centering on topic 'whether beer dehydrates the body or not', is a thread. Threads could be collected for analysis in class of language, style, or logic. This type of activity could be particularly useful in demonstrating the need for well-supported and logically coherent writing.

Most newsgroups are discussions groups in which any individual can participate. However, there are some exceptions. A few groups are moderated to ensure that groups stay on the topic. One such group is the example above of <rec.food.recipes>. This group is strictly for requesting and posting recipes; no discussion is allowed. A group of moderators filters the articles (all messages posted in newsgroups are known as articles) according to the group's guidelines.

In addition, there are a few newsgroups, such as news.answers and sci.space.shuttle which are strictly for posting FAQs (frequently asked questions) or informational bulletins. Groups such as these do not allow discussion. Newsgroups vary considerably as to what participants will tolerate; some groups are close-knit communities with very definite norms, while others are more tolerant, with less structure to influence behaviour. Search engines like Google.com and MSN search provide a list of newsgroups on any conceivable topic. These search engines encourage the visitors on their sites to form their own group and develop a community anchoring on any topic. One can form and manage one's own group at groups.msn.com.

Chat rooms cover online discussion. Even though the discussion is on the topics of interest but it is "often fantasy-oriented, social, sexual, and relational in nature" (Kozinets, 2002). A group manager may regularly schedule sessions with special guests. Some groups maintain photo albums of their members and even articles of common interest.

The second source of information which may be of interest to marketers on online communities are thematically linked web rings or even independent web pages. On sites like epinions .com one obtain information on discussion on a variety of topics and can even have information on the profile of the participant and the summary of his activity in discussions.

A listserv, another source of information on online communities is a way for a group of people to share information collectively through e-mail. Some listservs are participatory others are not. A listserv is a way for a group of people to share information collectively through e-mail. Once you sign up for the listserv, you will be sent instructions on how to address your future e-mail to everyone else in the group. When you want everyone on the listserv to receive your e-mail, as part of a discussion with everyone, you address it one way. When you want to respond to an individual about his or her comments, you address your e-mail just to that individual.

When you sign up for a listserv, you send a message to an e-mail address, following whatever instructions you are given by the keepers of the listserv. Sometimes you can subscribe to the listserv on a website. Within a day or so, you will receive a message back that you have been added to the mailing list, and there will be instructions on how to find out who else is on the list, how to unsubscribe when you want to, and many other basic instructions. Many sites maintain the archives and databases of past listservs on various topics which can be searched by keywords. CataList is one of such sites which maintains a catalog of more than 27,000 listserv mailing lists and can be reached at www.lsoft.com/lists/listref.html.

When suitable online communities have been identified the researcher can select them on the basis of the amount of traffic or activity in these self-segmented communities. The researcher can then collect information from these selected sources and then interpret the observations on the community.

RESEARCH METHODOLOGY

I had applied the qualitative method of "Netnography" to interpret the meaning of contemporary beer consumption to the online beer community, which is dedicated to the discussions related to the beer. This research could help the beer companies to have an insight into the new consumption trends.

The research began by connecting to yahoo Groups and coping the archives of the postings of newsgroup named beerlovers2 between 30th November, 2000 and 21st August, 2002. About 214 postings were copied on all threads between the above said time period. The site, BeerAdvocate.com Groups that manages private beer-related groups, which has heavy traffic was selected and information on various beerfests to be held was copied. Further relevant postings with good number of replies were chosen and 100 postings were downloaded. Another site Beer.com that maintains archives on beer discussion was visited and 303 postings were copied. The FAQs of newsgroups <alt.beer>and <rec.food.drink.beer> were copied to have an insight into the interests of the community and their areas of curiosity.

The postings of different sites were classified into different topics on the basis of relevancy to the research topic. The threads that were relevant and representative were chosen.

ANALYSIS AND INTERPRETATION

The different postings were categorized into different categories on the basis of comparison of their similarities and differences. The analysis is qualitative and unstructured interpretation is done.

The online beer community holds many beerfests and which are important to most of them. They provide the geographically dispersed members an opportunity for high context interaction (McAlexander, Schouten and Koeing, 2002). The rendezvous is announced and posted before hand and the "beer crawl" places are mentioned. The names of the active members who are expected to participate are announced. Beer companies may sponsor many beer festivals. These fests mainly focus on beer appreciation or craftsmanship behind beer but sometimes the fest may be held for charitable purposes and by a moral community (Kozinets, 2001) holds them as charitable acts as a posting for one of the beer festival says:

Beer for a Cure to benefit the Leukemia and Lymphoma Society. Kahn's, Chalkies, and World Class Beverage beer tasting at the Montage (Allison Pointe). $25 ($30 at door), 50+ beers, and hors d'oeuvres. Tasting will be arranged by style, with beers from: Bell's, Three Floyds, Rogue, Brasserie d'Achouffe, Upland, Corsendonk, Schneider, Spaten, North Coast, Arcadia, Rebel, Summit, Samuel Smith, Pyramid, Black Sheep, Brouwerij Van Steenberge and more. . . .

There is presence of shared rituals (Muniz and O'Guinn, 2001) as they discuss beer styles, glassware and how to pour, taste and store beer. In these communities as they discuss the taste of beer and discuss the various forms of beer like ciders, ales and lagers which may differ on the type of yeast for fermentation. The community has its own language which they use while discussing on any topic and includes terminology like beer crawls, beer tower, ciders, ales, lagers, porter, etc. In some beer fests souvenir like mugs and T-shirts may be distributed. There are brewing competitions held at the fests showing appreciation for home brewed beer. There is great interest shown by the community to home brew the beer, that is why one of the FAQs is "How do I make it?." The key values of reverence are "handmade over manufactured, do-it-yourself over purchased services" (Belk and Costa, 1998).

The community members have a sense of moral responsibility towards the community (Muniz and O'Guinn, 2002). The connoisseurs educate the members about the art of pouring, tasting and storing beer. The features of good bears along with the various brands are the one of the major topics of discussion. The members are taught the method to hold beer festivals and the art of brewing at home. The response to one of the question: "How do I judge a beer?" suffices the moral responsibility that members have towards their community in the following way:

Much has been written about wine tasting, and that technique and vocabulary apply quite nicely to beer, as well. Of course, beer is a more complex beverage and its evaluation covers some additional ground, but the concepts are the same. The biggest change most drinkers must undergo is warming up their beer. Ice cold beer numbs the taste buds and doesn't allow the beer to develop its full flavour potential. In general, pale beer is best served at cooler temperatures than dark beer, and lagers cooler than ales. Start with 40-50F (5-10C) for the cooler beers and 50-60F (10-15C) for the warmer ones.

Beer should be evaluated using four senses: sight, smell, taste, feel. Always drink beer from a clear glass to fully appreciate it. Look at it and note the color and clarity. Hold it up to a light if necessary. Take a good sniff from the glass to get the aroma or bouquet. Taste it, swishing it around in your mouth, and notice its body and flavours. After swallowing, notice any aftertaste or finish.

You should be noticing things like:

Was it golden, amber, black?
Clear or cloudy?
Did it smell sweet, malty, flowery, alcoholic?
Did it taste bitter, sweet, tart, smooth, roasty?
Did it feel "thick" or "thin" as you swished it around?
Did it leave a buttery taste, nutty, fruity?

With additional experience and some reading you will begin to develop not only a sense of what you enjoy, but what marks a truly good beer from a bland or mediocre one.

Also, it is usually a good idea to try a beer more than once. Get it from different sources, try it when your in a different mood or setting, wait for a full moon, whatever. Many factors will affect your overall perception, so be flexible. Be aware, as well, that tasting many beers at once is not a good idea. The taste buds begin to tire and send confusing impressions.

The members look for their solutions within the community. To a community member who is in a dilemma whether he should swirl beer or not, the solution is provided to him by a member in his community in the following way:

OK, this I know and know well since I used to wonder the same thing and came to learn it. If you're drinking wheat based beers like german wheats (Franziskaner, Schneider Wiesse, Aventinus, etc.) or belgian whites (Hoegaarden, Alagash White, Blanche De Chambly, etc.) than you DO want to swirl!! I makes a BIG difference if you swirl. If you don't the beer will be much lighter and weaker in taste. I pour the beer until there's about a half inch left then swirl it fast both clockwise and counter clockwise until ALL the sediment is mixed into the beer and there's none remaining at the bottom of the bottle. Then I wait a few seconds for the foam to settle a little then pour. If you swirl it with 1/3 still in the bottle you'll get too much foaming. Now, for Belgian beers like Dubbels and Tripples you do NOT want to swirl. It's not necessary at all anyway cause the beers are heavy enough and are meant to be drank without the sediment. That also goes for other beers that have sediment like England's Fuller's Vintage. So my general rule is to only swirl wheat based beers. Hope .this info is helpful

There is evidence of inflections of post-modernism on this community as one of the members calls it "unfortunate" that there is a policy of not to have beer during lunch. Some members' sentiments find a vent against the modern branding paradigm which is a "company-generated template" in the following lines:

You might as well ask In fact, any country in the world with a sufficiently large brewer is guilty of brewing beer that is (ahem) less than it could be. In an effort to boost profit margins and still be acceptable to the broadest possible market, the mega-brewers have resorted to using cheaper adjuncts, like corn and rice, instead of all barley malt. The resulting less-sweet beer doesn't need as much balancing bitterness, so they cut back on hops to save money and to make the end-product innocuous to the casual drinker. The change has been a gradual one, taking place in small increments over many years, so that most consumers would not notice the difference. These practices are followed up by huge, multi-media, marketing campaigns that attempt to sell brand image rather than beer flavour.

SUMMARY

The understanding of communities is one way in which marketers can look to achieve greater recognition and acceptance for their brands. The way in which a marketer becomes involved is crucial to the level of success that may be achieved. It is important to work with the community, not simply to broadcast advertising messages at the community in the hope that some of them stick. Genuine involvement in the community helps to build trust and encourage acceptance.

It has also been suggested that community involvement adds a human element to what may sometimes be viewed as a cold e-commerce environment. It provides the necessary personal interaction that is missing. If the product or brand involvement is genuine and relevant to the community, there is a possibility to synchronize the e-commerce offering and community involvement.

This is an evolving environment for brands. One aspect enabling the new communities to be formed and develop quickly is the use of newer communications channels. As Through the Loop's previous work on The Third Age of Internet shows, this channel evolution is continuing so these communities can be expected to utilise channels such as mobile phones, WAP, SMS messaging, Smart Home devices, etc. All of this means expanding opportunities for marketers. But it's not all about new channels. More traditional forms of marketing communication such as event marketing or ongoing sponsorship represent an often effective way of demonstrating involvement with the community.

References

Belk, Russell W. and Costa, Janeen Arnold (1998), "The Mountain Man Myth: A Contemporary Consuming Fantasy," *Journal of Consumer Research,* 25(3) (December) 218-29.

Boorstin, Daniel J. (1974), The Americans: *The Democratic Experience,* New York: Vintage.

Cova, Bernard (1996), "The Postmodern Explained to Managers: Implications for Marketing," *Business Horizons,* November-December.

Cova, Bernard and Cova, Veronique (2001), "Tribal Marketing: The Tribalisation Of Society and it's Impact on the Conduct of Marketing," *European Journal of Marketing* (January).

Foster, Gary S. and Hummel Richard L. (2001), "The Commodification of Body Modification: Tattoos and Piercings from Counterculture to Campus," Presented at the Annual Meeting of the Midwest Sociological Society, Chicago, Illinois (April 21).

Gupta, Inderjit and Rajshekhar, M. (2002), "Why is Marketing not Working," *Business World* (November) 28-36.

Holt, Douglas B.(2002), "Why Do Brands Cause Trouble? A Dialectical Theory of Consumer Culture and Brand," *Journal of Consumer Research* (29) (June) 70-89.

Kates, Steven (2001), "Marketing's Interpretive Communities: An New Form of Sociocultural Segmentation?", Monash University.

———(2002), "The Protean Quality of Subcultural Consumption:An Ethnographic Account of Gay Consumers," *Journal of Consumer Research,* 29 (December), 383-99.

Kozinets, Robert V. (1997), '"I Want to Believe': A Netnography of The X-Philes' Subculture of Consumption," *Advances in Consumer Research,* Vol. 24, ed., Merrie Brucks and Deborah J. MacInns, Provo, UT: Association for Consumer Researh, 470-75.

———(1999), "E-Tribalized Marketing?: The Strategic Implications of Virtual Communities of Consumption," *European Management Journal*, 17(3), 252-64.

———(2001), "Utopian Enterprise: Articulating the Meanings of Star Trek's Culture of Consumption," *Journal of Consumer Research*, 28(1), (June).

Muniz, Albert and Thomas C. O'Guinn (2001), "Brand Community," *Journal of Consumer Research*, 27(4).

Oliver, Richard L. (1999), "Whence Consumer Loyalty," *Journal of Marketing*, (63) (Special Issue), 33-44.

Rheingold, H. (1993), *The Virtual Community:Homesteading on the Electronic Frontier*, Reading, MA: Addison-Wesley.

Schouten, John W. and James H. McAlexander (1995), "Subcultures of Consumption: An Ethnography of the New Bikers," *Journal of Consumer Research*, 22 (June), 43-61.

Schouten, John W. and James H., McAlexander and Koeing, Harold F. (2002), "Building Brand Community," *Journal of Marketing*, 66(38-54) Janauary.

Sherry Jr., John F., *et al.* (2001), "Being in the Zone", *Journal of Contemporary Ethnography*, 30(4), (August) 465-510.

Shiffman, Leon G.and Kanuk, Leslie Lazar (2004), *Consumer Behaviour*, Delhi: Pearson.

Thompson, Craig J., and Troester, Maura (2002), "Consumer Value Systems in the Age of Postmodern Fragmentation: The Case of the Natural Health Microculture," *Journal of Consumer Research*, 28 (March), 550-71.

Venkataman, N. and Henderson, John C. (1998), "Real Strategies for Virtual Organizing," *Sloan Management Review*, Fall (40) 33-48.

Venkatesh Alladi (1999), "Postmodernism Perspectives for Macromarketing: An Inquiry into the Global Information and Sign Economy," *Journal of Macromarketing* (19), (December).

CHAPTER

21

Implementation of ERP Systems

Application of Multi-dimensional Approach

ASHIM RAJ SINGLA AND D.P. GOYAL

The Enterprise Resource Planning (ERP) software market has been growing at a very fast pace over the last several years and has been predicted to keep growing rapidly in the long-term. ERP systems are most integrated information systems that cut across various organizations as well as various functional areas. Also ERP software projects include the implementation of new internet-based IT architectures and business models. A successful ERP implementation can shorten production cycles, increase the accuracy of demand forecast, improve customer service, trim fat from operating expenses, and may lead to a reduction in overall information technology cost by eliminating redundant information and computer systems. It has been found that ERP systems prove to be a failure either in the design or its implementation. In this paper, we propose a framework for overall ERP system implementation and a design of program management that contributes to the success of complex ERP implementation. This framework is designed to facilitate small and medium level companies to implement ERP system of their own.

Keywords: Enterprise Resource Planning (ERP), Implementation, Planning and Implementation models, Information systems Implementation.

I. INTRODUCTION

Today's business and competitive climate requires more than just providing high-quality and, low-cost products to customers. Not only the customers and suppliers require information that is fully integrated throughout the supply chain or value chain, industries also require timely and flexible responses to changing market conditions. The implementation of an ERP software packages can help to enable or even drive the required changes towards faster, more accurate, and integrated information. ERP software can integrate various business processes and departments across the organization into a single computer system. It has potential to integrate database, data flows, and systems even across different companies, and to streamline operations and reporting. It is packaged software designed for a client-server/ distributed environment and preferably integrated with web-based environment. It allows integration of transaction processing and access to real time data. Moreever ERP system implementation provides one of the primary tools for Business Process Reengineering (BPR). Reengineering should be implemented along a spectrum of approaches that range from a technology enabled approach to a clean slate approach. A technology enabled approach limits the set of design choices and thus resulting in avoiding information overload and difficulty in choosing between particular choices (Daniel E. O'Leary, 2000). Similarly, one of the critical set of decisions that needs to be made in any ERP concerns the choice of common standard models, artifacts and processes. The quality of these has a huge impact on overall success of ERP implementation.

The implementation methodology of ERP system is greatly dependent on organizational size, complexity, structure and in terms of overall extent of the implementation. Keeping these factors in mind, an entire suite of ERP applications can be implemented at all locations at the same time or various applications/modules can be implemented one at a time in a group of modules, often a single location at a time.

SURVEY OF LITERATURE

Duration of implementing an ERP software project is related to size and complexity of client organization. Software implementers play a key role, not only in technical terms, but also in managerial and political terms, because they can help their clients in correcting their expectations and perceptions of ERP systems and ERP implementations (Frederic Adam, Peter O' Doherty, 2000). The teaching methodology of ERP system should focuses on three topics: The traditional management of operations in a functional organization; The integrated, dynamic approach to operations(including team development and process management); Use of advanced information systems to support the management of operations (Avraham Shtub, 2000). Success of ERP software implementation is dependent on design of program management. Three measures of ERP implementation complexity are: variety, variability, and integration. Variety reflects the number of elements, variability relates to dynamics over a time and integration of IT systems across business processes (Pieter Ribbers, Klaus-Schoo, 2002). A design interface with a process plan is an essential part of the system integration process in ERP. By interfacing with a process plan module, a design interface module helps the sequence of individual operations needed for the step-by-step production of a finished product from raw materials (Hwa Gyoo Park). Motivation for ERP system may be varied but their utility to the organizations can not be undermined. If organizations are not able to elicit meaningful and appropriate user involvement, user participation will tend to dilute the potential impact of ERP project. The source of such inadequate participation could well be the nature of the ERP implementation process itself wherein users are involved only after a decision to implement certain package has already been taken (Shivraj Kanungo, Shantanu Bagchi, 2000). Unique risks in ERP implementation arises due to tightly linked interdependencies of business processes, relational databases, and process reengineering (Sally Wright, Arnold M. Wright, 2002). Business risks drive from the models, artifacts, and processes that are chosen and adopted as a part of implementation and are generated from the firm's portfolio of MAP's with respect to their internal consistency and their external match with business partners. Organizational risks derive from the environment—including personnel and organizational structure—in which the system is chosen and implemented (Daniel E. O'Leary, 2000). ERP implementation failure rate is from 40% to 60%, yet companies try to implement these systems because they are absolutely essential to responsive planning and communication (Gray A. Langenwalter, 2000). A careful use of communication and change management procedures is required to handle the often business process reengineering impact of ERP systems which can alleviate some of the problems, but a more fundamental issue of concern is the cost feasibility of system integration, training and user licenses, system utilization, etc. needs to be checked (David Allen, Thomas Kern, 2002).

Knowledge of such factors is important in design of a framework for planning and implementation of complex ERP systems. But there are certain gaps in existing studies regarding ERP implementation.

Objective

Keeping in view the importance and gaps in research, a study was conducted with the objectives to find critical factors for ERP implementation in selected organizations and to present a framework for successful ERP implementation.

Scope

The study has been conducted in two large manufacturing public sector organizations PUNCOM (Telecom system) and PTL (Tractors) located in northern India. PUNCOM specialize in R & D as well as manufacturing in telecommunication systems and various related equipments. It has developed its enterprise-wide product to streamline the whole system. On the other hand PTL is large tractor manufacturing unit and is controlling its own several subsidiary units. One of its subsidiaries SWRAJ is developing mini trucks. PTL is using its self designed enterprise-wide product, but is planning to implement SAP.

Research Methodology

1. Secondary data for research was collected from related books, publication, annual reports, and records of organization under study.
2. Primary data has been collected through questionnaire-*cum*-interview technique. For this purpose questionnaire was created on already established models and survey of literature. Questionnaire was first pre-tested on 20 managers from the actual sample to be interviewed for checking its reliability and content validity. Cronbach's alpha test was applied, where the value of coefficient was 0.987. Thus pre-tested and modified questionnaire was administered to all the sampled respondents. For developing design model, all the managers in the EDP departments of each of the selected organizations were interviewed. Where as for the purpose of developing implementation model all the managers in the EDP departments along with an appropriate sample of the managers at the three levels of the management of each of the selected organizations were selected. The sample of the randomly selected managers was proportionate and statistically sound that represents the universe of managers of the selected organizations. 70 experienced respondents from both the companies who specialize in their related production skills and use of ERP system had participated in the study.
3. Data was collected on 5 point scale depending on the relative importance of a factor. Finally the factor analysis is applied to analyze the data to arrive useful conclusions using SPSS package.

FINDINGS

The thus collected data were subjected to various types of statistical methods to analyze the critical success factors in ERP system design and implementation. Table 1 lists the score for each of the 3 factors each in planning phase, project phase and critical success factors in ERP system implementation. Similarly Table2 gives the ranking of these implementation factors as calculated by the factor analysis. The rotated component matrix of factor analysis for all 3 classes of implementation factors is given respectively in Appendix Tables 1, 2 and 3. The analysis of Table1 reveals that Gap analysis is most important factor in ERP system implementation. It is important to identify which ERP modules are required to be installed and analyzing the current business processes to find the level of BPR required and on that basis creating project implementation plan keeping in mind shortened and eliminated business process cycles. User training (4.26) is ranked 2nd. ERP system training should be based on methodology, phases, tasks, deliverables and tools supporting the methodology. Implementation team set-up (4.19) is ranked 3rd according to the study. It is important to identify functional heads/project leaders, BPR consultants and team managers for successful implementation of ERP systems. Implementation constraints (3.93) ranked 4th includes consideration on financial constraints and training problems. Management support (3.76) is highly important in successful implementation. Similarly, Risk management strategy (3.59) includes factors like creating smaller user groups, minimal customization and un-complicated option selection, fewer modules for installation, which are followed by system configuration and design, package selection and system testing.

3. RECOMMENDATIONS

It emanates from the above study that ERP system links together an organizational strategy, structure and business processes with the IT systems. Based on the study, following recommendations are put forward for successful

TABLE I

Issues of Risks in ERP System Design and Implementation as Tested in PUNCOM and PTL (N=70)

Factors	*Issues*	*Average Score*
1	*2*	*3*
Planning phase factor for ERP Implementation		
Implementation team Set-up	Identifying functional heads/project leader.	4.26
	Appoint an outside ERP BPR consultant.	4.39
	Set BPR objectives and responsibilities.	4.21
	Assembly of steering committee.	4.40
	Determination of high level project scope and broad implementation approach	3.97
	Selection of a project team manager.	3.94
Gap analysis	Identification of ERP system modules for installation.	4.24
	Project team is selected and structured with appropriate mix of technical and business expertise.	4.43
	Analysis of current business processes.	4.13
	Creating a plan and understanding eliminated and shortened process cycles.	4.20
	Determine level of BPR required.	4.06
	ERP implementation resource determination.	3.71
	Organizations commitment.	3.80
	Clear communications of strategic goals.	
	View ERP as enterprise wide venture.	3.86
Package Selection	Selection of ERP package.	3.37
Project phase factor for ERP Implementation		
Testing	Population of test instances with real data.	3.13
	Building and testing the interface.	3.13
	Writing and testing reports.	3.13
	System and user testing	3.14
	Consultant performance.	3.63
Configuration and Design	Install ERP and map the modules with business processes.	3.93
	Apply high level design and detailed design subject to user acceptance.	3.80
	Apply interactive prototyping method in design	3.44
	Building network for ERP.	3.24
	Installation of various desktops.	3.06
	Vendor performance.	3.47
Implementation Constraints	Financial constraints.	4.11

(Contd.)

1	2	3
	Training problems.	4.00
	Management commitment.	3.70
Critical success factors for ERP Implementation		
User training	Training on methodology approach, phases, tasks and deliverables.	4.69
	Training on tools supporting the methodology.	4.36
	Set realistic milestones and delivery dates.	4.23
	Provide evidence of the value of new methodology.	3.74
Management support	Top management's advocacy.	3.71
	Provision for adequate resources.	4.01
	Steering committee/member of project core team are independent of taking decisions.	3.96
	In developing an internal training plan.	3.37
Risk management strategy	Minimal customization and uncomplicated option selection.	3.67
	Fewer modules and less functionality implemented	3.37
	The old system, including all informal system are eliminated.	3.13
	Training on benefits of reusability.	4.11
	Smaller user groups and fewer sites.	3.37
	Legacy system is working in parallel.	3.93

TABLE 2

Ranking of ERP System Implementation Factors as Tested in PUNCOM and PTL (N=70)

Implementation Factors	
Risk Factors	*Score*
Gap analysis	4.48
User training	4.26
Implementation team Set-up	4.19
Implementation Constraints	3.93
Management support	3.76
Risk management strategy	3.59
Configuration and Design	3.49
Package Selection	3.37
Testing	3.23

Average Score	**Importance Level**
4.00-5.00	Highest
3.00-4.00	Moderate
2.00-3.00	Slight
1.00-2.00	Least

TABLE 3

Recommendations for Successful ERP Implementation

Phases	*Issues*
Gap analysis	• Analysis of current business processes to understand their process flows and to determine level of BPR required. Thus implementation plan should be based on that, incorporating eliminated and shortened process cycles and generating required resources. • Moreover it is important to identify ERP modules required for installation. • Project team is selected and structured with appropriate mix of technical and business expertise. • View ERP as enterprise wide venture thus organizations commitment and clear communications of strategic goals is very important.
User training	• Training on methodology approach, phases, tasks, deliverables and tools supporting methodology with realistic milestones and delivery dates.
Implementation team Set-up	• Identifying functional heads/project leader, BPR consultant and thus constituting the steering committee. • High level project scope and broad implementation approach with clear cut BPR objectives and responsibilities.
Implementation Constraints Management support	• System implementation strategy should take care of risk factors like financial constraints, training problems and management commitment. • Top management's advocacy and support in implementation, creating provision for adequate resources and making steering committee independent of taking decisions.
Risk management strategy	• Minimal customization, uncomplicated option selection, smaller user groups and fewer sites, with fewer modules and less functionality. • Training on benefits of reusability. • Legacy system is working in parallel.
Configuration and Design	• Apply high level design and detailed design with interactive prototyping. • Install ERP and map the modules with business processes. • Building network and installation of various desktops.
Testing	• Building and testing the interface and reports by population of test instances with real data. • System and user testing

implementation of ERP systems in any organizations and specifically in selected organizations.

CONCLUSIONS

To conclude the study, it may be emphasized that a multidimensional approach in ERP system implementation, including issues like Gap analysis, user training, implementation team set-up, implementation constraints, management support, risk management strategy, configuration and design, package selection and system testing will surely help in smooth and successful implementation of ERP systems in any organization in general and in the selected organization in particular.

REFERENCES

Allen David, Kern Thomas Kern and Havenhand Mark (2002), "ERP Critical Success Factors: an exploration of the contextual factors in public sector institutions", Proceedings of 35th Annual Hawaii International Conference on System Sciences.

Avraham Shtub (2001), "A framework for teaching and training in the ERP era", *International Journal of Production Research*, 3, 567-576.

C. Boynton Andrew and W. Zmud Robert (1984): "An Assessment of Critical Success Factors", *Sloan Management Review*, University of North Carolina.

Colette Rolland, Naveen Prakash (2001), "Matching ERP system functionality to customer requirement", IEEE, 1090-705X.

Daniel E. O'Leary (2002). "Information system assurance for ERP systems: Unique Risk Considerations", *Journal of Information Systems*, 16, 115-126.

Davis, Gordon B. (1986): "An empirical study of the impact of user involvement on system usage and information satisfaction", Communications of the ACM, 29 (3): 232-38..

Elisabeth J. Umble, M.Michael Umble (2002), "Avoiding ERP implementation Failure", Industrial Management.

Franch Xavier, Illa Xavier and Antoni Pastor Joan (2000), "Formalising ERP selection criteria", IEEE.

Gibson Nicola, Light Ben and P. Holland Christopher (1999), "Enterprise Resource Planning: A Business Approach to Systems Development", Proceedings of 32nd Hawaii International Conference on System Sciences.

Goyal, D.P. (2000), Management Information System, Managerial Perspective. New Delhi: Macmillan India Ltd.

Keng Saiu, Jake Messersmith (2002), "Enabling Technologies for E-Comm and ERP integration", *Quarterly Journal of Electronic Commerce*, 3, 43-52.

Malik, Kamna and Goyal, D.P. (2001), "Information Systems Effectiveness—An Integrated Approach", IEEE Engineering and Management Conference (IEMC'01) Proceedings on Change Management and the New Industrial Revolution, Albany, NewYork, USA, pp. 189-94.

Ribbers, Schoo (2002), "Program management and complexity of ERP Implementation", *Engineering Management Journal*, 14, 2.

Shivraj, Shantanu (2000), "Understanding user participation and involvement in ERP use", *Journal of Management Research*, Vol. 1, No. 1.

Teltumbde Anand (2000): "A framework for evaluating IS projects", *International Journal of Production Research*, Vol. 38, No. 17.

Thomas L. Legare (2002), "The Role of Organizational Factors in Realizing ERP Benefits", Information System Management.

Wilhelm Scheer, Frank Habermann (2000), "Making ERP a Sucess", ACM, Vol. 43, 4.

Frederic Adam, Peter O'Doherty (2000), "ERP implementations in Ireland-towards smaller and shorter ERP projects", *Journal of Information Technology*, 15, 305-16.

Web Links

http://portal.acm.org

http://ieeexplore.ieee.org

www.proquest.com

http://ernesto.emeraldinsight.com

APPENDIX I

TABLE I

Rotated Component Matrix for Risk Factors in ERP System Implementation as Tested in PUNCOM and PTL (N=70)

Issues	*Component*		
	Factor 1	*Factor 2*	*Factor 3*
Selection of ERP package.	.108	.103	.870
Pre-evaluation screening and package evaluation.	.524	.121 .	.556
Identifying functional heads/project leader.	.849	4.603E-02	.187
Appoint an outside ERP BPR consultant	.799	.243	.213
Set BPR objectives and responsibilities.	.772	.333	.162
Assembly of steering committee.	.856	.125	.121
Determination of high level project scope and broad implementation approach	.786	.410	-5.472E-03
Selection of a project team manager.	.579	.535	.195
ERP implementation resource determination.	.423	.778	4.185E-02
Organizations commitment.	.359	.738	.231
Clear communications of strategic goals.	.156	.598	.555
View ERP as enterprise wide venture.	1.485E-02	.865	6.442E-02

Extraction Method: Principal Component Analysis.

Rotation Method: Varimax with Kaiser Normalization. A Rotation converged in 6 iterations.

TABLE 2

Rotated Component Matrix for Risk Factors in ERP System Implementation as Tested in PUNCOM and PTL (N=70)

Issues	*Component*			
	Factor 1	*Factor 2*	*Factor 3*	*Factor 4*
Identification of ERP system modules for installation.	.759	.166	.260	.140
Project team is selected and structured with appropriate mix of technical and business expertise.	.833	.109	-5.820E-02	.228
Analysis of current business processes.	.770	.201	.143	.299
Creating a plan and understanding eliminated and shortened process cycles	.854	.175	8.940E-02	.145
Determine level of BPR required.	.741	-6.089E-02	.433	3.355E-02
Install ERP and map the modules with business processes	.575	7.624E-02	.663	5.814E-02
Apply high level design and detailed design subject to user acceptance	.311	.316	.689	.240
Apply interactive prototyping method in design	.230	.475	.623	.214
Population of test instances with real data.	.133	.633	.540	.259
Building and testing the interface.	9.358E-02	.784	.298	.212
Writing and testing reports.	.142	.876	.248	4.432E-02
System and user testing	.254	.864	.112	9.383E-02
Building network for ERP.	.228	.443	.646	.130
Installation of various desktops.	.201	.478	.633	.200
Financial constraints.	.360	.149	5.691E-02	.823
Training problems.	.206	.258	.258	.765
Management commitment.	.264	8.581E-02	.566	.671
Vendor performance.	-.116	.493	.625	.154
Consultant performance.	-1.184E-02	.505	.420	.367

Extraction Method: Principal Component Analysis.

Rotation Method: Varimax with Kaiser Normalization. A Rotation converged in 16 iterations.

TABLE 3

Rotated Component Matrix for Risk Factors in ERP System Implementation as Tested in PUNCOM and PTL (N=70)

Issues	*Component*			
	Factor 1	*Factor 2*	*Factor 3*	*Factor 4*
Training on methodology approach, phases, tasks and deliverables.	.757	131	-.170	.328
Training on tools supporting the methodology	.774	.235	1.496E-02	.386
Training on benefits of reusability.	.604	.265	-4.951E-02	.610
Top management's advocacy.	8.836E-02	.833	8.514E-02	.345
Provision for adequate resources.	.284	.703	.161	.301
Steering committee/member of project core team are independent of taking decisions.	.439	.590	.375	.244
Set realistic milestones and delivery dates.	.811	.112	.324	-8.848E-02
Minimal customization and uncomplicated option selection.	.256	7.079E-02	.832	-3.198E-02
Fewer modules and less functionality implemented	-.123	7.743E-02	.838	.106
Smaller user groups and fewer sites.	.128	5.519E-02	.478	.763
The old system, including all informal system are eliminated.	3.299E-02	.469	.597	8.433E-02
Legacy system is working in parallel.	6.803E-02	.382	-.162	.667
In developing an internal training plan.	.168	.790	8.846E-02	2.131E-02
Provide evidence of the value of new methodology.	.550	.428	.372	-.161
Hosting training seminars to explore participants to the methodology.	.262	.165	.375	.417

Extraction Method: Principal Component Analysis.
Rotation Method: Varimax with Kaiser Normalization.
[a]Rotation converged in 9 iterations.

CHAPTER

22

Managing Processes for Business Excellence

The TQM Approach by PSU

PANKAJ MADAN

TQM is a systems approach to management that aims to continuously increase value to customers by designing and continuously improving the organizational processes and systems. TQM involves all the employees and extends backward and forward to include the supply chain and the customers. Intense competition has been stimulus for the spread of Total Quality Management (TQM) throughout the world. In addressing that theme, this is a comprehensive study of Management of Quality in Totality whose primary focus is on studying the processes which help in the implementation of TQ process in a Public Sector Unit. In our paper a relation between the increasing competition globally and process preparation of an Indian PSU in light of TQM approach has been focused.

World-class achievers follow world-class models. Japan achieved success by instituting the Deming Prize, the US by instituting Malcolm Baldrige Award, the Europe by the

European Quality Award, and now Indian organizations are striving for the success with instituting the CII Award for business excellence based on EFQM criteria. The process of implementing the TQM by rolling the model and than assessing it, offers the organization an opportunity to learn about its areas of improvement. During our research we have studied a Navratna PSU, which made its quality policy in 1993 and launched the concept of business excellence through EFQM model. In 2000 it applied for CII-Business Excellence Award and it the best-suited place to observe and analyze how this model is implemented, what are the impediments in its implementation.

With the entry in the new millennium a distinct shift from organizations' initial focus on solving task-related problems through people involvement to bring continuous improvement in processes have been felt significantly. They are moving ahead on the path of business excellence through integration of customer and improvement efforts with adoption of TQM, 5S, ISO 9000:2000 and ISO 14000. According to Total Quality Management (TQM) approach a nine point criteria have been laid in CII Model for Business Excellence and this paper has focused on various such measures which an organization has to implement to attain the business excellence. The organization under study is a PSU manufacturing heavy electrical equipments.

The Process of implementing the TQM by rolling the model and than assessing it, offers the organization an opportunity to learn, to learn about its own strengths and the areas for improvement. To learn about TQM means when applied in an organization it can know, how far down the quality road it has traveled, how much further it has to travel and how it can compare itself with others.

TOTAL QUALITY MANAGEMENT MODEL

The model which we are going to discuss is the CII Model for Total Quality Management which underlies the CII Award for Business Excellence and is based on the Europe Foundation for Quality Management (EFQM) criteria expressed graphically, the principle looks like this:

Fig. I

EFQM TQM Model

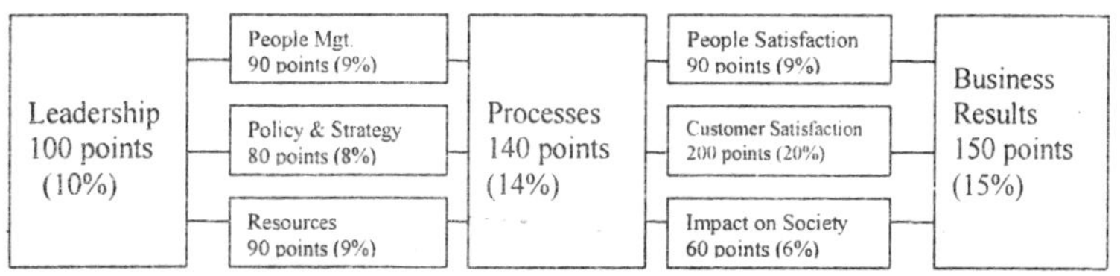

Each of the nine elements shown in the model is the criterion that can be used to assess the organization's progress towards the business excellence.

Enables

The Enablers criteria are concerned with how the organization approaches each the criterion parts. Each Enabler is broken down into the number of criterion parts and each criterion part does require a response, even if the response is not "non-relevant to our business."

Results

The Results criteria are concerned with what the organization has achieved and is achieving. The organization's results and trends for all Results Criteria should be addressed in terms of:

- the organization's actual performance
- the organization's own targets

And wherever possible

- the performance of competitors
- the performance of "best in class" organization

To successfully implement the above-mentioned TQM model, nine criteria have been laid by EFQM that has its own requirements to be fulfiled. In this paper we are going to discuss what the PSU under study has done in Process criteria to achieve the business excellence

WHAT THE COMPANY HAS TO DO UNDER THIS CRITERIA 5 OF PROCESSES

The management of all the value adding activities within the company, how processes are identified, reviewed and if necessary revised to ensure continuous improvement of the company's business. Evidence is needed of:

5A: How process critical to the success of the business are identified.
5B: How the organization systematically manages its processes.
5C: How process performance measurements, along with all relevant feedback, are used to review processes and to set targets for the improvement.
5D: How the organization stimulates innovation and creativity in process improvement.

WHAT THE PSU HAS DONE TO FULFIL THE CRITERIA 5 OF PROCESSES

5a. Processes are Systematically Designed and Managed

Designing Processes to Deliver Organisation's Policy and Strategy

The Key Business Process (KBP) are those significant and vital Processes, which are targeted to achieve and improve the performance Indicators necessary for satisfaction of all the stakeholders especially customers. Expert inputs from external consultants are also sought to identify and benchmark these processes. The KBP are derived from Critical Success Factors (CSF) identified by Management Committee (MC) during the formulation of Policies and Strategies of the company and are reviewed and updated on continual basis by TQ Core Group. The method for Identification of KBP are:

(a) Identification, review and updation of critical success factors by TQM core group.

(b) Brainstroming by Management Committee (MC)/ TQM core group to identify the Key Business Processes and related subprocesses.
(c) Formation of time and ownership based unit level TQM action plans through wider participation of executives in all functional areas, approved by TQM action plans.
(d) Linkage of TQ action plans with recently introduced Performance Management System for

FIG. 2

Key Business Processes for Benchmarking

	Process Champion
K1. Project Planning and Review	GM (T&D)
K2. Manufacturing Planning and Review	GM (FBM)
K3. Managing Materials	GM (CP)
K4. Response Mechanism	GM (Engg.)

executives.

KBP have been changing in the company through annual reviews based on the customer expectation and TQ Self Assessment Feedback. For example, in 1999-2000 major thrust was on cycle time reduction in material procurement and manufacturing, product aesthetic appearance, delivery of spares to enhance the customer satisfaction, etc. However, the Focus areas of 2000-02 were Quality, Delivery, Cost Optimization, Technology upgradation and Employees Satisfaction. For a more focused attention during the current year, PSU plant has adopted Benchmarking, modern and strategic management technique for increasing the operational effectiveness and efficiency. M/S Institute of Quality Limited, Delhi facilitated this process. Based on brain storming during one-day workshop of Top Management, PSU have identified KBPs (Refer Fig. 2) as benchmarking projects.

To integrate various processes and improvement activities related to KBP, process information data are periodically discussed and reviewed at different forums at unit as well as corporate level illustrated in framework of

Policy and Strategy. Improvements in the Key Processes are made based on learning, changing needs of stake holders And analysis of emerging market scenario done by MCM and MC. Additionally, improvements are benchmarked with respect Sister Units and Best in Class companies.

Example: Quality Improvement has been Identified as Critical Success Factor continuously for last 3 years. It was felt that measurement of Cost of Quality is a must to make further improvements. The procedure for capturing the cost of Rejection and Rework (Both internal and external) was developed by corporate (Cross Functional Teams) CFT having representation from Heavy Electrical Equipment Plant (HEEP).

On-line system for this has been implemented to measure rejection and rework cost.

Establishing Process Management System

Process Ownership and Process management has been established on the basis of Process Mapping through various system manuals like Quality System Manual, Functional Manuals, Systems and Methods Instructions (SMIs), Plant Standards/Specifications, Departmental Work Instructions, etc. The Process Owners set targets/performance standards of the processes and align it with the Company's Policy and Strategy and improvement plans. Review, updation and monitoring of these plans is done at the various levels in well-structured meetings e.g. Unit Head's and Functional Head/Process Owners meetings. To systematically manage critical Processes, 56 TQM Action plans were drawn and Cross Functional Teams (CFT) made with GMs as process owners during 1999-00. CFTs mapped the Process, resolved interface issues and submitted their recommendations for implementation to respective Process Owners. Unit's Capital Investment plans have also been aligned with these recommendations. TQM Council reviewed the progress made. Further TQM Self Assessment based on New Millenium Model for Business Excellence by inter-Unit team of PSU in July 2000 followed by shortlisting of HEEP for Site Visit by CII-EXIM Business Excellence Award Team in Sept. 2000. The feedback report of CII was received in January 2001. Based on the Feedback brainstorming sessions were conducted in major functional areas to identify the improvement plans. TQM core group reviewed plans and got approved by TQM Council and Executive Director.

To optimize an increase the efficiency of the processes, the activity based process management is implemented with the help of Primavera Software based on PERT/CPM Operational Techniques. To give further impetus to the process of cultural change in the Process Management, special training programs for Top Management are regularly organized with the help of leading faculties e.g. "TQM Orientation for Top Management" and "Project Management." Implementation of these plans and other major initiatives finalized after the Brain Storming Session of GMs and HODs together and separately with their subordinates. To spread TQ culture up to grass root level, every executive is being involved in at least two improvements.

System Standards in Process Management

Quality Management co-ordinates for ISO 9001 Quality Audits. HEEP was certified by BVQI for conforming to Quality systems as per ISO 9001 in November 1993. Internal/ external audits are carried out at an interval of every 6 months to assess the implementation status of Quality Management System. Further HEEP has been reaccredited ISO 9001 in Dec. 96 and Dec. 99. The effectiveness of these measures is clearly evident from continuous reduction in number of System NCRs. HEEP will be one of the first PSU units to adopt latest version of ISO 9001 (Rev. 2000) and to be audited by BVQI during May 2002 for certification to the latest version of ISO9001. PSU has been accredited with ISO 14000 Certification by M/S DNV in May 2000. Environmental Management System comprising of Apex Level EMS manual, Register of Regulations (ROR), Departmental Manuals and Work Instructions are fully integrated with Quality Management Systems and requirements of ISO 14001. Environmental Management Programs (EMP) has been implemented. Operation Control Procedures (OCP) has been implemented to keep various environmental aspects under control.

FIG. 3

Format of Weekly Audit Status Report

5-S Weekly Audit Status Report				*Production Week No. 5, 6*				
Work Area:				*Area Incharge: GM/DRO:*				
Incharge-				*Status of 5-S Non-Conformities Report (NCR)*				
Work Unit No.	*Name of the work unit*	*Work-Unit Owner*	*Work-Unit 5-S Coordinator*	*NCR Balance up to the week*	*NCR Generated up to the week*	*NCR Vacated up to the week*	*NCR Claimed Vacated but found not vacated Up to the week*	*NCR at the end of the Week commutative*
(A)	*(B)*	*(C)*	*(D)*	*(E)*	*(F)*	*(G)*	*(H)*	*(I)*
EMO1								
EMO2								
EMO3								
EMO4								

To improve the house keeping of the machines and offices, 5-S (Seiri, Seiton, Seiso, Seiketsu, Shitsuke) implementation has been given a special thrust during 1999-00. To being with SKODA machine Block-II was identified as Model machine. It followed by identification of 66 Model Machines and areas with Senior Executives including ED and GMs as Owners under implementation of Manager's Model. The implementation was extended form production shops to offices, township and even to schools located in PSU Campus. To further spread the 5S culture during 2000-01, all manufacturing shops have been divided into smaller work units having its owner and 5S co-ordinator. These work unit areas are audited on weekly basis and status report is available on-line (For the format of status report refer Fig. 3) To integrate improvement activities, the present and future competitive advantages are identified. To identify essential measures of bring business excellence in operations and integrate improvement efforts related to Key Business Process Committee was constituted having Management Representatives for TQM, ISO 9000 and ISO 14000 Implementation as its members and GM (P&A) as Chairman. The committee got implemented its Decisions for systems integration led to ISO 14000 Certification (Fig. 4). In Dec. 2000 it was Replaced with TQM Core Group to give a wider Coverage. The Owner of Safety Process is the Apex level Safety Committee with GM (T&D) as its Chairman. In addition, there are separate Departmental Safety Committees. A number of procedures addressing various aspects/elements of health and Safety have been developed and documented in SMIs 216, 217, 221, 222 and 511 including a committee for chemical hazards. Various statutory and regulatory requirements as per legislative acts e.g. Factory Act, Indian Electricity Act, Indian Explosives Act, Chemical Hazards (SMI 278), Fire Orders (SMI 511) and additional measures as per Safety Manual are also enforced effectively. All lifting equipment/tackles are inspected periodically as per Factory Act, 1948.

For continuous technological up-gradation, new state of art equipment are procured (Refer 4c) and maintained to establish the standard of operations. Technological

FIG. 4

Integration of ISO 9000, ISO 14000 and TQM

- Environmental Management System as per ISO 14000 have been formulated and fully integrated with Quality Management System.
- 5-S implementation efforts integrated with ISO 14000 implementation leading to faster improvements.
- Apex manual for ISO 14000 has been developed in the line of Quality System manuals. SMIs have been integrated for both ISO 9001 and ISO 14000.
- An Integrated business Excellence and Environmental Management Model has been developed to formulate review and monitor all excellence plans under various improvement process.

Development Department studies the requirements and regular feedback sessions are held for capital Investment (Refer 4b). Various improvement plans e.g. TQM Action Plans, Special Improvement Projects, Quality Improvement Plans, Productivity projects and TQM Excellence Plans, etc. lead to setting of higher standards of performance (Fig. 4.2d.2).

Process Measures and Performance Targets

Data related to Quality of the products during manufacturing is collected and collated to evaluate the performance of manufacturing processes. Quality being important focus area, PSU is in the process of implementing the concept of "Quality Though Measurement (QTM)" to identify, measure, analyse and continually improve critical to quality process through various quality indices. The QTM methodology is of its own kind and is one of the patent of PSU.

The System provides precise and apparent web based Management Information for review and control of process. Similarly measurement of delivery indices (Fig. 5) provide precise and apparent-based measurement information for continuous review and control of the delivery performance.

Customer and site Complaints are also analysed to take to take Corrective and Preventive Action at PSU's end. The above systems provide the opportunities to evaluate its processes and improve on continuous basis. Process performance is measured, reviewed and improved based on identification of Critical Success Factors and Key Business Processes.

Interface Issues

The process owners identified for KBP quantify the process performance measures and targets in the form of TQM Action Plans. Performance of these processes is reviewed in TQM Council meeting held regularly. Issues related to the adequacy/competency of the processes adopted to manufacture the product are resolved through various structured meetings like Monthly Shop Quality Review Meeting Convened by shop in-charges and attended by various functions of the organisation. Monthly site complaint meeting being held by respective product engineering takes care of necessary charges needed in the process to produce the higher quality product and satisfy the customer.

The Monthly Performance Evaluation of Vendors/ Subcontractors based on the feedback data of material inspection and its regular feedback to the supplier results in process improvement at supplier's works. Vendors Partnership Meet is also organized to educate the vendors in resolving issues related to product quality and the present market requirements. Issues related to external customers are taken up on regular basis through structure meeting at customer's end and/or at PSU's works. A 'Customers Meet' was also organized to understand and resolve the generic nature issues. A Corporate Quality Committee has been formed to take up issues related to customers in structured manner periodically.

5b. Process are Improved as needed using Innovation in Order to Fully Satisfy and Generate Increasing Value for Customers and other Stakeholders

Prioritising the Opportunities for Improvement

Continuous improvement is a natural and in-built phenomenon in Revenue/Capital/Performance budget exercises. Every year budgeting process is carried out under the framework for policy strategy. Inputs form Customers Satisfaction Survey, meeting with customers, Product Committee Meeting, Feedback through Customer letters and Third Party Inspections done on behalf of customers are used in identifying and prioritizing processes for improvements for better customer satisfaction.

On the basis of feedback of Customers, Govt. Agencies/Consulting Institutions, and Collaborators, etc. challenging targets are fixed. Challenging targets are set at Apex Level (TQM, PQC, etc.) and are integrated into normal working in a systematic manner.

FIG. 6

Action Plan to Improve Customer Satisfaction

Sl. No.	Projects
1.	Refinement in service to customers through single window.
2.	Formulation and implementation of procedure for prompt response to enquirer for service and spares.
3.	Ensuring timely submission of quality documents and their approval.
4.	Enhancement of satisfaction level of motor customers through faster response to complaint handling, customer education, increased interaction and better technical support.
5.	Improvement in packing and transportation and ensuring safe arrivals at sites.
6.	Coordination, interaction and monitoring for improve project management.
7.	Improved adherence to schedules and timely delivery of turbines and spares.
8.	Smooth clearance of customer hold points, faster and satisfactory resolution of NCRs.
9.	Faster and satisfactory resolution of technical deviations and customer complaints.
10.	Ensuring completeness of directly dispatched items, quality of documents for BIOs and transparency in sharing status of procurement with customers.
11.	Improvement is surface preparation in quality of painting.
12.	To reduce delivery time of motors and their spares.
13.	State of art improvements in respect of ease of operation/maintenance and for meeting specified level of its performance for AC and DC motors.

The targets are agreed based on PSU capability to meet the challenges. Inputs from Suppliers' e.g. Vendors' Participation meet, visits to Vendors, etc. are regularly used for making improvements. Many new improvement initiatives have been taken to improve Vendors relationship. Special emphasis is being given on "Time Cycle Reduction in Procurement of Critical Items."

Inputs from employees Satisfaction Survey, Suggestions, Quality Improvement Plan and Various Awareness Drives are used to identify the methods of improvement. A large number of Suggestions received in last 5 years have resulted in enormous savings.

Several improvement projects are taken in the form of QIP, PIR, SIP, BEP and Productivity Projects, etc. These projects cover different functions e.g. Quality, Engineering, Production, Technology and Material Management, etc.

Another example of in-building improvement in PSU's culture is special company wide emphasis on implementation of 5-S. Continuous improvement is facilitated through continuous nurturing of innovative potential of employees. They are encouraged to articulate their ideas for incremental improvements and impetus is provided through Suggestions Scheme, Quality Circles, Productivity, Value Engineering and Energy Projects, Self-inspection Scheme and various other forums. Major improvement was achieved in directly dispatchable assemblies of NTPC projects with respect to visual quality of welds, thickness of paints in Fabrication Area. Special task forces/committees constituted and project taken up to provide continuing support and guidance in these areas. For example, Fig. 6 gives the list of projects undertaken to improve customer satisfaction.

Establishment and Development of Technological Improvements

Technological development Plan, Suggestion Scheme, Quality Circle Concept and Shop/Site Feedback/BVQI Audit are the basic building block for changes required to be incorporated for process improvement, enhance the product quality level, reduce time cycle and cost of manufacturing. The changes suggested through any one of above system are presented to Apex Level of organization for approval and incorporated in the technology for future production. The records of changes are also maintained and controlled in a manner by respective agencies. The new or changed processes are piloted and implemented in a controlled manner before actually starting manufacturing.

- All Critical/CNC Machines are made to produce prototype before actually starting manufacturing.
- Development of on-line Quality Index for production and non-production areas.
- Discussions/review by all concerned deptt. before finalisation of SMIs for all functions.

- Computerisation of design documents in Engg. Department.
- Pilot testing has modified Process Steam Pipeline.
- Hydro Turbine Model testing in HTL at design stage.

Prioritising the Opportunities for Improvement

Processes are continuously improvised through various initiatives like TQM Projects, Quality Improvement Projects, (QIP), Special Improvement Projects (SIP), Productivity Improvement Projects (PIP), Quality Circles, Suggestions Scheme, etc. The system for identification, implementation and review of these improvement projects are well laid down. RMX and TQM department co-ordinates TQM Projects, PIP and Suggestions at Unit level. QM department coordinates QIP, SIP and Quality Circle at the Unit Level. The efforts of individuals and Terms carrying out improvements are also recognized by the Executive Director. The scope of improvement and level of involvement is also well defined for these activities as illustrated (Fig 7).

Piloting the Implementation of Improvements in Processes

The new and changed processes are piloted before its deployment in the plant. It is being done for both the Product related and the Non-Product related processes. For example Aesthetic improvement in the products was identified as Key Improvement area under TQM Action plan based on Customers' feedback. The improvement project was undertaken by a Cross Functional Team and piloted on Control Panels and Motors. After successful implementation, 11 aesthetic improvement projects have been identified for various products.

Process Changes

New/changed processes are monitored regularly and results are compared with set targets and benefits are evaluated. It forms the basis for affecting subsequent changes in process. The process changes are reviewed and approved for implementation by respective process owner/manager to ensure that predicted results are attained based on past

FIG. 7

Various Process Improvement Measures

Response	*Suggestion Scheme*	*Quality Circles*	*QIP*	*SIP*	*PIP*	*TQM Projects*
Focus	Incremental improvements related to work area	Incremental improvements related to work area	Problems solving related to products or system quality	Chronic/Generic Custcmer Complaint	Methods simplification and improvement	Critical process improvement
Action by	All employees	Workmen QC members	Task Performers upto DGM level			Senior Manager and above
Tools and Techniques	Simple problem solving tools	Simple problem solving tools	SQC Tools	Six Sigma Techniques, QFD	Error Proofing, SQC Tools	Process Mapping & Benchmarking

performance data. Process changes are reflected in respective document/systems and are communicated to all concerned agencies by issuing revised documents/systems. Process changes are communicated as per guidelines in quality Systems, SMIs and through circulars, letters, etc. Prior to implementation of Process changes, new skills, managerial, behavioural inputs are given through:

- Training by Foreign Experts/Suppliers at PSU's work/Collaborator's works/Supplier's works.
- Training at Sister Units, Educational/Research Institutions.
- On the job training by employees trained at Suppliers/Collaborators work to others.
- Encouragement to employees to become members of Institutions like AIMA, AMIE, IIIE, MA, etc.
- Training inputs arranged through HRDC/HRDI with help of Internal/External Faculty.

To develop a deeper understating of the quality aspects of its products, processes and services and to promote commitment towards quality down to the task performer level, training-*cum*-communication programe "Quality at Doorstep" was initiated and lunched in 1999-2000 to cover all level of employees. In all 5575 employees who constituted 83% of total eligible employees attended the progamme. During the interactive sessions, 599 suggestions were received from the participant, 73% suggestions have been implemented. As a benchmark now the other Unit of PSU have also adopted the concept of "Quality at Doorstep." Further Quality index is being measured and the report is available on-line helping in quality improvements. Additionally Weekly Root Cause Analysis based quality improvements are also taken up.

Process changes are viewed periodically in line with the requirement of ISO 9001 for the processes covered under it, in Plant Quality/Committee Meetings. Review of Quality Systems is done by Functional Heads and through audits. Executive Director also reviews these changes in various Boardroom review meetings.

5c. Products and Services are Designed and Developed Based

On Customer Needs and Expectations

In pursuit to become a world-class company and to maintain its competitive edge, PSU, Hardwar keeps abreast of the latest developments in design and technology. This is done through customer feedback (e.g. customer complaints, site problems, performance test results, etc.), customer requirements, benchmarking the developments made by the competitors, in-house R & D and new design and technology adopted by its collaborator M/S Siemens Germany, who is also a global player. The latest literature, national/ international seminars and conference are also source of new developments in design and technology. Engineering departments along with the technology departments assess the new design and technology available and introduce those found suitable.

Product Committees

In line with Corporate guidelines, Product Committees and Technical Committees for various products e.g. Turbines, Generators, Motors, Condensers, etc. meet regularly for assessing and incorporating new design features in the products. The members from various PSU Units, Business Groups and Power Sector Regions participate in these meetings. While Technical Committee reviews the purely Technical matters, the Product Committee decides the policy guidelines for the Products based on comprehensive information on market scenario, new design developments in the world, site feedback, manufacturing/technological capabilities available in various Units, etc. Product Committee approves the R & D Projects (commonly known as Project Initiation Report or PIR) identified by the Technical Committee. Product Committees also provide the direction for collaboration agreements, additional manufacturing facilities for new design developments and training of people to Benchmark the Product related improvements with respect to International competitors. Similarly for inducting new technologies, Technology Plan and Technology Development

Projects are prepared. Product committees also provide direction of collaboration agreements and training.

For example, cost Competitiveness has been identified as a Focus area for improvements. Engineering group undertakes Value Engineering, Productivity improvement and Import substitution projects under PIPS TQM Action Plans. The need-based help of the vendors is also taken by placing the developmental, orders on selected vendors and full technical support is provided to them. This process also helps in building the partnership relations with vendors.

All new design and developments are subjected to the in-built system of design review, verification and validation as per ISO 9001. Whenever required, designs are vetted by the collaborator to satisfaction of the customers. Customers are also educated on the benefits of the new design and usage of the products.

Realising the potential of information technology in effecting improvements, PSU has gone in a big way in introduction of IT in the field of design and development. Today design drawings, CBOMs, MIDs are prepared through computers and electronic drawing management system is under finalisation and will soon be implemented. All the employees are encouraged to make improvements in their respective processes based on feedback from customers, employ es, suppliers and other stakeholders by providing necessary help and resources. The open work culture of PSU has a high degree of freedom to work, which empower employees to contribute fearlessly, and confidently through their innovative and creative ideas. Employees are given training in the required field at our HRDC or at external sources. Engineers from concerned areas are also sent to collaborator's works for acquiring knowledge on new design and technology. The employees have also got free access to organisation's computerised information network. The engineers from engineering and other departments carry out various value engineering, indigenisation and cost reduction studies and participate in different competition in PSU and national level.

5d. Products and Services are Produced, Delivered and Serviced

Producing Products and Services in Line with Designs and Developments

Customer requirements are translated into technical documents in the form of drawing, specifications, technology, quality plans, etc. and products are produced in line with the technical inputs. Total manufacturing cycle time is maintained as committed to the customer by planning and monitoring all major processes.

The following activities are worth mentioning to deliver the products in time to the customer:

- Computerisation of design documents, material planning
- Material procurement: Rate contract
- Defect prevention
- Technology upgradation
- Continuous production review meetings to monitor the delivery commitments.

Marketing and Selling Products to Existing and Potential Customers

In line with our journey towards business excellence, "Business Potential for Spares and Modernisation" was identified as Critical Success Factor and TQM Action Plans were drawn during 1998 and CFT was made with Head of Sales and Services as process owner. The approach to tap the business potential for Spares, Repairs and Modernisation of Power. Plants was finalised by the CFT and reviewed by Units TQ Council and Apex TQ Council at Corporate level. The team members visited existing and potential customers to identify the potential business areas. The success of approach is clearly evident from growth in Spares business declined during 2000-01, as some of the expected orders did not mature due to recession in the market.

During installation of the product at site, the Site/Unit engineers resolve all field quality problems. The Service after Sale (SAS) department takes care of the spare and service requirements of customers during installation and commissioning of the product. After, commissioning, PSU provides services to the customer regarding operational problem.

Bench-Marking

Product Committee does benchmarking with respect to international competition for Products and Manufacturing Technology. In order to facilitate learning for Process Benchmarking and target setting for improvement of various parameters, PSU has become the member of IBM Club with CQA as co-ordinator for the same. The data on internal and external benchmarking is received form CQA for the same. The best practices/processes followed by the other PSU Units are compiled for internal benchmarking and concerned functional heads are advised to identify the benchmarking projects for setting the improvement targets. Four key Processes have been benchmarked with help of M/S IQL.

During 2000-01, based on Employees Satisfaction Survey results, Training has been identified as critical area of improvement. The benchmarking was done with respect to PSU Bhopal and 2.2 training days per employees has been achieved during 1999-00.

5e. Customer Relationship are Managed and Enhanced

PSU Corporation and PSU Hardwar Vision clearly emphasizes on Customer Focus. The Customer Focus has also been identified as Critical Success Factor and TQM Action Plans are being drawn for the same. In order to maintain a very cordial relationship with all its customers, PSU has been taking various measures. Its aim is to provide complete business solution to the customers.

Customer Satisfaction Survey

In order to assess specific needs and expectations, current level of specification of its customer, Internal or External Customer Satisfaction Surveys are conducted every year since 1997. So far 3 Internal Customer Satisfaction Surveys have been conducted in 1997, 1998 and 1999 (Refer 6a) based on Corporate Guidelines. Output of the Survey results is utilised in identification of TQM Action Plans. For example Aesthetic Improvement and Cycle Reduction Projects have been identified based on CSS results.

External Customer Satisfaction Survey

In order to assess specific needs and expectations, current level of satisfaction of its customer, PSU for the first time organised external Customer Survey in a structured manner, through M/s CSMM a unit of IMRB. The survey covering processes like Contact Project Co-ordination, Engineering/System and Manufacturing, Delivery, Erection and Commissioning. Equipment System performance, Services after sales and attitudes like overall image, price, value, etc. was based on "Customer Relationship Assessment" Model of M/s CSMM. This model ultimately determines "loyalty" of Customer through response given on PSU's performance, PSU's competitors (with whom Customer have dealt with) and overall images of PSU perceived by Customers.

Board conducted the survey on 'Project Specific' basis where separate instrument of survey were prepared and administered on selective customers of projects and select products—as decided.

The customers surveyed include entire customer profile with which PSU is dealing like NTPC, State Electricity Board, Corporations and Private Industries. The Customer profile surveyed covers projects marked by Power Sector and Industry Sector. This included Customers of Motors for Product Specific Survey and Supplies (covering most of the Products) made by PSU Hardwar to projects under 'Project Specific Survey'. The respondents interviewed by trained interviewers of M/s CSMM, cover Top Level Management of Customers (three levels from Top at Head Quarters have dealt with) was also obtained during same interviews. Areas for improvement have been brought out from survey, based on perceptions of Customer of PSU, Images of PSU as perceived by customers and competitors, performance on above mentioned process-using model of the consultant/ statistical regression analysis, etc.

The survey results have been presented to HMC followed by a Cross section of about 400 executives on July 7,

2000. The action planning is under progress with GM (E&CC) as Process Owner. Based on the detailed report submitted by CSMM, PSU has identified 13 nos. action plans to enhance customer satisfaction. TQC Council and Process Owners review the status of these action plans.

Customer Meets

With an objective of build partnership relations with its esteemed customers, Product wise, Customers meets are being organised both for external customers and internal customer.

Customer Complaints/"SAR" Handling System

To analyze the site feedback and customer complaints and to evolve corrective measures for preventing the reoccurrence of the problems in future, the procedures as per the Quality System SMI-806 are followed. The procedure covers site feedback of technical nature received from Power Sector through Site Action Requests (SAR), Commissioning Action Request (CAR) and the customer complaints received form the customer directly. The complaints are analyzed and corrective/preventive action is decided in the weekly/monthly meetings. The status of the actions taken on the important feedback is reviewed in the Plant Quality Committee meeting chaired by Head of the Unit.

In order to resolve the issues raised by customer representative with respect to shop practices, structured weekly meetings are organized by Head Quality with them to take corrective and preventive actions. The feedback on action taken is also given to are also invited to participate in the Corporate Quality committee (CQC) meeting being held on regular basis as per CQC terms of reference issued by corporate quality assurance. Quality heads of major Units are the members of committee. The meeting is held to listen the customer voice and to resolve the standing issues pertaining to all major units. The main objective of the committee is to modify or devise system to improve the quality of product/process to reduce the complaints of generic nature.

For the resolution of Generic problems, identified and classified based on various inputs like customer complaints, site failure reports, problems refereed to CMD/Director/Unit

Heads, etc. time bound action plans are made and reviewed for implementation as per the Documents.

Other Measures to Strengthen the Customer Relationships

- Regular visits to customer sites/offices by senior executives including Executive Director to discuss their needs and expectations and to take proactive actions in fulfiling the same. The feedback of the visits is communicated to concerned agencies through meetings.
- Structured meetings with customers to resolve the outstanding issues related to product performances: Regular corporate/unit level meetings are held with customers. The follow up issues brought out by the customer in these structured meeting are continuously monitored and resolved in time. These meetings are planned at different units of PSU to involve the local representatives of customers and PSU to understand each other and resolve all the issues.
- Project Manager Group is functional at PSU to promptly and expeditiously gives focused attention to the customers' commitments/ requirements against various projects.
- R and M Group (4 Nos.) have been created to tap the business potential in the field of renovation and modernization of power plants. Thus creating the customer needs in a better way.
- *Technical discussions with customer*: Manufacturing Quality Plan, Vendor Quality Plan, Vendor approval, Manufacturing processes, Repair procedures, etc. are discussed in detail and got approved by the customer as per their requirements.
- Prompt services are provided to the customers for improving the operational efficiency of supplied equipments Various life extension projects are being carried out in old power stations by PSU.

- *Quality Audits at sites as a proactive approach*: A task force has been constituted to look into the quality issues emerging during the erection and commissioning at various sites. The feedback of the team is conveyed to all the related departments to formulate the action plans and their implementation.
- Logistic supports of customers and their representatives like office facilities in PSU premises, housing, transportation, computer, etc. to enable them in carrying out the functions effectively and smoothly. The representatives of the different customers like NTPC, NPC, NJPC, LLYOD, RITES, etc. have been provided such facilities.

References

American Society for Quality Control (1988), 88 Gallup Survey: Consumers' Perceptions Concerning the Quality of American Products and Services, Milwaukee: ASQC 4.

Bass, B.M. (1976), "Leadership Good, Better, Best, Press: 189-207; *Organizational Dynamics,* 13 (Winter 1985): 26-40; N.M. Tichy and D.O. Ulrich, "The Leadership Challenge—A Call for the Transformational Leader," *Sloan Management Review,* 26 (Fall 1984), pp. 59-68.

Bowles, J. and Hammond, J. (1991), *Beyond Quality: How 50 Winning Companies Use Continuous Improvement,* New York: Putnam, pp. 193-94.

Band, W.A. (1991), *Creating Value for Customers,* New York: Wiley, pp. 168-69.

Carothers, G.H.; Bounds, G.M. and Stahl, M.J. (1991), "Managerial Leadership," in M.J. Stahl and G.M. Bounds (eds.), *Competing Globally through Customer Value: The Management of Strategic Suprasystems,* Westport, CT: Quorum Books, pp. 80.

Cole, R (Spring 1993), "Introduction", Special Issue on Total Quality Management, *California Management Review,* 35, No. 3: 8.

Deming, W.E. (1982), *Out Of the Crisis,* MIT, Mass. (USA), Cambridge, pp. 224.

Dale, B. and Cooper, C. (1992), *Total Quality and Human Resources,* Oxford, England: Blackwell, pp. 111-12.

Denton and Keith, D. (Summer Fall 1995), Ingraining employee involvement into corporate decision-making, *Business Forum,* pp. 11-14.

Dellana; Scott, A.; Hauser and Richard, D. (1996), Proceeding—Annual Meeting of the Decision Science Institute, Vol. 3, Atlanta, GA, USA, pp. 1736-38.

Dewan, P. (1996), *Quality in Totality: A managers' guide to TQM and ISO 9000,* New Delhi: Deep and Deep Publications.

"Dinosaurs: IBM, Sears, GM," *Fortune* (May 3, 1993), pp. 36-42.

Dingus, V. (August 10, 1993), "The Strategy for achieving Quality of Management," presentation at Eastman Chemical/University of Tennessee Continuous Improvement Workshop.

Ferguson, G. (Aug. 1990) "Printer Incorporates Deming-Reduces Errors, Increase Productivity," *Industrial Engineering*, pp. 32-34.

Garrett, H.E. and Woodworth, R.S. (1981), *Statistics in Psychology and Education, loth ed.*, India: Vakils, Feffer and Simons Ltd., p. 354.

Gumpert, D.E., "The Joys of keeping the Company small," *Harvard Business Review* (July/Aug. 1986): 6-14.

Gerhard, L. and. Sparrow, W.T. (June 1988), "Pride Teams, A Quality Circle that Works," *Journal for Quality and Participation*, p. 36.

Ghobadian, A. and Gallear, D.N. (1996) *Omega* Vol. 24 n 1: 83-106.

Herzberg, F (July/Aug. 1968), "One More Time: How Do You Motivate Employees?" *Harvard Business Review*, pp. 56-57.

Hackman J. and Oldham, G. (1980) *Work Redesign*, Reading, MA: Addison-Wesley.

How to operate Quality circle Activities, JUSE, Tokyo (1984).

Harrington, H.J. (1991), *Business Process Improvement: The Breakthrough strategy for Total Quality, Productivity, and Competitiveness*, New York: McGraw-Hill, pp. 9.

Harrington, J.H. (March 1990). "Work life in the Year 2000," *Journal for Quality and Participation*, pp. 56-57.

IBM: A Special Company, *Think* (September 1989): 51.

Joseph and Berk, S. (1995): *"Total Quality Management," Implementing Continuous Improvement*, New Delhi: Excel Books, pp. 84.

King, W.R. "Strategic Planning for Information resources," Information Resource Management Journal (F~111988): 2-3.

Kohnke, L. (July 1990), "Designing a Customer Satisfaction Measurement Program", *Bank Marketing*, pp. 24.

Lewin, K. (1951), *Field Theory in Social Sciences*, New York: Harper and Row.

Lansing, R.L. (Feb. 1989) "The Power of Teams," *Supervisory Management*, pp. 39-43.

Ludeman, K. (Dec. 1992), "Using Employee Surveys to Revitalize TQM," *Training*, pp. 51-57.

Levin, R. and Rubin, D. (1995), *Statistics for Management*, 6th ed., India: Prentice-Hall, pp. 397-402.

Mandl, V.J. (June 1990), "Team Up for Performance," *Manufacturing Systems*, p. 1.

Marchington, M. (1992), Managing the Team: *A Guide to Successful Employee Involvement*, Oxford, England: Blackwell, pp. 115-23.

Moskal and Brian (April 1995), S. Take a Walk on the Wild Side, Industry Week, pp. 3.

Mersha, Tigineh (1996), Proceeding—Annual Meeting of the Decision Sciences Institute, Vol. 3, Atlanta GA, USA, pp. 1754-56.

Nagendra, P.; Soni, R.; Das S. and Upadhyay, A. (1996) Proceeding -Annual Meeting of the Decision Sciences Institute, Vol. 3, Atlanta, GA, USA, p. 1663.

Parzinger, M.;Ramarapu, N. and Timmerman (1997) *Industrial Management and Data Systems,* Vol. 97, Nos. 3-4, pp. 125-30.

Rosseau, D. and Cooke, R. (1984), "Technology and Structure," *Journal of Management,* pp. 345-61.

Schein, E. (1985), *Organisational Culture and Leadership,* San Francisco: Jossey-Bass, p. 14.

Sovoie and Ernest, J. (1986), Creating the Work Force of the Future: The Ford Focus, Ford in house publication, p. 6.

Srivastava, U.K; Shenoy, G.V. and Sharma, S.C. (1989), *Quantitative Techniques for Managerial Decisions,* India: New Age, pp. 222-28.

Simmons, J. (June 1989), "Partnering Pulls Everything Together," *Journal for Quality and Participation,* pp. 12-16.

Soin, S. (1992), *Total Quality Control, Essentials—key elements, methodologies and managing for success,* New York: McGraw-Hill.

Schonberger (1992), Building a Chain of Customers, 83, Gravin, *Managing Quality: The Strategic and Competitive Edge,* New York: McGraw-Hill: 49.

Schmidt, W. and Finnigian, J. (1992), *The Race without a Finish Line: America's Quest for Total Quality,* San Francisco: Jossey-Bass, pp. 268-69.

Schnidt and Finnigan, *The Race Without a Finish Line,* pp. 272-79.

Sullivan (1992), "Japanese Management Philosophies from the Vacuous to the Brilliant," *California Management Review:* 66-87.

Sims, Jr. and Henry, P. (1995) *Journal of Quality and Participation,* Vol. 18, No. 2.

Tylor, F.W. (1911), *Scientific Management,* New York: Harper.

Townsend, P. and Gebhardt, J. (1992), *Quality in Action,* New York: Wiley, pp. 18, 96.

Yue, Z.; Mei, Z.; Cheryl, W. and Linda, S. (1996), Proceeding—Annual Meeting of the Decision Sciences Institute Vol. 3, Atlanta, GA, USA, pp. 1739-41.

Zairi, M. (1990), *Total Quality Management for Engineers,* Woodhead, Cambridge, Mercury Books.

CHAPTER

23

Manufacturing Excellence Leading to World Class Manufacturing

Japanese *v.* Indian Practices

RAJINDER KAUR, D.P. WARNE AND RAJWINDER SINGH

Manufacturing strategies provide tremendous growth potential to meet the challenges of ever increasing market demands. After successful emergence of Japanese manufacturers as a global market leader it has invariably captured the attention of Indian managers to scrutinize the factors of Japanese manufacturers. The most distinctive feature of Japan is lack of natural resources, which makes it necessary to import vast amount of materials. To over this handicap Japanese industries put forth their best efforts in order to produce better quality products, added values and at lower cost than those of other countries. This paper attempts to discuss Japanese and Indian manufacturing revolution and comparing the strategies (practices) adopted by these two countries.

INTRODUCTION

The development of the economy of any country is supported by the growth of its manufacturing industries. The excellence of manufacturing facilities and continuous improvement play a key role in the progress of any nation. Currently, the manufacturing industries are passing through very tough competition. The economic environment is becoming harsh. In order to survive every industry has to strive for improving productivity in all spheres of activities. What is required is, new ways of improving manufacturing performance by optimally utilizing the resources. In this context, World-class Manufacturing Systems (WCMS) provide organizations a significant competitive edge over its rivals. WCMS offer many benefits such as reduced cost, increased quality, improvement in competitive position, lower turnover of staff, and many more. World-class Manufacturing (WCM) is a term now widely recognized in manufacturing, covering a wide range of activities.

World-class means changing the way we view and operate all business functions. World-class manufacturing (WCM) is about using manufacturing successfully as a competitive weapon in global competition. Generally in WCM, customer focus is not only a sign but also a fundamental activity in world-class manufacturing. According to Collins and Porass, world-class organizations have to be visionary firms, which should be "crown jewels" in their industries and should be widely admired by their peer group and have a long track record of making significant impact on the world around them.

World-class manufacturing was described as collective term for number of production processes and organizational strategies which all have flexibility as their primary concern. Hays *et al.*, emphasize that it was necessary to have the capability to be a superior competitor to define World-class manufacturing. Womack *et al.*, stated a lead for quantifying World-class while defining lean production which uses less of everything (efforts, space, tools, time, etc.). Jestius' argued that WCM levels requires an over all willingness to establish closer connection with everyone from customer and suppliers to workers. The changing scenario in Indian market due to liberalization of economy is having its implication on Indian industries. Of late, Indian industries finding it difficult to reckon with their old manufacturing practices and are trying to look for new manufacturing systems to sustain competitive pressure.

HISTORY OF MANUFACTURING—AN OVERVIEW

Beginning of the Organized Effort

Man over generations have endured to carry out different tasks by harnessing human skills and developing appropriate tools. However, the first of the organized efforts to establish manufacturing as a functional activity can be traced to decade 1760-70 which bought contribution of James Watt and ushered in industrial revolution. The manufacturing practices centered around the deployment of skills of workman on appropriate jobs. Both quality and quantity of production came to depend on the skills of labour and the performance came to be evaluated in terms of efficiency.

Age of Scientific Management

F.W. Taylor differentiated the role of manager and workman. He advocated the management should take responsibility in planning, directing and organizing work and labour to carry out assigned task, called as scientific management (20th century). Management also brought in improved process quality resulting in better quality products with consistency in performance. Assembly lines helped the quality dimensions as it called for the use of interchangeable parts. Scientific methods of production and a motivated work force increased efficiency and brought down cost of production and the elements of cost emerged as another factor of competition.

Age of Mechanization

It emphasize the development of multi-disciplinary approach known as operation research. It developed models as linear programming, queuing theory, forecasting techniques, Monte Carlo, Simulation methods and these methods were used to minimize wastage of material, machine ideal time, distance to be traveled, etc. Here value added per man hour and value added per unit of material become other criteria to take competitive advantage.

Era of Mass Production

End of World War 2nd ushered in newer manufacturing concepts of faster assembly lines and high speed tools suitable for mass production. This technology was responsible for introducing consumer goods. Optimum utilization of hard assets, i.e. inventory, plan, machinery, building and land became important criteria. Material planning and inventory control came to be recognize as full disciplines.

Age of Automation

Late 1970s ushered in an age of automation. Consumer products had created a new market segment and a new class of customers. Factors that influence production are product and process technology, ability to innovate, a high emphasis on quality and a controlled cost of production.

Contemporary Manufacturing

The current scenario is changing rapidly. Global competitive equations and multifaceted constraints are propelling manufacturing in several directions. Revolution in IT and Telecommunications witness in the last decade a high customer expectation, service and satisfaction, ability to wide choice of branded and unbranded products, shirt product cycle, reduce lead time from concept to materialization of the product, quality and costs have necessitated reinventing manufacturing.

Manufacturing management is expected to compete globally for the survival of the organization. Global competition implies that manufacturing must possess the characteristics of World-class manufacturing.

World-class Manufacturing

To be a World-class organization the firm does not have to operate world-wide or even nationwide. It may be a small local organization, which leads in its area fields, embraces and actively demonstrates the characteristics of World-class performance.

World-class performance maintains continued success through the development of an organization environment, i.e. distinctly different to peer and competitor firms in its philosophy and wealth creating formula. The term WCM also means the pursuance of best practices in manufacturing.

Schoberger coined the term "World-class Manufacturing" in the year of 1986, and it is defined as the techniques and technologies designed to enable a company to match its best competitors. According to him, "Today there is a wide agreement that continual improvement in quality, cost, lead time and customer service is possible, realistic and necessary, and that one more primary goal, improved flexibility is also part of the package. In addition he also stated that with agreement on the goals the management challenge is reduced to speeding the pace of improvement."

WCM is commonly understood as advanced manufacturing technique that can be adopted and use to elevate a facilities manufacturing performance to World-class levels (Rubrich *et al.*, 1998). Quite often Japanese manufacturing techniques like Total Quality Control (TQC), Just in Time (JIT), Total Productive Maintenance (TPM), etc. were regarded as advanced manufacturing techniques, and an application of these implies World-class manufacturing. Subsequently, different techniques like Computer Added Design (CAD), Computer Added Manufacturing (CAM), etc. have also been added to the above set of techniques to be regarded as World-class Manufacturing (Nandi *et al.*, 2000).

MANUFACTURING INDIAN PERSPECTIVE

India and China were a head of Europe and America in industrial production. In 1750 India and China together controlled about 51% of the World production. European came here to purchase these products. Before the introduction of Macaulayan system of Modern English education, the literacy rate in India was 33% whereas Macaulays England it was only 17%. In 1947 when British imperialists left India, the literacy rate of India was 17% and that of England increased to 65%. At present more than 50% of the World's illiterates are in India. About 16% of the World population lives in India but GDP share is only a mere 1% and our share in world trade is only 0.8% of global trade.

History has witness that Indian industries right from their inception were the follower of Taylorism. At the time of independence India may have seemed a promising candidate for rapid industrial growth. The growth rate has lagged behind even with many other Asian countries. Indian industries did not support rapid technological changes due to failure of manufacturing structure. Most important is that there is little understanding of the central role of productivity and quality improvement in industrialization process. Also the factors like RND motivation, human resource management, Capital investment decisions, etc. have been the lagging factors for Indian industries.

Indian industries are trying to look for a new manufacturing order to sustain competitive pressure. After the emergence of WCM a formidable competitor and global leader, efforts are extended for the justification and design of WCM for Indian conditions.

Characteristics of WCM

Several authors have discussed WCM and they have brought out its characteristics in detail. Sardana (2000) has quoted Sahay and Saxena (1999), while emphasizing the importance and relevance of WCM to the industry in developing economies now exposed to the uncertain environment of global competition. Nandi (2000) has identified and summarized the characteristics of WCM as perceived by different authors. With this list as a sample, few more characteristics proposed by different authors have been identified and the same has been added to the list, to provide a comprehensive view about WCM.

Sl. No.	*Author*	*Year*	*Characteristics of WCM*
1	*2*	*3*	*4*
l.	Schonberger	1986	• CAD • TQM • Computer Aided Engineering (CAE) • Computer Integrated Manufacturing (CIM) • Flexible Manufacturing System (FMS) • JIT production • Supplier development • Employee involvement • Manufacturing strategy
2.	Gunn	1987	• CIM • FMS • CAD • CAE • TQC • JIT • Computer Aided Process Planning (CAPP) • Automated Storage and Retrieval System (AS/RS) • Improved supplier quality • Human resources • Manufacturing strategy
3.	Ettlie	1988	• CIM • FMS • CAD • CAE • CAPP • Quality systems • JIT in purchasing • Suppliers • Human resources
4.	Hayes, Wheelwright and Clark	1988	• Becoming the best competitor • Growing more rapidly and being more profitable than competitors • Hiring and retaining the best people • Developing a top-notch engineering staff • Being able to respond quickly and decisively to changing market conditions • Adapting a product and process engineering approach which maximizes the performance of both

(Contd.)

1	*2*	*3*	*4*
			• Continuous improvement in addition to • Learning • Human resource management • CAD/CAM • JIT • Information flow • Flexible Automation
5.	Huge and Anderson	1989	• Continuous improvement • Elimination of waste
6.	Giff *et al.*	1990	• Manufacturing cells • CAD • CAE • Quality management • JIT • Partnership • Human assets • Manufacturing strategy
7.	Maskell	1991	• Focus on process quality • JIT techniques • Workforce management • Flexibility in meeting customer requirements
8	Womack *et al.*	1991	• Relations with suppliers • Relations with customers • Concurrent engineering (CE) • JIT • Continuous improvement
9.	Kasul and Motwani	1995	• Management commitment • Quality • Customer service • Vendor and material management • Advanced technology • Facility control • Flexibility • Price/cost leadership • Global competitiveness
10.	Hupton	1995	• Training • Focused team initiatives • New processes and tools • Organization change • Knowledge development
11.	Aggarwal	1995	• CAD/CAM • FMS • CIM • JIT

1	*2*	*3*	*4*
			• TQM
			• Concurrent engineering
			• Total Productive Maintenance (TPM)
12.	Kinni	1996	• Customer focus
			• Quality
			• Agility
			• Supply management
			• Technology
			• Product development
			• Environmental responsibility
			• Employee safety
			• Corporate citizenship
13.	Bates and Flynn	1996	• Cellular manufacturing
			• CAD
			• CAM
			• TQM
			• JIT
			• Supplier management
			• Employee involvement
			• Manufacturing strategy
14.	Jetley and Catalano	1998	• Elements of WCM
			• Mission statement
			• Customer needs and expectations
			• Organization audit
			• Certification
			• Employee education and training
			• Communication
			• Philosophies
			• Dedication to quality
			• Reduction of lead time
			• Reduction of inventory
			• Employee involvement
			• Measurement
			• Continuous improvement
15	Sardana	2000	• Manufacturing strategy
			• Manufacturing technology
			• Manufacturing management principles
			• Human resource management

Growth of WCM

Farsijani H. and Carruthers A. (1996) has highlighted the growth of WCM and the following figure shows the growth. Each year, new concepts and philosophies were included with that of previous years.

Growth of World-class Manufacturing

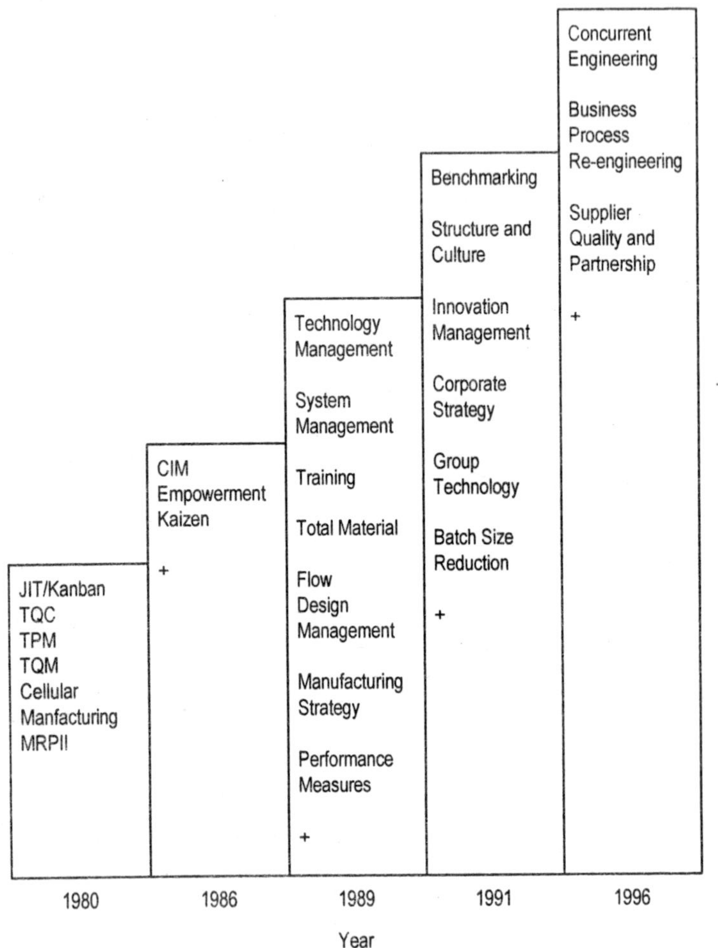

Objective

Total Customer Delite—"we advertise our technology to our customers."

Serve Customer Better Than Your Competitor.

World-class Manufacturing Framework (Giffi, Roth and Seal, Eds. Voss C.A., 1992)

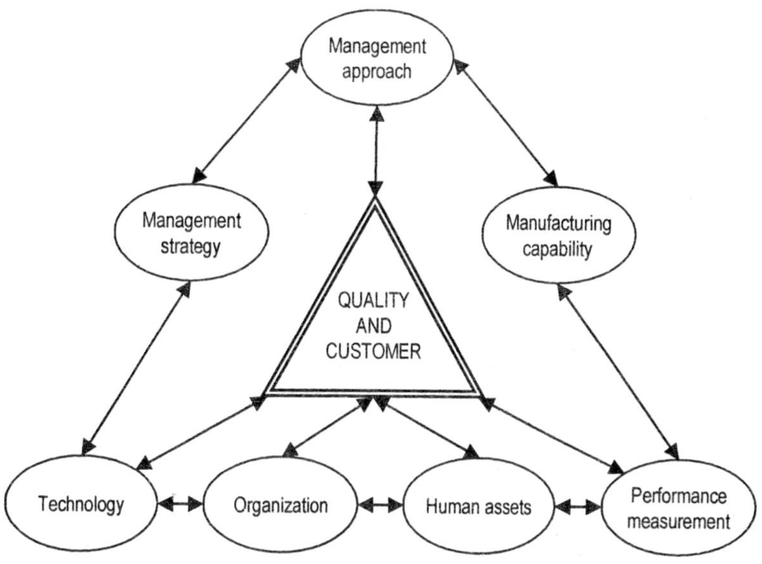

Best Practice Model of WCM (Nandi, 2000)

Total Quality

Innovation	Concurrent	Product Development
Concurrent	Engineering and Manufacturing Information Systems	Engineering
Logistics	Engineering	Lean Production

Business Performance → Customer Satisfaction

Organisation and Culture

Framework for Implementing World-Class Manufacturing (Schultz, 1998)

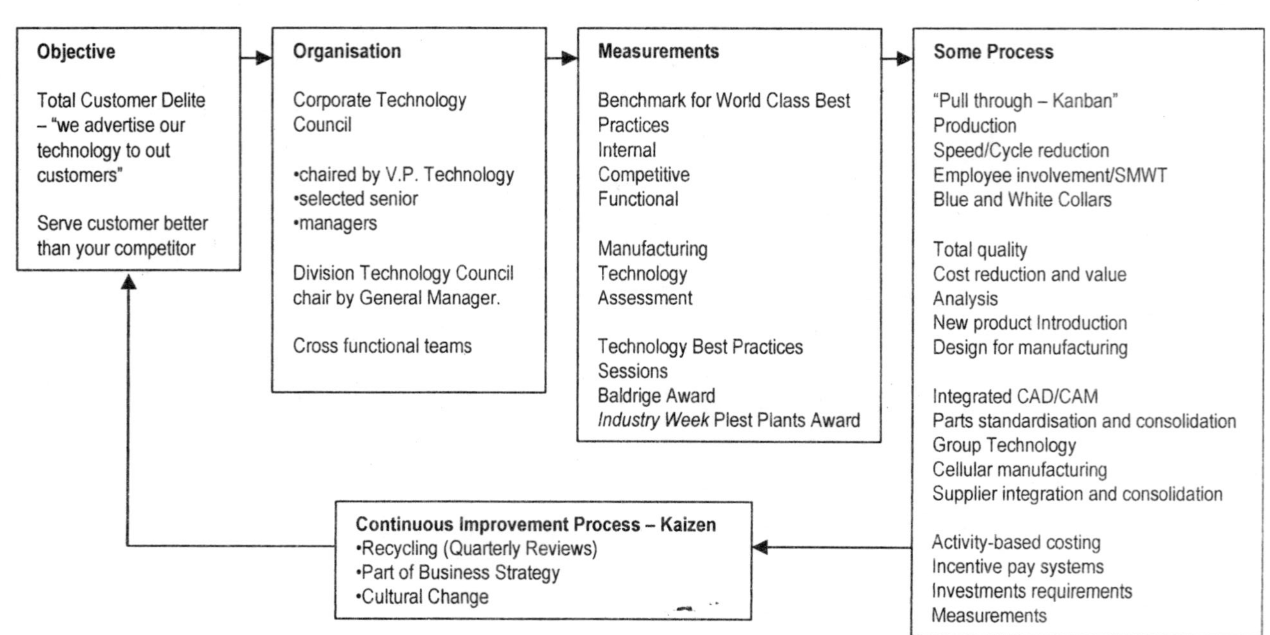

Comparative Study of Japanese and Indian Manufacturing Strategies

It is paramount to compare Japanese manufacturing with Indian counterpart for the better understanding of the distinction existing between them. There have been studies which have attempted to identify differences in socio-economic, quality, people, purchasing, production system and management practices of Japanese vis-a-vis traditional manufacturing practices (Prem Vrat 1993; Leavy 1994; Bounds 1994; Harrison 1992; Plratec 1994; Korgaonkar 1992; Ansari 1986; Hays 1981; Peter 1971; Peter 1980; Richard 1978; Howard 1978; Steven 1981; Skinner 1974; Cheng 1993). Comparison between Japanese and Indian manufacturing system is explicitly discussed here under in a very apropos manner. Depending upon the circumstances, type and operations of the organisations a methodology should be developed to adopt these strategies to reap out maximum benefits accrued in the novel concept of Japanese manufacturing. Each element of this novel manufacturing has a role to play, the choice you need to make depending upon circumstances. Priorities among feasible element can be established to achieve organisational goal objectively and effectively. Comparative studies of Japanese and Indian manufacturing strategies are presented in table below.

Comparison of Japanese and Indian Manufacturing Strategies

Attributes/sub-attributes	*Japanese manufacturing Strategies*	*Indian manufacturing Strategies*
1	*2*	*3*
1. Workforce and Organization		
• Multi functional Workers (Soiinka)	Flexible.	Specialized and rigid
• Attitude	Common values, facilitating cooperation.	Often divergent values, individualism sometimes hindering cooperation.
• Decision-making	Collective decision-making (ringi) with consensus.	Individual decision-making.

(Contd.)

1	2	3
	Change by consensus.	Change by edict.
	Involvement of many people in preparing and making decision.	Involvement of few people In making decision and "selling" the decision to persons with divergent values.
	Decision flow from bottom to top and back.	Dècision initiated at the top. Flowing down.
	Slow decision-making, fast implementation of the decision.	Fast decision-making, slow implementation requiring compromise, often resulting in sub-optimal decisions.
	Group activities and stressed.	Difficult to organize.
	Japanese disagree with their boss often but politely.	Indian will disagree with their boss rarely but violently.
• Willingness to change	Learn to accept.	Resistance to change.
• Loyalty	Loyal to company.	Loyal to profession
	Holistic concern.	Segmented concern.
• Employment	Life time employment, dedication and job satisfaction.	Short-term employment, Job security prevailing.
• Job design	Non-socialized carrier oaths.	Socialized carrier oaths.
• Training and education	Life time training.	Optimal training to meet immediate job need.
	Training and development considered long-term investment.	Training and development undertaken with hesitation.
	Broad skills.	Narrow skills.
• Motivation	Hard pace.	Easy Dace.
• Continuous Improvement (Kaizen)	Never rest on laurels.	Often rest on laurels.

(Contd.)

1	2	3
Organization		
• Organizational values and culture	Human resource management is connected with individual sense of purpose, emotions and social meanings.	Social and emotional issues are suppressed, politics and power dominates.
	Fix the problem not the blame.	Fix the blame not the problem.
	Saving face.	Fixing blame.
	Mistakes are treasures the study of which leads to process improvement.	Mistakes are inevitable and have to be inspected out.
• Enterprise unions	Labour union is not affiliated to political parties. Labour interest is foremost important during negotiations.	Labour union movement is strong with the unions having affiliation to political parties. Labour interest is subjugated by political parties.
• Industrial relations	Union fights management.	Union fights the company.
	Harmonic industrial relations	Belligerent
• Empowerment	Employee Empowerment to take right decisions	Total control to meet production targets.
• Organizational Structure	Flat management	Tall hierarchy
• Respect for human system	No status differentials	Status symbol pay privilege.
	Respect to humanity and creativity	Respect to status.
• Profit sharing	Sharing profit with labour	Making: profit for themselves
• Manpower planning	Work force is first built and workers are then placed in business hierarchy according to their abilities.	Required number of slots are created and then filled in.

(Contd.)

1	2	3
2. Quality		
• Quality management	Quality is free.	It cost money to make Quality
	Quality is built in.	Quality is controlled.
• Statistical Quality Control	Quality at the source is emphasized.	Inspection at large.
	Statistical study of variations to understand causes.	Scoring, reporting and evaluating,
	Process control	Acceptance sampling.
• Total quality control	Workers are on-the-spot trouble shooter.	Quality personal are responsible for quality problems.
• Total Quality Management (TQM)	Planning-oriented.	Control-oriented.
• Strategic Quality Management	Focused on broader systems, proactive to opportunities, big breakthroughs and small steps.	Focused new product development, reactive to problems, big breakthroughs only.
• Visually control	Control chart, poka-yoka system.	Only charts.
3. Plant and Equipment		
• Group technology (GT)	GT is highly used.	Reluctant to use.
• Automation	Automation is valued because it facilitates consistent Quality.	Automation is valued because it drives labour out of the product.
• House keeping	5'5 (Seiri, Seiton, Seiso, Seketsu, and Shitsuke) are used.	Comparatively untidy and disorganized work place.
• Displays	Light displays to highlight trouble spot.	Not used.
• Total Productive Maintenance (TPM)	Prevention mentality.	Corrective mentality.

(Contd.)

1	2	3
	Preventive maintenance.	Breakdown maintenance.
	Maintenance is regular, machine breakdown and tool failure must be eliminated.	Maintenance is done only after failure. Machine break down is not serious because of inventory.
4. Production system		
• Priorities	Priorities: limited market.	Accept all orders.
• Manufacturing system	Make to order.	Made to stock.
	Kanban (pul! system)	MRP (push system).
• Standardization	Standardized output	Customized output
• Capacity utilization	Capacity moderately utilized.	Highly utilized.
	Run equipment slow but for 24 hours.	Run equipment fast as long as it runs.
	Just-in-time production, no WIP.	WIP is needed to assure that machine utilization stays high.
• Engineering	Incremental design simplify, design for manufacturing.	Design from scratch.
	Standardized output.	Customized output.
• Set-ups	Low set-up time	High set-up time.
• Layout	Flexible layout.	Rigid layout.
• Material Handling System	Flow: use of gravity.	Less significant.
• Customization	Material handling system: customized, state-of-art technology.	Specific, standard items available in market.
5. Inventory System		
• Waste reduction	Inventory is an evil.	Inventory is an asset.
	Inventory is an evil it hides	Inventory is useful. It

(Contd.)

1	2	3
	problems that should be allowed to surface.	makes production rolling along.
	Every effort must be extended to minimize inventory.	It protect against forecast error, machine break down, and late deliveries.
• Queues	Once in motion, always in motion. Production should be just-in-time, there should be no queues of work-in-orocess.	Queues of work-in-process are needed to be sure that machine utilization stays high.
• Lot sizes	Keep reducing the lot size. The smallest quantity is desired for both manufactured and purchased parts.	Keep revising the optimum lot size based on some formulas.
6. Purchasing		
• Small lot purchasing	Small lots.	Large batches.
• Supplier-buyer Proximity	Frequent deliveries.	Few deliveries.
• Supplier selection	Supplier selection: long-term contract.	Short-term contract.
• Few committed suppliers	Single source supply.	Multiple source supply.
• Complimentary Concern	Work together to maximize the economies of co-operation.	Reduce supplier power, widen supbase; reduce buyer power, widen customer base.
• Buyer-supplier Cooperation	Win-Win situation.	Planning them off against each other competitors perspective.
• Buyer control over Freight	Transportation mode: concern for both inbound/outbound freight.	Outbound freight.
• Supplier evaluation	Supplier evaluation: includes: Quality, delivery and Price.	Mainly price.
• Zero defects.	No rejects acceptable.	Some percentage rejects are permissible.

(Contd.)

1	2	3
• Supplier as designer.	Loose specification, emphasis on performance.	Rigid specification innovations not encouraged.
7. Product and Price		
• Product design	Innovations.	Limitations.
	Customer-oriented product.	R and D lacking: product design depends upon what is available what the customer demands.
• Pricing strategy	Believe in long-term gains, low profit margin; sell high volume at lower price to make high profit.	Strive for short-term gain, sell a price to make high profit.

CONCLUSION

Manufacturing Excellence strategies have been proved more promising and challenging as compared to Indian manufacturing strategies (practices). It is very evident from the comparison that manufacturing excellence strategies have the larger potential to provide the companies with competitive advantages.

References

Aggarwal, S.C., "World-class manufacturing and benchmarking—The philopsophy of performance enhancement, *Productivity*, Vol. 41, No. 2, 2000, pp. 206-09.

Hays, R.H., 1981, "Why Japanese Factories Works", HBR, pp. 57-66.

Jately, S., Catalano, J., "World-class manufacturing", working paper, College of Technology, Bowling Green State University, 1999.

Nandi, S.N., "Manufacturing Strategy: A potent source of competitive advantage" Productivity, Vol. 34, No. 2, 1993, pp. 189-98.

Peter, F.D., 1971, "What we can learn from Japanese Management", HBR, pp. 110-20.

Sardona, G.D., " World-class manufacturing: A strategic Business Driver", Productivity, Vol. 41, No. 2, 2000, pp. 252-60.

Sharma, R.R.K., Upadhyay, S., "Manufacturing Strategy: Relating Process to content", Productivity, Vol. 39, No. 2, 1998, pp. 272-79.

Warne, D.P., 1997, "Monograph on Management Thoughts", Dept. of Business Management, PAU, Ludhiana.

CHAPTER

24

Trade Protection Measures

Challenges and Implications for Indian Business

RAJIV ARORA

The era of globalization under the aegis of World Trade Organization (WTO) and the emergence of technologies, which collapse the physical boundaries to cyber space interactions, have thrown tremendous challenge for the business organizations. The boundary to conduct business today is no longer the national domain but it is greatly influenced by the global environment. The liberalization on account of low tariffs and reduced quantitative restrictions (QRs) makes the competition domain global. The 4 P's of marketing are well known basics in business. In this basket of P's, the P pertaining to price had been a common leveraging element to penetrate markets. The present paper highlights the impact of a pricing policy of an organization on its business in the contemporary era of globalization where usage of WTO compatible contingency measures like Anti-dumping, anti-subsidy and safeguard is extremely high which not only equalizes prices to protect domestic industry but also makes business unpredictable. India has been an active user of AD and has also been a frequent target of AD on its exports. The impact of AD usage travels all along a value chain.

I. INTRODUCTION

It is a well known fact that World Trade Organization (WTO) is today steering and facilitating the process of global integration through its enshrined mandate of free and fair multilateral trade. India also initiated its march on to the process of liberalization, privatization and globalization (LPG) essentially since 1991. However, after the emergence of World Trade Organization (WTO) in 1995, this process of integrating with the global world gained momentum and India adopted a road map of gradual and careful integration. The process of global integration is recognized as an irreversible and an inevitable tenet of any nation's economic policy. The pace and extent of global integration through dismantling of Non- tariff barriers (NTB's), and reduction of tariffs has been calibrated by the nation states so that there are minimal shocks due to global exposure and the transition is smooth by a parallel development of resilience in the economy.

However, the process of globalization and the cherished goals of a free and fair trade are often under attack by unfair trade practices like subsidization and dumping. Member-states and organizations resort to such unfair trade practices so as to capture the market shares in the highly competitive world market. While subsidies are granted by the state, dumping of goods, a price discriminatory practice leading to injury to the producers of the importing country is followed by individual exporting organizations. The WTO's framework provides for trade remedial measures by way of anti-subsidy measures (AS measures), also known as Countervailing duty imposition measures (CVD measures) and anti-dumping (AD) measures which can be invoked whenever the unfair trade practices are resorted to. India along with other countries uses the anti-dumping instrument to correct the distortion in trade. India is recognized as an active user of anti-dumping measures next to USA. The AD measure happens to be an extremely potent instrument in this era of networked and integrated world, which can not only be used as a shield but also as a sword to regulate trade (unfair trade). It is this usage of AD as a double-edged sword, which is relevant for understanding the implications for trade and industry.

The exporters on account of their pricing policy and subsidization by the governments today face threat of various trade protection measures which are invoked under special circumstances. The three instruments are different in terms of their application and impact.

Dumping though in common parlance is sometimes understood as cheap, inferior and high influx of goods but is not the case so. It is technically referred to as the differential pricing policy of the exporter and that it indicates the difference between the domestic selling price (normal value) in the exporter's country and the export price to the importing country. Of course the comparison is a complex issue which calls for apple to apple comparison at an appropriate level of trade generally Ex-Factory level. The injury to the domestic industry (DI) is seen in terms of fifteen explicitly defined injury parameters comprehensively indicated under WTO articles. These parameters are the reduced profitability, market share, employment, cash flow, etc. of the domestic industry. Once an investigation is completed and the conclusions of dumping and injury to domestic industry attributable to dumping are conclusive, anti-dumping duty is imposed to the extent of injury but not exceeding the extent of dumping. The exporter can voluntarily give an undertaking not to sell at dumped price and can, therefore, get out of the dumping net or else the duty continues for five years until and unless reviewed. In this time review of the decision can be undertaken on request of any of the stakeholders or by the authority itself if the circumstances change, i.e. if dumping or injury ceases or increases. The dumping is thus an exporter specific phenomenon and the anti-dumping duties are exporter and product specific.

The counter vailing duties (CVD) duties are resorted to in event of exporter getting subsidies from the exporting country (government). The subsidies, which are not WTO compatible, are offset by an equivalent extent of CVD. It is thus directed against the government and is country specific.

Safeguard is technically not an unfair trade practice instrument and is resorted to when there is sudden surge in imports and cause not merely injury but serious injury to the

DI. Such duties are across the board on all countries and call for reciprocity and compensation by the importing country. The industry has to undertake a restructuring programme in a time bound manner.

All three measures can be challenged under the Dispute settlement mechanism viz. under the aegis of Dispute settlement Body (DSB) of WTO. The national legislation also provides for domestic appellate mechanisms to challenge the decisions of the concerned quasi-judicial bodies.

The salient attributes of the 3 measures are indicated comprehensively and comparatively in the Table 1.

TABLE I

Comparative Attribute Matrix for 3 Contingent Measures

Sl. No.	*Attribute*	*AD*	*Cvd*	*Sg*
1.	Rationale	Price discrimination	Subsidasation by governments	Sudden surge in imports
2.	Nature of phenomena	Unfair by exporter	Unfair by government	Trade eventuality
3.	Nature of measure	Exporter specific	Country specific	Across board
4.	Compatibility	Wto compatible	Wto compatible	Wto compatible
5.	Redressal	Dsb	Dsb	Dsb
6.	Extent of usage in world from 1995-2000	1441 cases	115	61
7.	Nature of institutional mechanism	Quasi-judicial	Quasi-judicial	Quasi-judicial
8.	Extent of criticism	Extremely high	Limited criticism	Rarely

Source: WTO data and concepts as conceptualized.

Thus it can be observed that AD mechanism is the most frequently used measure constituting almost 90% of the kitty as compared to the other two TPM measures. The key concepts of AD are also appended as Appendix 1.

2. AD USAGE IN INDIA

The AD usage in India since 1992—year-wise, product-wise and country-wise is as indicated in Tables 2(a), (b) and (c) below.

TABLE 2(A)

AD Usage Pattern in India—Year-wise Trend

Financial Year	*No. of cases initiated*	*No. of cases where Finalfindings/ Prliminary findings have been issued*	*No. of measures in force as on 31.3.2003*
1992-93	2	2	0
1993-94	1	1	0
1994-95	6	6	4
1995-96	5	5	1
1996-97	5	5	4
1997-98	14	13	11
1998-99	13	12	11
1999-2000	19	19	18
2000-2001	28	25	24
2001-2002	30	29	29
2002-2003	30	17	14
Total	153	134	116

TABLE 2(B)

AD Usage Pattern in India—Product-wise Trend

Product Category	*No. of cases*
Chemicals and Petrochemicals	70
Pharmaceuticals	28
Fibres/Yarns	14
Steel and Other Metals	14
Consumer Goods	13
Others	14
Total	153

TABLE 2(C)

AD Usage Pattern in India—Country-wise Trend

Country	*No. of cases initiated*
China	66
Taiwan	25
EU	25
Korea	24
Japan	19
USA	18
Singapore	18
Russia	14
Thailand	12
Indonesia	11
Brazil	6
Hong Kong	6
France	6
Iran	6
Canada	5
Malaysia	5
Germany	5
Romania	5
S. Africa	5
Others (include 28 countries)	58

The above usage pattern indicates a increased usage in last 4-5 years more on products which are intermediates, though there is also a shift towards the finished goods. The majority of cases are on imports from China and Southeast Asia.

3. ECONOMIC IMPACT OF AD

India has both been an active user and also a frequent target of AD Cases. As a user, the AD instrument has been able to provide level playing field to the domestic producers by protecting them from the unfair trade practice of dumping. The other stakeholders viz. the users and exporters have been a critique of the usage of AD instrument by India. The AD like any tariff tends to provide protection thus leading to improved prices and enhanced market share for the domestic producers. The two effects are referred to as price effect and volume effect respectively in the AD parlance. Besides this, the dumped imports, which are arrested by AD, levy decline, and its market share is distributed between the domestic industry and other non-dumped import sources. Thus trade diversion is also a common outcome in an AD measure imposition. Besides this, at times trade contraction is also witnessed. The mere initiation of an investigation slows down the imports thus leading to a trade chilling effect on imports. The impact of AD also gets transmitted to the upstream industries (suppliers) and downstream users in the value chain. The upstream industries are benefited by the protection given to their customers, as they are able to maintain sustained supply. The competitiveness of the downstream industries is greatly effected and at times the dumping point shifts upward to next value added product. The export competitiveness of user industry is also stated to be affected. The global perception and threat is that a rampant usage of AD instrument may lead to global wars and retaliation. Having identified the various effects in the industry value chain as a consequence of AD usage, some select results of a study on impact assessment of AD measures are reported here.

To collect the information on the above issues, a structured (with both closed and open-ended questions) questionnaire was administered to 40 industries out of a universe of 160 AD cases. The sample chosen was a purposive stratified sample. The questionnaire was validated by an expert group comprising of academicians, policy implementers and trade representatives. The questionnaire was also tested for reliability.

The issues, which are attempted to be covered through the questionnaire, are listed below:

(i) Volume and price effects of AD measures on the domestic producers.
(ii) Effect on quantum of dumped imports.
(iii) Effect on quantum of imports from the non-dumped sources (trade diversion effect).
(iv) Trade chilling effect subsequent to the initiation of an AD investigation.
(v) Effect on the user industry.
(vi) Effects by way of retaliation by the affected countries viz. trade wars.
(vii) Efficacy of AD measures by exploring extent of circumvention of AD measure.
(viii) Restructuring measures other than AD shelter taken by domestic industry for building resilience.

For the quantitative data actual figures were collected were subsequently normalized and indexed for a meaningful analysis as the economic data for different organizations was in different units of production and sales and for an apple to apple comparison normation was essential. The indexing of the data to a base of 100 for the first year of pre-AD measure era also ensures confidentiality of data of the respondent organizations.

3.1 The Perception of Efficacy and Desirability of AD Measures

As indicated above in the questionnaire format table, the perception on efficacy of AD measures has been captured. The results of the same are indicated in the Table 3.

The following are the learnings from the perception survey:

Uni-variate perception analysis

(i) 80% of the respondent organizations indicated that quality of their products were comparable to the international standards while 20% claimed it to even better than international quality. None of the respondents reported their product quality as below the international/world class standards.

TABLE 3

AD Efficacy: The Perception Analysis

Attribute of dumping	*Percentage of Respondents*	*Special Feature*
Dumping measure has benefitted	90% of respondents benefited	Economic effects reported by all. Price effects by 80% and volume effects by 60% of domestic producers.
AD measure should continue	100% Domestic industry desired continuance of AD	80% for years and 20% for 10 years.
Dumping is still continuing	75% reported continuance. 25% reported arrest.	Circumvention and repeated dumping reported as reasons
Measures other than dumping taken to build resilience	Cost cutting by process improvement HR restructuring. Captive power plants.	30% of domestic producers indicated such cost competitive measures being undertaken.
AD as an effective mechanism	90% of domestic producers felt that AD was effective.	Circumvention and repeated dumping were reported as eroding efficacy.
AD as a sustainable long-term solution	Only 60% of domestic producers felt AD as sustainable solution.	Circumvention and repeated dumping were reported as eroding efficacy.
Circumvention of AD	70% of the domestic producers reported circumvention.	Source shifting, modifying forms , 100% EOU sales, advance license sales etc were types of circumvention reported

(ii) 20% of respondent organizations reported that their cost of production is higher and can be reduced.

(iii) 60% of the respondent organizations reported high incidence of financial (interest) cost as a reason of high cost of production.

(iv) 50% of respondent organizations reported manpower as a reason of higher cost of production.

(v) 70% of respondent organizations felt that circumvention of the AD duty was happening and was a reason of evasion of AD duty thus undermining the efficacy of the AD measures.

(vi) 70% of respondent organizations reported that reduction of customs duty will increase dumping, 10% reported that it would decrease dumping while 20% reported no effect.

(vii) 20% of respondent organizations had AD duty also on their raw materials.

(viii) 30% of organizations reported that their products were attracting the AD duty

(ix) 40-50% of the organizations also reported the improvement in the financial health of their raw material suppliers.

3.2 The Normated Trend Analysis of Various Economic Parameters

As indicated earlier in this chapter, the comparative and overall composite analysis of impact of AD at the national level has been done by indexing the data captured for different respondent organizations. The timeframe for which the analysis is conducted is essentially five years (two years pre AD measure and two years after AD measure). The average trend of various normalized economic parameters is given in Table 4 as indicated below.

TABLE 4

The Normalised Average Trend of Various Economic Parameters

Parameter	*YOI(-2)*	*YOI(-1)*	*YOI*	*YOI(+1)*	*YOI(+2)*
Domestic production	100	122	149	159	185
Domestic sales	100	113	118	124	141
Domestic selling prices	100	104	103	112	115
Demand	100	122	165	141	159
Profitability	100	116	128	139	161
Dumped Imports	100	182	232	22	39
Other Imports	100	107	376	414	1078
Total Imports	100	175	223	21	38

YOI: Year of imposition of AD measure, YOI (-1, -2) (2 previous years) and YOI (+1, +2) (2 later years)

3.3 The Economic Effects of Anti-dumping Measures

3.3.1 The Volume Effect

The volume effect at a macro aggregate level is evidenced from the normalized average trends of production, domestic sales and demand. As can be seen from the Table 4 the production and domestic sales have shown a rising trend in both pre and post-AD measure period. The rate of growth of sales and production, however, remains almost same. The demand of the subject products has also increased during the period thus ruling out recession as a cause for injury to domestic producers. The Figure 1 depicts the rising trend of all the three economic parameters of volume effect. Thus dumping has not led to erosion or shut down of production by the affected industries. The level of AD duty as percentage of import price in the period of study ranged from 30% to 77%. The correlation coefficient of Production and domestic sales change over the entire period and also subsequent to the AD measure period respectively shows a positive correlation of 0.6 and 0.6 and 0.73 and 0.59 respectively with the level of AD duty. This establishes the relation that a high AD duty has a significant effect on the market share of domestic industry.

FIGURE 1

The Normalised Volume Effect Trend

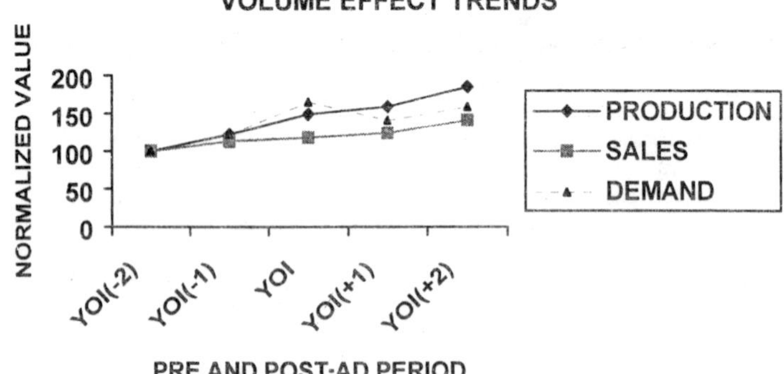

3.3.2 The Price Effect

The price effect of AD measure is captured through the selling price trend coupled with profitability as indicated in Table 4. The selling prices over the period have not risen significantly. However, the profitability has shown a significant increase. This implies that during the period of study, there has been decline in the average cost structure of the industry, which could be primarily due to the raw material costs or restructuring attempts by organizations for long-term sustenance. The correlation coefficients of AD duty level with the selling price and profitability comes to minus 0.53 and minus 0.36. The result implies erosion of AD benefit if the level of AD is high. As has also been indicated through the perception survey and the specific case studies that circumvention of duty is very significant, the higher AD duty results in circumvention thus leading to erosion of profitability which might accrue due to AD measure. The figure 2 below indicates the normalized price effect trends.

FIGURE 2

Price Trend

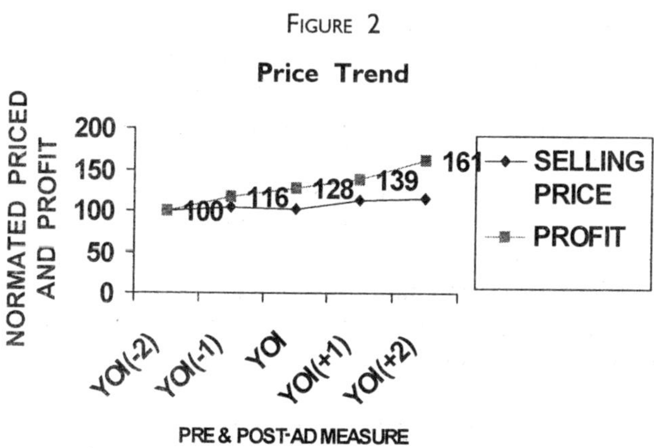

3.3.3 The Trade Chilling Effect

It is seen from some of the individual responses that volume of dumped imports between initiation and first AD measure imposition declines significantly. Thus, mere initiation of a measure can lead to slow down of dumped imports. Such an effect is clearly visible in case of sodium hydro sulphite and lead acid batteries. In case of sodium hydro sulphite the dumped imports from China declined by almost 56% on mere initiation of the case. The normated trend of imports from china of sodium hydro sulphite is as under in Figure 3.

FIGURE 3

Trade Chilling Effect

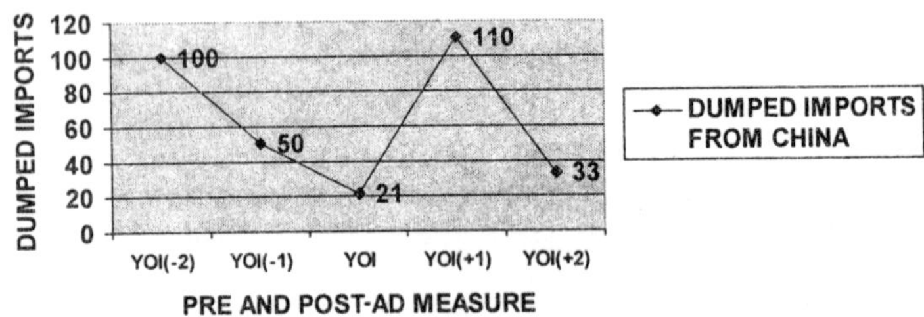

3.3.4 The Trade Diversion Effect

The trade diversion effect is analyzed at a global aggregate basis by comparing the trends of dumped and non-dumped imports. Table 4 indicated above depicts that the dumped imports fall significantly after the AD measure and the imports shift to the other sources significantly. Thus the trade diversion effect is explicitly visible. The correlation of change in total imports and dumped imports with the level of AD duty in the pre and post AD measure period comes to Minus 0.13 and minus 0.18 respectively. This indicates a feeble relationship and points to circumvention theory as was illustrated above in section 3.3.2. The Figure 4 indicates the trade diversion trend.

3.3.5 Effect on Downstream User Industries

The effect on the user industry has been captured in specific cases through the structured interviews and case studies. The price effect on domestic industry has led to increase in the price for user industry. However, the cost increase due to AD in many cases is absorbed since it is the supply stability which becomes vital concern for an user industry. In caustic soda, barium carbonate and lead acid batteries the AD duty has been absorbed with hardly any

FIGURE 4

Trade Chilling Effect

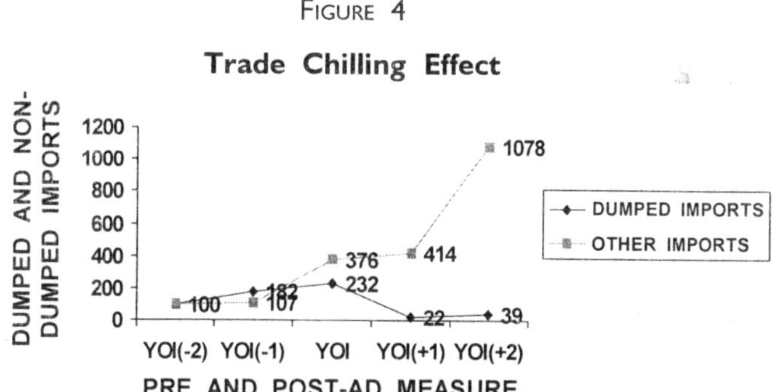

turmoil. The cost incidence of AD on barium carbonate in the caustic soda production is quite small. In case of strontium carbonate though the cost incidence could be borne by the user industry, the quality of domestic product was an issue. In fact in case of Lead acid battery, M/s Panasonic, the exporter from Thailand is proposing to set-up a battery plant in south India with an investment of Rs. 100 crores as the AD duty disrupts the dealer confidence and by setting a manufacturing facility in the AD user country itself can lead to a sustained solution to evade dumping investigations repeatedly. In case of SSI beneficiaries of AD, the price levels are generally kept under check by hard bargaining and arm twisting by the big user groups. Also, the internal competition in case of caustic soda industry prevents a sellers market to emerge even after the AD measure. In case of oxo-alcohols the user industry suffered as the dumping of downstream finished products started once the user industry became unviable. Thus it may be noted that the perception survey indicates that effect of AD on user industry is mixed and in most of the cases it is not significant.

One of the other significant effects of AD measures in case of lead acid batteries has been a decision by the exporter to set-up a manufacturing base in India with a collaboration with Indian partner so that AD can be escaped. The Indian partner feels that it is the dealer channel confidence and supply chain which gets disturbed by AD and, therefore, protection of this channel confidence is a priority of the exporter. The battery being a consumer product with a wide base, the consumer absorbs the AD levy. Thus a shifting of manufacturing base from abroad would no doubt be a better and useful economic gain at a macro-economic level as it would have its other spin off effects in terms of employment, competition, consumer choice, GDP augmentation by domestic and export sales and lastly providing reasonable prices to consumers.

3.3.6 Effect on Upstream Supplier Industries

The suppliers of raw materials to the AD beneficiary producers have also improved in terms of economic viability. Almost 65% of the respondents indicated that timely payments and the continuous and sustained production led to improvement in the financial viability of the upstream suppliers and also in turn ensured a stable supply to the domestic producers. The effects were clearly visible in case of salt suppliers to the soda ash industry.

3.3.7 Trade Wars and Retaliation

One of the criticisms of the trade protection measures, Anti-dumping in particular is that AD measures lead to trade retalizzation and trade wars. In order to test this research proposition, the WTO data on country-wise usage of AD measures from 1995 to June 2003 was referenced. The correlation between the AD initiations as user and target by the presumed retaliator and also AD measures as user and target by the presumed retaliator was carried out. The correlation coefficient in both the cases was very feeble viz. 0.29 to 0.22. Thus the retaliation of AD Practices on trade platforms is not established. However, retaliation does happen on other platforms. It is also a perception of trade and industry (that were interviewed) that Cancun outcome and present EU-India consultations on Anti-dumping are linked.

3.3.8 Effect on Export Competitiveness: India as an AD User

The effect on user industry has been illustrated above The trends of three user industries have been evaluated whose one or many inputs were subjected to AD measure.

These include Speakers (input hard ferrite magnets), Caustic soda (input barium carbonate) and Automotive tyres (input SBR/HSR). The normated trend of exports of finished goods is as under in Table 5 and Figure 5

TABLE 5

Normated Trend of User Indsutry Exports

Exports	*YOI(-2)*	*YOI(-1)*	*YOI*	*YOI(+1)*	*YOI(+2)*
	100	123	148	162	185

FIGURE 5

AD and User Industry's Exports

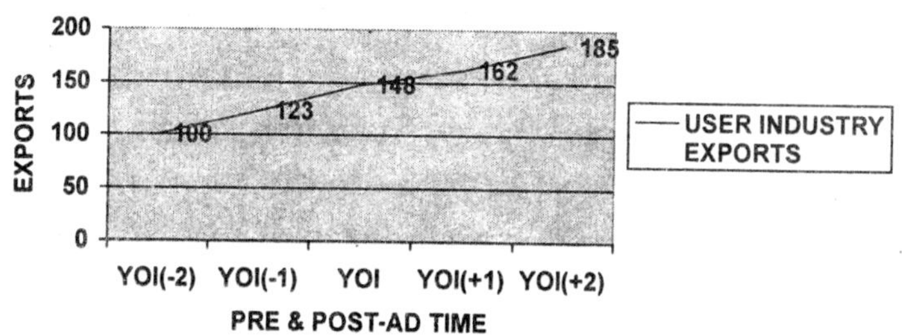

It can, therefore, be seen that export competitiveness of user industry has not got eroded. This is also supported by the fact that all duties on raw materials and intermediates, which go as inputs for export production, are refunded. This viewpoint also emerged in the pilot study conducted at FIEO as indicated in chapter four. A study by DGAD in 2001-02 also led to a similar conclusion. Thus one can conclude:

(i) Export competitiveness of user industry is not eroded by AD levy, as AD is refunded/not levied on inputs for export production.

(ii) The incidence of AD in production cost is reported to be not very significant on many products.

(iii) The AD levy helps in building supply chain stability thereby off-setting the price burden disadvantage if any.

3.3.9 Effect on Exports: India as a Target of AD Measures

The effect on exports due to AD and CVD measures has been significant. To evaluate this effect data from the Export promotion councils/FIEO is used. From the period 1998-99 to 2002-03, the normated exports of Indian products facing AD measures was considered and the trend analyzed. The products considered for testing this hypothesis are bed linen, polyester films and steel products. The normated exports for the last five years for these products, which have been severely hit is indicated in Table 6. The trend of impact on exports is depicted in Figure 6.

TABLE 6

Normated Trend of Exports Facing AD Measures

EXPORTS	*1998-99*	*1999-2000*	*2000-01*	*2001-02*	*2002-03*
	100	92	87	76	70

FIGURE 6

AD Effect on Exports

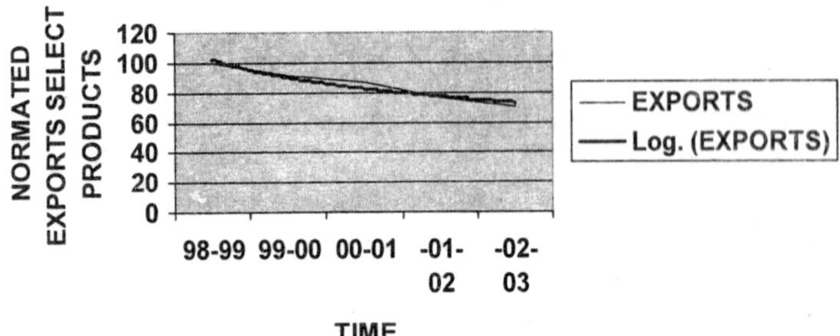

The above trend shows an overall 30% decline in exports due to the AD measures. In the last five years it is seen from WTO data that AD cases have increased by 150% while the CVD cases by 500% as compared to the previous five years.

3.3.10 The Overall Impact

In order to evaluate the overall economic impact three variables, viz. Domestic industry's sales, user industry's exports and exports of AD targeted products have been considered. These select variables are representative for the three vital stakeholders in the industry value chain who are affected by an AD levy. It is presumed that the upstream suppliers are benefited invariably along with the domestic producer who is the beneficiary of the AD levy. Such a positive effect on upstream industries is observed in the case of Chlor-Alkali industry. Hence effect of Domestic industry sales is presumed to include the upstream industry effects also. The average normated trend of overall impact on the variables as identified above is as under in Table 7 and depicted in Figure 7.

TABLE 7

Overall Impact: A Normated Trend

Overall Benefits	*Year 1*	*Year 2*	*Year 3*	*Year 4*	*Year 5*
	100	109.3	118	120.6	132

FIGURE 7

Overall Economic Impact

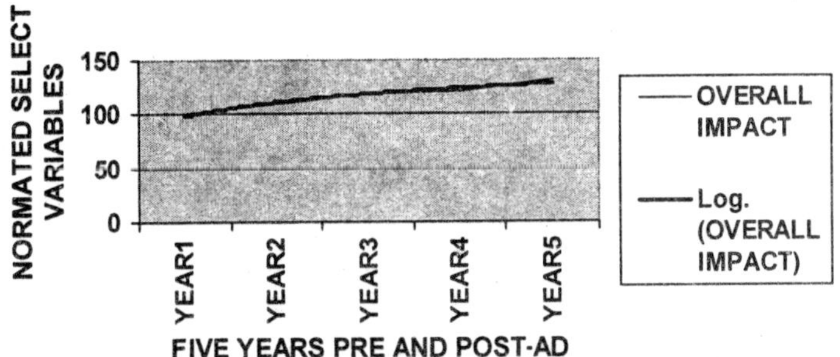

The trend/regression line on log (overall impact) also indicates a rising trend of overall economic impact of AD measures.

3.4 Synthesis of Empirical Results

The empirically tested economic effects of AD measures

conceptualized as various research issues are tabulated below in Table 8.

TABLE 8

Synthesis of Various Empirical Results

Research issue	*Result*
Financial Health of Domestic Producers	There is a positive volume and price effect coupled with profitability
Trade Chilling and Diversion effect	Both effects witnessed at specific industry and global level respectively.
Overprotection to domestic industry	The Net sales realization to the domestic producers shows negative relationship with the extent of AD duty which indicates that higher AD is counter productive and erodes overprotection through the market base structures and phenomena like circumvention.
Effect on export competitiveness of user industry and exports of AD targeted products	There has been no negative effect on the export competitiveness of the user industry products while exports of select products from India have declined by almost 30% due to levy of AD duty
Effect on upstream industries	The upstream industries as suppliers to the industries, which have benefited due to AD, have also witnessed growth and acquired viability. e.g. Chlor Alkali industry providing stability to salt and barium carbonate producers
Net effect on Industry	The overall impact is perceived as positive
Trade retaliation	The correlation coefficients between use and target is 0.29 to 0.2. Hence retaliation not upheld

The results of various research issues clearly bring out the positive effect the AD measures had on the domestic industry. It also highlights the negative impact on India's exports on account of usage of AD/CVD measures by other countries. The results also lead to a very significant finding about AD measure erosion when the level of AD protection is high. This implies repeated and renewed dumping coupled with circumvention phenomena, which has been mentioned by the domestic industry. One of the reasons of increased usage of AD in India is circumvention and trade diversion and shifting of dumped source.

3.4 Efficacy and Desirability of AD

The Figure 8 captures the various attributes of AD efficacy and desirability in light of the results of the study. The various aspects of the suggestive framework are illustrated below.

3.4.1 AD Usage

(i) The AD usage has increased on account of recent reduction in tariffs and QR's coupled with the global environment of recession in select product industries and also usage of AD and CVD tools as strategic trade policy instruments for curbing unfair trade practices.

(ii) The AD usage is handicapped by lack of appropriate data and cooperation from various stakeholders in particular exporters and importers. There is a need to re-engineer the AD MIS system through development of online DGCIS and customs link with improvised data captures.

(iii) The Indian exporters and other developing countries suffer immensely due to denial of constructive remedies like price undertakings in event of imposition of such measures. This needs to be taken up aggressively as a S and D treatment area at WTO forum.

3.4.2 AD Efficacy

(i) As can be seen from the price and volume effect trends, the AD efficacy is eroded by circumvention, which acquires various innovative forms like new sources, slightly differentiated product to evade the legal and technical nuances, diverting/conduiting material of export production (advance licenses or 100% EOU's), which has no AD levy to the domestic market.

Thus it is felt that AD investigation should not pick up too micro-level products which lead to data constraints, analysis complexity and also induce circumvention. The off loading of material under advance license and by 100% EOU's should be subjected to AD duty as applicable.

FIG. 8

A Suggestive Framework for AD Measures

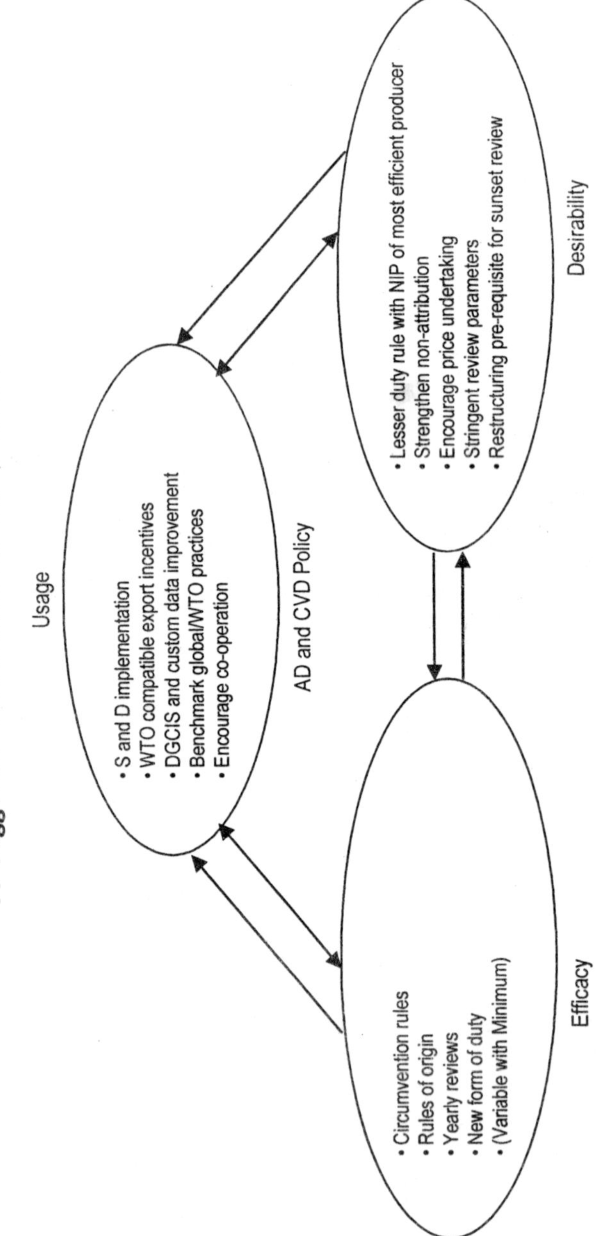

A significant result, which emanates from the study, is that level of AD measure and price realization by domestic industry is negatively correlated. This, therefore, implies that high level of an AD measure is counterproductive. This is also supported by the high extent of circumvention, which takes place eroding the efficacy of an AD measure. Also there has been increase in the repeated and renewed dumping cases increasing the usage rate of AD measures by India. Thus a moderate level of AD is recommended. This, therefore, gets linked to the issue of lesser duty rule and methodology to arrive at fair selling price, which is discussed later.

(ii) Keeping in view the fact that circumvention also takes form of duty absorption, the type of AD levy variable or fixed are circumvented or absorbed by the exporters. Thus a new hybrid form of AD levy is needed. A variable reference price with minimum fixed duty is suggested.

(iii) There is a need to address the issue of AD efficacy by putting in place circumvention rules along with rules of origin. The implementation of the measures needs to be stringent at the customs level.

3.4.3 AD Desirability

(i) As mentioned above, high level of AD can be counterproductive and the fact that the AD measure even though has not led to a turbulence in the user industry sectors, its effects are no doubt transmitted. Therefore, a lesser duty rule which is otherwise practiced in India, can be further improvised by making the fair selling price reference level instead on averaged normated industry level modified to the most efficient producer's cost of production with fair and reasonable profit level. This would then only subsume in the reference price the national structural cost disadvantages which are given to the industry and beyond their control but would eliminate the firm specific inefficiencies. The non-attribution analysis, which is intended to only, punish dumping and not reward organizational inefficiencies needs to be stringent and more elaborate. The fair selling price methodology as indicated above would be in the direction of strengthening the non-attribution analysis.

(ii) There is a need to encourage cooperation and accept price undertakings. The cooperation can be increased if the level of product investigated is not too micro defined and price undertaking are welcomed.

(iii) The reviews need to be carried annually since the arena of trade and economic environment is extremely dynamic.

(iv) The sunset reviews, which are mandated after the 5-year period, need to take into account the restructuring effort made by the benefiting industry. As the factor to be evaluated for the continuance of AD measure after 5 years is that discontinuance of AD measure would cause injury, the analysis of effort on restructuring by industry assumes significance.

5. CONCLUSIONS

The study of the AD measures indicates that AD measures impact through out the value chain. The price factor as a key driver to capture market is thus checked and negated. As the usage of such instruments is on increase, business needs to understand the technical nuances and also should guard themselves against such instruments. In the long-term, besides price the other aspects on quality, after sales support etc would need to be given more importance. The domestic producers in light of the frequent erosion of AD measures through circumvention needs to invest more in restructuring, cost reduction efforts and R & D to achieve a long-term sustainability.

References

Ahuja, Rajiv and Hoda, Anwarul, 2003, 'Agreement on Subsidies and Countervailing Measures: Need for clarification and improvement', Working paper 101, ICRIER, Delhi.

Aggarwal, A., 2001, 'Anti-dumping law and practice: an Indian perspective', Working paper 85, ICRIER, Delhi.

———, 2003, 'Patterns and determinants of Anti-dumping: A world-wide perspective', Working paper 113, ICRIER, Delhi.

Arora Rajiv, 2003, Threat of unfair trade practices: A conceptual framework for R & D and E-business', ICMARD, IIT Delhi.

Aggarwal, A., 2003, 'Anti-dumping code: Issues for review in post Doha negotiations', Working paper 99, ICRIER, Delhi.

Banik, Nilanjan, 2001, 'Anti-dumping measures: A critical evaluation', India biz news and research services limited.

Directorate General of Anti-dumping and Allied Duties (DGAD), Department of Commerce, New Delhi, 2002-03, Annual Report.

———, Custom tariff (identification, assessment and collection of anti-dumping duty on dumped articles and for determination of injury) rules, 1995.

Finger, J.M, 2001, 'Anti-dumping as safeguard policy, Working paper 2730,Washington DC, World Bank

Hufbauer, G.C., 1999, 'Anti-dumping, a look at US experience—Lessons for Indonesia', Institute of international Economics.

Ministry of Finance, Customs Tariff Act, 1995, India.

Thakaran PKM, 1996, 'Anti-dumping measures and strategic trade policy'.

———, 1995, 'Political economy of contingent protection', *The Economic Journal*, Vol. 105, No. 133, pp. 1550-64.

Viner, Jacob, 1923, 'Dumping, a problem in international trade', Chicago University Press, 1923.

Vermulst, E.A., 1997, 'Adopting and implementing Anti-dumping Laws: Some suggestions for developing countries', *Journal of World Trade*, Vol. 31, No. 2.

WTO Secretariat, 1998, 'Guide to Uruguay round Agreements'.

APPENDIX I

KEY CONCEPTS OF ANTI-DUMPING MEASURES

Under the agreement on implementation of article VI of GATT 1994, 'Dumping' is defined as introduction of goods in the commerce of another country by an exporter at a price less than the normal value of the goods in his domestic market. The various provisions on evaluation of injury to the domestic industry, establishing their *locus standi* and rules pertaining to imposing AD measures are defined. The custom tariff (identification, assessment and collection of anti-dumping duty on dumped articles and for determination of injury), rules, 1995 enacted under the Customs Tariff Act, 1975,as amended in 1995 are compatible with the 'AD Code under' WTO articles. It is the spirit of redressing the injury to the producers which is of primary concern rather than the effect on or welfare of the other value chain partners of the economic value chain. European Commission's regulation on AD measures include a community interest clause also. The key concepts in the AD measures revolve around Dumping, Injury and Causality of Dumping and consequential injury technically called as causal link. The AD rules in India are compatible with the WTO framework.

1.0 DUMPING

In common parlance dumping is sometimes referred to as sales of cheap and inferior quality goods, which is not correct. 'Dumping' is technically defined and determined as per the WTO rules. Under the Anti-dumping Rules, a product is considered to be dumped if its export price is lower than its normal value (loosely the domestic price but explained later in the text). The basis for assessing the normal value and the export price depend on the particular situation prevailing in the country of origin or export and the importing country. Thus, dumping is said to occur when the goods are exported from a country to another country at a price lower than its normal value. Therefore, the two fundamental parameters that are used to determine dumping are 'normal value' and 'export price'.

A fair comparison has to be made between the normal value and the export price. To this end, these elements are to be compared at the same level of trade, which is generally at the ex-factory level. The 'margin of dumping' is the quantity measure of dumping and is determined as the difference between the normal value and the export price of the goods under investigation. The dumping margin is also expressed as percentage of the export price.

The determination of 'normal value', 'export price' and 'margin of dumping' is done in accordance with Rule 10 of the Anti-Dumping Rules and the principles thereof as laid in Annexure 1 to these Rules. Dumping Margin of less than 2% is considered as *de-minimis* as per rules. If the margin of dumping is *de-minimis,* no anti-dumping duty can be recommended against the exporter.

Illustration: Say the 'normal value' is US $ 1000 Per Metric Ton (PMT) and the Ex-Factory Export Price is US $ 800 PMT. In the above illustration, the dumping margin in absolute terms is US $ 200 PMT that is also indicated as 25%, i.e. percentage of the Ex-Factory Export Price.

1.1 INJURY

It is not enough to allege and prove dumping. What is imperative is that such dumping must cause injury to the domestic industry. Under the WTO framework, international trade is to be conducted in as liberal a manner as possible and to prevent anti-dumping or countervailing measures from being applied merely as a means of eliminating undesirable competition, or of providing unjustified protection to an industry. It is, therefore, considered appropriate that these measures should be remedial, rather than punitive. It is for this reason that certain countries including India limit the amount of the duty to an amount less than the full margin of dumping, if the lesser amount would be sufficient to remove the injury caused to the domestic industry by the dumped imports. The injury to the domestic industry is generally considered in terms of all relevant economic factors and indices having a bearing on the state of the industry, including actual and potential decline in sales, profits, output, market share, productivity, return on investments, or utilization of capacity; factors affecting domestic prices; the magnitude of the margin of dumping; actual and potential negative effects on cash flow, inventories, employment, wages, growth, ability to raise capital or investments. This list is not exhaustive, nor can one or several of these factors necessarily give decisive guidance. The injury is particularly analyzed in terms of 'volume effect' and 'price effect' of the dumped imports. While the volume effect refers to fall in the market share, domestic sales, production, etc. the price effect refers to the price suppression and depression caused by the dumped imports which lead to low sales realization for the domestic industry. The injury could be material injury, threat of injury or material retardation to the establishment of an industry. The injury is determined in accordance with Rule 11 of India's Anti-dumping Rules and the principles thereof as laid in Annexure II to the Anti-dumping Rules.

1.2 CASUAL LINK

As already stated above, in an Anti-dumping proceeding, it is imperative to prove that the dumping has caused injury to the domestic industry. No anti-dumping duty can be recommended unless and until it is established that the phenomenon of dumping has actually caused injury to the domestic industry. A direct nexus between the phenomenon of dumping and injury, therefore, needs to be established. All factors other than dumping which could also have attributed injury to the domestic industry need to be analyzed and their effect, if any, on the state of health of the domestic industry has to be excluded in order to capture only that magnitude and incidence of injury which has been caused solely due to dumping. For establishing such a causal link in an anti-dumping proceeding, factors like effect of demand of subject goods, substitutability of the subject goods by other sort of goods, effect of any inefficiencies on account of low capacity utilization, ineffective consumption norms of raw materials and utilities, uses of inappropriate technologies, etc. is considered and eliminated in the injury determination exercise. The principles and parameters as laid down in Annexure II to the Anti-dumpingRules govern the establishment of the Causal Link.

1.3 NORMAL VALUE

'Normal value' is the comparable price at which the goods under complaint are sold in the ordinary course of trade in the domestic market of the exporting country or territory. Ordinary course of trade refers to such sales, which are profitable and are made to unrelated customers. The normal value has to be primarily determined on the basis of domestic market price for the like article in the country/ territory of export provided they have been made in the ordinary course of trade. However, there could be situations where there are no sales of the like product in the ordinary course of trade or because of the particular market situation or the low volume of sales in the domestic market or the exporting country/territory, the proper comparison may not be possible; then normal value may be determined on the basis of two alternative methods. It could either be determined by comparing with a comparable price of the like article when exported to an appropriate third country provided the price is representative; or it could be determined on the basis of cost of production in the country of origin plus a reasonable amount for administrative, selling and general costs and for profits (popularly called the constructed normal value method). Principles as laid down in Section 9A(1)(C) of the Customs Tariff Act and Rule 10 read along with Annexure I thereof govern the determination of normal value.

1.4 EXPORT PRICE

In order to determine whether or not dumping has taken place, the normal value is compared with the export price.

Section 9A(1)(b) of the Customs Tariff Act defines 'Export Price' as "Export price", in relation to an article, means the price of the article exported from the exporting country or territory and in cases where there is no export price or where the export price is unreliable because of association or a compensatory arrangement between the exporter and the importer or a third party, the export price may be constructed on the basis of the price at which the imported articles are first resold to an independent buyer or if the article is not resold to an independent buyer, or not resold in the condition as imported, on such reasonable basis as may be determined in accordance with the rules made under sub-section (6).

While the prima facie evidence in respect of the export price is taken either from the DGCI&S data or the data procured from the secondary sources e.g. customs daily lists; the export price is normally derived from the prices of actual transactions as verified from the exporters' invoices.

1.5 CONSTRUCTED EXPORT PRICE

The first footnote to Article VI of the GATT recognizes that when exports are made between associated companies, the importer may sell the product at a lower price than that invoiced by the associated exporter. The practice is referred to as hidden dumping, the presumption being that the loss incurred by the importer would, in fact, be borne by the exporter. In such cases, the note provides that dumping margins may be based on the lower price at which the goods are resold by the importer.

The Anti-dumping Agreement and the Indian Legislation extend this concept to all cases where there is no export price, or where it appears to the authorities concerned that the export price is unreliable because of an association or a compensatory arrangement between the exporter and the importer or a third party. In these situations, the export price may be constructed on the basis of the price at which the imported products are first resold to an independent buyer. In such circumstances, allowance has to be made for all costs incurred between the point of importation and resale.

1.6 DUMPING MARGIN

Margin of dumping is the difference between the normal value and the export price of the product under consideration. In order to have a fair comparison, the normal value and export price are considered at same level of trade, generally ex-factory. In relative terms, it is generally referred to as percentage of export price. Due allowance is made for the differences that affect price comparability. Margin of dumping can be determined on the basis of (a) comparison of weighted average normal value with weighted average export prices, (b) comparison of normal value and export price on a transaction to transaction basis, (c) comparison of normal value evaluated on weighted average basis with the prices of individual export transactions if the pattern of export prices differs significantly among different purchasers, regions and time period. Normally in the anti-dumping investigations conducted in India, the weighted average to weighted average method is resorted to. The principles as laid down in the Annexure I of the Anti-dumping Rules govern the choice of an appropriate method for evaluation of Dumping Margin.

1.7 INJURY MARGIN

Injury Margin is the difference between the Non-Injurious Price (NIP) for the goods under complaint as manufactured by the domestic industry and the landed value of the dumped imports. The 'Non-Injurious Price' is the level of prices, which the domestic industry would have charged under normal circumstances in the Indian market during the period chosen for investigation. This price enables recovery of cost of production with reasonable profits after taking into account the best consumption norms and practices of the domestic industry in terms of raw material, utilities and capacity utilization. The determination of NIP is done so as to eliminate impact of all those factors of production which could have adversely affected the company and for which the dumped imports cannot be held responsible. The 'Landed Value' for the purpose is taken as the assessable value of imports under the Customs Act and the applicable basic customs duties. Rule 17 of the Anti-dumping

Rules permits the Designated Authority to recommend lower Anti-dumping Duties than the Dumping Margin. The determination of injury margin is, therefore, an important parameter, which evaluates the extent of duty necessary to redress injury, which is considered for applying the lesser duty rule. The levy of Anti-dumping duty in India is on the basis of lesser duty rule, i.e., on the basis of injury margin or dumping margin which ever is less.

I.8 THREAT OF INJURY

The definition and concept of injury would be meaningless if it were possible to circumvent it by resorting to the concept of threat of injury when the actual injury sustained is insufficient to justify the application of anti-dumping measure. Both the Anti-dumping Agreement and Indian legislation aim to ensure, therefore, that this concept be not used as an excuse to justify the application of anti-dumping measures when there is no prospect of material injury being caused to the domestic industry.

Firstly, any determination of a threat of injury needs to be based on facts and not merely on allegation, conjecture or remote possibility. Secondly, the determination is made where a situation is likely to develop into material injury being caused. Thirdly, it needs to be ensured that the circumstances, which would lead to the injury, are both clearly foreseen and imminent.

Para (vii) of Annexure II of the Anti-dumping Rules enunciate the relevant provisions on the subject. It states that a determination of a threat of material injury shall be based on facts and not merely on allegation, conjecture or remote possibility. The change in circumstances which would create a situation in which the dumping would cause injury must be clearly foreseen and imminent. In making a determination regarding the existence of a threat of material injury, the designated authority shall consider, *inter alia*, such factors as:

(a) a significant rate of increase of dumped imports into India indicating the likelihood of substantially increased importation;

(b) sufficient freely disposable, or an imminent, substantial increase in, capacity of the exporter indicating the likelihood of substantially increased dumped exports to Indian markets, taking into account the availability of other export markets to absorb any additional exports;
(c) whether imports are entering at prices that will have a significant depressing or suppressing effect on domestic prices, and would likely increase demand for further imports; and
(d) Inventories of the article being investigated.

Thus, a determination of threat of injury could be justified, when there are convincing reasons for believing that there will be substantially increased imports of the dumped product. In addition, the rules mention that such factors as an increasing trend in exports to India, and the production capacity, either existing or planned to come into operation in the country of origin, together with the likelihood that the exports would be to India rather than to other export markets. A threat of injury could also be deduced from such factors as an increase in the inventory of the dumped products.

Although these criteria have been incorporated into the Rules but they by no means are exclusive.

1.9 DOMESTIC INDUSTRY

'Domestic industry' under the Anti-dumping Rules means Indian producers of the like article as a whole or those producers whose collective output constitute a major proportion of the total Indian production. The producers who are related to the exporters or importers or those who import the allegedly dumped goods may not be deemed to form part of the domestic industry if so considered by the Authority. Domestic Industry is defined as per Rule 2(b) of Anti-dumping Rules. As regards the 'Standing' requirement, the initiation of an investigation on behalf of the Domestic Industry can be done in accordance with Rule 5(3)(a) of Anti-dumping Rules which lays down that no investigation can be initiated unless the DA determines on the basis of an examination of the degree of support for, or opposition to the application expressed by domestic producers of the like product, that the application has been made by or on behalf of the domestic industry. In addition, no investigation is initiated if domestic producers expressly supporting the application account for less than twenty five percent of the total domestic production of the like article by the domestic industry. For instance, if a product X is manufactured by five producers, viz. A, B, C, D and E who account for 1000, 1500, 2500, 400 and 600 MT of the goods respectively, then producer(s) who account for 1500 MT or more of production which is 25% plus share of total production can file an Anti-dumping Petition on behalf of the Domestic Industry. While producer B only can file an Anti-dumping petition, D and E cannot do it even collectively, as they do not account for 25% of the production. In addition, the opposition to the petition, if any, by any of the domestic producers should not be more than the support extended to the petition, i.e. if supporting producers account for 2000 MT of production and opposing account for 2500 MT, then the petition cannot be initiated. The determination of this parameter is a challenge in a situation of dispersed industry like SSI, where the upstream input based linkages and downstream output based linkages are to be referenced to evaluate a realistic SSI production.

1.10 LIKE ARTICLE

Like Article refers to the subject goods manufactured by the Indian industry, which are being compared to the allegedly dumped imported goods. Such goods referred to as 'like article' imply goods either identical to the dumped imports in all respects or in the absence of such article, closely resembling those imported goods. The Like Article concept is defined in Rule 2(d) of the Anti-dumping Rules. The Like Article is established on the basis of technical and commercial substitutability of domestically produced goods with the imported goods. This concept ensures an apple to apple comparison.

1.11 PERIOD OF INVESTIGATION

The anti-dumping investigations are carried with respect to a specific time period for which all critical parameters like dumping (Normal Value and Export Price) and consequent injury are evaluated. As per the anti-dumping rules and the indicative guidelines of WTO on the subject, the period of investigation should be as recent as possible, subject to the availability of data and should not be less than six months in any case. In India investigations use a period of investigation of normally 12 months is preferred though depending on the specificity of the case in terms of data availability, price fluctuation, phenomenon of dumping, etc. even periods of shorter/longer duration are at times considered.

1.12 PRICE UNDERTAKING

As per the Article 8 of the WTO and Rule 15 of the Indian Anti-dumping Rules, an exporter after a preliminary determination of dumping may approach the anti-dumping authority and submit a price undertaking for not exporting the alleged dumped goods below a particular price level. After the Authority accepts such an undertaking, the investigation in respect of such an exporter is suspended and the undertaking is made operational.

For instance, consider a situation where the Authority has indicated a dumping margin specific to an exporter leading to an anti-dumping duty of US$ 0.2/kg. The exporter can undertake not to export below a landed value (CIF plus landing charges and basic custom duty except CVD, SAD and ADD) of say an agreed price level of 1$ per kg which would eliminate the extent of dumping so established for him. In case the exporter fails to adhere to such a landed price, the Authority can levy the appropriate anti-dumping duties after determining the same.

The price undertaking measure leads to an amicable settlement of the dumping disputes and brings in a fair playing ground for both the parties viz. exporters and the domestic industry. So far price undertaking have been accepted by the Anti-dumping Directorate in case of Black and White Photographic Paper from UK and Hungary, Polyester Films from Korea RP and Lead Acid Battery from Korea RP, Taiwan and Bangladesh.

CHAPTER

25

New Economic Environment and Employment in India

R.K. MAHAJAN

INTRODUCTION

The stabilization and adjustment policies in 1991 have set in new economic environment in Indian economy. The stabilization policies stand for a sharp reduction in fiscal deficit and adjustment policies advocate a wholesale privatization and marketization of the economy. They have brought a radical shift in the trade policy, industrial policy, fiscal reforms, financial sector reforms, etc. These changes have ended India's decades old import substitution policy and inward looking industrial policies. The economy has been open, though partially, to the global competition. In the mid-1990s Peter Drucker, a leading marketing expert, told us that from now on, "a country's competitive position in the world economy has to be the first consideration in its domestic policies and strategies."[1] Opening up the economy both internally and externally in a country like India (predominantly agrarian) poses many challenges.

The new economic environment has brought a paradigm shift in the growth strategy of India by increasing the role of private investment, foreign direct investment, liberalization and globalization. This has also resulted in the growth of the economy. But the position at the employment, poverty and economic inequality level has been dismal. Poverty alleviation can only be possible if output growth must translate into incomes of the poor by way of increasing employment both quantitatively and qualitatively. Employment is, thus, the key link between output growth and poverty alleviation.

Few would deny today that the new economic environment (i.e., stabilization and structural adjustment policies), currently being implemented in many developing countries including India, has been contractionary in nature and reduced employment opportunities. There may be a number of reasons for the same. Some of them are, first, stabilization policies often lead to decline in domestic saving and investment rates. Where this happens, the contractionary effect persists in the medium term and the employment conditions continue to worsen. Secondly, structural adjustment calls for rapid changes in the composition of output and in techniques of production, particularly in the modern organized segment of the economy. This leads to labour redundancy in the short-run and very slow growth of employment in the medium term. In some cases, as in India, a stock of redundant but employed labour is carried over from pre-reform days and the economic reforms threaten to transform this disguised unemployment into open unemployment. Thirdly, privatization of the economy has reduced the role of public sector. The public sector had begun shedding jobs and downsizing policies.

It may be interesting to see how the recent changes have affected the growth and structure of employment in the Indian economy. The main objective of the present study is to examine the impact of new economic environment generated by recent policy changes on employment in India. The data used in this study are compiled and collected from different studies and reports. The source of each table is given in the end of the table.

GROWTH OF GDP IN THE ECONOMY

The growth of gross domestic product is one of the indicators for reducing poverty and unemployment in an economy. While there is no easy answer to the question of how poverty and unemployment can be alleviated, various studies now provide a fairly strong indication about the role of overall economic growth in alleviating poverty. In Asia, for example, the countries that achieved notable success in poverty alleviation viz., the People's Republic of China (PRC), Indonesia, the Republic of Korea, Malaysia, and Thailand are also the ones that attained high rates of gross domestic product (GDP) growth. It must be noted, however, that a high rate of economic growth is only a necessary condition, not a sufficient criterion in itself, for reducing poverty. The nature and content of output growth and employment generated is also extremely important for achieving this goal.

India's GDP performance from 1951-80 was around 3.5 per cent per annum. It went up to 5.6 per cent during 1980-90. It averaged even higher at 6 per cent in the final decade up to 2000-01. Indeed, if the crisis-affected year of 1991-92 is omitted, GDP growth in the past nine years (1992-93 to 2000-01) averaged an unprecedented 6.3 per cent (Table 1). And between 1992-93 and 1995-96, the growth rate averaged even higher at over 7 per cent a year. Despite an unprecedented growth of GDP in India in the recent years, there has not been reduction in poverty. It may because of the fact that the

TABLE I

Average Growth of Real GDP over Fifty Years (Per Cent)

Sectors	*1951/52-1960/61*	*1961/62-1970/71*	*1971/72-1980/81*	*1981/82-1990/91*	*1991/92-2000/01*	*1992/93-2000/01*
Agri. and Allied	3.1	2.5	1.8	3.6	2.8	3.2
Industry	6.3	5.5	4.1	7.1	5.7	6.46
Services	4.3	4.8	4.4	6.7	7.8	8.1
GDP (factor cost)	3.9	3.7	3.2	5.6	5.8	6.3
Per Capita GDP	2.0	1.5	0.8	3.4	3.9	4.4

Source: CSO, National Accounts and Income Estimates, New Delhi, 2000.

growth of GDP has not been accompanied by growth of employment. It would be interesting to study the impact of recent changes on employment scenario in Indian economy.

GROWTH OF EMPLOYMENT AND GDP

A remarkable feature of the new economic environment has been that the GDP increased by 6.3 per cent in 1994-95 and grew at over 7.5 per cent per annum for three successive years 1994-95 to 1996-97. But after that growth decelerated mainly because of decline in industrial growth. However, inflation during this time remained under control. Foreign direct investment also continued in the country (Parikh, 1999). But, the growth of employment could not keep pace with increase in GDP. The employment growth rate was around 2 per cent during 1960s and up to mid-70s, after that it decelerated. It rose to over 2 per cent during 1992-97, after which it decreased to about 1 per cent (Table 2).

TABLE 2

Growth Rate of GDP and Employment

Plans	*Annual average growth rates*	
	GDP (1993-94 Prices)	*Employment*
1951-56 (First Five-Year Plan)	3.7	0.39
1956-61 (Second Five-Year Plan)	4.2	0.85
1961-66 (Third Five-Year Plan)	2.8	2.03
1967-69 (Annual Plans)	3.9	2.21
1969-74 (Fourth Five-Year Plan)	3.4	1.99
1974-79 (Fifth Five-Year Plan)	5.0	1.84
1980-85 (Sixth Five-Year Plan)	5.5	1.73
1985-90 (Seventh Five-Year Plan)	5.8	1.89
1992-97 (Eighth Five-Year Plan)	6.8	2.4
1997-2002 (Ninth Five-Year Plan)	5.6	1.1

Source: Economic Survey 2002-03.

The growth of employment may be better discussed in relation to demand and supply of labour. The supply of labour has been consistently rising around 2 per cent per annum, whereas the demand for labour depends upon rate and pattern of growth of GDP. Table shows that there has been significant increase in the rate of growth of output after mid-1970s, but the growth of employment has not picked up at that pace. It may be mainly because of the fact that growth of GDP may be due to increase in productivity. But the benefit of growth in productivity in GDP has increased the use of capital intensive and labour-saving technology. The decline in employment in the regime of new economic reforms can also be interpreted, despite capital intensity of the economy, because of the recent policies of globalization and downsizing of labour. It can be concluded that the employment generating capacity of the economy has substantially gone down.

SECTORAL GROWTH RATE OF EMPLOYMENT AND EMPLOYMENT ELASTICITIES

The most concerning issue is that there has been a substantial decrease in the share of agriculture and allied sector in GDP, but there has been a marginal change in the structure of employment in this sector over the last 40 years. The share of agriculture and allied activities has declined from about 55 per cent in the year 1960-61 to 26 per cent in the year 2000-01, whereas workforce in this sector has decreased from 76 percent in 1961 to about 60 per cent in 2000. The share of manufacturing sector in total employment has increased marginally from 9 per cent in 1972-73 to 11 percent in 1999-00. It is clear that there is less diversification of jobs outside agriculture. If the employment opportunities are not increased through non-farm sector in rural areas and agricultural sector is not diversified, there will be serious unemployment problem in India.

The perusal of Table 3 shows that the employment absorbability of agricultural sector has substantially decreased from growth rate of 1.51 per cent per annum during 1983-94 to -0.34 per cent during 1994-00. Due to stabilization and adjustment policies of the government Indian agriculture is facing crisis. therefore, there is no scope for the growth of

TABLE 3

Employment Growth and Elasticities in Different Sectors, 1983 to 2000

(Usual Principal and Subsidiary Status)

Sector/Year	*Annual Growth Rate(%)*		*Employment Elasticities*	
	1983-94	*1999-00*	*1983-94*	*1999-00*
Agriculture	1.51	-0.34	0.50	0.00
Mining and Quarrying	4.16	-2.85	0.69	0.00
Manufacturing	2.14	2.05	0.33	0.26
Elect., gas and water supply	4.50	-0.88	0.52	0.00
Construction	5.32	7.09	1.00	1.00
Trade	3.57	5.04	0.63	0.55
Transport, Storage, etc.	3.24	6.04	0.49	0.69
Financial services	7.18	6.20	0.92	0.73
Community, social and personal Services	2.90	0.55	0.50	0.07
All Sectors	**2.04**	**0.98**	**0.41**	**0.15**
Labour Force	2.43	1.31		
GDP	5.2	6.7		

Source: Planning Commission (2001), NSSO and Economic Survey.

employment growth of additional employment in this sector. There has been a substantial decrease in capital formation in agriculture in public sector. The gross capital formation in agriculture in public has decreased from Rs. 4467 crore in 1993-94 to Rs. 4007 crore in 2000-01 at 1993-94 prices. There is need to enhance employment opportunities in the rural sector through diversification of agriculture and promoting the non-farm sector so that the produce of the farmer is utilized in rural areas itself. There has been a substantially increase in employment in the sectors like trade, construction, financial services and transport. The employment in sectors has grown faster than the average and share of these sectors in total employment has increased. Total employment growth has decreased from 2.04 per cent per annum during 1993 to 1993-94 to mere 0.98 per cent during 1993-94 to 1999-00. This is a substantial decline. No doubt, labour force has also declined during this time, but, if the growth of employment is less than the growth of labour force, there will be bound to be increase in unemployment.

Employment elasticity is measured as the ratio between the growth in employment to growth in output. Simply stated, it indicates employment per unit of output. As Prof. Bhalla noted, elasticities that approach unity are not desirable. High elasticities may imply very low productivity and, therefore, wage rates. He maintains that under Indian conditions, elasticity of the order of 0.5 to 0.6 at the aggregate level is sufficient.

The overall elasticity of employment has recovered during the period 1983-94. But at 0.41 for all sectors it is still not ideal for India according to Bhalla's parameters. Agriculture, construction and services led the recovery of elasticities during this time. The elasticity of manufacturing has persisted at about the same low level. The big swing in elasticity for construction is a result of the 1987-88 drought (Table 3), which made many workers from agriculture move to construction and then move back again once the drought was over.

There has been a substantial decline in the employment elasticities in new economic environment, i.e. in post-reform period. The employment elasticity of primary sector has become nil. It means that the growth of income in primary sector is not giving additional employment to the labour force. This is disappointing and disgusting because new economic reforms are not doing anything for the development of agriculture and rural areas. The elasticity of manufacturing has persisted at low level as established in the 1983-94. Another sector which has stagnated is services. As a matter of fact, agriculture and services provide a large share of employment, but their employment elasticity has gone down considerably as against more than 0.50 during 1983-94. Employment in sectors like construction, trade, transport, storage and financial sector has grown faster than overall average elasticity.

It is concluded that the rate of growth in employment has been positive over time, although more modest than economic growth in pre-reform period. It actually declined between 1994 and 2000, at a time when rates of economic growth were increasing in most of the sectors. The distressing situation causing employment elasticity to fall to such a low level is agriculture. While the primary sector average growth has been around 3 per cent for the last 20 years, the growth of employment has gone down recently almost nil in this sector. There has also not a considerable growth of employment sector in the manufacturing sector due to capital intensity in the post reform period.

EMPLOYMENT IN ORGANIZED SECTOR

Another important aspect of discussing employment in a development policy change is the distinction between employment in organized and unorganized sectors of the economy. There is higher earnings and job security in the organized sector than in unorganized sector. But the organized sector constitute very small portion of total employment (its share was about 12 per cent in pre-reform period but decreased to around 7 per cent in post-reform period.

Government is slowly and silently withdrawing from the public sector by selling its stakes to general public. Here again, only the stakes of profitable companies are sold to public. All these policies have resulted in slow increase in employment in public sector. Table 5 gives the percentage change in employment over the previous year both in public and private sectors. The perusal of Table 4 shows that there has been a considerable decline in percentage increase in employment in public sector after 1991 as compared to earlier years, i.e. declined from 2.5 per cent in 1984 to 1.7 per cent in 1990, to 0.1 per cent in 1995 and –0.91 per cent in 2001. In case of private sector, there was an increase in employment from 1.7 per cent in 1990 to 2.2 per cent in 1992, but this per cent fell in 1994 but again increased in 1995 and became negative in 2000. It can be said that the increase in employment has been slow in organized sector after 1991. Since 1990-91, there has been a very sharp decline in the growth of public sector employment, falling from 1.6 per cent growth per annum between 1984 and 1990 to 0.4 per cent between 1991 and 2001. In the private sector, however, there

TABLE 4

Employment in the Organised Sector

(Lakh persons as on 31st March)

Year	Employment In Public sector	Per cent Change over the previous year	Pre-reform % Change	Employment in Private Sector	Per cent Change over the previous year	Pre-reform % Change	Total Employment	Per cent Change over the previous year	Overall change
1	2	3	4	5	6	7	8	9	10
1981	154.89	2.73		73.95	2.32		228.84	2.60	
1982	159.46	2.95		75.47	2.06		234.93	2.66	
1983	164.57	3.20		75.52	0.07		240.09	2.20	
1984	168.69	2.50		73.46	-2.73		242.15	0.86	
1985	172.7	2.38	2.11	73.09	-0.50	0.25	245.79	1.50	1.51
1986	176.84	2.40		73.74	0.89		250.58	1.95	
1987	180.24	1.92		73.64	-0.14		253.8	1.32	
1988	183.2	1.64		73.92	0.38		257.12	1.28	
1989	184.47	0.69		74.53	0.83		259.00	0.73	
1990	187.62	1.71		75.82	1.73		263.44	1.71	

(Contd.)

TABLE 4 *(Contd.)*

1	2	3	4	5	6	7	8	9	10
Post-reform change									
1991	190.58	1.58		76.77	1.25		267.35	1.48	
1992	192.1	0.80		78.46	2.20		270.56	1.20	
1993	193.26	0.60		78.51	0.06		271.77	0.45	
1994	194.45	0.62		79.3	1.01		273.75	0.73	
1995	194.66	0.11		80.59	1.63		275.25	0.55	
1996	194.29	-0.19	0.04	85.12	5.62	1.15	279.41	1.51	0.36
1997	195.59	0.67		86.86	2.04		282.45	1.09	
1998	194.18	-0.72		87.48	0.71		281.66	-0.28	
1999	194.14	-0.02		86.98	-0.57		281.12	-0.19	
2000	193.14	-0.52		86.46	-0.60		279.60	-0.54	
2001	191.38	-0.91		86.52	0.07		277.90	-0.61	

Source: Calculated from different issues of Economic Survey.

is different trend. Employment growth rate was 0.45 per cent per annum between 1984 and 1990, rising to 1.15 per cent between 1991 and 2002. Overall, organized sector shows a dismal picture. In pre-reform period, the employment was growing at 1.51 per cent per annum, which decreased to 0.36 per cent in post-reform period. These results clearly show that increment in employment in organized sector is very low which would not bring significant change in employment position.

Above discussion shows that in the first 11 years of reforms there has been a slow increase in employment in organized sector. The track record of the growth in economy is not consistent. The pressure on agriculture would once again increase. There would be further increase in casualization of workers in rural areas.

STATUS OF EMPLOYMENT

It is not that availability of employment matters, the status of employment also very important. It is also interesting to note that what sort of opportunities new economic environment has provided to the economy. Let us discuss the status of employment as self-employment, regular employment and casual employment.

Various NSSO survey tables show a lot of information regarding the changing status of employment. The Table shows that most part of the workforce is engaged in self-employment. Self-employment category comprises of heterogeneous units such as rich people, like big cultivators, high income earning professionals, as well as poor people like marginal farmers, artisans, hawkers, shopkeepers, etc. However, the share of self-employment has declined from around 59 percent in 1977-78 to 56 per cent (Table 5) in the pre-reform period to 53 per cent in the post-reform period. The decline is mainly in the rural areas. Regular salaried employment is considered as the best form of employment. It is mainly because it gives assured income and security of job. However, the share of this category of employment is around 14 per cent. There is a likelihood that its share in the future may go down mainly because of increase in employment on

TABLE 5

Distribution of Workers (Usual Status) by Status of Employment (per cent)

Year	*Self-Employment*			*Regular Salaried*			*Casual*		
	Rural	*Urban*	*Total*	*Rural*	*Urban*	*Total*	*Rural*	*Urban*	*Total*
1977-78	62.6	42.4	59.9	7.7	41.8	13.9	29.7	15.8	27.2
1983	61.0	41.8	57.4	7.5	40.0	13.9	31.5	18.2	28.7
1987-88	59.4	42.8	56.0	7.7	40.3	14.4	32.9	16.9	29.6
1993-94	58.0	42.3	54.8	6.4	39.4	13.2	35.6	18.3	32.0
1999-00	56.0	42.1	52.9	6.7	40.1	13.9	37.3	17.8	33.2

Source: Various NSSO Surveys on Employment and unemployment.

contract basis and casual employment. The table also shows that there is substantial increase in the share of casual employment. Casual employment share was only 27 per cent in 1977-88 which increased to 29.6 per cent in pre-reform period increased to 33.2 per cent in 1999-00. This type of trend is found in both rural and urban areas. This may be explained because of displacement of marginal farmers and casualization of employment in the urban areas.

SUMMARY AND CONCLUSION

The stabilization and adjustment policies started in 1991 have paved a way for new economic environment in Indian economy. How far these policies have affected employment in the economy? The analysis of the pre and post-reform periods reveal that the growth of GDP picked up and was around 6 per cent per annum in post-reform period. Despite this impressive growth of GDP, the employment has not been picked up during the same time. Primary sector which constitute about 26 per cent of the total GDP in the year 2002 still provides employment to majority of the people. The growth rate of employment of people in agriculture sector has been negative. It clearly shows that the primary sector is not absorbing additional workforce. Rather existing force is displaced by this sector. Its elasticity of employment is also nil. It can be said that agriculture and allied activities are mainly suffered the burnt of decline in employment. The manufacturing sector is also slow in generating employment. There has been above average elasticity of employment in sectors like construction, trade, transport, storage and financial sector. The study also shows that employment in the organized sector is increasing at a very slow pace. It may be mainly due to the policies of downsizing, privatization and increase in capital intensity of the economy.

REFERENCES

Bhalla, Shiela (1997), "Trends in Poverty, Wages and Employment in India", *Indian Journal of Labour Economics*, Vol. 40, No. 2, April-Jane.

Chadha, G.K. and Sahu, P.P. (2002), Post-Reform Setbacks in Rural

Employment: Issues that Need Further Scrutiny, *Economic and Political weekly*, Vol. 37, No. 21, May 25.

Chandrasekhar, C.P. (1996), "Explaining Post-Reform Industrial Growth", *Economic and Political Weekly.*

Datt, Rudra (2003), Economic Reforms, Labour and Employment, New Delhi, Deep and Deep Publication Pvt. Ltd.

Drucker, Peter (1994), The Age of Social Transformation, *The Atlantic Monthly*, November, p. 77.

Ghosh, Jayati (1997), India's Structural Adjustment: An assessment in comparative Asian context, *Economic and Political Weekly*, May.

Krugman, P. (1994), The myth of Asia's miracle, *Foreign Affairs*, Vol. 73, No.6 November/December).

Ozler, B., Datt, G. and Ravallion, M. (1996), A Database on Poverty and Growth in India, World Bank, January.

Sen, A. (1996), Economic Reforms, Employment and Poverty: Trends and Options, *Economic and Political Weekly*, Special No.

CHAPTER

26

New Economic Environment and Trade Unions in India

KESAR SINGH BHANGOO

The gradual transformation of industrial societies from their earlier elemental foundations has been accompanied by a phenomenon of the rise of the associations of labour to a position of considerable prominence in the institutional and industrial structure of the modern economies. In the wake of liberalization, privatization and globalization, with growing emphasis on flexibility and downsizing in the name of reorganization of work, labour market institutions particularly trade unions have been under severe stress and pressure (Reddy, 2003). New economic environment not only in India but also throughout the world is not hospitable to trade unions and labour movements. Either they are no longer capable of protecting the interests of their members in particular and workers in general or they have no role in this 'new world' of constant flux and change (Yates, 2001). If this is true then trade unions will have to reorganize and reconstitute themselves thoroughly. Historically, trade unions have been instruments of class struggle, having anti-capitalist and pro-worker ideology; their basis is the clash of interests of workers and employers. In India, the deplorable and miserable conditions in which workers lived were responsible for the origin and growth of trade unions. Because strong employers backed by the state renders them impotent, individual workers must join together in a common mass to confront their employers to secure improved wages, reasonable working hours, better terms and conditions of employment, dignity and respect through struggle by forming trade unions (Bhangoo, 1995). But, in the new economic environment all of this is changing. The thrust of this paper is to study the new emerging trends in new economic environment and need and relevance of trade unions in this environment. The paper is divided into four sections. First section presents briefly the new emerging economic environment. In the second section the trends of weakening and declining of trade union movement has been discussed. Third section attempts to explore and inquire into the need and relevance of trade unions in new economic environment and in the final section conclusions has been made.

I. NEW EMERGING ECONOMIC ENVIRONMENT

Today, we hear a lot of talk about the changing economic scenario. The new emerging economic environment revolves around the concepts of liberalization, privatization, globalization, flexibility and reorganization of work, along with stiff economic competitiveness and free interplay of market forces at national and international levels. This phenomenon saw increasing linkages between markets across countries and across regions, as result of which workers and enterprises in the remote rural areas of the developing countries were affected (Jhabvala, 2002). The linking of markets is accompanied by new ways of production as enterprises moved to lean production, decentralized production and flexible methods of production. This requires, managerial freedom to rationalize costs and optimize productivity of resources with no or minimum interference from other stakeholders including governments and trade unions (Sheth, 1996). This resulted in employment of new and advanced technology for improvement of output with guaranteed high quality to compete globally. Rapidly changing technology continually creates new high quality products, so consumer choices and needs are perpetually changing as well; this places new demands on businesses (Yates, 2001). As a result, firms stuck with the mass production technology of old, with enormous fixed capital and rigid assembly lines, are doomed to lose the competitive struggle. Due to the freedom to innovate, so that these firms can rapidly introduce new technology and products to satisfy swiftly changing consumer choices and demands, adopted modern sophisticated technology, management and production practices involving the use of specially trained and educated workforce in the production and marketing of goods and services. All this resulted in the manifold increase in international trade flows during the emerging new economic environment. (see Table 1)

TABLE I

Trade Flows as a Share of GDP

(per cent)

Region	*1970*	*1990*
Industrialized Countries	28	45
Developing Countries	24	45

Source: Richard Anker (1990), Gender and Jobs, ILO, Geneva.

These rapid changes resulted in labour reforms aiming at to liberalize the existing labour legislation in favour of capital and against labour. In India, in the new economic environment government and employers are continuously striving to carry out labour reforms in the country. (see note 1) Second National Labour Commission (Report, 2002-03) recommended to limit the purview of Industrial Disputed Act, 1947 from existing 100 workers to 300 workers, this is in favour of employers, i.e. capital. Government has contemplated an exit policy to enable incurably sick enterprises to close down without hurdles from unions and the law. Government freely allowed the use of the National

Renewal Fund, created mainly for generation of new employment, for voluntary retirement scheme (VRS) and retrenchment of workers (Singh, 1995). This emerging new economic environment brought new balances of power within the economy. The balance of power between capital and labour shifted decisively in favour of capital, as workers became increasingly disempowered in the new economic environment. Which had been maintained by the existence of strong trade unions affiliated to political parties in the pre-reform period.

II. DECLINE OF TRADE UNION MOVEMENT

Strong trade unions often affiliated to political parties were able to bargain with employers and government in fovour of workers and to secure a decent standard of living. The global nature of the new economic scenario is hostile to unionization. Mobile capital will simply run away from unions or create conditions in which they cannot survive (Yates, 2001) by providing workers with a panoply of benefits like on the job training, stock options, profit sharing, etc. As production became decentralized, as the demand for flexible labour grew, and as capital and production moves to counties and areas where trade unions were weak or non-existent, the power and effectiveness of trade unions began to decline and weaken (Jhabvala, 2003). The decline and weakening of trade unions in the era of globalization is widely acknowledged. As the organized sector shrunk the number and numerical strength of trade unions also declined (Table 2). Further world wide turning of leftist and social democratic parties towards market oriented policies, growing hegemony of the market, failure of the left and opponents of globalization to put forward viable alternatives to the market principles, alienation of unions from political parties, availability of large number of workers, liberalizing and repealing of labour legislations in favour of employers, the practices of contract and casual labour eroded the strength and bargaining leverage of trade unions in India (Chowdhury, 2004). Therefore, it is clear that the very survival of trade union movement and its emergence as a socially relevant institution

TABLE 2

Number of Unions Registered, Submitting Returns, Membership and Average Membership

Years	*Registered Unions*	*Unions Submitting returns*	*Membership ('000)*	*Average membership*
1951	3714	1976	1750	817
1961	11416	6954	3960	576
1971	22122	8909	5431	606
1986	48030	11363	8190	721
1987	49329	11063	7959	719
1988	50048	8730	7073	810
1989	52210	9758	9295	953
1990	52016	8828	7019	795
1991	53535	8418	6100	725
1992	55680	9165	5746	627
1993	55784	6806	3134	460
1994	56872	6277	4094	652
1995	57952	8162	6538	801
1996	58988	7242	5601	773
1997	60660	8872	7409	835
1998	61692	7403	7249	979
1999(P)	64817	8152	6407	786

P – provisional.

Source: Various Issues of Indian Labour Year Book, Labour Bureau, Shimla.

needs and depend upon its ability to evolve alternative strategies to face the emerging evils and challenges of the new economic scenario.

This is a worldwide phenomenon most clearly seen in the declining membership of trade unions in countries where they were strong. The World Labour Report revealed that it is generally agreed that the trade union movement has fallen on hard times but sometimes the extent of its difficulties may be exaggerated by overemphasizing adverse national situations or for ideological reasons or for the sake of convenience. Nonetheless, trade unions are losing members and some even have doubts about their future. The recent years, it seems, were particularly bad (ILO, 1997). Data on membership and density of trade unions, generally speaking, out of a sample of 92 countries, only 14 had a rate of more than 50 per cent in 1995; in 48 the rate was less that 20 per cent (ILO, 1997). In France, trade unions lost 25 per cent membership during 1975-85, in England the trade unions lost 3 million members in five years, in USA the percentage of the workforce who were the members of unions dropped from a peak of 35 per cent in 1953 to less than 17 per cent in 1983 and in Japan it dropped from 55 per cent in 1949 to 29 per cent in 1985 (Jhabvala, 2003). Similar phenomenon is clearly evident in India (Table 2) trade union membership declined from a peak of 92.95 lakhs in 1989 to the lowest 31.34 lakhs in 1993. The strength of the trade unions fell as the production became decentralized and lean and employers and industrialists began adopting the practices of contract and casual labour with the help of state and legislation. The available data indicate that in the new economic scenario, the power and influence of trade unions is dwindling (Table 3). The equation between labour and management has altered dramatically (Table 4) and in several organizations, the managements has begun to flex muscle by locking out units rather than the workers forcing the hand of the managements through strike actions (*Business India,* 1996). To remain competitive, employers are forced to transform the organization into a leaner for more cost effective entity. On the other side, the aspirations of the workers for upward mobility and better life style has increased their financial commitments as a result workers began to opt for money and benefits rather than working class rights (*Business India,* 1996). All these emerging issues of new economic scenario had extremely adverse effects on trade unions all over the country. The trade union movement in the country built during the first quarter of the last century. By the last quarter of the 20th century, trade union movement had grown economically and politically powerful. But, during the 1990s they rapidly lost their membership and prominence (Table 2) and decline in their activities like protest, strikes, workers involved in strikes, man days lost due to strikes, etc. (Table 4), thereby weakened the trade union movement as a whole.

TABLE 3

Number of Disputes, Workers Involved and Mandays Lost

Year	No. of Disputes	Workers involved, (000)	Mandays Lost, (000)
1951	1071	691	3819
1961	1357	512	4919
1971	2752	1615	16546
1989	1786	1364	32663
1990	1825	1308	24086
1991	1810	1342	26428
1992	1714	1252	31259
1993	1393	954	20301
1994	1201	846	20983
1995	1066	990	16289
1996	1166	939	20285
1997	1305	981	16971
1998	1097	1289	22062
1999	927	1311	26787
2000	771	1418	28763
2001 (P)	674	688	23767

P – provisional.

Source: Various issues of Indian Labour Year Book, Labour Bureau Shimla.

III. DIRE NEED AND RELEVANCE OF TRADE UNIONS IN THE NEW ECONOMIC ENVIRONMENT

The decline and weakening of trade union movement and erosion of their membership and functions in the new economic scenario have often raised the questions of their need, survival and relevance. It has been argued that trade unions has became redundant or irrelevant. But, if poverty, destitution, deprivation and injustice exist in the society, trade unions's presence is vitally needed and relevant according to trade unions original mandate (Sheth, 1996). In such a situation, there is a dire need of trade unions in the new economic environment to confront the new problems and challenges posed by liberalization, privatization and globalization. Precisely problems and challenges are, to protect workers and trade unions from the negative effects of

TABLE 4

Industrial Disputes Classified by Strikes and Lockouts

Year	Strikes No.	Strikes Worker Involved	Strikes Mandays Lost, (000)	Lockouts No.	Lockouts Workers involved	Lockouts Mandays Lost, (000)
1961	1240	432000	2969	117	80000	1950
1966	2353	1262000	10377	203	148000	3469
1971	2478	1476000	11803	274	139000	4773
1976	1241	551000	2799	218	186000	9947
1991	1278	872482	12428	532	469540	14000
1992	1011	767484	15132	703	484741	16127
1993	914	672024	5615	479	281843	14686
1994	808	626326	6651	393	220103	14332
1995	732	682595	5720	334	307100	10570
1996	763	608673	7818	403	330631	12467
1997	793	637480	6295	512	393787	10676
1998	665	800778	9349	432	488145	12713
1999	540	1099240	10625	387	211455	16162
2000	426	1044237	11959	345	374062	16804
2001	372	488596	5563	302	199182	18204

Source: Various issues of Indian Labour Year Book. Labour Bureau, Shimla.

decentralized production and lean production, to combat the corporate-state alliance that has wreaked havoc on their living standards through trade agreements, to resist anti-labour legislations, refusal to enforce labour laws, the destruction of welfare state, to resist disinvestments of public sector, to make them more secure, guarantee of safe workplace and ensure their futures (Yates, 2001).

In the most fundamental sense, i.e. social relations, there is nothing new in the today's economy, i.e. new economic environment or 'New Economy'. Capitalist are busy in accumulating capital, in the wake of intense competition, which is made possible by extraction of surplus labour time from workers. When during 1970s capital accumulation slowed down markedly (Yates, 2001), capital went on attack, scrapping labour accords and intensified its pressures on the state to clear the way for more rapid and profitable accumulation. Capitalism is all about market dependence, we are all dependent on the market not just for the necessities of life but also for our livelihood (Wood, 1999). Capital accumulation and its market dependence are reaching into the far corners of the globe and in our personal lives. In the wake of universalizing of market dependence, comes the monetization and depersonalization of daily life, alienation at work, production of debased products, rising unemployment and destruction of environment. Trade unions and labour movements have historically been important and necessary for ordinary workers and people to fight against these inevitable consequences of the new economic scenario.

In certain quarters, there is also a misplaced impression that trade unions should have been replaced by some new forms of organizations, such as non-government organizations (NGOs), self-help groups (SHGs), etc. which is not true, right and possible. In the new economic scenario trade unions are badly needed as human defense mechanism, but with some sort of new orientation and improvements, there is much room and scope for improvements in house of labour. Trade unions would function confining to themselves traditional roles of organizing the formal sector workers along with bargaining over issues of concerns to workers, involving themselves largely in the issues, exercising pressures through legislation actions and required to be complemented by other issues and initiatives (Reddy, 2003). Future emerging issues and initiatives would be unionization of neglected workers (women, unorganized or informal sector workers), forming of new alliances and coalitions in the struggle, broadening of union functioning and initiating efforts towards national, regional and global solidarity of workers. The global nature of the capital in the present scenario demands the globalization of trade unions, so that flight and mobility of the capital on this count be arrested. International and regional trade union associations and alliances (NAFTA, SAFTA, ASEAN, EU, etc.) might seem to be helpful to trade unions in the new economic environment. But the barriers in terms of language, culture and distance make this unlikely prospect. A new emerging labour movement trend must be one that recognizes and takes as its basic position that nothing is inevitable and reconstruct an anti-capitalist and pro-worker ideology and organize trade union movement around it (Yates, 2001). In future trade unions and labour movements must struggle for employment as right, meaningful work, sharing of society's more onerous tasks, a good deal of consumption fully socialized such as education at all levels, health care, child care, care for aged, maximum democratic control of production by workers or community or both, no discrimination of any kind and equality of every kind. Trade unions must be more responsive to their members and work for complete democratization of labour movement and spreading the democratic impulse to the workplaces.

IV. CONCLUSIONS

It is beyond doubt that economy had changed and changing fast towards a 'New Economy'. New and advanced technology accompanied by new forms of organizations and reorganization of work has changed the things. Changing production system and changing consumer tastes and preferences put new demands on the businesses and people identify happiness with consumption. In this emerged and emerging new economic scenario the working class, labour movements and trade unions suffered hard and severely stressed. As for as trade unions are concerned, it has often argued in the capital and supporters of globalization circles, that they became redundant and irrelevant. In academic circles also, it has been advocated to replace the trade unions with new forms of labour organizations such as NGOs, SHGs, etc. One thing is clear and evident that market forces and these changes has weakened the labour movement and trade unions and eroded the power and influence that they have wielded ever before. It is also clear that to replace the trade unions with the new forms of labour organizations is a misplaced impression. It has been concluded that trade unions are badly needed in the new economic environment, but they must improve themselves and reorient their functioning and functions according to the new pressures, challenges and stresses of the globalization. It is also evident from the analysis that today role, need and importance of trade unions has increase manifold to protect the economic as well as non-economic interests of the working class and society from the onslaught of globalization. Today, new economic scenario demands that trade unions must function with alliances and coalitions at national, regional and global levels to achieve solidarity to mitigate the problems of the workers of the world.

Note and Reference

1. Indian government in 1994, 1998 and 2003 tried to amend the major labour legislations like Industrial Disputes Act, 1947 and Indian Trade Union Act, 1926 under the pressure of capital and in line with liberalization, privatization and globalization.

References

Reddy, D. Narsimha (2003). Changing World Economic Order and World of Workers. *The Indian Journal of Labour Economics*. 46(2).

Yates, Michael D. (2001). The 'New' Economy and Labour Movement. *Monthly Review*. 52(11), pp. 28-42.

Bhangoo, K.S. (1995). Dynamics of Industrial Relations. New Delhi: Deep & Deep.

Jhabvala, Renana (2003). New Forms of Workers' Organisations: Towards a System of Representation and Voice. *The Indian Journal of Labour Economics*. 46(2).

Seth, N.R. (1996). WE, The Trade Unions. *Indian Journal of Industrial Relations*. 32(1).

Report of Second National Labour Commission. (2002). New Delhi: Academic Foundation.

Singh, G. (1995). Who Needs An Exit Policy Any Way? *Economic and Political Weekly*. Jan. 10, pp. 1359-60.

Chowdhury, Supriya Roy. (2004). Globalisation and Labour. *Economic and Political Weekly*. 39(1), pp. 105-08.

ILO, (1997). World Labour Report: Industrial Relations, Democracy and Social Stability. Geneva: ILO.

Business India, (1996). Trade Unions Losing Clout? Nov. 6-9, pp. 54-60.

Wood, Ellan. (1999). The Origin of Capitalism, New York: *Monthly Review Press*.

CHAPTER

27

Problems and Prospects of BPO Industry in India

PRATIBHA GOYAL AND AMIT SIKKA

In a global market place, managing a business is increasingly becoming complex as it pulls the company leaders in many directions, multiplying their responsibilities, dividing their attention and often hindering their efforts. The convergence of telecommunication, information technology and media has redefined the way we do business. In the changed environment it is essential to focus on some core competency rather than to get involved in activities that are non-core to their business. The non-core activities are being increasingly outsourced to a specialized service provider or an outsourcing vendor who can perform these tasks more cost effectively. Business process outsourcing is the long-term contracting of a company's business processes to an outside service provider to help increase shareholder value. It enables companies to shatter the boundaries of their traditional business, and to build long-term strategic partnerships with outside professional service firms for managing in the new millennium. Globalization, competitive markets, and mergers and acquisitions are the primary stimuli for BPO. The ITES industry, of which BPO forms a very important part, is expected to be a $ 17 billion industry in India and will generate over 1.1 million jobs by 2008. Given the critical changes taking place and effect that BPO is going to be the industry of the decade and will, therefore, generate huge revenues and employment for India. The present paper, based on study of literature and discussions with executives of BPO industry in India, presents a SWOT analysis of this industry in India.

The convergence of telecommunication, information technology and media has redefined the way we do business. In a global market place, managing a business is increasingly becoming complex as it pulls the company leaders in many directions, multiplying their responsibilities, dividing their attention and often hindering their efforts. In the changed environment it is essential to focus on some core competency rather than to get involved in activities that are non-core to their business. The non-core activities are being increasingly outsourced to a specialized service provider or an outsourcing vendor who can perform these tasks more cost effectively.

Business process outsourcing is the long-term contracting of a company's business processes to an outside service provider to help increase shareholder value. It enables companies to shatter the boundaries of their traditional business, and to build long-term strategic partnerships with outside professional service firms for managing in the new millennium. Globalization, competitive markets, and mergers and acquisitions are the primary stimuli for BPO. The ITES industry, of which BPO forms a very important part, is expected to be a $ 17 billion industry in India and will generate over 1.1 million jobs by 2008. Given the critical changes taking place and effect that BPO is going to be the industry of the decade and will, therefore, generate huge revenues and employment for India. The present paper based on study of literature and discussions with executives of BPO industry in India, presents a SWOT analysis of this industry in India.

The ITES industry, of which BPO forms a very important part, is expected to be a $ 17 billion industry in

India and will generate over 1.1 million jobs by 2008. Given the critical changes taking place and effect that BPO is going to be the industry of the decade and will, therefore, generate huge revenues and employment for India.

BPO includes:

Customer Service Interaction including Call-centres

Call centres are expected to grow to Rs. 3000 crore in 2002-03 and maintain a 45% growth rate for the next few years. With the advantage of English speaking population, low cost manpower and quality service, many companies are increasingly outsourcing their operations to India.

Back Office Operations/Banking/Revenue/Accounting/Data Conversions/HR, etc.

Verticals such as banks and aviation require large-scale data processing and data based decision-making capabilities. Raw data or paper documents are sent to remote locations (IT-enabled destination) where data entry and necessary reconciliation is carried out.

Transcription Services

Medical transcriptions involve the transcribing of medical records from audio format or dictated by doctors or other healthcare professionals into either a hard copy or electronic format. Doctors overseas record their findings into a dictaphone or any other such device and the sound tracks are transferred through datacom links to IT Enabled services (ITES) companies specializing in this area.

Content Development/Animation, etc.

India's strength lies in her low cost, high quality manpower. The same applies in these two fields. With the animation industry stated to be to the tune of 70 billion by 2005, much of the work will be outsourced to countries like India.

Data Research, Market Survey, Consultancy, Management, etc.

The organisations are also outsourcing their businesses for market survey, data research and consultancy, etc.

FIG. 1

BPO Ladder

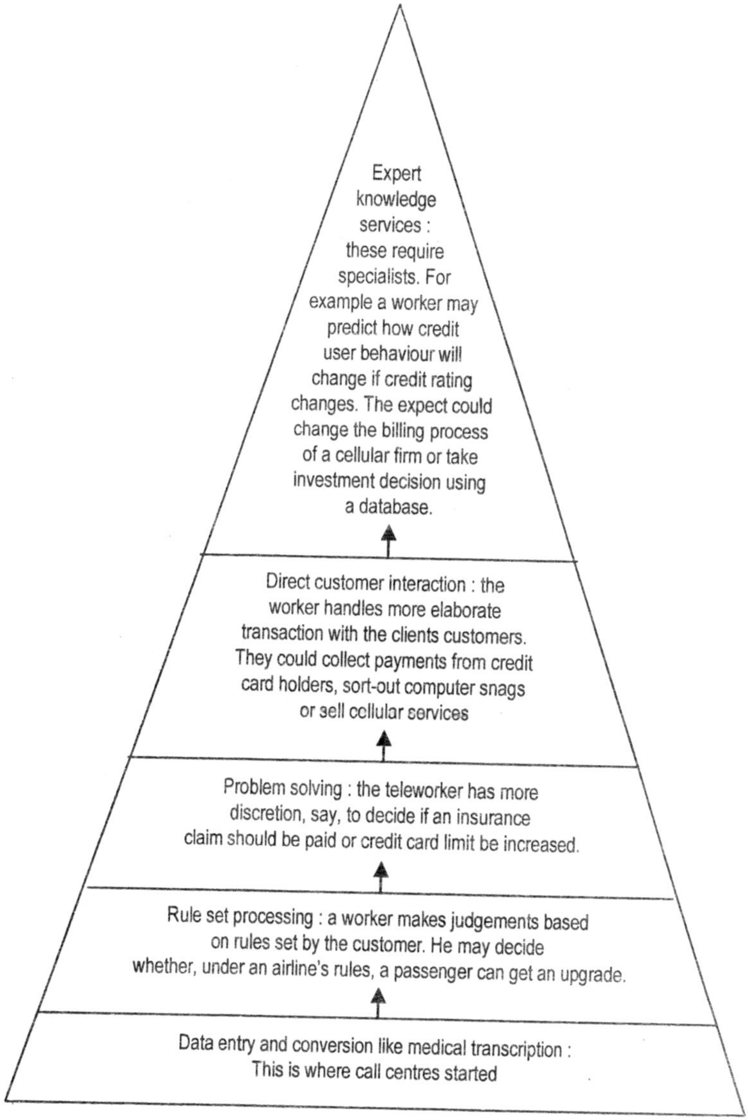

Source: Singh and Jayashankar (2002).

Fig. 1 explains about the BPO ladder as it starts from Data entry and this moves up towards rule set processing, problem-solving, customer interaction and at the top end is expert knowledge services.

Major Processes Outsourced in India

It can be readily observed that information technology (IT) still remains the favourite function for outsourcing to specialized external vendors. However, companies are now increasingly outsourcing their finance and accounting functions followed by Human resource (HR) outsourcing (Fig. 2).

TABLE I

Genres of Outsourcing that Constitute India's ITES Companies

Genre	*Examples*	*Number*	*Employees*
Backoffice Behemoths	GE, American Express, HSBC, Citibank	30+	30,000+
Software Converts	Progeon (Infosys), E-Serve (HCL Tech.), Spectramind (Wipro)	30+	6000+
The true third party companies	Daksh, EXL, Transworks, customer asset com.	100+	45000+
Global ITES companies	Convergys, ACS, Sitel, Teletech	10+	6000+
The consulting cheer leaders	Accenture, CSC	2+	500+

Source: Mahanta (2002).

The survey done by Price Water House Cooper of about 300 executives from various MNCs reveals that within the IT services, there is vast scope for data entry and conversion to be outsourced. Only 10% of the respondents are engaged in full IT outsourcing. Call centres and networks (both local and wide area) are also being increasingly outsourced. Within financial services, most companies are outsourcing internal audit processes followed by taxation and payroll processing. The trend of outsourcing financial information systems that is quite popular among multinational companies is yet to pick up in India. In the field of HR, recruitment and staffing activities are being outsourced the most, followed by consulting and training activity. However, the worker compensation is still not being outsourced to specialised HR firms. Companies are outsourcing a large number of processes in India (Table 2).

FIG. 2

Percentage of Business Processes Outsourced in Various Sectors in India (2002-03)

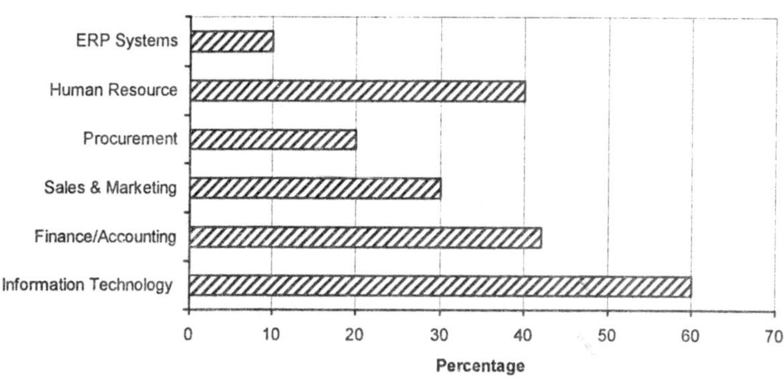

Source: Kumar (2002).

When outsourcing first made appearance in US in early 1990s, it quickly became the most common and most controversial form of carving up the corporation. The range of outsourcing possibilities is widening and critical activities like manufacturing, distribution and logistics, finance and even, HR came under its ambit (Table 3). Employment in this industry is expected to increase many folds in the coming years. BPO companies of India are providing services to many leading client organizations abroad.

POTENTIAL OF BPO IN INDIA: A SWOT ANALYSIS

This sector has grown by 73% during the last fiscal and recorded revenues of Rs. 7100 crores. Spending by US organizations on outsourcing increased from $ 100 billion to 318 billion in 2002. About 825 of the US companies rank India as the first choice for BPO. In view of the critical changes taking place and the effect that BPO is going to be

TABLE 2

Some Companies Outsourcing their Business Process and their Core Competencies

Company/institute	*Core competency*	*Functions it outsources*
Pfizer	Marketing	Manufacturing, tech. support, building maintenance, travel, cash management
Airtel	Business planning, market planning, network planning	Payment collections, bill printing, customer service, distribution.
LG	Marketing and R & D	Manufacturing, Logistics
Pizza Corner	Making Pizzas	Tech. support, security, food process, house keeping, database management and promotions
IIM-Bangalore	Teaching	Tech support, maintenance
Samsung (IT and telecom division)	Planning and strategic decision-making	Distribution, promotion, marketing, Logistics, collections
Eli Lilly	Marketing	Manufacturing, distribution, claims processing logistics, payroll, tech. support, patient education
Max. NY Life	Making Insurance products, marketing, services	HR, data entry
Safe express	Transport, logistics management	IT, data warehousing, HR consulting

the industry of the decade and will generate huge revenues and employment for India.

Strengths

India offers many advantages to serving as an ITES destination for major companies. These include:

1. The abundant skilled manpower has made India a target destination for multinationals to back end their operations in India. India ranks high in areas such as qualification, capabilities, quality of work, linguistic capabilities and work ethics, and thus is ahead of competitors such as China, Ireland, etc.

TABLE 3

Areas of Outsourcing

Areas	*Applications*	*Major players and market*
HR	Payroll, retirement benefits, medical benefits	India Life Hewitt, Cross Domains, Ma Foi. Market growing at above 25-40% annually
Finance	Billing, cash management, fund accounting	Deutshe Bank, HDFC, ABN Amro. Market figure not available
IT	Hardware and software maintenance, ERP and database management, network management	Wipro, IBM, Infosys, EDS, TCS, CMC, HCL. Market size in 2001 was Rs. 2300 crore; growing at 15% annually
Logistics	Transport from factories to warehouse to markets, inventory management	TCI, Safexpress, Speedage, Gati, Lemuis, Market size about Rs. 5000 crore, growing at 35-40% annually
Facilities Management	Property management, house keeping, help desk, maintenance, electrical	CB Richard Ellis, Insignia, Jakson and Knight Frank. Organised sector manages about 20 million sq. ft. Market growing at 65-70% annually
Marketing and Sales	Distribution, brand building, channel management	Solutions, systems research, JL Marketing market figure not available

Source: Singh 2002.

2. India's unique geographic positioning which enables it to offer a 24 x 7 service and reduction in turnaround times by leveraging time zone differences, i.e. a virtual 12 hour time zone difference with USA and other major markets.
3. Cost of qualified personnel is amongst the lowest in the world. About 100000 engineers graduate from India every year, and many of them are employed with call centres for providing technical support at salaries that are dramatically lower as compared to the pay scales in US.
4. India has stable legislative and economic framework. India announced a special incentive and infrastructure for setting up ITES, for example tax incentives and multiple licenses.

5. India enjoys very strong brand equity in major markets, thanks to its growing and globally competitive software industry.
6. Thrust by government to make India an IT-driven nation with a focus on service sector where potential for value addition, and thus premium higher.
7. The proliferation of ITES and its continuing demand led growth may well emerge to be a strong opportunity for India, both in terms of generating employment and export.
8. As evident, ITES is a major boon for India as it provides tremendous potential to attract foreign investments.
9. Indian centres have achieved higher productivity levels for example, the number of transactions per hour to back office processing, than their western counterparts.

Weaknesses

Several negatives that may impact India's BPO industry are :

1. Undercutting by smaller players keen to get business could undermine the profitability of the sector.
2. A bad experience at the hands of price warriors could erode the brand equity of India as an ITES destination.
3. The overcapacity in the industry could act as a deterrent to the entry of companies with a long-term perspective.
4. Regulatory and Infrastructural issues could see countries like China and Phillippines replace India as the preferred ITES destination.

Opportunity

Some of the opportunities which India has still to tap are human resource BPO and Finance BPO. HR BPO is one of the biggest chunks of the global ITES sector and India hardly has a piece of the market. Nasscom, Gartner, international Data Corporation, Ernst and Young, Goldman Sachs, Edelwins Capital and Their ilk put the Human Resource Outsourcing (HRO) opportunity for India at $ 3.5 billion to 5 billion by 2008. By 2008, the global HRO market is expected to be $ 44 billion, say Nasscom-McKinsey. If even less than 10% comes to India, it will mean 56000 jobs. And if third party players take up 5% of this, they will earn revenues of $ 70 million.

So why have Indian companies not tapped this potential goldmine? The key thing here is delivery capability and domain knowledge. For, in HRO, the higher one may go up the value chain, the more complex the processes get and the more entrenched the players in the US. In HR, there is no methodology that one can uniformly implement in all companies for example performance appraisal.

Finance BPO is the 2nd largest business process outstanding opportunity. To make big money, Indian companies selling outsourced finance processes will have to get hold of the high-value assignments.

Threats

The biggest threat, which India may have to face, is unionism shown by US states not to outsource business processes to India, as this is causing unemployment in the US. Threats from the new entrants like China and the established players like Ireland and Phillipines can be a big trouble for India in the future. These threats are discussed as follows:

China

In the outsourcing field, China is the biggest challenge in the future and the largest threat to India. With the largest population and fastest economic growth, The main advantages of China are its lower manpower costs and Japan advantage. The Chinese Workers cost about 15 percent less than equally qualified Indian workers and China is likely to grow through the Japanese outsourcing route. The advantages that China has are Japan's proximity to China and similarity of the languages. India currently offers almost no BPO services in Japan. Also it has extremely low cost real estate and power. These costs are lower than in India. This can be a big attraction to the US companies, which are looking for cost cutting due to the downturn. The government is very friendly to this sector and has taken steps to teach English and other skills. Over $ 5.4 billion was invested in nine universities in China to promote English language and other skill sets. Government is targeting at increasing telecom density and PC Penetration. China scores over India in these aspects and intends to further increase the gap.

Philippines

The country is getting business from nearly 70 companies employing more than 12000 people with revenues of US $250 million. The Philippines government has initiated a number of policies by which the skills can be provided to a larger population. It has improved telecom and office infrastructure and Philippines scores over India in it. It is the third largest English-speaking nation in the world. It is considered 2nd only to India due to performance in software. Costs of technology workers is only around 16% to 25% in the Philippines to that of comparable workers from the United States.

Phillipines has been an American Colony. American Culture and language are widely emulated here. These cultural and communications skills could prove to be so appealing to American firms that they may outweigh slightly higher labour costs in the Philippines.

Ireland

It was one of the front-runners in the BPO and started much earlier than India. Thus, it has built a good brand equity in US. It has a very conducive regulatory framework and is known for excellent quality standards. The country has strategically pursued developing outsourcing services market and is planning to invest heavily in telecom infrastructure ($5 billion over 10 years). In the late 1990s India emerged as an ITES option. Infact, since 1999, India's attractiveness has improved (Figs. 3 and 4).

FIG 3

India's Attractiveness in 1990

High
Singapore
Hong Kong
Ireland
Australia
Netherlands
UK
India
Philippines
Mexico
China
Location Attractiveness
Low
People Attractiveness
High

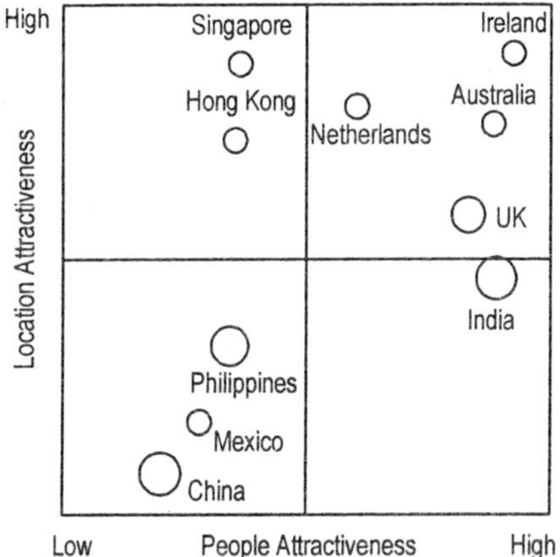

FIG. 4

India's Attractiveness in 1999

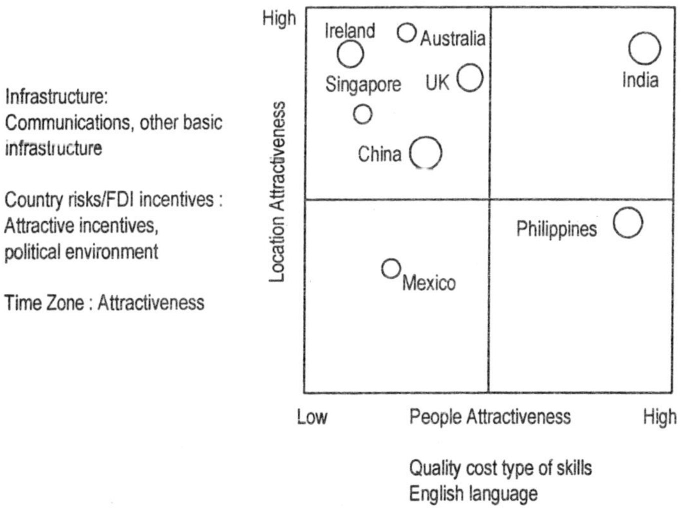

Infrastructure:
Communications, other basic infrastructure
Country risks/FDI incentives :
Attractive incentives, political environment
Time Zone : Attractiveness
High
Ireland
Australia
Singapore
UK
China
India
Philippines
Mexico
Location Attractiveness
Low
People Attractiveness
High
Quality cost type of skills
English language

Note: Size of circle indicates quantity of knowledge workers.

Source: Mahanta (2002).

Anti-Outsourcing Campaign

The anti-outsourcing cry in the US is a mere murmur today. But it could rise to a rumble unless India takes action now. This has happened because US people are loosing jobs and ITES/BPO employees in India are growing at the rate of 50-55% a year. According to Forester research 3.3 million number of jobs would move out of US, half to India by 2015. On Dec. 2002 New Jersey Almost passed a bill preventing outsourcing of government contracts to Indian IT firms. The bill is finally put in hold following hectic lobbying by Nasscom. But still now there is no trouble as ITES of India can breathe easily.

Bottlenecks and Pitfalls in the System

In this section we will discuss some of the bottlenecks and pitfalls in the BPO system. If we can remove these problems then India will remain undoubtedly the leader in the ITES industry.

1. Nascent Industry

Getting business from customers abroad is not easy for Indian companies, as the BPO industry is in a very nascent stage, and the concerns expressed by potential customers can range from concerns about the partner's lack of experience to the reliability and scalability of service and financial ability of organization.

2. Trust issues

Outsourcing can only take place if the MNCs trusts an Indian partner because the Indian partner would get access to sensitive areas of the business, some MNCs are using a mix of capitive and outsourced services, with some of more sensitive and complex process done in house.

3. Communication cut-off

Communication cut-off between the US or Europe and India. The Indian facility may be closed or made inaccessible. If all communications links are cut-off between Europe and India or the US and India, offshore resources will not have access to the systems.

FIG. 5

The Offshore Wave: What's at Stake

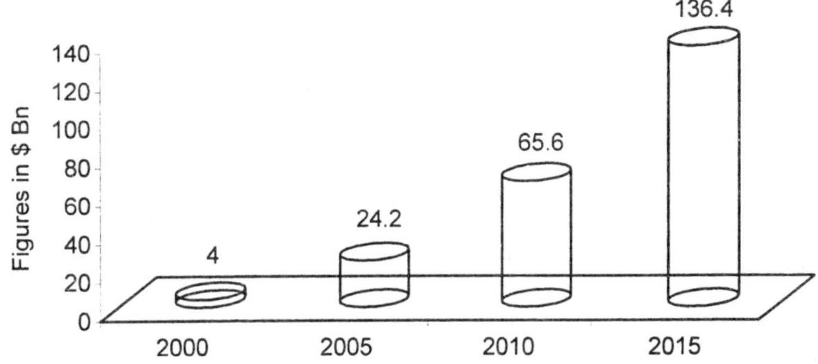

Total wages associated with US jobs moving off share

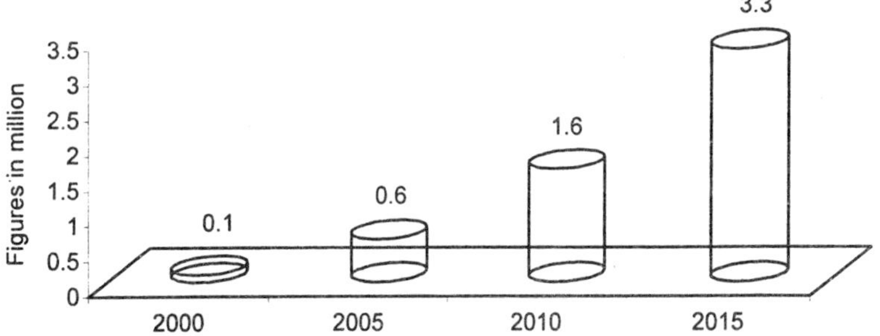

Number of US jobs expected to move off shares

Source: Srinivisan (2003).

4. Terrorists getting access to mission critical systems

This has always been a concern. During the period of concern about Y2K, variety of self-proclaimed experts prophesied that 'back doors' would be programmed into code and companies critical systems would be explored to the world. As far as we know, this has not happened yet. But, most companies that use offshore resources already adhere to very strict security policies and require their vendors to do the same.

5. Creates confusion whether in India or America

This is one of the major problem, it is something which we can say as juggling of personalities. Employees lose their identity with a changed name and changed accent. Names are changed from Jayanti to Jessie, Roshan to Roger. In this way employeess' social life is disturbed as sometimes they start behaving like Roger, Jessie, Arnold, etc. with their friends and this creates in a person a case of dual personalities.

Dasgupta (2002) in her article studied the process of training and developing a call centre employee and found that it involves giving them a completely new identity-names, accents and attitudes. It is a tough life but it has its compensations. The average call centre employee start out with Rs. 8000-11000 and this could double within two years. Call centre trainers earn well, from a minimum of Rs. 15000-18000, the money could go as high as Rs. 45000-50000 a month. Call centre employees are encouraged to watch baseball games and TV movies to give them a feel for life in America. Though call centres create an atmosphere of fun for employees yet attrition rate is very high in ths industry. Bakaya (2002) in his article has described that attrition rates shoot up to almost 60% as more and more companies enter the BPO foray. It is the highest employee turnover India has seen in any Industry, ever and that too in a dismal job market. In the past 6-9 months, attrition rates in BPO operations have scaled new heights, from 30% to a peak of 60%.

6. Hostility created in body-clock

As the call centre work starts around 6 in the evening at India, where it is around 8 am in the US, so the call centre employees have to work mostly in night shifts, their days ends with a hurry to go home and catch some sleep, when the world around you is headed for work. So your body-clock is disturbed and cause stress in your minds and may also cause physical problems.

7. Availability of reliable telecom bandwidth

This is one of the major concern for India, as this issue can pose a threat to Indian reputation. As currently VSNL is the sole provider and this eliminates the possibility of two independent providers connecting to US and UK.

8. Extra competition around

The BPO industry in India is at its mascot stage and the presence of too many players is a stumbling block for quality standards in the industry. The new entrants have to find a niche for themselves.

9. Tension between India and Pakistan

The lingering conflict between India and Pakistan over Kashmir, or threats from guerrilla groups is also a major bottleneck. The issue of nuclear warfare tends to frighten people away from coming to India.

10. Clients very demanding

Clients are very demanding and want full security about data and have very tough quality standards, which can differ from one project to another. The clients are also demanding about cultural differences and high STD rates prevailing in India. The provider can not disclose about the client's name because of confidential reasons.

11. Grooming middle level managers

As the industry is at its nascent stage, so the need of the hour is grooming the middle level managers, also these managers don't want to join BPO of less career development and the kind of job profile which is not suitable for highly qualified MBAs, MCAs and Cas, etc.

RECOMMENDATIONS

The following are some of the recommendations for improving the system:

Business Continuity Plan (BCP)

In case of communication cut-off between India and US there should be a business continuity plan. There should be spare resources in the US for this eventuality and that those resources can quickly acquire the appropriate application knowledge The other way out should be instead of one communication, a back-up link from another provider can be used.

Moving up the BPO Ladder

This is the need of the hour, as Indian ITES companies are only at data entry levels, they should move up towards expert knowledge services. This will reduced high attrition rate and will also help highly educated professional in ITES sector.

Develop Manpower in Relation with ITES

There are very few institutes offering training in these services. institutes need to offer skill sets in accent training, accounting systems, basic know how of different business segments like Real estate, insurance, customer can, etc. The gaps in skilled labour can be filled up by establishing dedicated courses in soft skills (Accent training, language skills in Spanish, French and Arabic), technical skills and financial skills (tele-marketing, secretarial services, customers care).

Improve Infrastructure

This is the weakest area of India. The weakest links in this segments which should be taken up at the earliest is to reduce the cost of real estate, improve telecom reliability and bandwidth and improve availability and quality of power.

Improve Regulatory Framework

The government has done a lot in the past one year in the area of telecom liberalization. However, there are various licensing and connectivity issues in the BPO sector, which require policy amendments by the government. It is imperative that the government encourages sustained growth in this sector by streamlining procedural bottlenecks and providing a progressive policy framework to encourage investments.

References

Bakaya, M. (2002). Mr. BPO's Savvy. *Business Today* 11(25): 146-48.

Dasgupta, A. (2002b). Hello Jessie, Goodbye Jayanti. *Journal of Indian Management*. 41(6): 36-40

Kumar, A. (2002). Assocham study. http://www.indiainfoline.com/bisc/leve.html.

Mahanta, V. (2002). Glut!. *Business Today*. 11(20), 52-56.

Singh, S. (2002). Lean and mean. *Business World*. 22(12), 28-36.

Singh, S. and Jayashankar, M. (2002). The BPO Boom. *Business World*. 21(33), 28-37.

Srinivisan, P. (2003b). Backlash. *Business Today*. 12(7), 102-05.

CHAPTER

28

ITES and BPO

A Boost to Indian Economy

BIKRAM SINGH VIRK

Services formed a mere 5 per cent of total GDP of India in post-independence days. The economy was largely agriculture dependent giving employment to more than 80 per cent of Indian populace. However, the shift in the scenario was witnessed after the planned economic growth and more and more people became dependent on industry and slowly growing service sector. By the end of the century, the Indian economy witnessed a complete shift in the GDP structure and at present 46 per cent of it is being contributed by the services. But this is far behind from developed economies of US and UK, where the service sector is contributing more than 80 per cent of GDP.

Since the last 10 years, a new dimension has been added to the Indian service sector and India has been recognized a knowledge economy world wide, thanks to its contribution to Information Technology Services (ITS) and Information Technology Enabled Services (ITES). Since 1990s India has been known as the tech Mecca for the Western companies that want good programming done on cheap. The latest addition to this growing sector is Business Process Outsourcing (BPO), where the business processes are being outsourced to the Indian companies by customers in the developed countries. India is a preferred destination for outsourcing of accounting, financial, health care and personal services which can be transferred through OFC wires. The low wages, IT friendly and fluent English speaking youngsters are highly acceptable to the customers from these developed nations as they fit very well in their business matrix. Apart from outsourcing their services, many a companies are establishing their back home offices in India to reap the benefits of cheap, qualified and IT savvy workforce available in India. Intel has 1000 engineers in Banglore and plans to increase them to 3000 by 2005. Accenture and IBM too have more than 2000 engineers working in India and plan to increase their number to 20000 during the next three years. In the similar way, many other companies are also following suit.

WHAT IS OUTSOURCING?

The word outsourcing means purchasing a significant percent age of immediate components from outside suppliers. The term was commonly used in buying and assembling segment of industry. In broader sense the practice of transferring in-house work to an outside vendor is outsourcing. The work is key component in the whole process of outsourcing.

However, this simple definition does not elaborate the true nature of the practice. A complete definition in documentation and training industry may further categorize it into three levels, the Project Level, Program Level and Department Level. In the first category, it involves all those activities needed for release of a single product and may include designers, technical writers, graphic designers and editors. In the second level, services needed to support the life cycle of product are included and in the third category it amounts to transfer of all the work in the department at a single location or across several locations. It involves the transfer of in-house resources to the supplier.

But in the IT industry, the outsourcing is the transfer or delegation to an external service provider the operation and day-to-day management of a business process. The customer receives the services that perform a destined business function that fits into the customer's overall business operations.

The IT companies in India these days are resorting to this kind of BPO, where they are holding the day-to-day operations of the overseas multinationals and other companies in the field of accounting, finance, personal care and telemedicine. Apart from this, the Indian IT companies are also providing ITES in a big way. Even the first category of outsourcing, i.e. the project outsourcing is also in the news and some of the multinationals are also seeking the help of Indian designers for their product designs. The publishing jobs are also being got done from India in this category.

CONTRIBUTION OF IT AND ITES TO INDIAN ECONOMY

Over the last one decade, India has emerged as an IT giant in the world. It has the same name in the IT field as Japan has in the field of Electronics and Germany in cars. As per the Nasscom-McKinsey study of 2002, IT industry will become the largest sector in the Indian economy. The share of this industry was 1.4 percent in 1999, which is expected to go up to 7 percent by 2008. Moreover, it is expected that it will contribute 19 percent of incremental GDP growth between now and 2008. The share in foreign exchange contribution from the export of ITES, which is 8 per cent today, shall grow up to 30 per cent by 2008. ITS and ITES shall be contributing to employment scenario in a big way. Currently 0.5 million people are employed in this industry and by 2008, it shall give employment to 2 million people directly and to another 2 million indirectly thereby generating employment avenues for 4 million people. The largest job segment shall be customer care, which shall provide 0.39 million jobs, followed by HR and administration, which shall create 0.16 and 0.1 millions respectively. The IT services, which include the development of product and technology services, shall create a combined of 1.2 million jobs.

Call Centers are also proving to be good job generators as there are 0.21 million seats the these at present. The number of Call Center seats last year was 0.14 million and has shown an increase of 50 per cent over last year. Most of this increase is from Indian vendors and captive units. The share of captive units in these seats is between 65 to 70 per cent and is expected to grow further. Mergers and acquisitions are also taking place and many Indian and foreign companies are involved in this exercise. More than 12 M&A have taken place recently.

Technology and manufacturing hubs have emerged across many industries. India has already effected the cycle for customized application development and succeeded in capturing a 15 percent market share. Since India possessed the ingredients and knowledge to repeat the cycle, it has the potential to enlarge as hub for other IT services like packed software installation and support, system integration software development and ISV back-ending. In terms of market share, India has the potential of having 4 per cent of IT globally.

At present, the world wide spending on BPO, which was 166 bn. US $ in 1999, is expected to rise to 177 bn US $ by 2008 at 69 per cent CAGR. According to the report of Gartner, India shall be able to wrest 13.5 bn of it, which is 17 per cent of the total world's BPO. This is in contrast to the world market in product sector, which is worth 180 bn US $ and the share of India in this is just 0.2 per cent.

FUTURE POTENTIAL AND CHALLENGES

Indian companies have been dependent so far on the largest IT services markets of US and UK. They have yet to catch up with some other English speaking economies like Canada, Australia, Sweden and Netherlands. Some non-English-speaking territories of Japan, Italy, France and Germany are also under-penetrated. The size of US economy alone in the IT sector is US $ 207 bn, out of which India has been able to explore only 1.7 per cent. Similarly, it has only taken 2.4 per cent from 28 bn worth market of UK. English-speaking markets of Canada, Netherlands, Sweden and Australia, have a combined IT market of 29 bn US$. Indian companies have so far catered to only 3.3 per cent of it. The combined ITES market of non-English-speaking countries of Japan, Germany, Italy and France is 116 bn $ and India has shared only 1.4 per cent of it. India can capture up to 4.6 per cent of it by 2008 as per the study of Nasscom-McKinsey.

But the fast growing BPO and ITES industry in India has recently got a jolt by certain unsavory events. The passing of anti-outsourcing laws in some 20 states of US have shaken the myth of free trade and posed a question mark on the outsourcing activity from US to India. This has happened at a time when US is witnessing a situation of unemployment and 8.7 million of its people are without work. If the US remains successful in its bid to ban the outsourcing activities, many other countries may also follow suit. In these conditions, the booming sector of Indian IT may have to face hardships.

But contrarily, the positive side of the picture is that 90 per cent of BPO revenue to Indian companies from the private sector in US. The loss of business is estimated to be to the tune of 24 million US $, if the US government bans the BPO and it is only 1 per cent of the total revenues to India from US. Another study on the industry has shown that the company that outsource gains much more than the company to which it is outsourced. For every 1$ job outsourced by the US the American Company receives $1.14 out of the $1.49 value created for the global economy. The share of developing countries in this trade in services is only $0.35. Thus after the ban, the ultimate loser will be the US taxpayer, who will now pay more for the government services.

Another challenge before the Indian IT sector is a parallel emerging market of China and other countries, which can compete with Indian companies on the cost front. According to KPMG study, both China and Israel are the major competitor of India in the field of ITES.

Poor spending on IT and wire line networks are also a problem for Indian IT. India is spending on IT is only $ 4 per capita per annum in comparison to $ 64 by a country like Mexico. Similarly the wire lines, which by the end of year 2001 were 3.4 per cent or 34 million lines against 66.5 per cent 190 million lines in US, are also inadequate. If the country is to harp on this newly emerging technology job sector, it shall have to lay more stress on providing good infrastructure in the form of OFCs and wire lines. The development of HR is also of equal importance to make them well versed with English language apart from technical handling of computers. For this purpose, IT spending shall have to be increased substantially. Penetration in the markets of France, Germany, Japan and Italy is possible only by making learning of these languages. India can hope to lead in the IT sector only by resorting to these measures.

References

'Ites-BPO seats to touch 2.1 lakh by Mar-Nasscom', *Economic Times*, Feb. 24, 2004.

Kanavi, Shivanand, 'Coming of Age', *Business India*, Feb 16-29, 2004.

Sehgal, Madhuri, "Anti BPO Bill may hurt in long-run', *Economic Times*, Feb. 24, 2004.

www.bpoindia.org/news

www.nasscom.org/MediaRoom.asp

www.nasscom.org/artdisplay.asp

www.iata.org/itserv/headline.cfm

www.ciol.com/content/e-ent//default.asp

CHAPTER

29

Preparedness of the Indian Textile Industry for the Post Quota Regime

Opportunities and Challenges

SANDEEP KAPUR, BABITA KUMAR, GAGANDEEP BANGA AND MANVEEN SAINI

Textiles are one of the major areas of interest for India, since this sector accounts for about 15% of our industrial production and about one-third of our export earnings (Alva, 1998). Our strong raw material base and the wealth of craftsmanship as well as the relatively cheap labour available in the country highlight the potential for a tremendous increase in our performance in this sector. Presently there are several factors—some external and some internal—that restrict both our production and exports.

INDIA'S POSITION IN WORLD MARKET

In the early 1980s, the Multi Fibre Agreement (MFA) emerged as a major impediment to the full realization of textiles and clothing exporter's potential of many developing and least developed countries. Dismantling the MFA became a common demand of a large number of developing countries during the Uruguay round of multilateral trade negotiations and many of them considered the Agreement on Textiles and Clothing (ATC), which will phase out quotas by 2005—the most significant of all agreements resulting from those negotiations.

The Agreement on Textile and Clothing (ATC) stipulates how the quotas on textile trade would be regulated from 1995 to 2004 and that they would be abolished thereafter. It envisages that the quotas established under the Multi Fiber Arrangement (MFA) would migrate to WTO at the time of its establishment in 1995 and then would be phased out during a 10-year period during which products would be progressively integrated into WTO, i.e., removed from restrictions. The restraint levels would grow faster on the products that continue under restriction during this period than what MFA had provided for. For calculating the percentage of products to be integrated, the base year has been stipulated as 1990. Thus on 1.1.1995, each importing country's operating quotas had to integrate, products representing 16% of its imports of textile products in 1990. Similarly, 17% of such products had to be integrated on 1.1.1998 and another 18% on 1.1.2002. The remaining 19% (Sorenson, 1995) would be integrating on 1.1.2005, when the operation of MFA quotas would end. The importing countries are free to choose the products for integration within these percentages. There is no stipulation that the products integrated should be the ones on which quotas actually operated before the establishment of the ATC. Though it is stipulated that such products should include yarn, fabrics, made-ups and garments in each case, there is no stipulation of any proportion for these products. The result is that at least in the first two stages, both USA and EU have by and large integrated items on which quotas had never operated, that too more of yarn and fabrics and very little of made-ups and garments. In the third stage, which began in 1.1.2002, there was a marginal effective integration of products in the USA because there were very few unrestricted textile items left for them to integrate. In the EU there was no such constraint and, therefore, no effective integration is likely.

The crucial question is how the abolition of quotas would impact India's exports of textiles and clothing beyond 2005. Indian exporters have virtually no experience of handling the European or American markets without quotas. Many critics are of the opinion that quotas actually is helping countries like India to develop its export market. They cite the example of Japanese market to prove this point. They are of the opinion that, in a quota free market of Japan, China has overtaken all other countries in terms of exports and has a share of around 80.5% (Figs. 1 and 2).

FIG. I

Principal Exporters of Knitwear to Japan

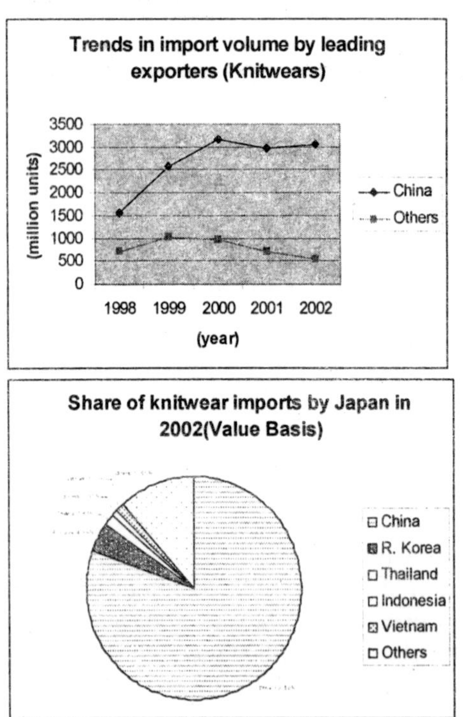

Source: JETRO Marketing Guidebook for major imported products.

FIG. 2

Principal Exporters of Woven Wear to Japan

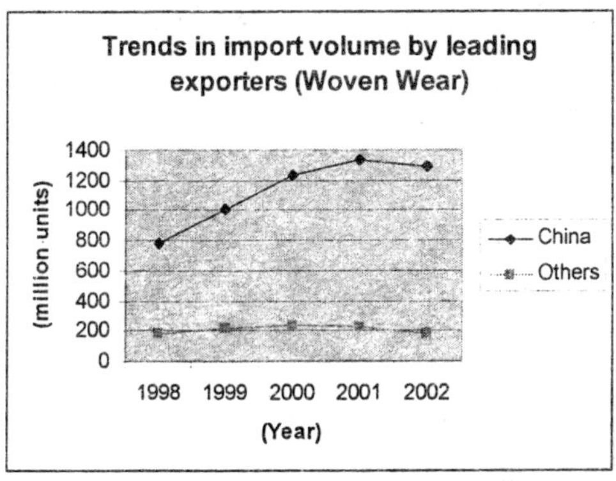

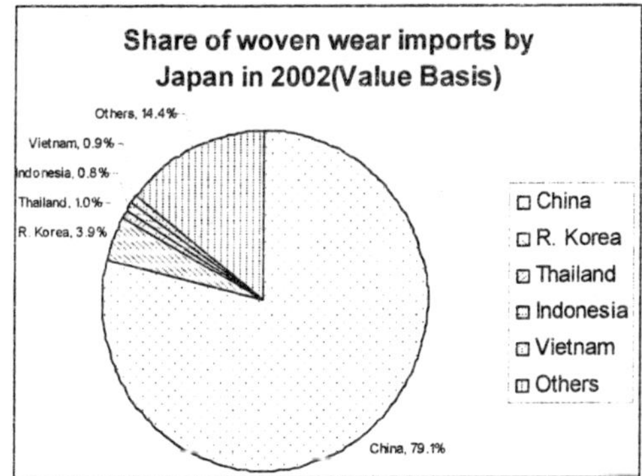

Source: JETRO Marketing Guidebook for major imported products.

Analyzing Figs. 1 and 2 in detail, it is observed that China has an overwhelming lead as an exporter of apparel to Japan accounting for 80.5% in knitwear and accessories and 79.1% in woven wear and accessories on a value basis in 2002. On volume base, China has a much higher share with 85.2% and 88.0% respectively. Tremendous growth in export of both knitwear and woven wear is seen in the last 4 to 5 years. In both the cases, there is a marginal decline in exports of other countries to Japan. India's share in Japanese market is negligible. Another example is of Australia where tariffs fell from 130% in 1986 to 25% in 2000. Tariffs will be further reduced in 2005. China was the main beneficiary contributing 69% of clothing and 21% of Australia's all textile imports. Critics are of the opinion that the same situation may be repeated in other developed markets of US and EU in the post quota era.

FIG. 3

Leading Textile and Clothing Import Markets, 2001

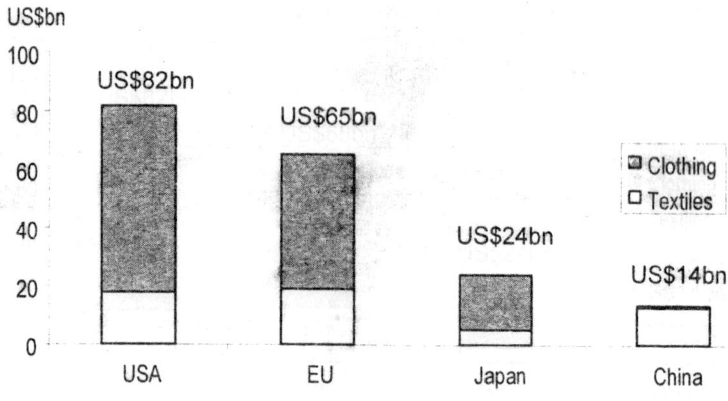

Source: WTO.

Fig. 3 reveals that US, EU, Japan and China represent the world's leading importers of textile and clothing. In US the opportunity to export clothing is higher whereas Chinese market throws open opportunities in textile. In future this trend is going to continue as China will depend on more of textile to cater to the international apparel trade therefore, an opportunity for India.

Another school of thought is that with the quotas being phased out, India has ample of opportunities in certain product categories (where the quota utilization is higher) and in some others it may not do so well (where quota utilization is lower). For example, EU Quota saturation for category 4 shown in Fig. 4 reveals that in the category 4 (Shirts, T-shirts) 11/2002, India is ahead of all other countries except for Vietnam. But in category 5 (Pullovers, Jackets, Coats) 11/

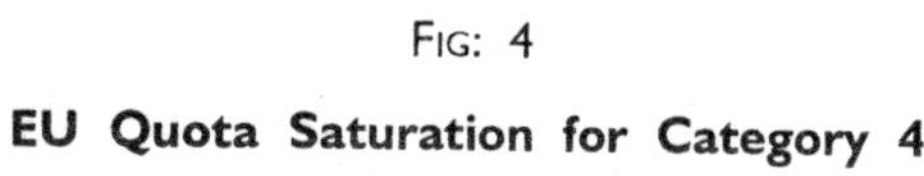

FIG: 4

EU Quota Saturation for Category 4

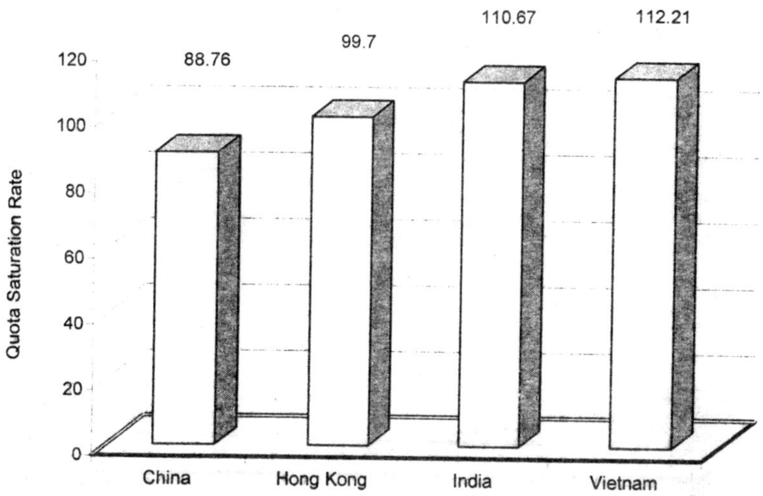

Source: www.textilesintelligence.com

2002, India is not going to gain much because it is already far behind other countries.

Fig. 5 reveals that the quota utilization in case of restrained levels during the calendar year 2000, 2001, 2002 has been fluctuating. It is noticed that except in the year 2001 (both Gr.-1 and Gr.-2) the utilization has been more than 100%. Therefore, an opportunity for India to excel in these categories.

In yarn, especially cotton yarn, India has been quite successful in the international markets, in spite of quotas. In fabrics, our exports are mostly in low value grey goods because of the inadequacies in our processing facilities. In areas like clothing and home furnishing, India's potential is perhaps substantially more than what our exports have allowed us to achieve so far. Especially in clothing, India's exporters have been procuring quotas at as much as 50% of their export prices in categories where some of the larger quota holders in South East Asia have quotas which remain under-utilized (Nair 2000).

FIG. 5

Utilisation of Restrained Levels during (Jan.-Dec.) 2000, 2001 and 2002

Country Category	*Unit*	*Year*	*Level*	*Shipment Passed*	*% Utilisation*
USA—Gr.-I	000SME	2000	291882	309205	105.93
		2001	314729	308939	98.16
		2002	346103	379412	109.62
Gr.-II	000SME	2000	80000	99003	123.75
		2001	85000	89079	104.8
		2002	85000	82328	96.86
TOTAL	000SME	2000	371882	408208	109.77
(Gr.-I and II)		2001	399729	398018	99.57
		2002	431103	461740	107.11

Source: aepcindia.com

CHANGING SCENARIO OF WORLD MARKET IN TEXTILE AND APPAREL

World Apparel and Textile market is changing at a rapid pace. To design suitable strategies, it is important to understand these changes and the trends in the world market. In this section, four aspects studied are:

1. Falling Prices
2. Multi-Base Imports
3. Ethical Sourcing
4. Pace

All the above mentioned aspects are dealt in greater detail below.

1. Falling Prices

From the year 2005 onwards, the market forces will determine the market prices and the market shares. The product categories in which India is already exporting more than the allocated quotas will act as competitive edges for India. As per a study done, the prices of US textile and clothing import are likely to go down (Fig 6). If the prices go down, only the countries that are able to provide good quality at cheap prices will survive the competition, because in competition one can always find someone offering lower prices. Falling prices will further fuel future growth in consumption, therefore, rising the demand.

FIG. 4

Trends in US Textile and Clothing Import Prices, 1983-2001

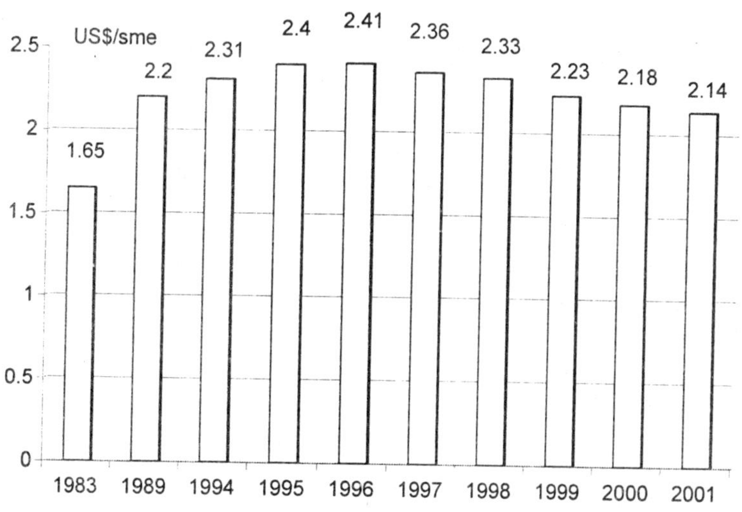

Source: Textile Outlook International, NB sme: square metres equivalent www.textilesintelligence.com

2. Multi-base imports

After 2004, the US Congressional Textile Caucus states that the US sourcing pattern will change a lot. Till now the US sourcing is driven by quota constraints and the retailers buy from about 40-60 countries. Many big retailers have to source from about 50 countries individually. This makes their task of outsourcing very difficult as a number of problems related to logistics, quality control, lead time, etc. crop up. This will be cut to half by end 2005-06 and will further drop from 1/3rd to 1/4th by 2010. As a result of all this, the least developed Countries (LDCs) will especially be the hard hit. According to US International Trade Center survey, US retailers will source from fewer countries, focus on those that are fully integrated with emphasis on speed, quality, legal compliance, logistics and product cost. As a result, the countries surviving only on quotas instead of competitiveness will be wiped out of the market. Moreover, for a particular country only those product categories will remain in competition where it is doing exceptionally well and is exporting more than quotas fixed.

3. Ethical Sourcing

Another change which is noticed in world textile and apparel business is that apart from prices guiding the global sourcing process, codes of conduct will also guide the business. That is, global sourcing will become ethical sourcing and social sourcing will become criteria for the trade. There is going to be increased insistence on social responsibility of manufacturers/suppliers. The corporate code of conduct and business values will act as guarantee to certain standards. Among other things a few things that will be considered for judging standards will be no child labour, working conditions, no forced labour, compensation, no discrimination, working hours, minimum wages and freedom of associations.

The European Business Social Compliance has taken initiative for this. The Foreign Trade Association (FTA) brings together retailers and provides them a common system for moving towards social compliance. It has recommended the use of standardized questionnaire for social audits and mutual recognition of company audits. The countries and the organizations have to gear up to meet the social compliance to get the edge in the international business. Many of the retailers have set their own standards for these compliance. Many exporters see social compliance as a method to restrict free trade in the area of Textile and apparel.

4. Pace

International trend in business suggest that the lead time for the exporters between the orders and the dispatch has declined. This is further going to go down in the years to come. The exporters have to gear up for faster and reliable deliveries. Any hindrance because of any reason will hamper the export opportunities of the country. For this the countries have to concentrate on developing effective supply chain management system to be able to gear up to the expectations of the importers.

ROLE OF INDIAN SMALL AND MEDIUM ENTERPRISES IN TEXTILE TRADE

Textile and apparel industry is exporting products worth Rs. 25,000 crores approximately. Out of the total Rs. 25,000 crore, Rs. 12,000 crore is contributed by large organizations. These organizations have large production facilities and sound financial backing. They are in the process of modernizing/equipping themselves and they have chalked out their plans to face the onslaught of coming quota free regime. It is believed that this large sector of the Indian apparel and textile sector will be able to cope up with the competition in the future. Another Rs. 6,000 crore export is location specific like apparel/textile export of Kanjivaram sarees of South India and textile designs from Jaipur. Since they do not have competition, these industries will survive. The major problem lies with the remaining approximately Rs. 7,000 crores Small Scale textile industry.

A very large section of the textile industry and knitwear industry in particular is built around thousands of small and tiny enterprises that form the backbone of textile economies in the region providing intensive employment and livelihood to lacs of people besides contributing to direct and indirect exports. Yet it is this section of the economy that faces serious challenges drawing attention of all those concerned with the well-being of the industry. The current policy framework surrounding the sector is out dated and itself needs repairing to build potential competitiveness. Small and tiny firms in the policy framework have so far not been the focus of the cooperation framework to build competitiveness.

SMEs do not operate in vacuum. Their problems and potential needs to be integrated with their larger counterparts and needs to build on its strengths rather than artificial crutches in a market based economic framework. Therefore, SMEs in a sectoral framework presents itself possibly as one of the best ways to enable it to become a vibrant and competitive component of the regional economy.

To improve competitiveness of Indian Garments in the world market, SMEs need to develop and cooperate with each other. For doing this, benchmark tools need to be introduced all over India to enhance quality and competitiveness. Value chain management is a concept that needs to be taught to SMEs and for this a strategy development tool kit needs to be introduced in SMEs. Product and Market Development activities including marketing missions, business contacts and design need to be introduced in SMEs.

CONCLUSION

Indian exporters have no prior experience of developing its export markets without quotas. After 2004 they will face an entirely changed and competitive environment. Market forces will determine the prices. In the countries where India is exporting more than the allocated quotas, it will survive. Whereas in other countries it faces the danger of being wiped out. Only those countries will survive who will be able to supply quality products at competitive rates. Hence, India needs to gear up wholeheartedly to face the challenges of post quota regime. Especially the SMEs which contribute a substantial portion of the textile exports. To keep up to the pace SMEs, need to modernize their production facilities so that they are able to meet the quality standards of importers and they should gear up to make their products available fastly and timely. Cluster approach to meet the forthcoming challenges is suggested. Collectively they shall be able to meet the requirements of post quota regime.

REFERENCES

Alva, D.S. (1998), The Changing Face of Asia—Impact on World Trade, Clthln 18 (4): 74-78.

Anonymous (2002), JETRO Marketing Guide for Major Imported Products. www.jetro.go.jp

Anson, R. (2002), Textile and Apparel Sourcing Options to 2005 and Beyond: Can Asia Compete with Mexico, Sub-Saharan Africa and Euro-Pheriphery. www.textilesintelligence.com

Nair, D.K. (2000), ATC and Indian Textile Industry. Background Paper of Seminar at Small Industries Service Institute, Ludhiana on 7th April, 2000.

Sorenson, J.E. (1995), WTO as Guarantor of World Trade. ITS Text Ldr. 16 (8): 31-38.

www.aepcindia.com

www.wto.org

CHAPTER

30

Developing an Effective Knowledge Management Strategy

SHAILENDER SAINI AND GIANETAN SEKHON

INTRODUCTION

The corporate sector has embraced KM and learning with the aim of improving organizational efficiency—measured in metrical figures of production and profit. In the development sector, organisational efficiency is also important, but it is far from the only aim. Many development agencies today work towards the Millennium Development Goals (MDGs) and measure their degree of success in terms of their impact on poverty reduction and policy change. In order to work towards these larger objectives, agencies not only need efficient internal coordination, but also increased ability to be responsive to the situation of the poor, and ability to influence debates and policy processes. The KM and learning needs of the development sector are Therefore, different in certain respects from those of the mainstream corporate sector, and recommendations from the corporate KM literature cannot be transferred indiscriminately. In recognition of this, development consultants and authors have started writing about KM and learning specifically in relation to different types of development organisations.

While in principle many executives accept the fact that "in an information economy, improving the utility of information is synonymous with creating economic value" (Sawhney, 2001) and that a "high stock of knowledge portends tremendous wealth-creating potential" (Kim and Mauborgne, 1999), in practice their actions and strategies demonstrate that they really don't know how to do this yet. A recent study by Ernst and Young shows that 94% of firms feel they could be making better use of knowledge (DeTienne and Jackson, 2001). Zack (1999a) writes that few organizations today are fully capable of developing and leveraging critical organizational knowledge to improve their performance. Knowledge management (KM) is supposed to address this situation. However, for many firms, despite massive investments in knowledge management initiatives, to date business performance improvements have been modest at best (Donohue, 2001). A key reason for this is that too many companies treat knowledge management as an end in itself. They create a KM program because they think it will pay-off eventually or because they think an effective organization should have one (Dixon, 2000). Thus, "the number one reason KM initiatives may not function in an organization is that the 'evangelists' fail to connect with the real business issues. . . . [They are] a solution looking for a problem" (O'Dell, 1998). The goal of KM should *not* be to make KM happen, but to deal with the organization's most pressing issues and to use KM where appropriate (Dixon, 2000). This means that KM strategies and actions must be closely coordinated with those of the enterprise. Unfortunately, studies show that alignment with business strategy is usually not a motivating factor or a key evaluation criterion of KM in most companies (Davenport *et al.*, 1998). Too many KM initiatives undertaken today are not explicitly linked to or framed by the organization's business strategy and knowledge managers are unable to articulate the links between knowledge and strategy. As a result, many executives are unsure of how to translate the goal of becoming a 'learning organization' or a 'knowing organization' into a strategic course of action (Zack, 1999a).

To explore how to develop and implement a KM strategy that is properly aligned with that of the business, Queen's University's Centre for Knowledge-Based Enterprises convened a day-long focus group of practicing senior knowledge managers from a variety of industries in the United States and Canada. They were asked to explore several questions, including How do you develop your KM strategy? Is there a direct relationship in your organization between KM strategy development and business strategy development? If so, how are the two sets of plans integrated? If not, why not? Is there a direct relationship in your organization between KM strategy execution and business strategy execution? If so, how are the two integrated? If not, why not? How could KM and business strategy be better aligned in your company? In what areas would your CEO and/or executive team like to see KM better aligned with business strategy? To establish a common frame of reference for understanding KM strategy and its relationship to business strategy, this paper first looks at the role and purpose of business strategy. Then it examines how a KM strategy can and should fit conceptually with a business strategy. Next, it discusses how a KM strategy should be developed for a firm and suggests some ways to ensure that it is effectively aligned with business strategy. Finally, it presents some factors which should be considered in executing a KM strategy.

WHAT IS STRATEGY?

In the most general terms, a competitive strategy is an approach to doing business (Gebauer, 1996). At its highest level, a strategy can be conceived of as an overarching set of values and objectives on which more specific business strategies are built (Hitt, 1998). The challenge for managers today is that strategy formulation is considerably more complex than it once was.

Traditionally, developing a competitive business strategy has involved influencing one of five market forces in an industry:

- The competition in the industry,
- New entrants to the industry,
- New or substitute products or services,
- The bargaining power of suppliers, and
- The bargaining power of customers regarding quality and conditions of goods and services delivered (Gebauer, 1996).

A successful strategy addressed one or more of these forces in a way which was favourable to the business (e.g., limiting the ability of new companies to enter the market) which in turn, positively affected the competitive position of the firm in the industry and its market share. Ideally, the ways a company improved its competitive position created significant difficulties for others to copy (e.g., making it too expensive) which resulted in a long-term or sustainable competitive advantage.

However, in the last decade with substantial upheavals in many business environments, this type of strategizing has been largely rejected as too static for today's dynamic environment and changing technologies (Porter, 1996). Instead, many companies are emphasizing a new set of strategic imperatives such as flexibility, continuous improvement and the development of core competencies. Thus, there are today two philosophies which form opposing perspectives on strategy:

Strategy as Capabilities

The prevailing wisdom of this "new economy" perspective is that a sustainable competitive advantage is no longer possible. It is, therefore, the capabilities of a business to respond to a changing environment which give it a strategic edge. This view of strategy suggests that firms should begin to compete on the basis of one or more organizational capabilities which, if combined and adapted effectively to current environmental conditions, enable a company to create a stream of short-term advantages (Mohrman, 1998).

Much of the writing about competency-based strategy is directed at companies that are making new markets with goods and services based on knowledge. Certainly, firms face significantly more opportunities in these types of markets with the advent of technologies and information management capabilities. Furthermore, the ownership of intellectual capital can be an important source of differentiation for companies and can be a key starting point in determining a competitive strategy (Gebauer, 1996).

This view of strategy suggests that the careful positioning of the past must be replaced by a more dynamic and disorganized approach which emphasizes strategy-making throughout the organization and continuously over time. The key building blocks of strategy from this point of view include: improvisation; experimentation; adaptation; and regeneration. The result is a semi-coherent direction that emerges over time which is not integrated across the company. More than anything else, this strategic perspective emphasizes a company's ability to change and continually reinvent itself. This is what gives it an 'edge' in the marketplace these days. Strategy is, therefore, about getting and keeping this edge in whatever way a company can, rather than creating and maintaining a clear position in a market (Brown and Eisenhardt, 1998).

Strategy as a Position in the Marketplace

The opposing and more traditional view of strategy suggests that the rules have not changed as much as the pundits of the new economy say they have. What has happened, says Harvard's Michael Porter, is that people are confusing *operational effectiveness* with *strategy*. He writes:

> "Ultimately, all differences between companies... derive from the hundreds of activities required to create, produce, sell, and deliver their products or services. . . . Operational effectiveness means performing similar activities *better* than rivals perform them. . . . In contrast, strat egic positioning means performing *different* activities from rivals' or performing similar activities in *different ways*." (Porter, 1996).

Because companies do not distinguish between these two concepts, they end up competing on the basis of operational effectiveness, which is a no-win situation. Strategic positioning on the other hand, is about being different from others, not the same. Managers must decide how they are going to preserve their company's distinctiveness or in what ways they are going to differentiate the firm in the market.

This approach to strategy formulation involves tailoring a company's activities to address its chosen position in the marketplace. However, to guarantee a *sustainable* competitive advantage, companies must also address two further issues. First, they must make trade-offs, i.e., choose what *not* to do, because some competitive activities are not compatible with each other. Second, they must also focus on creating a fit (or alignment) among all their activities so that they will reinforce each other. When activities mutually reinforce each other, competitors cannot easily imitate them. Only when these things all work together effectively, is sustainable competitive advantage possible (Galbraith, 1995; Porter, 1996).

KM AND BUSINESS STRATEGY

The starting point for any discussion of KM strategy must be the business' strategy and how to support it going forward. Zack (1999a) explains, "If KM is to take hold rather than become merely a passing fad, it will have to be solidly linked to the creation of economic value and competitive advantage." As the discussion above illustrates, if the KM function sees its role as developing new capabilities, while the rest of the business is trying to create a distinctive position in the marketplace, KM and business strategies are going to be seriously misaligned. Thus, the overarching consideration for any KM strategy is that it must be *appropriate* for what the business is trying to accomplish with its strategy. It follows that there are two broad perspectives on KM strategy, which parallel the two general approaches to business strategy:

TABLE I

Summarizes the Differences between these Two Strategic Philosophies

Strategy as Capabilities	*Strategy as Positioning*
There is no sustainable competitive advantage for a company	A unique competitive position is possible for a company
Companies must be flexible and able to respond rapidly to changing markets and competition	All company activities should be designed to support a coherent strategic position
Emphasis on improvisation, adaptation and reinvention throughout the organization	Clear trade-offs and choices must be made compared to competitors
Advantages rest on core competencies—key resources and capabilities	Competitive advantage arises from a fit across activities
A company's 'edge' derives from continual reinvention and lots of different moves.	Sustainability derives from an entire system of activities
Emphasis on best practices and benchmarking to keep ahead of or keep up with competitors	Operational effectiveness is assumed.

Source: Alternative Perspectives on Strategy (adapted from Porter, 1996).

Knowledge as an Input to Business Strategy Development

If a business strategy takes a "strategy as capabilities" approach, KM plays an important role in building the capabilities and providing the knowledge-creation capacities needed to support the ongoing development of business strategies. This type of KM strategy, therefore, seeks to help develop a sustainable competitive advantage by building a broadly-based, hard to imitate set of Queen's Centre for Knowledge-Based Enterprises Capabilities (e.g., learning) that are transportable across products and markets and which can then be used to adapt or develop new business strategies.

The key question knowledge managers need to ask of business strategy is, therefore,: "What sorts of competencies are worth developing and sustaining?" They can then approach KM strategy formulation by understanding the knowledge content of the company's desired core capabilities and trying to disseminate and grow them (Martin, 2000).

What a firm knows and knows how to do shapes the way it can compete (Zack, 1999a). Specific KM strategies could, therefore, focus on helping business gain strategic knowledge in one of the following ways:

Value innovation

Here, KM seeks to help organizations identify new opportunities for value by redefining business problems and finding new opportunities where others see problems. This could be innovation in products and services, but it could also be innovation in processes and structures as well. KM can identify and implement applications, structures and technologies that can help knowledge workers to dramatically leverage their creativity and ability to deliver new business value (DeTienne and Jackson, 2001). For example, consulting firms that develop highly customized solutions to unique problems have adopted this approach to KM. Their strategies encourage value innovation by promoting the exchange of tacit knowledge through knowledge networks (Hansen *et al.*, 1999).

Environmental scanning

Increasingly, the need to thoroughly understand and interact with the external environment is coming to be seen as a critical piece of any organization's design. In a world of continuous change, a key management skill is, therefore, the ability to understand what is going on in the broader world of business, technology and society and to determine its relevance to the firm in order to be able to develop a coherent response companies must learn to recognize new competitive positions as they open up and become more aware of how changes could affect them and their competition. And they must be able to do this more quickly than their competitors (Price, 1996). New ways of competing could come from new customer groups, new needs, new technologies, new materials or a combination of these. KM strategy can be designed to develop scanning capabilities and provide the mechanisms to disseminate such environmental information to various business units.

Strategic experimentation

To become more adaptive, organizations can use a series of strategic experiments which help them gain knowledge to support subsequent decisions about where to move in the future. Properly designed, these experiments create new knowledge about markets, proposed strategies and process changes, and also help to begin to develop new competencies. Experiments are thus an opportunity for creating new strategic knowledge which can help shape a company's future (Hatten and Rosenthal, 2001). KM can be used to help grow such strategic knowledge over time by building an organizational memory. This knowledge will then provide the input into the design of further strategic experiments.

Knowledge as a Support for Business Strategy

On the other hand, organizations which base their business strategies on a position in the marketplace will look for a KM strategy which helps them maintain and strengthen this position. KM strategies will, therefore, be more specific to immediate business needs and focus on adding a unique layer of knowledge which enhances the platform on which company products and services are delivered. They will be designed to apply knowledge more directly to the tactical needs of the firm. These types of strategies usually start with a business problem that KM can help solve. Many of the successful initiatives mentioned by the focus group fall into this category.

There are two key ways that KM can be used as a support to business strategy:

Support for performance

Knowledge can be used to help organizations improve their quality and service. For example, KM can help a company serve its customers better by providing improved customer information at every step of the value chain from sales to service. KM can help facilitate processes by ensuring the right information is available for every part of them. Information can be 'mined' to provide self-help facilities to empower both employees and customers. In this way, a KM strategy is designed to facilitate information linkages throughout many processes and functions in the organization (Duffy, 1999). Such context-specific knowledge built into organizational routines can be an excellent way of strengthening an organization's strategic position because it tends to be unique and difficult for others to duplicate (Zack, 1999b).

Support for productivity

Systematically applied, knowledge can help organizations to shorten cycle times for both development and delivery by capturing and sharing such things as best practices, lessons learned and other reusable assets. A successful KM strategy in this area would not only create repositories of information, it would also work to make people aware of what is available and to promote sharing and reuse behaviours (Duffy, 1999). Some consulting firms have built an effective KM strategy using this approach. They extract knowledge from the people who develop it and codify it in repositories so it can be reused by others. Their KM functions support the codification process, manage repositories and provide sophisticated help and search facilities (Hansen *et al.*, 1999). While *all* of the KM strategies outlined above are desirable, group participants and the experts emphasize that a KM strategy must be largely focused in a single area if it is to be successful. Hansen *et al.* (1999) note that effective firms pursue a single knowledge strategy primarily and use others in a minimal fashion as complements to their main strategic thrust. Similarly, DeTienne and Jackon (2001) caution that KM organizations must resist the temptation to be all things to all people and build focused strategies which yield useful results. As one group member explained, "We need to pick and choose the strategies we can support."

DEVELOPING A KM STRATEGY FOR YOUR BUSINESS

While creating an effective KM strategy for a business starts with understanding your business' strategy and how KM can best contribute to it, lasting positive results from KM come from two further actions: detailed planning and attention to execution (DeTienne and Jackson, 2001). Articulating a specific KM strategy requires careful analysis within the broad understanding of the business' competitive position to determine exactly where and how KM can best support the particular goals of the organization. One focus group member defined a KM strategy as "a specific plan of action. . . which will create a picture of how the organization's KM capabilities will be integrated into a cohesive whole." Building this plan consists of addressing a number of elements.

Strategic Goal

The ultimate strategic goal for any organization, business unit or function, regardless of their approach to strategy formulation, must be superior profitability. "If you don't start with that goal and seek it directly, you will be led to actions that undermine strategy." (Porter, 1996). As described so effectively in *The Goal,* failure to keep this principle in mind can lead to sub-optimization of efforts throughout an organization (Goldratt and Cox, 1984). Unless the KM function understands how their business makes its profit (i.e., its value model) and focuses its own strategies accordingly, there is a significant possibility that it will end up concentrating on strategic blind alleys, which at best will be irrelevant to the business and at worst, can bleed time and resources away from making money.

Strategic Analysis

The next element of developing a KM strategy is to understand the knowledge that already exists in the organization and how it contributes to the firm's overall strategic goal and strategic philosophy (i.e., through strategic capabilities or competitive positioning). Since there may be a discrepancy between current knowledge and what is needed to achieve these, a gap analysis can be helpful to highlight any knowledge deficiencies. Zack (1999a) suggests undertaking a knowledge-based SWOT (Strengths, Weaknesses, Opportunities and Threats) analysis to map knowledge resources and capabilities. This will help managers to better understand where KM can best add value. Another approach is to examine organizational initiatives (e.g., re-engineering initiatives, globalization of a line of business, mergers, acquisitions or joint ventures) which are currently underway to determine if they can be accelerated or improved through KM (Seeley and Dietrick, 1999). Price (1996) recommends sitting down with business leaders and doing an "if-only" analysis and using this as a guide for where KM could add value. Focus group members suggested taking a more direct approach and simply asking business leaders to identify their biggest area of "pain" and then analyzing the root causes and drivers of these problems to determine whether KM could make a difference. When strategic analysis is complete, knowledge managers should have identified a number of crucial business areas where KM could make a significant difference.

Strategic Direction

At this point in a KM strategy's development, managers need to resist the urge to begin designing an implementation plan to solve the business' problems with knowledge. They must still determine which problems are most important to be worked on, in what ways they should be addressed, and with what resources. Strategy is about making decisions and deciding what *not* to do is frequently as important as deciding what *to* do. Porter (2001) states that many managers feel they just have to "go out there and implement like hell", forgetting that if they don't have a direction which is clearly linked to strategy, they will be unlikely to be successful. Thus, one of the most critical jobs for the KM leader is to act as the "guardian of trade-offs" ensuring that the activities that make it into the KM strategic plan are aligned with the key business strategic direction. Alignment is the term used to refer to how well different activities support and complement each other. In a well-aligned company, therefore, all types of strategy should complement and support each other relative to the organization's overall business objectives. What we know about ensuring alignment at a strategic level mainly comes from our understanding of the relationship between business and IT. We have learned that there are three ways organizations should promote alignment. First, connection at senior management levels is important. Having the CKO sit in on business strategy meetings means that he/she is privy to the detailed analysis and assumptions which go into developing business strategy and this is a crucial way to identify specific directions for KM strategy development (Frohman, 1982; Henderson and Venkatramen, 1999). Second, KM plans should be explicitly coordinated with the organization's overall strategic plan and with IT and HR strategies as well. That is, these plans should be synchronized, working towards the same priorities and time frames. Developing such plans in isolation from each other will lead to a much greater risk that their benefits will not be realized (Hansen *et al.*, 1999). Third, although business plans have traditionally been developed first, and other plans expected to follow, there is today a wide variation of sequencing which takes place in organizations. Frequently, it is no longer desirable or appropriate for planning to take place in such a sequential fashion since a more iterative approach helps business strategy to be informed by the strategic possibilities available (Seeley and Dietrick, ?).

Specific KM Initiatives

The envisioning of specific initiatives within a KM strategy should take place iteratively in conjunction with strategic analysis and direction setting. Seeley and Dietrick (1999) identify six components which must be addressed for any KM initiative:

Governance

The KM plan should identify where the funding for the initiative will come from and how the people working on it (if any) will be managed. Sponsorship at the highest possible levels in the organization must be identified.

Culture and Behaviour

Frequently, knowledge initiatives miss their mark because they are conceived of as technology projects and there is only a vague understanding of the importance of changing culture and behaviour (Zack, 1999a). What behaviours need to change and how this will be accomplished should be at least generally articulated in a strategic plan.

Content

A plan should identify the type of content and expertise that will be needed as it will affect the scope of the effort, its costs and the risks involved. There are a variety of dimensions to content. For example, a specific initiative may exploit already existing knowledge and capabilities or be designed to explore new ones (Zack, 1999a). They can also come from a number of sources both from inside the organization and from outside. The desirable breadth and depth of content and expertise must be identified as well. Finally, how they will be maintained should also be articulated.

Technology

Technology is frequently the 'muscle' behind KM efforts and KM managers must clearly identify how and where it fits into each initiative and whether a particular initiative can take advantage of the company's existing technology infrastructure or requires further investments in hardware or software. Queen's Centre for Knowledge-Based Enterprises

Application

There should be a clear understanding of what the initiative is going to accomplish and how this particular project links specifically to the company's overall strategic goal and specific strategic perspectives and objectives.

Measurement

While knowledge managers often have difficulty linking their efforts to quantifiable results (Smith, 2000), this task is considerably easier when a KM initiative is linked to a specific business strategy. Measurement helps managers learn what is working and enables them to make necessary modifications to their strategic plans. To this list, focus group members suggested adding two further issues.

Scope

Organizations must be clear about where a KM initiative fits into the big picture. Some focus group members were implementing enterprise-wide projects, while others were more focused on functional or divisional opportunities. Some knowledge initiatives may be highly context-specific to a particular business unit, whereas others may be designed for national or global use.

Dissemination

Finally, companies need to identify how broadly specific knowledge can or hould be disseminated. This is particularly (but not exclusively) true in certain industries involved in technical or scientific research and development where knowledge is viewed as a proprietary asset to be protected with barriers to diffusion and transfer (Zack, 199b). Other organizations may not be as concerned with the dissemination of knowledge within or outside the firm. Understanding this dimension will impact the types of KM strategy that are appropriate for a firm as well as the scope and cost of particular initiatives.

Strategic Case

Strategic plans frequently end up being nothing but a list of bullet points documenting "good things to do" to make the company stronger. Shaw *et al.* (1998) suggest that the case for a particular strategy is better made by using a strategic narrative. They explain that bulleted lists have three problems:

They are typically too generic to give people a clear picture of what will be done and why it needs to be done, e.g., "reduce process and product costs", "accelerate the development and introduction of new products."

They leave critical relationships unspecified. Sequence, priority and relationship to other items are all essential to understanding a strategic plan. Lists only present one of these dimensions at a time, leaving it difficult to understand exactly what the plan proposes doing.

They omit critical assumptions about how the business works. All plans make assumptions. Without knowing which ones the planners are making, it becomes difficult for senior managers to evaluate or modify plans. In contrast, a strategic narrative addresses each of these flaws making the reader privy to the author's thought processes and reasoning. It is designed like a traditional story. First the stage is set by describing the current situation in an insightful and coherent manner. Then, dramatic conflict is introduced, for example the challenges the company is facing. Queen's Centre for Knowledge-Based Enterprises.

Finally a resolution is introduced to describe how the company can overcome these obstacles and win. The power of narrative is already well-known among knowledge managers as an effective way to communicate complex information (Stewart, 1999; Snowden, 1999). At 3M, the use of strategic narratives is enabling planners to communicate complicated plans and strategies first to executives and ultimately to the people who must make the plans happen. Given the complexity of KM strategies and the challenges many knowledge managers have in communicating these in their own organizations, a strategic narrative has the potential to document a KM strategy extremely effectively and to educate people about where and how KM fits into the larger picture of organizational strategy (Greco, 1999).

EXECUTING A KM STRATEGY

While strategy has a *formulation* component (i.e., the decisions pertaining to being competitive in the marketplace) it also has an *implementation* component (i.e., the capabilities of the firm to execute its strategy decisions) (Henderson and Venkatramen, 1999). Clearly, there must be a coherence or fit between these two components or a strategy will not be effective. Thus, fit is dynamic. As strategic choices evoke imitation over time, strategic responses will be needed from the company in a process of continuous adaptation and change (Henderson and Venkatramen, 1999). The more precisely all parts of an organization are tailored to a particular business strategy the more difficult it will be for competitors to copy a competitive position. Thus, strategy is not a one-time or short-term thing but an ongoing and interactive process of ensuring an organization's activities and functions closely support a business' strategic approach. "The success of a strategy depends on doing many things well. . . and integrating them. If there is no fit. . . there can be no distinctive strategy and little sustainability." (Porter, 1996). Focus group members agreed that it is in execution where strategy bears fruit. "Often, our objectives may be well-aligned with those of the business," stated one member "but not our implementation strategies." After a thorough analysis of the what and the why of KM during strategic planning, implementation must emphasize a practical approach to the how. To align mission with practice, a KM execution plan needs to be thoroughly grounded in reality. Steps to implementation need to be clearly spelled out, a schedule established, and a budget created. While most would agree that overseeing KM implementation is not the same as building a new facility or developing an IT system (although IT *may* be an important component), there are many good project management disciplines that can be beneficially adopted from these types of projects. For example, one KM manager has created a six step methodology, complete with inputs, tools and outputs which he uses to plan and implement his KM initiatives. Other advice on effective implementation from the focus group and the research includes:

Have an executive sponsor

Any knowledge initiative should have a sponsor who understands what the project is trying to accomplish and who is willing to lead the communication effort and support the changes that will be necessary to implement the project effectively. "Getting buy-in from senior management at the outset may not be easy," said one manager, "but it is critical to successful implementation." "Without it" another Queen's Centre for Knowledge-Based Enterprises noted "you will feel like you are pushing a string." The sponsor must take a leadership role to ensure that everyone understands the strategic goal the initiative is trying to accomplish. Even more so than on other types of projects, everyone affected by a KM initiative must understand how it creates value for the organization because it is this understanding which informs each of the many thousands of choices and actions which get done in the organization every day and which can make or break the success of the endeavour (Porter, 1996).

Think Big, Start Small

While a KM initiative may start out with a goal of "fixing the whole world" said one manager, "you need to start implementation in a small, manageable way." This allows managers and staff to learn as they go and to make sure the project is actually producing the value for which it was designed. Where you start should depend not only on your strategic objective but also on the practical limitations of how much can be done at any one time. Thus, even a global enterprise-wide initiative should start with a single region and/or a single process and grow from there. It is especially important that an implementation plan be appropriate for both the initiative and the culture of the organization. Some firms have found it effective to start implementation from the top down; others from the bottom up. Still others have found a "middle out" strategy to be best.

Emphasize Culture and Behaviour

There is a natural tendency to gravitate towards the technological side of a KM project since it is more achievable and tangible. This is a mistake. As even technologists have found out, successful change cannot be achieved unless the people and processes with which they interact are taken into consideration (Markus and Benjamin, 1997). This is even more true of KM initiatives. Thus, it is critical that companies support KM projects with corresponding change management initiatives designed to create the proper environment for KM to flourish. Involving users in planning and development, rewarding and promoting success and linking content to work processes are just some of the ways this can be done (Seeley and Dietrick, 1999).

Know What Success Looks Like

It is essential that regular assessment of a project's effectiveness be undertaken. This is not only to reinforce the project's value to senior management but also to understand *how* and *why* the project is successful and/or not successful. "We must analyze and build on the pieces that work" stated one focus group member. As Porter (Hammonds, 2001) explains, "Strategy is complex. . . . Even successful companies almost never get everything right up front." In fact, even very successful companies only get a few pieces of a strategy right at the start. They then clarify and modify their strategy over time. An effective KM implementation will, therefore, include analysis of the success of all elements of an initiative and development of plans for continuous improvement to the project. "Strategic direction and continuous improvement in how you do things. . . . are absolutely consistent with each other. . . . They are mutually reinforcing." (Hammonds, 2001). Queen's Centre for Knowledge-Based Enterprises

CONCLUSION

Today, while many firms are toying with the idea of knowledge management, very few are actually approaching it in a strategic, disciplined way and linking KM initiatives directly to business strategy. While not all KM initiatives link directly to the corporation's bottom line, all can and should be designed to directly support a business' strategic objectives, whether these involve improved capabilities or a competitive position in the marketplace. To date, developing and aligning KM strategy in most firms has suffered from a poor understanding of what strategy is, and the lack of a systematic means of approaching it. Developing an effective KM strategy requires careful analysis and thorough planning as well as alignment with the organization's overall strategic plans and with other functional strategic plans (e.g., IT). An iterative approach to strategy development is, therefore, highly recommended. In addition, KM managers must remember that strategy execution is at least as important as strategy development and balance their efforts accordingly. Queen's Centre for Knowledge-Based Enterprises.

REFERENCES

Argyris, Chris (1992), *Overcoming Organizational Defences: Facilitating Organizational Learning*. Boston: Allyn and Bacon.

Binney, Derek (2001), 'The Knowledge Management Spectrum—Understanding the KM Landscape', *Journal of Knowledge Management* 5(1): 33–42. (available at www.bellanet.org/km)

Brown, S.L., Eisenhardt, K.M., "Competing on the Edge", *Harvard Business School Press*, Boston, 1998.

Davenport, T., D.W. De Long, and M.C. Beers, "Successful Knowledge Management Projects", *Sloan Management Review*, Vol. 39, No. 2, 1998, pp. 43-58.

DeTienne, K.B. and Jackson, Lisa Ann, "Knowledge Management: Understanding Theory and Developing Strategy", *Competitiveness Review*, Indiana, 2001, Vol. 11.

Dixon, Nancy, *Common Knowledge: How Companies Thrive by Sharing What They Know*, Boston, Harvard Business School Press, 2000.

Donahue, Kristen B., "Knowledge Management Beyond Databases", *Harvard Management Update*, May, 2001.

Duffy, Jan, "Harvesting Experience: Reaping the Benefits of Knowledge", *Arma, International*, Prairie Village, Kansas, 1999.

Frohman, A.L., "Technology as a Competitive Weapon", *Harvard Business Review*, January-February, 1982, pp. 97-105.

Galbraith, J.R., "Designing Organizations: An Executive Briefing on Strategy, Structure, and Process", *Jossey-Bass Publishers*, San Francisco 1995.

Gebauer Judith, "Virtual Organizations from an Economic Perspective", *Proceedings of the 4th European Conference on Information Systems*, Lisbon, Portugal, 1996.

Goldratt, Eliyahu, M., and Jeff Cox, "The Goal Excellence In Manufacturing", *North River Press*, Inc., 1984.

Greco, JoAnn, "Knowledge is Power", *The Journal of Business Strategy*, Boston, March-April,1999, pp. 18-22.

Hammonds, Keith H., "Michael Porter Big Ideas", March 2001, pp. 152-55.

Hansen, Morten T., Nitin Nohria and Thomas Tierney, "What's Your Strategy for Managing Knowledge?", *Harvard Business Review*, March-April, 1999.

Hatten, Kenneth, J. and Stephen R., Rosenthal, "Reaching for the Knowledge Edge,"*Amacon*, 2001.Queen's Centre for Knowledge-Based Enterprises

Hitt, M.A., Keats, B.W., DeMarie, S.M., "Navigating in the New Competitive Landscape: Building Strategic Flexibility and Competitive Advantage in the 21st Century," *Academy of Management Executive*, Vol. 12, No. 4, 1998, pp. 22-42.

Henderson, J.C., Venkatraman, N., "Strategic Alignment: Leveraging Information Technology for Technology for Transforming Organizations," *IBM Systems Journal*, Vol. 32, No. 1, 1999.

Kim, W. Chan, and Renee Mauborgne, "Strategy, Value Innovation, and the Knowledge Economy", *Sloan Management Review*, Cambridge, Spring, 1999, pp. 41-54.

Markus, L. and R.I. Benjamin, "The Magic Bullet Theory in IT Enabled Transformation", *Sloan Management Review*, Winter, 1997, pp. 55-68.

Martin, Bill, "Knowledge Management within the Context of Management: An Evolving Relationship", *Singapore Management Review*, Singapore, 2000, pp. 17-36.

Mohrman, S.A., Galbraith, J.R., Lawler, E.E. III, "Tomorrow's Organization: Crafting Winning Capabilities in a Dynamic World," *Jossey-Bass Publishers*, San Francisco, 1998.

O'Dell, Carla, C.J. Grayson Jr. and Nilly Essaides, *If Only We Knew What We Know: The Transfer of Internal Knowledge and Best Practice*, Free Press, 1998.

Porter, Michael E., "What is strategy?", *Harvard Business Review*, November-December 1996,79 p. Porter, Michael E., "Strategy and the Internet", *Harvard Business Review*, March, 2001, pp. 62-78.

Price, Robert M., "Executive Forum: Technology and Strategic Advantage", *California Management Review* , Vol. 38, No. 3, Spring, 1996, pp. 38-56.

Sawhney, Mohanbir and Deval Parikh, "Where Value Lives in a Networked World", *Harvard Business Review*, January, 2001, pp. 79-86.

Seeley, Charles P. and William M. Dietrick, "Crafting a Knowledge Management Strategy", *KM Review*, Nov./Dec. 1999 pp. 18-21.

Shaw, Gordon, Robert Brown and Philip Bromiley, " Strategic Stories: How 3M is Rewriting Business Planning, *Harvard Business Review*, May-June, 1998, pp. 4-8.

Smith, H.A., "Valuing the Knowledge Management Function", Queen's KM Forum Working Paper 2000, Queens Centre for Knowledge-based Enterprises, Kingston, 2000. Queen's Centre for Knowledge-based Enterprises.

Snowden, David, "Story Telling: An Old Skill in a New Context", *Business Information Review*, March, 1999, pp. 30-37.

Snowden, David J., "The art and Science of Story or "Are you sitting uncomfortably?", *Business Information Review*, Hartlepool, December, 2000, pp. 215-26.

Stewart, Thomas A., "Telling Tales at BP Amoco, *Fortune*, New York, June 7th, 1999, pp. 220-24.

Zack, Michael H., and Davenpat *et al.*, "Developing a Knowledge Strategy", *California Management Review* , Berkeley, Spring, 1999a, pp. 125-45.

Zack, Michael H., "Managing Codified Knowledge", *Sloan Management Review*, Cambridge, Summer, 1999b, pp. 45 -58.

CHAPTER

31

Industrial Sickness in Punjab

A Case Study of Punjab State Industrial Development Corporation (PSIDC)

Sarupinder Singh and Parveen Gill

Though the small-scale sector has acquired a prominent place in the socio-economic development of India during the past four and a half decades, but now it is facing relatively harsh times. Researchers have analyzed each and every issue and aspect related to small-scale sector in India. Centre and State Governments are always concerned regarding the incentives and promotion policies for this sector. The Ministry of Small Scale Industries and Agro and Rural Industries (SSI&ARI) was created on 14th October, 1999 as a nodal Ministry for formulation of policy, promotion, development and protection of small-scale industries in India. The Ministry was bifurcated into two separate ministries namely, Ministry of Small Scale Industries and Ministry of Agro and Rural Industries on 1st September, 2001. No such special attention is being given to the large-scale sector by the central or state governments. Researchers recently take up no issue and aspect related to large-scale industry. The prosperity of the small scale to a large extent depends upon the success of large-scale industries, because, majority of small-scale units serve as ancillaries to the large-scale sector. But the number of large-scale units is not increasing in proportion to increase in the small-scale units. An attempt has been made to explore industrial sickness among large and medium unites assisted by PSIDC.

I

Business cycles are an integral part of any market-dominated economy. Western economies have faced many business cycles and learnt many lessons over the last two centuries. The modern Indian economy is relatively young. The process of industrialization and modernization in India started around the first Five-Year Plan, that is, in 1951 and got a boost from the second Five-Year Plan, that is, 1955 onwards. From 1985, the economy started moving towards market-oriented systems, and this process accelerated after the crisis of 1991. Dominance of market forces resulted into industrial slowdown, especially since 1997-98.

The real growth rate of manufacturing sector peaked in 1995-96 at 14.9 per cent and fell to 9.7 per cent in 1996-97. In 1997-98,the performance was minimum at 1.5 per cent. It picked up to 2.5 per cent in 1998-99 and to 6.8 per cent in 1999-2000. The year 2001-2002 was characterised by a slowdown in world output. India also witnessed a weak industrial growth of 2.7 per cent during this period, as measured by Index of Industrial Production (IIP). In India the concept of sick units pertains to economically non-viable firms that are kept alive in the public interest through massive subsidies of all kinds. In 1980's this practice became more than casual phenomenon. The voice for industrial sickness rose. The process of liberalisation, privatisation and globalisation has been further weakening the Indian industrial sector since 1991.

The small-scale sector has acquired a prominent place in the socio-economic development of the country during the past four and a half decades. It has contributed to the overall growth of the gross domestic product as well as in terms of employment generation and export. Performance of the small-scale sector, which forms a part of total industrial sector, therefore, has direct impact on the growth of the national economy. There has been a steady increase in the number of SSI units, their production, employment and exports over the years. From 19,58,000 units in 1990-91, the number of units has increased to 33,70,000 units in the year 2000-01. On the production front also, there has been a steady increase over the previous years ranging between 7%-10% during the period 1990-91 to 1994-95. The increase was 11.4% and 11.3% in 1995-96 and 1996-97 respectively. In 1997-98 the increase over the previous year was registered at 8.43%. The increase in the year 1998-99 and 1999-2000 were 7.7%, and 8.16% respectively. The estimated increase for 2000-01 is 8.09%.

Small-scale industries (SSI) sector is facing relatively harsh times. The SSI sector constitutes 95 per cent of the industrial units in India. To quote S.P.Gupta member of Planning Commission, "The major problem facing small industry is that banks have virtually stopped lending to them. Against an average of 16 per cent lending in the past, SSI got just 4 per cent of total bank credit in last quarter." Finance ministry studies show that the sector gets loans at around 17-18 per cent per annum compared with 7-8 per cent for large industry. As per bank rules getting a loan require not more than 60 days, but processing in some cases took more than six months. Generally speaking, one needs 76 permissions in all from central government, state government and finally local government to set-up a unit. Thus the phenomenon of industrial sickness did not arise by surprise but eventually emerged from four decades of unhealthy policies. Sickness is a process and no unit becomes sick overnight; rather it becomes sick over a period of time.

Industrial undertaking, in which the investment in fixed assets in plant and machinery, excluding land and building, whether held on ownership terms or on lease or on hire purchase, does not exceed Rs. 1 Crore (One crore).

Magnitude to sickness

Sickness in the SSIs financed by banks during the last eleven years is given in Table 1.

TABLE I

Sickness IN SSI Sector

As at the end of March	*Total sick units*		*Potentially viable*	
	No.	*Amount (Rs. Crore)*	*No.*	*Amount (Rs. Crore)*
1990	218828	2426.94	16451	590.50
1991	221422	2792.00	16140	693.12
1992	245575	3100.00	19210	728.90
1993	238176	3442.97	21649	798.79
1994	256452	3690.37	16580	685.93
1995	268815	3547.16	15539	597.93
1996	262376	3721.94	16424	635.82
1997	235032	3909.201	16220	479.31
1998	221536	3856.64	18686	455.96
1999	306221	4313.48	18692	376.96
2000	304235	4608.43	14373	369.45

Note: These units include Village and cottage Industries.
Source: RBI.

A unit becomes sick when it fails to generate internal surplus funds to honour its obligations towards its suppliers and creditors in time. *The Tiwari Committee (1985)* defined industrial sickness as, "A doubtful account remaining overdue for more than two and half years and erosion in net worth and accumulated cash losses." As per the recommendations of The Tiwari Committee the government of India has set-up a board for industrial and financial reconstruction (BIFR) in 1987. The main objective of BIFR is to determine the remedial measures to deal with the problems of sick unit. If the industrial company becomes sick as per the definition it is the obligation of such company to make a reference to BIFR within 60 days from the date of finalization of the duly audited accounts of the company for the financial year at the end of which the company has become sick. *The Nayak Committee (1993)* revised the definition as," An industrial unit may be classified as sick when any of its borrowal accounts has become a doubtful advance, i.e. principal in respect of any of its borrowal accounts has remained overdue for a period exceeding two and a half years and there is erosion in the net worth due to accumulated cash losses to the extent of 50 per cent or more of its peak net worth during the preceding two accounting years." Further *Kapur Committee* reviewed the definition and remarked, "the non-performing period of SSI account from two and a half years to one year."

The definition of sick industrial company has been given under the provisions of Section 3(1)(0) of SICA (The Sick Companies Act, 1985 which got amended in 1993). As per this,

1. The company should be in an existence for at least 5 years since the date of incorporation.
2. The company should have an accumulated losses equal to or exceeding its net worth at the end of any financial year. (Net worth means the total sum of paid up capital and free reserves).

Potentially Sick Industrial Company means an industrial company whose accumulated losses are more than 50 per cent of its Peak net worth during the immediately preceding four financial years.

II

The Punjab State has lop-sided growth. Punjab industry could not develop in tune with the agrarian transformation. Although Punjab is primarily an agrarian State, the future lies in the development of Industry, by harnessing the synergies in agriculture and industry through the development of agriculture-based industry, by further strengthening base of manufacturing industries, and by rapid development of service and knowledge-based industry. Due to socio-political and economic reasons, industrial growth of the state has never been the priority of the Central or State governments.

Punjab witnessed heavy destruction and damage during partition, yet it is one of the most affluent states in the country today. The mainstay of Punjab's economy, and the source of its affluence, is agriculture. Nearly 84 percent of the total geographical area of the state is under cultivation. Punjab alone contributed about 62 per cent of wheat, and 50 per cent of rice, to the central pool in the 1994-95 seasons, despite the fact, that it comprises only 1.53 per cent of the area in the country. Besides wheat and rice, the other crops grown in the state are maize, gram, pulses, cotton, oilseeds, sugarcane, potato, onion, mustard and sunflower.

Decade long militancy lasting till 1990's deflected the priorities of the state government and its focus shifted towards maintenance of law and order. Self-preservation and survival instinct overtook the investment sentiment hence slowing down industrial development.

During the past few years, industry has been feeling the pressure of the liberalized economic regime. Resultantly, there has been declining trend in the industrial growth during the past five years. In the year 1996-97, 2497 new industrial units with investment of Rs. 854.47 crore, were set-up in the State. But the number came down to 1187, with investment of Rs. 622.41 crore, during the year 2001-02. The average growth rate of the secondary sector (comprising of manufacturing), which was 11.78% in the year 1998-99, declined to 5.90 and 5.73 in the years 1999-2000 and 2000-01, respectively.

This has also resulted in industrial sickness in the State. As per data compiled by the Reserve Bank of India, out of 1,06,329 SSI units financed by the banks in Punjab, 6304 units, with investment of Rs. 233.57 crore, have gone sick as on 31st March 2002.

Factors Affecting Industrial Sickness

The internal factors include:

- Technical causes such as obsolete technology and non-availability of skilled labour,
- Financial causes such as poor resource management, diversion of funds and deficiency of working capital and other funds, and
- Managerial causes such as lack of entrepreneurship lack of professionalism and marketing problems.

The external factors include:

- Economic causes such as high cost of inputs, uneconomic size of the project, over estimation of demand and high break-even point, and
- Socio-political causes such as Government controls and its fiscal policies such as taxation and non-payment of subsidies and incentives in time, and lack of physical and social infrastructure.

III

Punjab State Industrial Development Corporation Limited (PSIDC) was established in the year 1966 to promote planned industrial development in the organised sector and to speed up industrialisation in the State of Punjab. Today, PSIDC'S name is synonymous in the corporate world and it is engaged in the promotion of large and medium scale projects. PSIDC is responsible for making major projects happen in the new economic environment.

Broad Objectives

- Promotion of industrial and infrastructure projects in Assisted and Joint Sector.
- Extending of term loan assistance under IDBI Refinance Scheme to projects promoted by private sector.
- Providing of escort services to projects initiated through private sector.

The maximum number of units assisted by PSIDC is in Patiala/Sangrur region and minimum is in Jalandhar. The percentage of sick becoming units also varies from region to region. The nature of industry in these areas also varies.

The above tables are summarised form of the data provided by PSIDC. As per the classification standard units are those which are doing satisfactory and returning their instalments on time. Sub-standard (10 per cent) means the units having six months delay in their instalments. Similarly,

TABLE 2

Units given Financial Assistance by PSIDC at end of the year 2002-03

	Number of Units						
	Standard	*Sub-Standard*	*Doubtful—20%*	*Doubtful—30%*	*Doubtful—50%*	*Loss—100%*	*Total*
Patiala/Sangrur	7	6	12	10	23	20	78
Ludhiana/Hoshiarpur	2	6	6	10	17	15	56
Amritsar	2	0	1	5	5	6	19
Bhatinda/Ferozepur	6	1	1	1	1	7	17
Jalandhar	2	1	1	3	2	2	11
Ropar/Gurdaspur	2	2	0	2	7	17	30
Total	21	16	21	31	55	67	211

Source: PSIDC, Chandigarh.

TABLE 3

PATIALA/SANGRUR: Dues Outstanding on 31.03.2003

(Rs. Lacs)

	Outstanding Principal (2001-02)				*Outstanding Principal (2002-03)*			
	TL	*BL*	*CCA*	*Total*	*TL*	*BL*	*CCA*	*Total*
Standard	526.02	20	0.05	546.07	359.67	20	0.12	379.79
Sub-Standard (10%)	433.76	48.94	0.04	482.74	449.28	48.94	0.08	498.3
Doubtful (20%)	1598.37	48	0.45	1646.82	1535.07	48	0.58	1583.65
Doubtful (30%)	1354.63	153.67	1.07	1509.37	1047.47	94.14	5.29	1146.9
Doubtful (50%)	3344.78	322.15	27.47	3694.4	3344.78	322.15	46.26	3713.19
Loss (100%)	1828.04	114.03	48.4	1990.47	1818.04	114.03	64.76	1996.83
Total	9085.6	706.79	77.48	9869.87	8554.31	647.26	117.09	9318.66

TABLE 4

JALANDHAR: Dues Outstanding on 31.03.2003

(Rs. Lacs)

	Outstanding Principal (2001-02)				*Outstanding Principal (2002-03)*			
	TL	*BL*	*CCA*	*Total*	*TL*	*BL*	*CCA*	*Total*
Standard	424.85	0	0.02	424.87	97.25	0	0.02	97.27
Sub-Standard (10%)	112.4	0	0.01	12.41	112.4	0	0.01	112.41
Doubtful (20%)	51.44	0	0.05	51.49	28.11	0	0	28.11
Doubtful (30%)	444.21	20.67	0.06	464.94	439.61	20.67	0.06	460.34
Doubtful (50%)	399.74	0	2.6	402.34	399.74	0	2.69	402.43
Loss (100%)	229.9	0	5.33	235.23	299.9	0	7.94	234.84
Total	1662.54	20.67	8.07	1591.28	1377.01	20.67	10.72	1335.4

TABLE 5

BATHINDA/FEROZEPUR: Dues Outstanding on 31.03.2003

(Rs. Lacs)

	Outstanding Principal (2001-02)				Outstanding Principal (2002-03)			
	TL	BL	CCA	Total	TL	BL	CCA	Total
Standard	590.53	100	0.08	690.61	417.04	100	0.07	517.11
Sub-Standard (10%)	20	0	0.04	20.04	20	0	0.12	20.12
Doubtful (20%)	122.05	0	0.05	122.1	122.05	0	0.21	122.26
Doubtful (30%)	67.8	31.76	0.2	99.76	39.6	31.76	0.01	71.37
Doubtful (50%)	7.87	0	0.36	8.23	7.87	0	0.39	8.26
Loss (100%)	541.09	540	11.68	1092.77	541.09	540	12.4	1093.49
Total	1349.34	671.76	12.41	2033.51	1147.65	671.76	13.2	1832.61

TABLE 6

LUDHIANA/HOSHIARPUR: Dues Outstanding on 31.03.2003

(Rs. Lacs)

	Outstanding Principal (2001-02)				*Outstanding Principal (2002-03)*			
	TL	*BL*	*CCA*	*Total*	*TL*	*BL*	*CCA*	*Total*
Standard	37.31	0	0	37.31	17.41	0	0	17.41
Sub-Standard (10%)	801.43	35.26	0.08	836.77	785.03	35.26	1.61	821.9
Doubtful (20%)	435.05	30	0.28	465.33	410.74	30	1.61	442.35
Doubtful (30%)	609.79	14.78	2.59	627.16	474.62	14.78	8.11	497.51
Doubtful (50%)	1916.57	124.87	15.86	2057.3	1882.72	124.87	22.14	2029.73
Loss (100%)	1541.19	191	22.34	1754.53	1535.98	191	31.76	1758.74
Total	5341.34	395.91	41.15	5778.4	5106.5	395.91	65.23	5567.64

TABLE 7

ROPAR/GURDASPUR: Dues Outstanding on 31.03.2003

(Rs. Lacs)

	Outstanding Principal (2001-02)				Outstanding Principal (2002-03)			
	TL	BL	CCA	Total	TL	BL	CCA	Total
Standard	142.1	0	0	142.1	17.1	0	0	17.1
Sub-Standard (10%)	450	0	0.1	450.1	450	0	0.1	450.1
Doubtful (20%)	0	0	0	0	0	0	0	0
Doubtful (30%)	320.56	0	4.93	325.49	320.56	0	7.2	327.76
Doubtful (50%)	773.91	147.47	5.14	926.52	773.91	147.47	9.06	930.44
Loss (100%)	1724.36	2592.36	24.81	4341.53	1724.36	2612.96	30.27	4367.59
Total	3410.93	2739.83	34.98	6185.74	3285.93	2760.43	46.63	6092.99

TABLE 8

AMRITSAR: Dues Outstanding on 31.03.2003

(Rs. Lacs)

	Outstanding Principal (2001-02)				Outstanding Principal(2002-03)			
	TL	*BL*	*CCA*	*Total*	*TL*	*BL*	*CCA*	*Total*
Standard	5.64	0	0.15	5.79	0.57	0	0.15	0.72
Sub-Standard (10%)	0	0	0	0	0	0	0	0
Doubtful (20%)	6.9	0	0.08	6.98	3.94	0	0.08	4.02
Doubtful (30%)	517.8	135.88	0.82	654.5	517.8	135.88	3.07	656.75
Doubtful (50%)	500.52	100.73	6.79	608.04	500.52	100.73	9.25	355.15
Loss (100%)	466.17	49.59	7.18	522.94	466.17	49.59	10.82	526.94
Total	1497.03	286.2	15.02	1798.25	1489	286.2	23.37	1543.58

six months are added doubtful 20 per cent and doubtful 30 per cent. The units failed to return their instalments for more than one and half year fall under the category of doubtful 50 per cent. Then the category is regarding 100 per cent loss making units.

Outstanding Principal for the year 2001-02 and 2002-03 are given under the sub categories Term Loan (TL), Bridge Loan (BL) and Cash and Current Account (CCA). The tables depict that once the firms started delay in repayment of loans, the interest and hence principal amount got accumulated. It becomes difficult to get out of the trap. Recovery of loans for the PSIDC is a big problem. This becomes a sunk investment. Thus, eventually the units become sick. A few cases are handed over to BIFR by PSIDC.

IV

Therefore, concerted efforts are required to be initiated by the government and other concerned agencies for timely detection of sickness at its incipient stage. To facilitate the revival of viable sick industrial units, Government of India have set-up a statutory board viz. Board for Industrial and Financial Reconstruction (BIFR) under the Sick Industrial Companies (Special Provisions) Act, 1985 (BIFR is now being replaced by Tribunals). Small Scale Industries do not, however, come under the purview of BIFR or said Tribunals. To help this sector, Reserve Bank of India (RBI) has issued guidelines to the scheduled commercial banks for rehabilitation of sick units. But the approach has not yielded the desired results and Non-Performing Assets (NPAs) have piled up year after year. State Government has thus deemed expedient to set-up a State-Level Institutional mechanism, associating concerned state government departments, institutions, banks and industry associations to tackle this issue. The banks will be persuaded to voluntarily join this scheme and will also provide for timely identification of potentially viable sick units before it is too late for any revival. This mechanism will assist in formulating a revival package for such closed down units, which can be economically viable.

For this purpose a State-Level Industrial Revival Forum comprising of such institutions and agencies will be constituted which will consider concessions as provided in this scheme for the rehabilitation of the unit.

The Industrial Policy of Punjab 2003 has provided following guidelines in regard to revival of the sick units:

- State level Industrial Revival Forum headed by Principal Secretary Industries and Commerce to be set-up.
- Deferent of recovery of arrears of Sales tax, Electricity duty, Power bills, House Tax, Building tax.
- Exemption from power cuts and minimum charges during closure period.
- Permission for sale of surplus land.
- Permission for retrenchment/layoff.
- Reduction of Interest on delayed payment to PSEB to 12 per cent.
- 20 per cent of the revival cost to be shared by the owner.

References

A.S. Feroz, 'Steel Industry in Turmoil: Structural Crisis of *1990's, Economic and Political Weekly,* April 12, 2003.

Bimal Jalan (1992), *The Indian Economy,* Penguin Books India, New Delhi.

Dunlop, John (1958), Industrial Relations System, Free Press, New York.

Eswar Prasad and Kenneth Rogoff (2003), 'Effects of Finacial Globalisation on Developing Countries—Some Empirical Evidence', *IMF Working Paper,* April.

Government of India (1999), *Manual on Industrial Policy and Procedures in India,* New Delhi.

Ishwar Judge Ahluwalia (1993), *Policy Reforms in India,* Oxford University Press, New Delhi.

K.C. Reddy (1988), *Sickness in Small Scale Industries,* South Asia Books, Columbia.

M.S. Narayanan (1992), *Industrial Sickness in India: the role of BIFR,* Konark Publishers, New Delhi.

Prasanna K. Biswasroy (1993), *Corporate Sickness and Institutional Financing in India,* Ashish Publishing House, New Delhi.

R.K. Panda, R.K. Meher (1992), *Industrial Sickness: A Study of Small Scale Industries*, South Asia Books, Columbia.

S.S. Khanka (1994), *Industrial Sickness in India: Causes, Consequences, and Curses*, Commonwealth Publishers, New Delhi.

V. Janardhan, 'Arguing for Industrial Relations', *Economic and Political Weekly*, August 2, 2003.

Index